ARTHUR SYMONS: SELECTED LETTERS, 1880–1935

Arthur Symons (1910)
(*Courtesy of Princeton University Library*)

Arthur Symons: Selected Letters, 1880–1935

Edited by
Karl Beckson
and
John M. Munro

University of Iowa Press ᴪ Iowa City

International Standard Book Number 0–87745–213–X
Library of Congress Catalog Card Number 87–51647

University of Iowa Press, Iowa City 52242

AL Printed in Hong Kong

Contents

List of Plates

Acknowledgements

In the process of locating, gathering, and editing the letters for this volume, we have received the generous assistance of many who informed us where letters were, allowed us to examine letters in their collections, sent us photocopies, or, on occasion, the letters themselves. Our greatest debt is to the late Mrs Lucy Featherstone, Symons's sister-in-law, who kindly allowed us to examine and make copies from well over 1000 letters then in her possession. Mrs Hope Rutherford, her daughter, also kindly granted us access to these letters after they had passed on to her. We are also indebted to Mrs Nona Hill, Mrs Rutherford's sister, who over the years encouraged us in this project.

The Featherstone collection, purchased by Mr Kenneth A. Lohf, Librarian for Rare Books and Manuscripts at Columbia University, includes not only 1017 letters written by Arthur Symons but also 1044 letters written to him by his wife, Rhoda, in an exchange that spans some thirty-five years. These letters have been donated to the Columbia University Library by Mr Lohf. We are indeed grateful to him for granting us access to this extraordinary collection and for permission to publish selected letters by Symons and excerpts from Rhoda's letters. We also wish to acknowledge the kindness of Mr Brian Read (Dorset, England), owner of the Symons copyright, for permission to publish the letters and excerpts included in this volume.

Of those who responded to our queries and requests, we are especially grateful to the late Professor Peter Irvine (University of Cincinnati), who read the manuscript at an early stage and offered valuable suggestions for its improvement, and to Dr John Stokes (University of Warwick), who kindly consented to read the manuscript in its pre-publication stage. Others to whom we are grateful, who provided us with copies of photographs, photocopies and microfilms of letters, transcripts where access was impossible, or, in several instances, the original manuscripts themselves, include: Mrs Summerfield Baldwin, Professor Haskell Block, Professor P. G. Castex, Dr Thomas F. Conroy, Mr Edward A. Craig, Professor Ian Fletcher, the late Mr James Gilvarry, Sir Rupert Hart-Davis, Mr Michael Holroyd, Mr Clinton Krauss, Professor Mary Lago, Mr Robert Lowery, Ms Madeline Mason, Mrs Diana P. Read, the Reverend Herbert Boyce Satcher, Professor Stanley Weintraub, and Mr Michael Yeats.

To those who provided us with miscellaneous assistance and information we wish to acknowledge our deep appreciation: Professor Edward Baugh, Mr R. M. Busby, Ms Margaret Campbell, Professor A. E. Carter, Mr Alexander P. Clark, Dr Carl Dolmetsch, Professor

Charles Duffy, Mr J. A. Edwards, Professor Lawrence Evans, Dr Malcolm Easton, Professor Jules Gelernt, Professor Randolph Goodman, Professor Giovanni Gullace, Professor H. Pearson Gundy, Mrs Marinka Gurewich, Professor C. Michael Hancher, Ms Mary M. Hirth, Mr R. I. Kamp, Professor Frederick R. Karl, Professor Norman Kelvin, Professor Bettina Knapp, Professor Dan Laurence, M. Michel Legagneux, Professor James G. Nelson, Professor Robert L. Peters, Professor B. L. Reid, Mr Jack Russell, Professor Arnold Schwab, Dr Pamela Shelden, Professor Richard Sogliuzzo, Dr R. K. R. Thornton, Ms Ann Thwaite, and Professor Martha Vogeler.

To the following institutions, we are grateful for their permission to publish letters located in their respective libraries: Bibliothèque Royale de Belgique, British Library, Bryn Mawr College, Cambridge University, Case Western Reserve University, Library of Congress, Cornell University, Dorset County Museum (Dorchester, England), Bibliothèque Littéraire Jacques Doucet (Paris), Harvard University, Museum of the City of New York, New York Public Library (Manuscript Division and the Henry W. and Albert A. Berg Collection), Northwestern University, Princeton University, Queen's University (Canada), State University of New York at Buffalo, University of Iowa, University of Leeds, University of London, University of Pennsylvania, University of Reading (England), University of Texas, and Yale University.

We are also grateful to Dame Janet Vaughan for permission to publish extracts from two hitherto unpublished letters written by her grandfather, John Addington Symonds, to Symons; to the Bodleian Library, Oxford, for permission to quote from John Davidson's reader's report on *London Nights*; to the Society of Authors on behalf of the Estate of Havelock Ellis for permission to publish letters by Havelock Ellis in Appendix C; to Ms Janet Medley for permission to publish the George Moore letter to Symons (Letter 146); and to Ms Jennifer Gosse for permission to publish Letters 73 and 114, written by her grandfather, Edmund Gosse.

Finally, we wish to acknowledge the generosity of Brooklyn College of the City University of New York for providing Karl Beckson with released time and a summer research grant with which to pursue this work; to the American University of Beirut for providing John M. Munro with financial aid in the preparation of a portion of the typescript and to the Fulbright Program for a summer grant to enable him to complete work on the annotations.

Introduction

I ARTHUR SYMONS: HIS CAREER AND INFLUENCE

Arthur Symons is no longer a neglected figure, for since 1953, with the publication of Ruth Z. Temple's *The Critic's Alchemy: A Study of the Introduction of French Symbolism into England*, which contains five chapters on Symons, an increasing number of scholars and critics have asserted his claim for serious recognition as a writer of undoubted talent and considerable significance. It is true that Symons had some perceptive admirers of an earlier date – Howard Mumford Jones, for example, who in 1920 wrote that 'none . . . in the scanty array of authentic English criticism . . . of our contemporaries is more nearly assured of a permanent place than he'[1] – but such opinions were, until recently, comparatively rare. However, once regarded as little more than a daring hothouse poet and author of several volumes of impressionistic criticism, a credulous imitator of the French Decadent poets and an uninspired disciple of Walter Pater, Arthur Symons is now recognised as perhaps the most influential critic of the 1890s.

As a poet, Symons strove, particularly in *Silhouettes* (1892) and *London Nights* (1895), to free himself from the discursive mode of his Victorian contemporaries, focusing on a central image or situation and transforming it into a symbol in imitation of the French Symbolists, though lacking their complex technique. Of his prose, *Spiritual Adventures* (1905), a volume avowedly modelled after Pater's *Imaginary Portraits* (1887), is a noteworthy fictional achievement, which, in its exploration of the relationship of art to life, Ezra Pound contended, was 'worth all the freudian tosh in existence'.[2] More notably, Symons's criticism, especially that of the French Symbolists, has exerted a profound influence on several major writers of our time. Indeed, it was his *Symbolist Movement in Literature* (1899), enthusiastically acclaimed by such critics as Edmund Gosse and James Gibbons Huneker,[3] which attracted the attention of T. S. Eliot at a significant moment in his literary career and directed his subsequent development.[4] W. B. Yeats also profited from what Symons had to say about Symbolism in general and the French Symbolists in particular, a debt he acknowledged in his autobiography,[5] while Joyce's linguistic experiments in *Finnegans Wake* (1939) were inspired, at least partially, by what Symons had written about Mallarmé in *The Symbolist Movement in Literature*.[6] Finally, Pound, in a letter to René Taupin in 1928, noted that Symons was an important influence in the development of the Symbolist aesthetic,[7] and more specifically, in a letter to Floyd

Dell, Pound made the striking assertion that Symons was one of the few writers in whom he found his 'sanity'.[8]

Thus, Symons's influence extends far beyond the so-called 'Decadent Nineties'. In spite of his preoccupation with alluring *femmes fatales*, with unmentionable sins, with the cultivated artifice of the music-hall, and with *la vie de Bohême*, Symons was not merely a characteristic figure of that decade, for when we survey the whole of his literary career, it is apparent that his Decadent period was only a phase in his development.

In the 1880s he was writing poetry in the manner of Browning and criticism in the manner of Pater, maintaining that both writers were concerned with essentially the same thing: the isolation of significant moments of intensity in which the essence of a character or situation became apparent. During the late 1880s he became interested in contemporary French literature, and in an essay titled 'The Decadent Movement in Literature', he stated that, like Browning and Pater, such writers as Verlaine, Huysmans, and Mallarmé were also concerned with significant moments of intensity and revelation in which they perceived 'the very essence of truth – the truth of appearances to the senses – and the truth of spiritual things to the spiritual vision'.[9] As a result of his close friendship with Yeats,[10] whose interest in Symbolism Symons shared, he looked anew at those writers he had previously called 'Decadent', finding that it would be more appropriate to call them 'Symbolists', because in their pursuit of the significant moment they made one aware of other-worldly, extra-sensory existence.[11]

Soon Symons was applying Symbolist doctrine to the study of arts other than literature, writing about painting, sculpture, handicraft, architecture, the theatre, dance and music, even extending it to his vision of cities and people as well. Working intensively and unceasingly, beset by constant financial pressures and by disappointments in the development of his career as a playwright, he suffered a mental breakdown in 1908, from which he only partially recovered. He continued to write, but the later work is undistinguished, his poetry preoccupied with sin and damnation, reflecting the Nonconformist faith of his childhood.

Symons's friends and acquaintances included an extraordinary variety of literary and artistic figures. He could claim either friendship or an acquaintanceship with Browning, Swinburne, and Pater (three whom he admired deeply) as well as Hardy, Wilde, George Moore, Dowson, Symonds, Beardsley, Havelock Ellis, Augustus John, Conrad, and Joyce. He was also on familiar terms with such musicians as Paderewski, Vladimir de Pachmann, and Arnold Dolmetsch; actresses such as Mrs Patrick Campbell, Lily Langtry, Ellen Terry, Ada Rehan, and Eleonora Duse; and such music-hall performers as Yvette Guilbert, Minnie Cunningham, and Katie Lawrence.

Furthermore, Symons was also well known on the Continent. When in Paris, he would attend Mallarmé's Tuesday evenings in the rue de Rome, and he was especially intimate with Verlaine, whose lecture tour in England he helped to arrange. He also knew Huysmans, Rodin, Gide, Verhaeren, and d'Annunzio. Indeed, there were few notables in the world of art and literature whom Symons did not know. But after the period of his mental collapse, he made few new friends and took remarkably little interest in literary and artistic developments between the two world wars: his letters, for example, make no mention of such figures as T. S. Eliot, D. H. Lawrence, or Virginia Woolf. He continued to follow Joyce's career, for he had met the young Irishman in 1902 and assisted him in placing his first book with a publisher at a time when Symons was at the centre of London's literary world.

Because of the variety and number of his friendships, Symons's letters are studded with celebrated names, and for this reason alone his letters make fascinating reading. From them we learn what it was like to be a literary journalist at the turn of the century and of the pressures under which writers worked who lived by the pen. We inevitably hear gossip of writers and of books, of the lives led by the great, the near-great, and the obscure whose paths crossed that of Symons in the course of his long life. Perhaps Symons's letters are less full of his literary and artistic views than one would wish, for once his career was under way his letters became more functional. Whereas he had written pages of criticism in the correspondence of early years, as he grew older and leisure time diminished, he confined his literary theories to his published work.

As personal documents, Symons's letters are of particular interest, for in them we may trace the growth of his personality, understand something of the nature of the disaster that struck him in 1908, and follow the painful decline of his powers in the long years following. The record is not as detailed as one would wish. The period when Symons and Yeats were most intimate is not exhaustively detailed in their correspondence; indeed, relatively few letters seem to have been written to Yeats by Symons. It is also unfortunate that we have been unable to discover more than a few brief communications (not included in this volume) between Symons and Havelock Ellis, a close friend for over forty years. One would also like to know more about Lydia, the dancer at the Empire Theatre, who exercised a lifelong fascination over Symons, whose letters to her appear to have vanished, as have Symons's letters to Beardsley during the crucial year of 1896, when *The Savoy* was published (indeed, Beardsley's letters to Symons have also vanished). Finally, Symons's letters to his immediate family are not extant.

Nevertheless, much of Symons's correspondence has survived, sufficient to reveal the growth and development of one of the most complex personalities and perceptive minds of the late Victorian and Edwardian periods.

II SOURCES OF LETTERS

As might be expected of one who travelled widely and formed such wide-ranging friendships, Symons's extant correspondence is to be found throughout Great Britain and Europe, the United States and Canada, much being accessible in public and university libraries but much also remaining in the hands of private collectors. In many collections of his letters, there are, inevitably, unidentified, and perhaps unidentifiable, correspondents (such as the ubiquitous 'Sir'), whom we omit in the following survey, designed not to be exhaustive but briefly descriptive.

The largest single repository of Symons's letters – of more than 1000 letters at Columbia University – has already been described (see the Acknowledgements). In the Arthur Symons Papers (twenty-eight boxes) at the Princeton University Library (the largest library collection of Symons letters, manuscripts, photographs, and notebooks), there are over 200 letters to such correspondents as Ernest Rhys, Thomas B. Mosher, Mabel Beardsley Wright, Edward Martyn, A. H. Bullen, Elkin Mathews, Ada Leverson, and, most notably, Charles Churchill Osborne, to whom 121 letters are addressed. The Sylvia Beach Collection at Princeton contains six letters to Miss Beach. In the J. Harlin O'Connell Collection at Princeton, there are twenty letters, most of them to Elkin Mathews. The Manuscript Division of the British Library houses approximately 200 letters to James Dykes Campbell and approximately 100 to such figures as Swinburne, Theodore Watts-Dunton, Edmund Gosse, A. R. Waller, Ernest Rhys, 'Michael Field', Havelock Ellis, and George Macmillan; the Berg Collection of the New York Public Library has 138 letters, of which 119 are to J. B. Pinker and Sons (Symons's literary agents), the remainder to such figures as John Lane, Elkin Mathews, Lady Gregory, Swinburne, and Mrs Pearl Craigie ('John Oliver Hobbes'); the Manuscript Division of the New York Public Library contains 126 letters, postcards, and telegrams to John Quinn, thirteen to H. L. Mencken, twelve to Gertrude Norman, and four to Richard Watson Gilder and the editor of *The Century*; the Queen's University (Canada) has 101 letters and post cards, of which eighty-eight are to Henry-D. Davray, five to J. B. Pinker, and three to Bliss Carman; the Houghton Library of Harvard University has sixty-five letters to Edward Hutton, thirteen to William Rothenstein, and nine others to such correspondents as Montague Summers, James Russell Lowell, G. E.

Woodberry, Thomas B. Mosher, Frederick J. Furnivall, and T. W. Higginson; the Brotherton Library of the University of Leeds has sixty-seven letters, sixty of which are to Edmund Gosse and six to Clement Shorter; the University of Iowa Library has forty-three letters to such correspondents as George Sylvester Viereck, Leonard Smithers, Elkin Mathews, Gleeson White, and John Lane; the University of Texas Library (Austin) has approximately forty letters to such figures as Richard Garnett, Maire O'Neill, Olive Schreiner, Nancy Cunard, Gleeson White, Frederick J. Furnivall, J. Dykes Campbell, and Ernest Hartley Coleridge; the State University of New York at Buffalo has twenty-nine letters to such figures as James Joyce, Grant Richards, Holbrook Jackson, and George Sylvester Viereck; the Beinecke Library of Yale University has twenty-seven letters to such correspondents as Joseph Conrad, James Gibbons Huneker, John Drinkwater, Leonard Smithers, and Francis Viélé-Griffin; New York University has nineteen letters, of which ten are to Elizabeth Robins and four to Alice Meynell; the Bodleian Library of Oxford University has seventeen letters to such figures as John Lane, Christopher Millard ('Stuart Mason'), Gilbert Murray, and 'Michael Field'.

There are smaller collections at the following libraries: Cornell University, which has eleven letters to Joyce and four to George Jean Nathan; University of Pennsylvania, which has fourteen letters, of which ten are to Van Wyck Brooks; Bibliothèque Littéraire Jacques Doucet (Paris), which has five letters to André Gide, six to Paul Verlaine, and two to Alfred Vallette; University of London, which has eleven letters to Austin Dobson and one to Florence Farr; International Museum of Photography (Rochester, New York), which has twelve letters and postcards to Alvin Langdon Coburn; Dorset County Museum (Dorchester, England), which has ten letters to Thomas Hardy; the Armstrong Browning Library, Baylor University, which has ten letters, five of them to Frederick J. Furnivall; Theater Collection, Museum of the City of New York, which has ten letters to Julia Marlowe and one to Edward Sothern; Temple University, which has eleven letters to Constable & Co.; University of Toronto, which has seven letters to James Mavor and four to Herbert Thompson.

Other libraries having fewer than ten letters: Alfred University; Arizona State University; Bibliothèque Nationale (Paris); Bibliothèque Royale (Brussels); Brown University; Bryn Mawr College; Case Western Reserve University; William Andrews Clark Memorial Library, University of California (Los Angeles); Cambridge University; Dartmouth College; Dunedin Public Library (New Zealand); Dolmetsch Library (Haslemere, Surrey); Folger Shakespeare Library (Washington, DC); Huntington Library (San Marino, Calif.); Indiana University; King's College, University of London; Library of Congress; Loyola University

(Chicago); McGill University; National Library of Ireland; National Library of Scotland; Northwestern University; Pennsylvania State University; Primoli Foundation (Rome); Southern Illinois University; Swarthmore College; Trinity College (Dublin); University of Birmingham; University of British Columbia; University of Chicago; University of Iowa; University of Kansas; University of Liverpool; University of Michigan; University of Reading (England); University of San Francisco; University of Victoria (Canada); Westfield College, University of London.

Of private collections, the following should be noted: Mrs Summerfield Baldwin (New York) has thirty-three letters to Katherine Willard; Mrs Diana P. Read (Dorset, England) has twenty letters and notes to the Symonses' housekeeper, Mrs Bessie Seymour; Mr Kenneth A. Lohf has twenty-two letters to such correspondents as Vincent O'Sullivan, Augustus John, Selwyn Image, Leonard Smithers, and others; Sir Rupert Hart-Davis has eighteen letters to such correspondents as Robert Ross (eight of these letters remain the property of Mr J.-P. B. Ross), John Lane, and Allan Wade; Mrs G. Dugdale (London) has sixteen letters to Herbert Horne; the Reverend Herbert Boyce Satcher (Philadelphia) has sixteen letters to Kineton Parkes and one to Herbert Thompson; and Mr Michael Yeats has twelve letters to William Butler Yeats and one to John Butler Yeats.

Smaller private collections, varying in number from one letter to no more than a dozen, are in the possession of Mr and Mrs Peter Astwood; Mr Brian R. Banks; Professor Karl Beckson; Mr Lafayette L. Butler; Professor P. G. Castex; Mr Norman Colbeck; Mr Edward A. Craig; Professor Benjamin Franklin Fisher IV; Professor Ian Fletcher; the late Mr James Gilvarry; Romilly and Sir Caspar John (former owners); Dr G. Krishnamurti; Professor François Lafitte; M. Roger Lhombreaud; Mr Roger Lonsdale; Ms Madeline Mason; Mr Robert Mowery; Professor John M. Munro; the late Mr J. M. Purnell; Mr Stephen Sandy (on deposit at Harvard University); and Professor Stanley Weintraub.

III EDITORIAL PROCEDURES

Faced with such an overwhelming abundance of letters, much of it of interest only to the highly specialised needs of a biographer or bibliographer, we had to be rigorously selective in preparing the present volume. Our final decision as to what to include was based on the following criteria: the importance of the person to whom the letter was addressed; the importance of the persons mentioned in the letter; the letter's significance as a literary document, in so far as it illuminates the work of a particular writer or the nature of literature; the letter's importance as a record of the contemporary social or cultural milieu; and, finally, its biographical significance. We have, in these matters, kept in mind the intrinsic interest of the letter for the general reader. Recognising the desirability of providing a continuous record of Symons's development, we have also selected letters written after his mental breakdown in 1908 which reveal his sexual and religious preoccupations – crucial for an understanding of Symons's career as poet and critic.

In preparing the letters for publication, we have kept the ideal of readability in mind while preserving the original intent of the writer. For convenience, we have placed dates to the left, above the salutation, and we have indicated the source of the manuscript or text by an identifying word or phrase (explained in the 'Index of Sources', Appendix B) under the recipient's name. Around the turn of the century, Symons habitually began a new paragraph by extending the first sentence to the left of the margin; in conformity with habitual practice, we have indented the first line of each new paragraph. We have also italicised titles of books and journals (Symons was inconsistent in his practice), normalised punctuation when clarity demanded it, changed '&' to 'and' (again, Symons was inconsistent), corrected silently only obvious slips of the pen, and, occasionally, when we have inserted a word or phrase to clarify meaning or identify an allusion, we have placed such additions in square brackets. We have expanded the often used 'wd' to 'would' but retained the abbreviation 'vol.' as visually less odd in print. In the letters written in 1908 and later, where there is evidence of Symons's mental decline or disturbance, we have transcribed them as they appear in their original form, believing that their orthographic peculiarities should be preserved to reflect the writer's state of mind. We have, finally, striven for accuracy in transcription (a major problem with Symons's post-breakdown handwriting). Where doubtful readings occur, we have so indicated by question marks. A grave deficiency of Roger Lhombreaud's *Arthur Symons: A Critical Biography* (1963) is the great number of errors in transcriptions of Symons's letters. Some of these we point out in our edition.

In our annotations, we have kept the requirements of the general reader in mind, a reader who may have no great knowledge of the period or of the many minor figures to whom Symons alludes in his letters. For the reader's convenience, we have indicated in boldface type in the index the page number of the biographical annotation for each figure mentioned in the letters. Furthermore, in these annotations, we have quoted from Symons's unpublished prose and from other letters not included in the present selection when such material contributes to understanding. All such quotations are, of course, documented. In the biographical 'links' between sections of letters and in the annotations and notes, we have used abbreviations of titles of Symons's works, journals, and newspapers, the key to which is given in section IV of this Introduction.

Unless otherwise indicated, books cited in prefaces and notes were published in London. Finally, we have included a select bibliography of Symons's major works, arranged chronologically, at the end of this volume.

IV KEY TO ABBREVIATIONS

AM	*Atlantic Monthly* (Boston and New York)
Beckson	Karl Beckson, *Arthur Symons: A Life* (Oxford: Clarendon Press; New York: Oxford University Press, 1987)
CaR	*Café Royal and Other Essays* (1923)
CR	*Contemporary Review*
CSI	*Cities and Sea-Coasts and Islands* (1917)
CSP	*Colour Studies in Paris* (1917)
DN	*Days and Nights* (1889)
DP	*Dramatis Personae* (1923)
ER	*English Review*
FR	*Fortnightly Review*
FSC	*Figures of Several Centuries* (1916)
FTTR	*From Toulouse-Lautrec to Rodin* (1929)
IGE	*Images of Good and Evil* (1899)
KH	*Knave of Hearts* (1913)
LN	*London Nights* (1895)
LQR	*London Quarterly Review*
Memoirs	*The Memoirs of Arthur Symons: Life and Art in the 1890s*, ed. Karl Beckson (1977)
MM	*Macmillan's Magazine*
NAR	*North American Review* (New York)
PAM	*Plays, Acting and Music* (1903; rev. edn 1909)
PMG	*Pall Mall Gazette*
PN	*Parisian Nights* (1926)
QR	*Quarterly Review*
RMEP	*The Romantic Movement in English Poetry* (1909)
SA	*Spiritual Adventures* (1905)
SED	*Studies in the Elizabethan Drama* (1919)
SML	*The Symbolist Movement in Literature* (1899; rev. edn 1908)
SMP	*Studies on Modern Painters* (1925)
SPV	*Studies in Prose and Verse* (1904)
SR	*Saturday Review* (London)

SSA   *Studies in Seven Arts* (1906; rev. edn 1925)
SSS   *Studies in Strange Souls* (1929)
STL   *Studies in Two Literatures* (1897)
VF   *Vanity Fair* (New York)

Notes

1. See H. M. Jones, 'An Aristocrat of Beauty', *The Freeman*, 1 (1920) 45–6. Edith Sitwell also admired Symons: see *A Poet's Notebook* (1950) pp. 159, 166, 211, 222, 226, 228.
2. Ezra Pound, *Guide to Kulchur* (1938) p. 71. Frank Kermode calls *Spiritual Adventures* 'an unjustly neglected book' in *Romantic Image* (1957) p. 72.
3. See Gosse's letter to Symons (Letter 73); Huneker hailed *The Symbolist Movement in Literature* as 'the most important book of humanist criticism since Walter Pater's *Renaissance*' (quoted by Jones, 'An Aristocrat of Beauty', p. 45).
4. See T. S. Eliot's 'The Perfect Critic' in *The Sacred Wood* (1920) p. 4.
5. *The Autobiography of William Butler Yeats* (New York, 1965) pp. 213–15.
6. See David Hayman, *Joyce et Mallarmé* (Paris, 1956) vol. I, pp. 27–34; James S. Atherton, *The Books at the Wake* (New York, 1960) p. 49.
7. *The Letters of Ezra Pound*, ed. D. D. Paige (New York, 1950) p. 218.
8. G. Thomas Tanselle, 'Two Early Letters of Ezra Pound', *American Literature*, 34 (1962) 118.
9. Arthur Symons, 'The Decadent Movement in Literature', *Harper's New Monthly Magazine*, 87 (Nov. 1893) 858–67; rptd, rev., in *DP*.
10. See Yeats's *Memoirs*, ed. Denis Donoghue (1972) pp. 86–7, 89–94, 97–8, 99–102.
11. Frank Kermode, who devotes a chapter to Symons in his *Romantic Image* (1957), refers to the 'crucial' role that Symons played in the development of Modernism. See also John M. Munro, 'Arthur Symons and W. B. Yeats: the Quest for Compromise', *Dalhousie Review*, 45 (1965) 137–52, and his critical study, *Arthur Symons* (New York, 1969); see, also, Karl Beckson and John M. Munro, 'Symons, Browning, and the Development of the Modern Aesthetic', *Studies in English Literature*, 10 (1970) 687–99.

Biographical Chronology

1865   (28 Feb.) Symons born at Milford Haven, Wales.

1866–73   Family moves, as a result of the Revd Mark Symons's change of circuits, to Guernsey, Channel Islands; Alnwick, Northumberland; St Ives, Cornwall; and Tavistock, Devonshire.

1874   Begins formal schooling.

1876   Family moves to Tiverton, Devonshire.

1879   Family moves to Bideford, Devonshire. Symons enrolled in Mr Jeffery's school, where Charles Churchill Osborne is a master.

1881   (summer) Joins London Browning Society and begins correspondence with Frederick J. Furnivall.

1882   (June) Ends his schooling at Mr Jeffery's.

    (31 Aug.) Family moves to Yeovil, Somerset.

    (Dec.) Symons's first published article (on Browning) appears in the *Wesleyan–Methodist Magazine*.

1884   (30 Jan.) His 'Is Browning Dramatic?' read by Furnivall at a meeting of the Browning Society.

1885   Edition of Shakespeare's *Venus and Adonis* (in Quarto Facsimile Series, ed. Furnivall) appears, with Symons's introduction. Other editions of Shakespeare's quartos appear over the next few years with Symons's introductions and notes.

    (3 Sep.) Family moves to Nuneaton, Warwickshire.

1886   (Nov.) *An Introduction to the Study of Browning*, Symons's first book, is published.

1887   (5 Aug.) Meets Furnivall.

1888   (7 Aug.) Meets Walter Pater.

    (Sep.) Family moves to Buckingham, Buckinghamshire.

    (early Oct.) Meets Havelock Ellis.

1889   (Mar.) *Days and Nights*, Symons's first volume of verse, is published.

    (10 June) Meets Olive Schreiner.

    (25 Aug.) Meets Robert Browning.

    (20 Sep.) Leaves England for eight days in Paris with Ellis, Symons's first trip abroad.

1890   (Mar.–early June) In Paris with Ellis. Meets such figures as Verlaine, Mallarmé, Maeterlinck, Huysmans, as well as George Moore.

(June [?]) Becomes a member of the Rhymers' Club. Meets Yeats, Dowson, Lionel Johnson and others in the club over the next year.

(late June) Meets Katherine Willard.

(1–25 Aug.) Edits *The Academy*.

1891 (Jan.) Moves into rooms in Fountain Court, The Temple.

(spring) In Provence and Spain with Ellis.

(July–Aug.) In Berlin with the Willards.

1892 (4 Mar.) *The Minister's Call*, Symons's first play, produced by the Independent Theatre Society.

(May) Meets Rodin in Paris. *Silhouettes* published.

1893 (Nov. [?]) Has love affair with Lydia until early 1896.

(late Nov.) Helps to arrange lecture tour for Verlaine in England.

1894 (Mar.) In Italy.

1895 (May) *London Nights* published.

1896 (Jan.–Dec.) Edits *The Savoy*.

(late July–Aug.) In Ireland with Yeats, including a visit to the Aran Islands.

(late Dec.–May 1897) In Italy. Meets d'Annunzio.

1897 (Aug.–Sep.) With Ellis in Paris, Moscow (Ellis attends the International Medical Congress), Munich, Bayreuth (to see *Parsifal*), Warsaw, St Petersburg, Prague, Budapest, Vienna, and the Rhine.

1898 (May) Meets Rhoda Bowser.

(Oct–April 1899) In Spain, Italy, Paris.

1899 *The Symbolist Movement in Literature* scheduled for publication, but distribution delayed until March 1900.

1900 (4–7 Aug.) Meets Thomas Hardy, with whom he stays at Max Gate.

1901 (19 Jan.) Marries Rhoda Bowser. Moves into a flat in Maida Vale.

1902 (Sep.) In Constantinople and Budapest.

(2 Dec.) Meets James Joyce, who is brought to Maida Vale by Yeats.

1903 (July–Dec.) In France, Switzerland, and Italy.

1905 (Oct.) *Spiritual Adventures*, his only work of short fiction, is published.

1906 (July) Moves into Island Cottage (a seventeenth-century structure), Wittersham, Kent.

1908 (mid Sep.) Leaves with Rhoda for Italy.

(late Sep.) Has mental breakdown in Bologna.

(early Oct.) Brought back to London. Hospitalised in Crowborough, Sussex.

	(2 Nov.) Certified as insane upon his transfer to Brooke House, Clapton.
1909	(Sep.) *The Romantic Movement in English Poetry*, completed before his breakdown, is published.
1910	(7 April) Returns to Island Cottage.
	(summer) Meets Joseph Conrad.
1913	(Nov.) *Knave of Hearts* published.
1914	(May) In Paris.
1915	(winter) In Cornwall with Ellis.
1916	(9–10 July) *The Toy Cart* produced.
	(Dec.) *Figures of Several Centuries* published.
1918	(Oct.–Nov.) *Cities and Sea-Coasts and Islands* and *Colour Studies in Paris* published.
1919	*Studies in the Elizabethan Drama* published.
1920	(May–June) In Paris.
	(Dec.) *Charles Baudelaire: A Study* published.
1921	(Dec.–Jan. 1922) In Cornwall with Ellis.
1922	(Nov.–Mar.) In Cornwall.
1924	*Collected Works* published.
	(Aug.) In Paris and Burgundy with Ellis.
1925	(late May–late June) In Paris and southern France.
1927	(10 Aug.) Meets Arnold Bennett.
	(winter) In Cornwall.
1930	*Confessions: A Study in Pathology* published.
1936	(3 Nov.) Rhoda dies.
1945	(22 Jan.) Symons dies.

Selected Letters

1

The Shaping of Talent: 1880–9

Arthur William Symons, born on 28 February 1865, at Milford Haven, Wales, was the son of a Wesleyan minister who rode the circuits and about whom he later wrote in his fictional autobiography: 'He was quite unimaginative, cautious in his affairs . . . he never seemed to me to have had the same sense of life as my mother and myself . . . he never interested me'.[1] Symons's mother, however, had a 'thirst' for life: 'she had the joy, she was sensitive to every aspect of the world . . . I think no moment ever passed her without being seized in all the eagerness of acceptance'.[2]

Symons's fictional autobiography, like Joyce's *A Portrait of the Artist as a Young Man*, takes liberties with fact in order to dramatise the artist's plight when young (Reverend Symons, for example, took an interest in his son's literary career by reading his book on Browning and following its progress in the reviews; moreover, he read proofs of his son's first volume of verse). Yet the fundamantal division that Symon perceived in his parents – the pious, devout father and the passionately responsive mother – seems to have been reflected in his own personality; certainly, it had a profound and disastrous effect on his own development.

His early schooling was uneventful, though he was later to write: 'I could not read until I was nine years old, and I could not read because I absolutely refused to learn.'[3] However, at that age he had already begun to write verse – his first poem was titled 'The Lord is Good' – and by the age of ten, according to his own account, he had already read *Don Quixote*. By the age of thirteen, he had completed a sufficient number of poems to refer to them as 'Poetical Works: Volume One' and 'Tales', modelled after Byron. The poems reveal, as one might expect, his pious upbringing but, at the same time, a yearning for forbidden experiences. By 1880, he had composed his fourth 'book' of verse, influenced by such poets as Browning and Tennyson.

In that year, when his family was living in Bideford, Devon, he began to study the piano seriously, and he began a lengthy correspondence with the former 'Third Master', Charles Churchill Osborne, six years his senior, who had left the private school where Symons was enrolled in order to become a journalist. To Osborne, Symons revealed his musical and literary enthusiasms, prevailing upon him to send information about composers and authors. Osborne, who became editor of the *Salisbury and Winchester Journal* in 1884, provided Symons with a steady stream of books, newspapers, and music. He also introduced Symons to such writers as the novelist 'Leith Derwent' and the blind poet Philip Bourke Marston; Osborne also published two reviews by Symons in the paper.

In 1882, at the age of seventeen, Symons ended his formal schooling when the family moved to Yeovil, Somerset, where they remained for three years. During this time, he suffered from intense loneliness, relieved only by his writing and study of the piano. To Osborne, he wrote on 5 September 1885 (MS., Princeton) that, in Yeovil, he had 'not a single friend in the town'.[4] But he was also aware, at that young age, as he later wrote in *Spiritual Adventures*, that the developing writer is naturally isolated: 'I wanted to write books for the sake of writing books; it was food for my ambition, and it gave me something to do when I was alone, apart from other people. It helped to raise another barrier between me and other people.'[5] His first success as a writer occurred in 1882, when an article on Browning was accepted by a magazine,[6] for which, as he reported with excitement to Osborne on 2 January (MS., Princeton), he had received his 'first cheque' (of twenty-three shillings), 'not the last, I hope'.

In 1884, a significant opportunity presented itself when the distinguished scholar Frederick J. Furnivall invited Symons to write an introduction to the First Quarto of *Venus and Adonis* for the 'Shakespeare Quarto Facsimiles'. Furnivall, a founder of the Browning Society in 1881, had known the young Symons, a member of the Society since its inception, and indeed, at one of its meetings, had read a paper to the members written by Symons. Furnivall was convinced by Richard Garnett, Assistant Keeper of Printed Books at the British Museum, who also knew Symons, that the introduction would be in capable hands. Though only nineteen, Symons received the commission, and Furnivall was sufficiently impressed with his work to ask him for introductions to *Titus Andronicus* and *Henry V* as well.

Meanwhile, Symons was publishing reviews in the *London Quarterly Review* and in *Time*. In preparing a review-article on Tennyson, Browning, and Swinburne,[7] he solicited advice from Osborne, to whom he wrote on 7 May 1885, saying that he had attempted to model his style on that of Pater, 'the most exquisite critic of our day'.[8] In the following year, Symons began a correspondence with the 'Master' (as he sometimes referred to him, not without, one gathers, a trace of amused affection).

As a result of an article on the Provençal poet Mistral,[9] Symons was invited in 1886 by Havelock Ellis, editor of the Mermaid Series of Elizabethan dramatists, to edit a volume on Massinger. It would be two years, however, before they met at the National Gallery when Symons was in London on a visit: this was the beginning of 'a long and close friendship', Ellis later wrote, 'which was still continuing forty years later'.[10]

Early in 1886, Symons was engaged on his first major critical effort, *An Introduction to the Study of Browning*, which Furnivall had suggested to him late in 1885. Through him, Symons met James Dykes Campbell, a critic and Honorary Secretary of the Browning Society, who offered him much advice and encouragement in the writing of the book. Published later that year, the book brought praise from Pater, Browning, and Meredith, to whom it was dedicated.

As a result of his extensive literary work, Symons began to spend more time in London, frequenting its theatres, for which he developed a deep love, and the British Museum, where he spent much time in research and reading. It was there that he met Ernest Rhys, then editor of the 'Camelot Series', who recalled his first meeting with Symons: 'It was on the broad steps to the colonnade of the British Museum I first saw him, a handsome youth some twenty-one or -two years old. He was almost pretty to look upon – rosy cheeks, light-brown hair, blue eyes, and peculiarly white skin.'[11]

The writing of poetry preceded Symon's other interests. In 1886 and 1887, he began to submit poems to Pater for his judgement. Though finding in them 'a poetic talent, remarkable, especially at the present day, for precise and intellectual grasp on the matter it deals with', Pater recommended that Symons make prose his principal *métier*, poetry second.[12] In practice, Symons followed Pater's advice that he make prose a fine art, but he had confessed to James Dykes Campbell, in a letter written on 26 April 1887: 'I do not at all despise prose criticism in general or my own prose criticism in particular; but I wish my life's work to be, as far as possible, poetry.'[13]

In August 1888, Symons finally met Pater after two years of correspondence. He wrote to Campbell that Pater was 'a curious personage',[14] and of his fourth visit, Symons wrote to Osborne that Pater was 'the kindest-hearted of men'.[15] To the youthful Symons, such visits were equivalent to pilgrimages to the Delphic Oracle.

Early in 1889, Symons's first volume of verse, *Days and Nights*, appeared, dedicated to Pater, who reviewed it favourably.[16] Other accolades followed: John Addington Symonds, who had been corresponding with Symons for some time, wrote to praise the volume, and George Meredith sent a word of appreciation for a presentation copy. But the major literary journals ignored it; thus, like the Browning study, *Days and Nights* did not reach the attention of the larger reading public. Writing to Campbell on 19 May (MS., BL), Symons lamented: 'I can scarcely as yet lay claim to anything even of a succès d'estime.'

But, largely as a result of the volume, Symons's circle of friends widened suddenly when he met the two Pre-Raphaelite painters Holman

Hunt and Madox Brown, Olive Schreiner, Mathilde Blind, William Michael Rossetti, Edmund Gosse, and Michael Field, among others. In August, he was introduced to Browning by Campbell just months before the great poet's death.

In September, 1889, Symons spent a week in Paris with Ellis, who acted as his guide. Disappointed at not finding the critic Gabriel Sarrazin at home, they spent their time as typical tourists, visiting the Exhibition and the picture galleries. However, when they revisited Paris in the following year, they met many of the leading literary figures, an experience that had a profound effect on Symons during the 1890s and for many years thereafter.

On the threshold of the 1890s, Symons, now known as a scholar, critic, and poet – all accomplished by the age of twenty-four – was prepared to enter the new decade with substantial achievements behind him and with a distinguished circle of friends taking note of his considerable talents.

Notes

1. 'A Prelude to Life', *SA*, p. 21. Symons's fictionalised autobiography, 'A Prelude to Life', exaggerates his distance from his father (see Beckson, pp. 6–7, 9–10). The Reverend Mark Symons (1824–98), having decided at the age of twenty to become a Wesleyan minister, entered Didsbury College, Manchester, a training seminary. He retired from the ministry more than forty years later.
2. 'A Prelude to Life', p. 22. Symons's mother – Lydia Pascoe (1828–96), the daughter of a farmer – married Reverend Symons in 1853.
3. Ibid., p. 5.
4. In later years, Symons told Rhoda Bowser, his future wife (MS., postmarked 27 April 1900, Columbia):

> Remember that, till nearly your age, *I* had to endure what was purgatory to me compared with your life to you – without friends, without amusements, with a father whom I rarely spoke to and a sister with whom I only argued myself frantic. There was indeed my mother, but there was nothing else, and I did not realise at the time quite all *she* meant to me. Except her I hadn't a single person with whom I could exchange an idea. And there I was in small country towns, bursting with the desire of life, with ambition, with the longing to travel, hating the fields I walked in and every human being I saw. Rhoda, you have never had to suffer what I have suffered. But – when I look back now, I see that it made me, made for me a foundation which makes me at least *different* from everybody else. Life did the rest. But without that enforced loneliness, that thinking, that immense reading, that learning of languages, that ceaseless writing of verse and prose (not a line of which ever got published) I should never have been even the little that I am.

5. Arthur Symons, 'A Prelude to Life', *SA*, p. 41.
6. Arthur Symons, 'Robert Browning as a Religious Poet', *Wesleyan–Methodist Magazine*, 6 (Dec. 1882) 943–7.
7. Arthur Symons, 'Three Contemporary Poets', *LQR*, 65 (Jan. 1886) 238–50.
8. See Letter 4.
9. Arthur Symons, 'Frederi Mistral', *National Review*, 6 (Jan. 1886) 659–70.
10. Havelock Ellis, *My Life* (1939; 1967, ed. Alan Hull Walton) p. 169.
11. Ernest Rhys, *Everyman Remembers* (1931) p. 110.
12. *Letters of Walter Pater*, ed. Lawrence Evans (Oxford, 1970) pp. 79–80.

13. See Letter 9.
14. See Letter 15.
15. See Letter 17.
16. See Letter 19.

1   To Churchill Osborne[1]
(MS., Princeton)

Friday [late May 1880]   [Bideford]

My dear Mr. Osborne

Thank you for the two books you sent me: the *British Dramatists* is a book I have wished to read for some time.[2]

Wuthering Heights [1847] must be a strange thing – I have scarcely glanced at it yet, but anticipate a feast of horrors.

In the *British Dramatists* I think the best play is Webster's *Duchess of Malfi* – the best by head and shoulders. I have never seen a play that comes nearer, in my opinion, to Shakespeare, – at least, a play of the Elizabethan age. There is such concentrated tragedy in certain passages – that passage, for instance, where the Duchess protests to Cariola that she is not mad:

> "The heaven o'er my head seems made of molten brass,
>   The earth of flaming sulphur, yet I am not mad"
>
>   [IV.ii.7–8]

and again, in a part of the death-scene, and the scene after – Ferdinand's remorse and ingratitude; first his hurried utterance of anguish:

> "Cover her face; mine eyes dazzle: she died young"
>
>   [IV.ii.264]

and then the wild, mad accusation of the less-guilty Bosola for merely carrying out his own orders: – scenes like these are not often found. I should like to read the rest of Webster's works.

I was interested to read [Jonson's] *Every Man in his Humour* for the sake of the celebrated Captain Bobadill, whom one meets so often. The *Philaster* [Beaumont and Fletcher] of the "twin-souled brethren of the single wreath" also interested me, with parts of other plays. Marlowe, as you are aware, I had read before.

I return with the *Dramatists* some other books which I have finished: Carlyle's *Heroes and Hero-Worship* I like and admire exceedingly.

I suppose you know that Swinburne has just published his *Songs of the Spring-Time*, and that he will review Victor Hugo's new poem ("Réligions et Réligion") in the *Fortnightly*.[3] In Swinburne's book there is a sonnet on the proposed erection of a monument to Prince Louis Napoleon in Westminster Abbey which contains a most fiery protest against it. I don't know whether you have seen the sonnet; it is given in the "Literary Table-Talk" of the new number of *Literary World*.[4]

You may imagine how delighted I am to hear that Browning will shortly publish a new book – a companion volume to his recent *Dramatic Idyls*.[5] Speaking of Browning, I don't know whether you have noticed the fine portrait of him in Miss Williams' window – it is a face worth looking at. I had never seen his portrait before, consequently was very glad when Miss Williams put it in her window. Browning's is one of the finest, most massive heads I have ever seen; finer, I consider, than Tennyson's.

I have just finished *Esmond*.[6] I feel much more admiration for it than I had felt before. I think it a great book – but I cannot say I consider it the greatest of novels. That there are magnificent scenes in it I grant, and also that it is very beautifully and calmly written, but there is nothing I dislike more than over-elaboration, and that I consider a fault of it. Perhaps you may say it is merely an additional grace – but I think it stands rather in the way of true eloquence and genuinely forceful tragedy, not that I deny there is both eloquence and tragedy in *Esmond*, but I think there might have been more and grander but for that elaborateness. I suppose you don't think so.

I daresay you will allow me to keep Plato a little longer: I have read the *Phaedo* (with the greatest admiration) but I want to read some of the other dialogues.

Yours very truly
Arthur W. Symons

Notes

1. American-born schoolmaster and journalist (1859–1944), who was a master at Mr Jeffery's school in Bideford. In that year, he left for Cardiff, Wales, to devote himself to journalism as sub-editor and music critic of the *Western Mail*. When he became editor of the *Salisbury and Winchester Journal* in 1884, he published reviews by Symons: see Letter 3, n. 1. In 1888 he lost his position: see Letter 14.
2. *The Works of the British Dramatists* (Boston, Mass., 1870).
3. Symons errs in the title *Songs of the Springtides* (1880). See Algernon Swinburne's review, 'Victor Hugo: "Réligions et Réligion"', *FR*, 33 (1880) 761–68; rptd in *Les Fleurs du Mal and Other Studies* (1913).
4. Swinburne's 'Sonnet on the Proposed Desecration of Westminster Abbey by the Erection of a Monument to the Son of Napoleon III' appeared in 'Literary Table-Talk', *Literary World*, 21 (1880) 333.
5. *Dramatic Idyls, Second Series* (1880).
6. W. M. Thackeray's *Henry Esmond* (1852).

2   To Churchill Osborne
(MS., Princeton)

1 March 1883   Yeovil

My dear Mr. Osborne

You can imagine my delight a few nights ago when, as I was reading Picton's *Cromwell*,[1] I heard the post at the door, and, hurrying out, recognized your familiar but so long-unseen handwriting. I only wish your letter had been three times as long as it was, but how can I hope or expect you to write at all while you are so busy and overburdened? I am exceedingly sorry to hear that your health has not been so good as it should be, and especially that you are beginning to feel the attacks of Rossetti's curse and Herbert Spencer's enemy, insomnia.[2] A newspaper-life must be too hard for any man. I am very sorry also to hear your bad news of George Goss.[3] You do not think him very seriously ill, do you? I hope he will soon recover.

I am exceedingly obliged to you for your kindness in connection with my foolish offer of a review of Browning's new vol. Your information is quite new and most valuable to me. I had not the least idea that newspapers *never* reviewed books not sent to them. Of course I knew that such was the custom; but I supposed that they were at liberty to do as they pleased. Do magazines and reviews act on the same principle?

You will, I hope, have ere long an opportunity of seeing in print my opinion of the book. I have promised the *London Quarterly* to review it for them; also another book.[4] If space serves I shall possibly attempt to indicate my opinion of Br[owning]'s later books in connection with my notice of the new one.[5]

I was greatly interested in your account of Browning as he appears to you, however much at variance that is from his appearance to me.[6] I do not think you do him justice; I believe, – I know, rather, – that you would admire him infinitely more if you read his works carefully right thro' from beginning to end, as I have done. His earlier style I can call neither obscure nor unmusical, on the whole. His later style bears, in my opinion, much the same relation to his earlier that Wagner's later style does to *his* earlier.[7] It is a development, a growth. More and more he flings aside all impediments and scorns all restraints that would hamper or hinder him in his soul-analysis, his dramatic rendering into speech of the inmost nethermost thoughts and impulses of human heart and mind. Surely you could not withold your admiration from such works as *The Ring and the Book* [1868–9] and *The Inn Album* [1875], two of the most extraordinary and perfect achievements of dramatic art? It has been said and rightly, "What he loses in grace, he gains in strength." Of course, I do not deny his faults; they are obvious. But I think his excellencies so immeasurably preponderate over his defects, that, take him *all in all*, I know no poet his equal since Shakespeare. By the way, I cannot agree with you when you say "he *studies* to make his thought obscure." Surely no man ever did that! His obscurity (which is not so great as people suppose) arises from various causes, one of the chief of which seems to be that because he sees a thing clearly, he imagines everyone else will do so with merely a hint. He leaves too much in his work to be filled up by the imagination.

But I have been writing enough and too much on the subject; and have not, I fear, given you any idea of what I mean, in my rambling remarks. I wish I could see you and talk with you on the subject.

This reminds me of your very, very kind invitation; but I fear I shall not be able to come, as I should like to do. I do no visiting. If I ever went to see anyone I would certainly come and see you, and wish I could do so now.

I have been reading lately an infinity of books of all sorts. I have re-read Swinburne's *Essays and Studies* and read (among others) *Victor Hugo and his Time, John Inglesant, Miss Misanthrope, The Revolt of Man,* Ebers' *Only a Word* (a masterly work), *Recollections of Rossetti,* Miss Hickey's *Sculptor and other Poems* (it is a very fine *first* book; I wish you would read it.[8] You know Miss H. is Hon. Sec. of the Br. Soc.) Besides the above I have read George Meredith's extraordinary *Shaving of Shagpat.*[9] About G.M. I am in the greatest perplexity. You know I admire him very much, and I want to write an article on his works, calling attention to them: they are so sadly and incomprehensibly neglected. I have read some and know the names of others, but I do *not* know and see no means of knowing, the names and publishers of *all* his books. He publishes with several firms, and I have never seen a complete list of his works. I believe he is going to publish a new vol. of poems soon.[10] If I knew what other poetry he has written I should have a fine opportunity (just what I have wanted) of writing an article for some magazine on "The Poetry of George Meredith."[11] I know of one vol. only *Modern Love and Poems of the English Roadside* [1862]. Do you know of any other?

What a calamity is the death of Wagner! Have you seen Swinburne's poemlet on his death, in the *Musical Review* for Feb. 24? it is just eleven lines long, I think![12]

As to *my* poems, to which you refer, – when I get one printed in any magazine, I will send it to you. If it cannot attain that distinction, it will hardly be worth your reading. Of course, anything I thought would *really* give you pleasure I would send at once. But these are doubtful blessings.

> With kindest regards
> Believe me ever truly yours
> Arthur W. Symons

Notes

1. *Oliver Cromwell: The Man and His Mission* (1882) by James Allanson Picton (1832–1910).
2. Herbert Spencer (1820–1903), philosopher and author, best known for his application of evolutionary principles to the social sciences.
3. A 'boarder' at Mr Jeffery's school in whom Osborne had taken an interest because of his extensive knowledge of science and whom he had taken on expeditions in search of fossils. Goss – a delicate, thin lad – was of Symons's age.
4. Symons reviewed the anonymous *Bone et fidelis*, 'a versified account of the life and labours of a deceased Wesleyan minister apparently by his son', in *LQR*, 60 (Apr. 1883) 229–30; another unsigned review by Symons of Lewis Morris's *Songs Unsung* appeared in *LQR*, 61 (Jan. 1884) 384–5.
5. See Symons's unsigned review of Browning's *Ferishtah's Fancies* (1884), *LQR*, 63 (Jan. 1885) 370–1.
6. Osborne had responded to Symons's article on Browning, published in Dec. 1882.
7. Richard Wagner (1813–83) was important to Symons in his own developing theories of the interrelation of the arts. See Symons, 'The Ideas of Richard Wagner' in *SSA*.
8. *Victor Hugo and His Time* (English trans. 1882) by Alfred Barbou (1846–1907); *John Inglesant* (1880), a novel by John Henry Shorthouse (1834–1903); *Miss Misanthrope* (1878), a novel by Justin McCarthy (1830–1912); *The Revolt of Man* (1882), a novel by Walter Besant (1836–1901); *Only a Word* (English trans. 1883), German fiction by George Ebers (1837–98); *Recollections of Dante Gabriel Rossetti* (1882) by Hall Caine (1853–1931); *A Sculptor and Other Poems* (1881) by Emily H. Hickey (1845–1925), a co-founder of the Browning Society with Frederick J. Furnivall (1825–1910), scholar and editor.
9. George Meredith, *The Shaving of Shagpat: An Arabian Entertainment* (1855, 2nd edn 1865).
10. George Meredith, *Poems and Lyrics of the Joy of the Earth* (1883).
11. In the following year, Symons published 'George Meredith's Poetry', *Westminster Review*, 128 (Sep. 1887) 693–7.
12. Algernon Swinburne, 'The Death of Richard Wagner', *Musical Review*, 24 Feb. 1883, p. 128; rptd in *A Century of Roundels* (1883).

3   To Churchill Osborne
(MS., Princeton)

5 August 1884   Yeovil

My dear Churchill

My notice of *Harper* is in good company. I like your review of *Wind Voices*:[1] it generates as I hold all reviews should, just such another atmosphere as that of the book itself. It is sympathetic, and a review is worth little if not sympathetic. But it is sometimes difficult, when one writes sympathetically, to be keen over the shades and distinctions. Thus you do not so much as touch on what seems to me very apparent in P. B. Marston: the limitation of workmanship, which sets him so far off from the uniformly perfect workmanship of Rossetti and Swinburne. His hand is very delicate and fine, but it easily gets exhausted, and the result, to my mind, is that there are one or two dead flies in every pot of precious ointment which he sets before us. Some word or tone or touch of weakness comes, inevitable as fate, in the midst of the most exquisite passages, so that one can rarely feel that complete satisfied pleasure which his models constantly give us, and which Swinburne generally gives us even when his thought is trivial and his similes the cast[-off] clothes of twenty preceding poems. But of course I only say he is not R. or S.; and who is?

One of Swinburne's models I am now studying, to my great profit I think – Gautier. I have just bought his *Émaux et Camées*, translated several of them, and read a good many.[2] Scarcely since I first came across Rossetti have I received so new, so fresh, so powerful an impression from any work or style of verse. I have added a new string to my bow. I see now, quite clearly how certain things I have wanted to do, and been unable to do can be done. I can't say however that I unreservedly admire everything in Th. Gautier. But many of his things are superb. There is a very fine piece called "Coquetterie Posthume." The last verse has for me a strange fascination; but I think the effect can only be understood in connection with the whole poem. It runs:

> "Je l'égrènerai dans la couche
> D'où nul encor ne s'est levé;
> Sa bouche en a dit sur ma bouche
> Chaque *Pater* et chaque *Ave*."

Which I render:

> "I will lie down then on that bed
> And sleep the sleep that shall not cease;
> His mouth upon my mouth hath said
> *Pater* and *Ave* for my peace."

The thought of love's lips felt or fancied in the coffin, with kisses that were *Paters* and *Aves* for this worldly soul, is perfect. And the sound! I cannot understand the mystery of these quiet lines which thrill one like strains of strange and subtle music.[3]

I have actually reached my second sheet without a word on *King Lazarus*,[4] about which I meant to write, and which I am now returning, with most grateful thanks. I have greatly enjoyed reading it. I wish it were all like the 3rd vol. You told me it was written for 2 vols. I suppose the greater part of vol. 1 was written to fill it out? So I should judge. If Busby Tickell is an afterthought, he is a very good one. And Mrs. Sprott – what a charming being! But there is nothing in all the book like the description of the Commune[5] and the death of Roland. Most vivid and masterly. But tho' Roland in war is so good, Roland in love seems to me very unsatisfactory. The love-affairs of Roland, Clifford and Mabel seem to me inextricably confused: I at least fail to unravel them in any completely satisfactory way. The last chapter in vol. 1 is written in L[eith] D[erwent]'s very best style: vivid, intense, suggestive. But I think he writes too excitedly in what should be the quieter portions. He is always at his best in scenes of passionate emotion. How fine now is the whole scene of Roland's execution!

Is Wastwater or somewhere about there Mr. Veitch's birthplace?[6] It looks to me as if he is writing of his home – scenery he has known and loved from a boy – when he bursts into rhetoric on the Lakes. If not, it is uncommonly well simulated.

Is there any poet in the world but Shelley? Not for L.D.

I have been having some negotiations with Mr. Tucker:[7] nothing settled yet, but he is very kind.

Truly yours
Arthur Symons

By the way, – is P. B. Marston still young? I have no idea how old he is.

Notes

1. Symons's unsigned review of a recent issue of *Harper's Magazine* appeared with Osborne's reviews of *Wind Voices* (1883) by Philip Bourke Marston (1850–87), the blind poet, and the anonymous *Confessions of an English Hashish Eater* in 'Literary Column', *Salisbury and Winchester Journal*, 2 Aug. 1884, p. 3. Osborne's enthusiastic review noted that *Wind Voices* was 'the most varied and sustained volume of poetry given to the world since the death of Rossetti'.
2. Théophile Gautier (1811–72), French poet, novelist, and critic, advocated the doctrine of 'art for art's sake' in the Introduction to his novel *Mademoiselle de Maupin* (1835). In the 1858 edition of *Émaux et Camées*, Gautier added 'L'Art', his poetic creed advocating impersonal, sculptured verse, a precursor to Parnassianism. Impressed by Gautier, Symons wrote 'Venus of Melos', celebrating art's timelessness, included in *Days and Nights* (1889).
3. Symons's translation was included in *Days and Nights*.
4. *King Lazarus* (1881), a novel by 'Leith Derwent', the pseudonym of John Leith Veitch, in whom Symons saw great promise.
5. A portion of the novel takes place during the establishment of the insurrectionary government in Paris – the Commune – at the end of the Franco-Prussian War (1871).
6. The biographical details for Veitch remain unknown.
7. Unidentified.

4   To Churchill Osborne
  (MS., Princeton)

7 May 1885   Yeovil

Dear Churchill
  Thank you for your very kind invitation, which at first I had hoped I
might in some measure accept – that is, not go to Stonehenge, but come
some other day to meet Mrs. Garnett,[1] – but unfortunately I have got
such a bad cold that I shall be quite unable to come. I have had but few
colds lately, and have generally contrived to get rid of them pretty
quickly by taking a little care: if I don't do this they are sure to hang
about me a long time. With my cold, and in the present weather, I
couldn't venture to come over to Salisbury. But it was very kind of you
to ask me to meet Mrs Garnett, whom I should so much have liked to
have met. I have heard a lot about her from Mrs. Bradford[2] as well as
from you. – If I had been able to come, should I have had the additional
pleasure of seeing Mr. Veitch? You don't mention him, but I thought
he was to be with you about this time.
  I was very sorry, as well as very grateful, when I saw how much
trouble you had taken about my MS. of Mistral.[3] I never thought of
giving you such a job. But of course that makes it all the kinder of you.
  I am afraid I can't agree with a great many of your strictures. First, I
don't see that the style, as a style, is bad. It is of course different from
that of the "Three Poets,"[4] for instance; but I don't call the one bad and
the other good, – each is quite different in intention. There is as much
rightness in being ornate as in being concise. I don't hold to one style
only, but practise several. Then as to your revisions etc. of particular
phrases – some of them are very keen and true, but others, if adopted,
would quite throw out the particular rhythms I attempted, and render
the whole thing colourless. You have done me a great service by pointing
out many slipshod expressions, which I will do my best to correct; but I
think it a pity that you tried to make one style conform to the laws of
another style. To take one slight instance, you object to the use of "I"
and seem always to wish to turn round a phrase in order to avoid it.
Now here I quite disagree with you. It is a perfect torture to me to have
to write for a quarterly or a newspaper, in which "I" is inadmissible. So
far from being ostentatious, it is modest. It is surely humbler to say '*I*
think this' – implying, "it may be wrong, I don't declare it to be true,
but it is what seems to me correct," than to say roundly 'This *is* so and
so', as if there were no doubt about the fact, and only one opinion was
even possible. When I am writing I never pretend to infallibility: I give
every statement, not as an absolute fact, but as my individual opinion,
which may be taken for what people choose to think it worth.

In this essay I attempted to model my style on that of Walter Pater (to whom I refer in a phrase you query as 'the most exquisite critic of our day' – a phrase which I think fits him exactly). I don't myself think that I succeeded very well on the whole, but at any rate it was an attempt towards a good end, and not a mere deflection into the flowery paths of sprawling verbosity.

You are curiously incorrect in thinking that the essay was written off at a rush. The fact was I took great pains about it, was months and months studying up the subject, and wrote very slowly. What I do best *is* written at one dash. As far as I remember, the Browning paper[5] took me very little trouble, *Venus and Adonis*[6] was written in a tearing hurry, and the "Three Poets" took a night each. I can only write well when I am in such a state of excitement that I can scarcely get the words down on paper. If I have to stop and think and plan and worry I can never write properly.

You see I acknowledge a certain faultiness in the Mistral, – but more in the conception than in the style. I had *not*, as you truly say, a thorough mastery over my subject, – that is, I did not feel fired with it. I'll see what I can do to improve it, but I fear it is too late now to do very much.

I'm sorry you don't like my telling of his story: I do. I think it is the best part of the essay. As to translations, I was and am too lazy to do any into verse.

I feel sure you will not be vexed by my frankness in objecting to some of your objections. It must seem very ungrateful, but be sure I am not so. I have never been more obliged to you, and I am venturesome enough to hope that you will add to the kindness of offering criticisms the kindness – still greater, because more difficult – of not minding when I can't see any way to believe in them.

I shall put aside this essay until I have done *Titus Andronicus*,[7] which ought to be ready by June; and then I shall see what I can do.

I think you will like the article on Meredith that I shall send you as soon as I can get a copy of the mag. in which it appears.[8] It is more in the style you like.

Best regards to yourself and Mrs. Osborne.

Very truly yours
Arthur Symons

Notes

1. Olivia Narney Garnett (d. 1903), described as 'warm-hearted, witty, vivacious, and with the Irish gift as a raconteur' (George Jefferson, *Edward Garnett: A Life in Literature* [1982] p. 8). In 1863, she had married Dr Richard Garnett (1835–1906), scholar, author, Keeper of Printed Books, and later Supervisor of the General Catalogue of Books in the British Museum, best known for his fables in *The Twilight of the Gods* (1888). See Symons's obituary, 'Richard Garnett', *The Speaker*, 14 (21 Apr. 1906) 59–60.
2. According to the novelist Simon Jesty, who knew Mrs Bradford (d. 1930), it was she

'who gave Arthur Symons a letter of introduction to a friend of hers, no less a one than Richard Garnett, and this took the young poet up to the town and opened doors'. See Jesty, 'Letters to the Editor: Arthur Symons', *Times Literary Supplement*, 24 Feb. 1945, p. 91.

3. Frédéric Mistral (1830–1914), French author and member of the Félibrige, a group of writers interested in restoring Provençal as a literary language. See Symons's 'Frederi Mistral', *National Review*, 6 (Jan. 1886) 659–70.

4. See Symons's unsigned article on Tennyson, Browning, and Swinburne: 'Three Contemporary Poets', *LQR*, 65 (Jan. 1886) 238–50.

5. Symons's 'Is Browning Dramatic?' was read by Furnivall at the Browning Society meeting of 30 Jan. 1885, and published in the *Browning Society Papers*, 2 (1885) 1–12. For its reception, see William S. Peterson's *Interrogating the Oracle: A History of the London Browning Society* (Athens, Ohio, 1969) p. 73.

6. Symons's 'Introduction' to Shakespeare's *Venus and Adonis* (Shakespeare Quarto Facsimiles prepared under F. J. Furnivall's direction) appeared in 1885.

7. Symons's 'Introduction' to Shakespeare's *Titus Andronicus* (1886); introduction rptd as 'Titus Andronicus and the Tragedy of Blood' in *STL* and *SED*.

8. Symons's review of *Diana of the Crossways*: 'Mr Meredith's Latest Novel', *Time*, 1, n.s. (May 1885) 632–6.

5 To James Dykes Campbell[1]
(MS., BL)

114, Abbey Street
24 October 1885   Nuneaton

My dear Sir

I post to you the *House on the Beach*.[2] I am sorry for your peace of mind in reading it, that it should be dotted and dashed in the margin – a failing of mine.

I was deeply grieved to learn the other day in the papers that Meredith had lost his wife. Must he not have had her in mind when depicting Lady Dunstane in *Diana*?[3] That is a strangely beautiful and touching portrait – unlike anything else I know in Meredith's works. I notice that in his early novels his portraits of sickly or suffering women are keenly touched with a sort of contempt – think of Juliana in *Evan Harrington* [1860]. But in this last work there is a really wonderful sympathy and tenderness toward the suffering Lady Dunstane. Does it not seem as if she may be, at least in some points, his wife? I should like to think so.

And I like always to trace the course of a man's work in the circumstances of his life – to see, when it is possible to do so, how such a result came from such a cause. Of course in the case of a living man this is mainly impracticable. But it is sometimes practicable. For instance – you know how great Thomas Hardy[4] is in describing fairs, and suchlike congregations of country-folk. Well, an acquaintance who knew him when he was living at Sturminster Newton told me that Hardy would go to the fairs and markets, stand up by the side of the most eccentric-looking people, and listen to their talk and study them. One sees after hearing that how he does the thing so well.

My great puzzle in regard to Meredith is – What *can* he have done with himself from 1866 to 1871? Up to *Vittoria* in '66 he wrote a novel a year. Then comes a blank of 5 years before *Harry Richmond* [1871]. Not a published word can I hear of beyond an article and a few poems in the *Fortnightly*. And I certainly don't think *Harry Richmond* a book that would take five years to write. Then there were 4 years before *Beauchamp's Career* [1875]. It is difficult to understand blanks like these in the career of a brilliant and earnest writer.[5]

Very truly yours
Arthur Symons

Notes

1. Author and Honorary Secretary of the Browning Society (1838–95), who knew many of the leading literary figures of the day, including Pater and Browning. For an account of Campbell's association with the Browning Society, see William S. Peterson, *Interrogating the Oracle: A History of the London Browning Society* (Athens, Ohio, 1969) *passim*.
2. George Meredith, *House on the Beach: A Realistic Tale* (1877).
3. Lady Dunstane was in fact modelled on Meredith's friend, Lady Lucie Duff Gordon (1821–69), author and literary hostess. Symons had recently reviewed *Diana of the Crossways*. See Letter 4, n. 8.
4. For an account of Symons's later friendship with Hardy (1840–1928), see Michael Millgate, *Thomas Hardy: A Biography* (1982) *passim*.
5. From 1866 to 1871 Meredith wrote little, partly because he devoted a great deal of his time to politics, but also because he was disheartened by unfavourable reviews of his previous work.

6 To Churchill Osborne
(MS., Princeton)

16 October 1886   Nuneaton

My dear Churchill

Best thanks for your letter, which with much pleasant news contains tidings I was very sorry to get of Marston.[1] I do hope however it is not so bad as you intimate. You will perhaps have seen him since writing; and can judge more for yourself. I am glad to say that my mother, about whom you so kindly inquire, is getting on quite as well as we could expect; that is to say, her eyes are not *worse*, nor likely to be (a great comfort), and give her but little or occasional pain: whether she will ever regain quite her former eyesight is questionable, I fear, though with the aid of much stronger glasses – recommended by the best oculist in Birmingham, whom she consulted – she is able to see almost as well. – Symonds, I am afraid, must be still having trouble with his eyes, for I have not heard from him for some time, except that he sent me his *Ben Jonson*, in the English Worthies series, the other day. It is a capital little book. By the way did you see the pictures of Davos in last week's *Pictorial World*?[2]

I mentioned you to Ellis and he has promised to send you some prospectuses of the Mermaid series when they are ready.[3] (I fancy, by the way, I gave your office address.) Don't abuse Ernest Rhys,[4] the esteemed editor of the Camelot Classics, for whom I am at present toiling and moiling over Leigh Hunt.[5] He isn't much of a fellow as a writer: *I* can't stomach his style; but he is very friendly disposed to-mewards [?], and it was he – a friend of Ellis – who recommended me for the Mermaid series.

I hope to see my Browning out next week. It has been practically ready for no end of time: but these delays! Browning has read the proofs and sent me a delightfully kind and gratifying letter. He is "delighted with" the book, Furnivall says.[6] I hope the public will be so too! By the way, you will not mind – will you? – having the copy I should of course send you, sent through the publishers as a review copy? With the limited number of copies I get gratis, I am obliged to save all I can. So I asked them to send a copy to the ed. of *Salisbury Journal* for review,[7] and thus I pay for it out of their pocket! You will please take it as from me, with all manner of kind wishes and regards.

I have not heard from Veitch for an age – tho' I believe, after all, *he* was the last to write. So he has given up Margate, I infer; is it teaching work that he is doing abroad? I should be glad if you could give me his address.

Did I tell you – no, I could not have done so – that George Meredith has accepted – "with a full sense of the distinction," as he politely puts it – my dedication to him of the *Introduction to Browning*. "My love of Browning runs beside yours," he told me; so you see the dedication is particularly appropriate.[8] Have you seen his delicious little poem – "Mother to Babe" – in the new number of the *English Ill[ustrated] Mag[azine]*?[9]

At Coventry I have quite made a friend in the Librarian of the splendid Free Library there; a library which I often go to consult. He is one of the best-read men I have ever met; and as kindly as he is intelligent.[10]

I was almost going to finish my letter without asking you a question I have wanted to ask for some time past. Do you, as a Sarisburiensis, know such a place as The Manor House, Bemerton, Salisbury, or such a person as a Miss Ferrant, therein living? A little while since I advertised in the *Exchange and Mart* for some old magazines I wanted; and comically enough the only person who replied was the above near neighbour of yours. I wonder if you know anything of her?

With best remembrances to Mrs. Osborne,

Most truly yours

Arthur Symons

Notice in today's *Athenaeum* the quaint and characteristic account of old Barnes, by his nearest neighbour Thomas Hardy.[11]

Notes

1. Marston was seriously ill at this time.
2. 'Some Continental Resorts', *Pictorial World*, 30 Sep. 1886, p. 332. John Addington Symonds (1840–93), historian, critic, and poet, best known for his seven-volume work, *The Renaissance in Italy* (1875–86). When Symons sent him a copy of *Titus Andronicus* (with his Introduction) in 1886, Symonds began a correspondence with him; they met in London in 1889. See Beckson, pp. 28–9, 51.
3. Havelock Ellis (1859–1939), later an authority on the psychology of sex, was at this time editing the Mermaid Series of Elizabethan dramatists and studying medicine. In the early 1890s, he sublet two of Symons's rooms at Fountain Court, The Temple, and periodically lived there when in London. For Symons's impressions of Ellis, see Letter 7. For Symons's friendship with Ellis, see Phyllis Grosskurth, *Havelock Ellis: A Biography* (1980) *passim*.
4. Author and editor, poet, essayist, and novelist, Ernest Rhys (1859–1946) was later the general editor of the Everyman Library. On 18 October 1887, Symons wrote to Churchill Osborne (MS., Princeton): 'Ernest Rhys is another of the younger men who has that same incapacity to put his thoughts into form, or even to get them quite clear and separate in his own head.' Rhys is best known for his memoirs, *Everyman Remembers* (1931) and *Wales England Wed* (1940), both of which contain accounts of his friendship with Symons.
5. Leigh Hunt's *Essays*, with introduction and notes by Symons appeared in 1887. On 22 Mar. 1886, Symons confessed to Osborne (MS., Princeton): 'Entre nous, I have never read a page of Leigh Hunt in my life!'
6. See Symons, *Memoirs*, p. 26. Symons had sent Browning the proofs.
7. Osborne reviewed it favourably: see Letter 7, n. 2.
8. Symons had sent Meredith a proposed dedication, which contained a description of him as the 'greatest of living novelists'. Meredith responded, in a letter dated 14 Sept. 1886, that the phrase 'rings invidiously'. Symons altered the dedication to read: 'To George Meredith, Novelist and Poet, this little book on an Illustrious Contemporary is with deep respect and admiration inscribed', which Meredith in a letter dated 18 Sept. 1886, found 'entirely acceptable'. See Symons's 'George Meredith: With Some Unpublished Letters', *Forum*, 68 (1922) 817–34; also published in *FR*, 119 (Jan. 1923) 50–63.
9. 'Mother to Babe', *English Illustrated Magazine*, 4 (1886) 26; rptd in Meredith's *A Reading of Earth* (1888) p. 50.
10. Edward Brown (1842–1931), the first City Librarian of Coventry, appointed to the post in 1868, when the Free Library was established, until his dismissal in 1908 for alleged incompetence in maintaining records and accounts and failure to implement up-to-date procedures.
11. See Hardy's 'The Rev. William Barnes, B.D.', *Athenaeum*, 16 Oct. 1886, pp. 501–2. Barnes (1801–86), Dorsetshire poet and philologist, was the author of *Poems of Rural Life in the Dorset Dialect* (1854, 1859, 1862; coll. edn 1879). Hardy edited Barnes's *Selected Poems* (1908).

7   To Churchill Osborne
(MS., Princeton)

3 January 188[7][1]   Nuneaton

My dear Churchill

Many thanks for your kindly thought in sending me so substantial a Christmas greeting. I have never seen [Thoreau's] *Walden*, and I have heard much about it; so you will see the book is very welcome.

I hope you have all had a merry Christmas, and are entering gaily on the New Year. As for me, I am twice as well as I was at this time last year; in fact, I have not had a cold worth speaking about since last Spring, and am quite enjoying the frost and snow. Here, and I suppose with you, there has been what one always considers the ideal Xmas weather – snow on the ground, and clear sharp air.

I am wondering what you think of my Browning, if you have had time to read it yet.[2] I shall have another book to send you soon – Leigh Hunt's *Essays*. As before, I shall ask the publisher to send it to you, and I shall at the same time give a hint – whether it will be acted upon I can't of course say – that they would find it advantageous to send *all* the "Camelot" vols to you for review.

I have just been reading one of the most wonderful novels I have ever come across – Flaubert's *Madame Bovary* [1857]. Have you read it? If not, do.

I wonder if you have ever met with a book called *Story of an African Farm* by Ralph Iron (Olive Schreiner)?[3] Havelock Ellis, the 'Mermaid' editor, quite raves about it. I have not yet seen it, so can't say if he is right.

By the way, Ellis is a remarkably clever and interesting fellow. He is just your age; lives at home studying surgery, reviewing theology for the *Westminster* – odd combination! – and writing essays to please himself. He is something of a Socialist besides, is writing a novel, and is very friendly with Michael Field.[4] I learnt from him that the "E. Nesbit" who writes poems in the magazines, and who has just published a volume, is a Mrs. Bland, who with her husband writes stories under the name of Fabian Bland.[5] I rather like some of her verse that I have seen.

Have you seen Tennyson's new vol.?[6] [J. Dykes] Campbell writes me that it is a "personal political pamphlet, and as such, utter trash." That is a hard saying. By the way, in Watts's review of the poem in *Athenaeum*, isn't that a delicious bit about the ratcatcher and Browning?[7]

Did I tell you I have been studying Italian lately? I have just subscribed for an admirable little Italian weekly paper – the *Fanfulla della Domenica*: it is capital practise to read it, and most interesting in itself – critical articles, stories, poems, by their best writers. I am hoping that Nencioni, the best Italian critic, a great admirer of Browning, will review my book either there or in the quarterly *Antologia*.[8] When are the English papers going to notice me?

Best regards, wishes, and seasonable compliments!

Yours ever

Arthur Symons

Notes

1. Symons inadvertently wrote '1886'.
2. When Osborne reviewed *An Introduction to the Study of Browning* (1886) on 12 Feb. 1887 in the *Salisbury and Winchester Journal*, Symons responded (MS., 14 Feb. 1887, Princeton): 'Now let me thank you for your review: I can quite understand its delay. Now it comes it is worth waiting for. It is discriminating as well as kindly, and I am all the better pleased with you for having given your own opinion of things. It is lordly in length too; and as my father said to me five minutes ago, it "goes into" the book as no other reviewer has yet done.'
3. South African novelist and feminist (1855–1920), who lived in England from 1881 to 1889, and, as 'Ralph Iron', published her most widely acclaimed work, *Story of an African Farm* (1883). She met Havelock Ellis in May 1894, in London, after a brief correspondence (Ellis had written 'an admiring but critical letter' about her novel), a relationship that progressively became emotionally intimate, though 'their own sexuality proved to be unexpressed'. See Ruth First and Ann Scott, *Olive Schreiner* (New York, 1980) pp. 124–33. Symons met her in early June 1889. See First and Scott, pp. 184–5.
4. 'Michael Field' was the pseudonym of Katherine Bradley (1846–1914), known as 'Michael', and her neice Edith Cooper (1862–1913), known as 'Field' (also as 'Henry'), who collaborated on twenty-seven plays and eighteen books of verse. Their posthumously edited diaries, *Works and Days: From the Journal of Michael Field*, ed. T. and D. C. Sturge Moore (1933), are drawn from the twenty-six folio volumes in the British Library. See Symons's 'Michael Field', *Forum*, 69 (June 1923) 1584–92.
5. Edith Nesbit (1858–1924), a Fabian Socialist, poet and author of children's books, married Hubert Bland (1856–1914), journalist and founding member of the Fabian Society, in 1880.
6. Alfred Tennyson, *Locksley Hall, Sixty Years After* (1886).
7. Walter Theodore Watts (1832–1914), author and reviewer for the *Athenaeum* from 1876 to 1898, added his mother's maiden name, 'Dunton' (with a hyphen), to his surname, apparently to conform to the terms of a family legacy. See Mollie Panter-Downes, *At the Pines: Swinburne, Watts-Dunton, and Putney* (Boston, Mass., 1971) p. 16. He is best known as Swinburne's guardian. In his review, Watts describes an East Anglian ratcatcher who, on being interviewed on his ninety-fifth birthday, said, 'I'm stun deaf, thank God, an' I'm stun blind, but as long as I've got a full belly an' a ferrit to nuss I means to be loively' – a story which Watts offers as an analogy to Browning's optimism in old age. See 'Literature: Locksley Hall, Sixty Years After', *Athenaeum*, 1 Jan. 1887, p. 32.
8. Enrico Nencioni (1837–96), Italian poet and critic, reviewed Symons's book on Browning in 'Rassegna di Letteratura Straniera', *Nuova Antologia* (Rome) 8 (1887) 365–6.

8   To James Dykes Campbell
(MS., BL)

8 January 188[7][1]   Nuneaton

My dear Mr. Campbell

   I am delighted to hear of the Leigh Hunt rarity you have secured: if it is unknown to Mr. Ireland[2] it surely *must* be rare!

   With your letter this morning came a second hand *Fortnightly* for Oct. '78 containing Pater's essay on Charles Lamb – an exquisite and most characteristic piece of work which I had never before read.[3] I was amused when Pater's name greeted me next moment from your letter. Next to Browning and Meredith, he is perhaps the living English writer whom I most admire, and whose acquaintance I should most like to make.[4] Did I tell you that in acknowledging my *Browning*[5] he most kindly asked me to call on him if I were in London during the vacations? I have always been very curious to know what sort of man he is, in the flesh: really I can scarcely conceive him as a man in the flesh at all, but rather an influence, an emanation, a personality, quite volatilised and ethereal! You would confer a great pleasure on me if you would tell me your impression of him – the most difficult thing to put into words, I know.

   I was glad to see in today's *Athenaeum* an advt. of my book – very distinct. There was a good advt. too in that immensely popular thing *Yuletide*. I see Browning's new poem is advertised:[6] that will further call attention to the book about him.

   In the same *Athenaeum* I observe a severe onslaught on J. A. Symonds' last work, *Sidney*.[7] Mr. Symonds sent me a copy of the book, and I read it the other day. I confess I was rather disappointed. It was not up to *Ben Jonson* [1888] and that was not up to his true level. I believe however that the true cause of the inequality was more than usual ill-health last winter when the book was written.

   The old people here say (but then they always do say) that the snowstorm last night was the most severe they have known since they were young. The aspect is superb – still, ten inches of snow are not pleasant to step in.

                                                Very truly yours
                                                Arthur Symons

Notes

1. Inadvertently, Symons wrote '1886'.
2. Alexander Ireland (1810–94), publisher of the *Manchester Examiner* and author of the *List of the Writings William Hazlitt and Leigh Hunt* (1868).

3. Written on the side of the letter adjacent to this: 'I am collecting all P.'s scattered articles, and I have now more than half'. See Walter Pater, 'The Character of the Humourist: Charles Lamb', *FR*, 30 (1878) 466–74; rptd in *Appreciations* (1880).
4. Symons met Pater on 7 Aug. 1888. See Letter 15.
5. Arthur Symons, *An Introduction to the Study of Browning* (1886).
6. Robert Browning, *Parleyings with Certain People of Importance in Their Day* (1887).
7. See 'Literature', *Athenaeum*, 8 Jan. 1887, pp. 55–6, for the review of *Sir Philip Sidney* (1886).

9 To James Dykes Campbell

(MS., BL)

26 April 1887   Nuneaton

My dear Mr. Campbell

Let me thank you first for your supplementary note containing [an] extract from Mr. Lowell's letter.[1] Nothing of course could be nicer – and from such a man. Before seeing that, I had been thinking of sending him a copy of my Massinger;[2] for I have just been reading a report of a lecture he has delivered on M. in the course of some lectures on the dramatists which he has been giving in Boston.[3] Don't you think it would be timely, and worth doing? If you think so, will you let me have his address. I have a single copy of the book left.

Did you see the review (headed "Browningismus") in the last *Saturday*? It is by no means soothing, but will do me, I think, no sort of harm. Whoever the reviewer may be, he seems to know pretty exactly about my age. Poor Prof. Corson – what with the "little hymn" etc. – comes off very badly.[4] The *Saturday* has now noticed Browning, Hunt and Massinger – which is more than any other weekly has done.[5] Neither *Athenaeum* nor *Academy*, nor yet *Spectator* has devoted a line to any one of them. Long live W.H.P.![6]

Yesterday I walked over to Hinckley, where I saw that battered copy of *Melincourt*,[7] and hunted it up again. It has become mine for the sum of 9d – not exactly exorbitant – and I shall send it to Nevett Bros. to rebind in one vol., half calf, which they would do I fancy for 2/- or 2/6. The pages are in very fair condition indeed. I also bought a few 1878 and 1879 nos. of the *Contemporary* (1d. each!). Among them was an article by Mrs. Orr on [Browning's] *Dramatic Idyls*, and another, which if you have not seen I will send for you to glance at, on "The Text of Wordsworth's Poems," by Dowden, an extremely interesting collation of various editions.[8] This reminds me that I most criminally forgot in writing my last letter to thank you for the articles on Beddoes.[9] Out of sight at the moment it was out of mind; but I had read it with deep interest in the quotations and biographical facts. I shall very gratefully accept your offer to lend me his plays by and by: let your binder bind as he listeth, he will not take too much time as far as I am concerned, for I am deep in Miss Rossetti's poetry just now.[10]

I saw your note in the *Athenaeum*.[11] Did you see, in the same number, the announcement, at last, of Pater's *Imaginary Portraits*, the first of which "The Child in the House" was printed 10 or 12 years ago?[12] And Meredith too is about to publish a new vol. of poems.[13] From Mr. Pater, by the way, I had a kindly line the other day in acknowledgment of the Massinger.[14]

Now let me turn to your delightful last letter – or I might as truly say your last delightful letter. I have to thank you for reading the proof, for the sermon, and for the "lively hope" of some realisation of you in the shape of a photograph. Pray do not on any account forget that when you get home.

As to the "Sermon," I am still unregenerate and unconvinced. Frankly, and *altogether apart* from a personal wish to see my verses "in print," I think you are wrong. And for this reason. When you say, Wait till your name is better known than it is now, you forget that prose is one thing and poetry another, and that no one was ever received more graciously as a poet because he was well-known as a prose-writer: but quite the contrary. If I go on editing and publishing prose books, and writing prose articles in the magazines, and then in a year or two's time bring out a volume of poems, people will receive the volume as the by-play or "lyrical recreation" of a critic, and they will say, "Here's this critic of poetry thinking he can write it too! Let him stick to his proper trade." Such a view – and I feel sure it is a likely view to be instinctively taken – would be fatal, simply fatal. I do not at all despise prose criticism in general or my own prose criticism in particular; but I wish my life's work to be, as far as possible, poetry. Prose I shall be *obliged* to do – for money; and I should in any case do it more or less – for pleasure. But there is a vast difference between seeming to the public a poet who also writes criticism and a critic who also writes poetry. I consider myself, and I wish to be considered, the former: if I bring out a volume of poems now soon, *before* I have made much of a name as a prose-writer, there will be some chance of my getting my wish: let the quality of the poetry quite alone, let the book be received as it may chance – that is no matter; I shall be able to show *something* for myself as poet. I may say that Mr. J. A. Symonds, with whom I had about this time last year a good deal of correspondence in regard to this matter, has *recommended* me to publish a volume if I can do so without paying a publisher to bring it out. He said at first exactly what you do, but after seeing more pieces reversed his judgment.[15] The MS [*Days and Nights*] is now with

Chapman & Hall, who have written to say it shall "receive their careful consideration."[16]

I hope you spent a pleasant evening with Coventry Patmore[17] on Saturday, and that the talk did *not* run on politics. That is very romantic about his house – more romantic than his poetry, I should say. Have you ever seen Swinburne's coarse but clever parody, "The Person in the House"?[18]

Sincerely yours
Arthur Symons

Notes

1. James Russell Lowell (1819–91), American poet, critic, Professor of Modern Languages at Harvard University, 1853–76, and Minister to Great Britain, 1880–5.
2. Symons edited *Philip Massinger* for the Mermaid Series, 2 vols (1887); Introduction, 'Philip Massinger', rptd in *STL* and *SED*.
3. Lowell gave six lectures on English dramatists in 1887 at the Lowell Institute, Boston. They appeared in *Harper's New Monthly Magazine* (New York) between June and Nov. 1892; rptd in Lowell's *The Old English Dramatists* (Cambridge, Mass., 1892).
4. 'Browningismus', *SR*, 63 (1887) 596, which contains a review of Symons's book, states: 'Compared to Professor Hiram Corson, of Cornell University, Mr. Symons is a Longinus, doubled with a Sainte-Beuve'. Corson (1828–1911), an ardent Browningite, founded the earliest known Browning Club in 1877, a small group of Cornell faculty members and their wives. See William S. Peterson, *Interrogating the Oracle: A History of the London Browning Society* (Athens, Ohio, 1969) pp. 91–6.
5. See 'Books on Shakespeare and His Contemporaries', *SR*, 63 (1887) 562; review of Symons's edn of Hunt's *Essays*, ibid., p. 208.
6. Walter H. Pollock (1850–1928), poet, journalist, and editor of the *Saturday Review*, 1883–94.
7. *Melincourt, or Sir Oran Haut-on* (1817) by Thomas Love Peacock (1785–1866), a satirical *roman à clef* of some leading Romantics, such as Southey and Coleridge.
8. Edward Dowden (1843–1913), critic and Professor of English at Trinity College, Dublin. See 'The Text of Wordsworth's Poems', *CR*, 33 (1878) 734–57, and Mrs Orr's 'Mr. Browning's "Dramatic Idyls" ', *CR*, 35 (1879) 389–402. Alexandra Sutherland Orr (1828–1903) was a generous supporter of the Browning Society. See Peterson, *Interrogating the Oracle*, pp. 167–70.
9. Thomas Lovell Beddoes (1803–49), poet and dramatist with a taste for the macabre and supernatural, best known for *Death's Jest Book, or the Fool's Tragedy* (1850).
10. Christina Rossetti (1830–94), the sister of Dante Gabriel Rossetti, was a poet whose *The Goblin Market and Other Poems* (1862), was the first literary achievement of the Pre-Raphaelites. Her lifelong religious devotion is reflected in her brother's painting *Ecce Ancilla Domini* ('The Annunciation'), in which she posed as the Virgin Mary, the painting now in the Tate Gallery, London. See Symons's 'Christina Rossetti' in *STL*.
11. See Campbell's letter, 'The London Magazine', *Athenaeum*, 23 Apr. 1887, p. 546.
12. Walter Pater, 'The Child in the House', *MM*, 38 (1878) 313; rptd in *Imaginary Portraits* (1887).
13. George Meredith, *Ballads and Poems of Tragic Life* (1887).
14. Pater's letter, dated 19 Apr. [1887], is in the Department of Special Collections, University of Kansas.
15. See Symonds's letters to Symons, dated 5 Apr. 1886 and 26 June 1886, in *The Letters of John Addington Symonds, 1885–1893*, ed. Herbert M. Schueller and Robert L. Peters (Detroit, 1969) Vol. III, pp. 130–1, 152–3.
16. *Days and Nights* (1889) was eventually published by Macmillan and Co.
17. Poet and critic (1823–96), best known for his long poem on the theme of wedded love,

The Angel in the House (1854). Symons, who met Patmore through J. Dykes Campbell, wrote to Michael Field on 4 Aug. 1889 (MS., BL): 'I spent two afternoons with Coventry Patmore, who lives at Hastings – a man much more interesting than his work, utterly un-"angelic," a narrow but fierce and keen personality.' See Symons's 'Coventry Patmore' in *FSC* and *DP*.

18. 'The Person of the House: Idyll cccLxvi', *Specimens of Modern Poets: The Heptalogia; or the Seven Against Sense, A Cap With Seven Bells* (1880) pp. 51–62; rptd in *The Complete Works of Algernon Charles Swinburne*, ed. Edmund Gosse and Thomas J. Wise (New York, 1925 and 1968), vol. v, pp. 273–7.

10   To Churchill Osborne
   (MS., Princeton)

Coton Road

7 August 1887   Nuneaton

My dear Churchill

You will be glad to hear that my *Introduction to Browning* has attained a second edition, which means that 2000 copies have been sold – apart from the sale of the American edition. The new ed. will have a notice of the *Parleyings*.[1] It's very gratifying – the sale of so many in about 8 months.

Friday I spent at Little Alne, a tiny village near Stratford, with Dr. Furnivall, who is spending August there, with his cracked cousin. The Dr. is one of the most charming and at the same time eccentric men I have ever come across – wears no hat, for instance, at all, no waistcoat, no collar, light alpaca coat and gray knickerbockers – goes everywhere on his bicycle. His plainness of speech is something astounding, yet all said so simply and sweetly that you hardly realise it. As a specimen phrase – it hardly bears reporting, but it is very characteristic – 'What is Robert Buchanan[2] doing now?' I said. 'Oh,' replied the Dr. serenely, as if stating the most obvious and palatable truism, 'fornicating about and writing plays!' He told me no end of tales about everybody whose name one cares to know – some very amusing and some very astounding. You know very well that anything he says about Swinburne is not likely to lean to mercy's side; but he assured me that Th. Watts literally saved S.'s life some 8 or 9 years ago, when the man had drunk himself into such a state that the doctor didn't give him 3 days chance of life. Watts heard of it, rushed off to him, took him home and has kept him ever since. – What do you think of the "Whitmania" article? – and the *P.M.G.* comments on it?[3]

About 3 weeks ago I had a very pleasant day in London – spent the first part with the Campbells (whom of course I hadn't seen before) and the latter part with my cousin Will – whose musical wife I hadn't seen either.[4] I hoped to have spent a little time with Pater too: he asked me to lunch, – that I couldn't do, as I was pledged to Campbell's, and when I called, about 3, he was out. I was sorry to miss him. Did I tell you I have an article on his new book in this month's *Time*?[5] I will send you the number when I can.

You can fancy how pleased I was to meet Campbell, after having corresponded with him so long. He is a most agreeable man, and his wife, who is, by the way, a niece of the Col. Chesney who wrote *The Battle of Dorking*,[6] is really charming. Campbell's collection of books – rare 1st eds., annotated copies and the like, – is such as I have never seen before, in a public or private library. I don't know whether you would at any time care to look at a little book he edited in 1862 – he has just given me a copy of it – a reprint of Tennyson's vols of '30 and '32, or rather of all the poems that have been altered or omitted.[7] Some of the first draughts are simply inconceivable. "The Dream of Fair Women" for instance began originally:

"As when a man who sails in a balloon"![8]

One might make an amusing article out of the variations.

I mustn't forget to tell you that when in London I had the singular good luck to see Browning – driving up the road near the Albert Hall – just in the neighbourhood of his new house.

What do you think of the Sharps,[9] now you have had them with you? I shall like to have your impressions.

Arthur O'Shaughnessy's work[10] I know very little of. The song you have copied for me, has a certain charm, tho' the workmanship and the emotion is a trifle thin. I have just been reading a little of Beddoes – a singular genius. Do you know his work?

Thanks for the *Vox clamantis* – adini! Joseph Ellis[11] is nothing to do with my friend Havelock – I am thankful to say. Have not you had the Middleton and Beaumont & Fletcher?[12] I might give a hint to Ellis.

I suppose I told you I was to do Hawthorne for the Great Writers. As Lovell's biography[13] is just coming out I have taken up Poe instead. If you know any useful books etc. I shall be glad to know.[14]

Could you sometime lend me Sharp's Marston memoir?[15] This reminds me I must apologise for not sooner returning Clarke's notice of P.B.M.[16] which got quite overlooked under some things. I send it now.

What did you mean by saying the *L.Q.R.* came from me? It was sent you by Ellis! and you didn't know my writing any better than that – let alone the postmark!

I have no room left for more. Best of all possible wishes to (and from) all. You do not tell me how your aunt is doing? I hope Mrs. Osborne and the boy will enjoy their Brighton visit, and be nicely set up by it. Pity you are not going.

Yours ever

Arthur Symons

Notes

1. In the second edition of his *Introduction to the Study of Browning* (1887), Symons included a review of Browning's *Parleyings with Certain People of Importance in Their Day*, pp. 199–203.
2. Scottish writer and critic (1841–1901), who achieved notoriety with his attack on Rossetti in 'The Fleshly School of Poetry: Mr. D. G. Rossetti', *Contemporary Review*, 17–18 (1871) 334–50; rptd, expanded, in *The Fleshly School of Poetry and Other Phenomena of the Day* (1872).
3. Swinburne had written of the 'noble army of Whitmaniacs' infected with a 'singular form of ethical and aesthetic rabies', noting that the American poet 'seldom writes well . . . bound in to the limits of a thoroughly unnatural, imitative, histrionic and affected style'. The *Pall Mall Gazette* commented that 'if Mr. Swinburne is to be accepted as a critical guide, a good many other idols will have to be knocked down and some others set up'. See Algernon Swinburne, 'Whitmania', *FR*, 42, n.s. (1887) 170–6; rptd in *Studies in Prose and Poetry* (1894). 'Mr. Swinburne on Walt Whitman', *PMG*, 30 July 1887, p. 13.
4. William Christian Symons, who was a painter, had recently married Cecilia Davenport, a composer of songs.
5. Arthur Symons, 'Walter Pater: "Imaginary Portraits"', *Time*, 6, n.s. (Aug. 1887) 157–62. Symons sent the review to Pater, who replied that it was 'the work of a really critical mind and a well-skilled pen'. See *Letters of Walter Pater*, ed. Lawrence Evans (Oxford, 1970) p. 75.
6. Sir George Tomkyns Chesney (1833–95), an Army officer, published *The Battle of Dorking* (1871), a brief account describing an imaginary invasion of England, designed to draw attention to the inadequacy of the nation's military preparedness.
7. *Suppressed Poems of Tennyson: A Pamphlet Privately Printed under the Supervision of J. D. Campbell* (1862).
8. In the 1832 version, the first line actually reads: 'As when a man, that sails in a balloon', which was subsequently omitted with the four opening stanzas. See *The Poems of Tennyson*, ed. Christopher Ricks (1969) pp. 440–1.
9. William Sharp (1855–1905), Scottish poet, critic, and biographer, in the 1880s and 1890s, of such figures as Browning, Heine, and Shelley. In 1894, he emerged as the major figure in the Scottish Celtic movement with his romances published under the pseudonym of 'Fiona Macleod', his dual identity revealed on his deathbed to his wife, Elizabeth Sharp (1850–1932), translator and author of *William Sharp (Fiona Macleod): A Memoir* (1910). See Flavia Alaya, *William Sharp – 'Fiona Macleod'* (Cambridge, Mass., 1970) pp. 6–7.
10. Arthur O'Shaughnessy (1844–81), Pre-Raphaelite poet, best known for *Songs of a Worker* (1881), was a herpetologist at the British Museum and Philip Bourke Marston's brother-in-law.
11. Poet (1815–91), the subject of a study by the poet Eric Mackay (1851–98), *Vox Clamantis: A Comparison Analytic and Critical Between the 'Columbus at Seville' of Joseph Ellis and the 'Columbus' of the Poet Laureate (Lord Tennyson)* (1887).
12. *Thomas Middleton*, 2 vols, ed. Charles Algernon Swinburne (1887); *Beaumont and Fletcher*, 2 vols, ed. J. St Loe Strachey (1887), both editions in the Mermaid Series.
13. Presumably a reference to the *Life of Nathaniel Hawthorne* (1890), by Moncure Conway, published by Lovell & Co., New York.
14. Symons never completed his projected study of Poe.
15. William Sharp's memoir precedes Marston's *For a Song's Sake and Other Stories* (1887);

a revised version precedes Marston's *Song-Time: Poems and Lyrics of Love's Joy and Sorrow* (1888).

16. An obituary notice written by Marston's friend, the poet Herbert Clarke, quoted in Louise Chandler Moulton's 'Philip Bourke Marston: A Sketch', preceding Marston's *Garden Secrets* (Boston, Mass. 1887). When Marston died in February 1887, Symons wrote to Churchill Osborne (MS., postmarked 17 Feb., Princeton): 'I saw the sad news on Tuesday . . . with what regret I need not tell you. But I could not be sorry, for his sake, that he was not left, as many are after a stroke, a sort of living corpse – that, with blindness, would be far worse than any death.'

11   To Herbert Horne[1]
(MS., Dugdale)

19 September 1887   Coton Road

Dear Mr. Horne

Do you remember, in a note to Havelock Ellis the other day, referring in a postscript to Simeon Solomon?[2] Oddly enough, I had just been writing to Ellis, asking for information about that very man. I knew nothing about him but his name, but the references to his pictures which I came across now and then in looking into old periodicals had made me curious about him, and when the other day at Manchester I saw half a dozen pictures of his in the Exhibition, I was so impressed with their beauty and originality, and a certain morbid grace they have, that I asked one or two people about the man, and finally got the lamentable story from Ellis. One cannot wonder that he has dropped out of sight, and foregone his future; but it is an infinite pity. Do you know him? You say "he is glad to sell a pencil drawing for a few shillings": what sort of drawings does he do? Is he still capable of fine work? I judge from your remark that he must be almost in destitution: how is that? – would no one patronize or employ him, or has he neglected his art? If you really know much about him you will do me a favour by telling me a thing or two. He *had*, at any rate, a remarkable genius; and there is nothing in this world so pitiful as a shipwreck of genius.

I write to you without apology. I have heard a good deal of you, and you may have heard something of me. Besides, are we not comrades at the sign of the Mermaid?[3]

Yours truly
Arthur Symons

Notes

1. Architect, poet, art historian, and biographer (1864–1916), who was editor of the *Century Guild Hobby Horse*, 1886–92, and its successor, the *Hobby Horse*, 1893–4. Symons's relationship with Horne deteriorated as time went on, but the reason remains obscure: see Beckson, pp. 161–4. See, also, Ian Fletcher's 'Herbert Horne: The Earlier Phase', *English Miscellany* (Rome) 21 (1970) 117–57.
2. Pre-Raphaelite artist and writer (1840–1905), a friend of Pater and Swinburne, introduced erotic and Hellenic themes and symbols into his paintings and prose poem *A Vision of Love Revealed in Sleep* (1871). His arrest for homosexual solicitation in 1873 lost him friends and reduced him to begging. Dissipation led to St Giles's workhouse for most of the remaining years of his life. See Philip Henderson, *Swinburne: The Portrait of a Poet* (1974) p. 183.
3. Symons, Ellis, Horne were co-editors of *Nero and Other Plays* (1888) for the Mermaid Series; Symons edited John Day's *The Parliament of Bees* (1607?) and *Humour Out of Breath* (1608) for the volume.

12   To James Dykes Campbell
(MS., BL)

3 December 1887 Coton Road

My dear Mr. Campbell

I am well repaid for a little waiting: if all expected letters could only be as good as this of yours! Very good indeed it was of you to show the poem to Browning, and how delightful that he seemed really to like it![1] Of course, after such an opinion as his I can laugh 'able editors' to scorn – however trying, in the practical way, they may be. As for that bad rhyme, – tho' no doubt a 'trifle' to *him* to remove – it was a thorn in my side during a whole afternoon's walk yesterday and it sticks there still: I *cannot* think of anything else. And yet I hate an imperfect concord almost as much as he does, and the rhyme had always grated on my ear. I could bring forward eminent "instances" for even greater atrocities. Curiously enough, of Shelley's two poems in the decasyllabic couplet-rhyme, "Epipsychidion" *begins* and "Julian and Maddalo" *ends* with an imperfect rhyme – 'one' and 'on', and 'how' and 'know.' There is a fine shield for me, you will confess – and even Browning might; tho' the retort is both easy and just – 'Imitate great men's virtues, not their faults.' Can *you* think of any other way of expressing just that sense? If RB thought it a 'trifle,' I wish he had said how the trifle could be managed?[2]

You suggest the *Spectator*: perhaps I will try there. I have at one time or another tried them two or three times, but without success. A few days ago I sent something to Herbert Horne, for the *Hobby Horse* if he will have it – improbable enough, for our canons of poetry are far apart.

But I should like to appear in those aesthetic pages. The thing I sent was a dramatic scene called "A Bridal-Eve."[3] I wrote the first draught of it more than two years ago: the subject is striking (a story I met with), but I did not consider the style sufficiently good to have it copied when a number of my pieces were copied out for the publication that did not come. Last Saturday I took it up and completely rewrote it, making 125 lines out of what was but 83, and quite transforming the whole thing. I think it is now one of my *very* best things – quite as good, in a different style, as the "Revenge." I very much wish Horne would accept it. Do you know his verses? or him? He has written some little things that would quite deceive one if quoted as Herrick's, who seems to be his great model.[4] I also sent Oscar Wilde (who has been asking me to write him) half a dozen stanzas, but don't know yet whether he will take them.[5] I am very glad you liked my "Opium" sonnet, which Havelock Ellis, who has seen a great deal of my verse, thinks the best sonnet I have done.

Now after all this about my own affairs, let me turn to yours. I can't at all see why you should "hate" your writing in print. You ask me to tell you quite candidly if your review does not look "crude and unworkmanlike" and a lot of other horrible things. I say, "quite candidly," no it doesn't, it looks clear and businesslike. I hardly think this one is equal, in point of verve at least, to that in which you pursued poor Brandl through all his burrows.[6] But thinking of the two, – which are all I know of your printed work, I believe, – I should *criticise* (as you wish it) just thus. For one thing, you are rather too avid of facts (now I hate facts, I may be allowed to observe, mildly, in a parenthesis) – one would like a little more butter with such thick bread. In other words, you might allow yourself room to think more about *how* things should be said, and to dress up the naked shivering little bodies – facts. I do not think you have "lack of skill in grouping facts"; but I do think that in what I have seen you have been so bent on putting a great number of them into a small space that the general impression of the whole has been somewhat sacrificed to the details. Then in your style there is *now* and *then* a little stiffness – the stiffness that comes to anything, pens or legs, from want of exercise. Now what you want to do is to write when you are writing for the press *exactly* as you would if you were writing a letter to a friend. Your letters are always models of that kind of writing – like what Pater would call *select* talk. Nothing could be better from a literary point of view than, to take the latest instance, your account of Browning reading the poem. It has the very tones of voice of one speaking, and it is as vivid as life. Then you are constantly hitting on epigrams that, as I told you before, fill me with envy – a characteristic that stamps your style with something individual. I sometimes fancy that if you had gone in for literature your style would have been something like that of Frederick Wedmore[7] – gently humorous, mildly poignant, a winnowed colloquialism. As it is, when you sit down to write for print, you feel burdened with a sense of responsibility – perhaps you write slowly and correct much – you set aside this phrase and that as not dignified enough for what is going to be printed. Well, if a man chooses to write in filigree, as Pater does, that course is all very well; but otherwise, it is fatal. The spontaneous words that one throws over are generally the best words, and the result of our labour is that we smother a live man into a very decent and orderly corpse. I almost always write best when I write fastest; and yet my style (in prose) is not what I should call exactly a simple one – at least simplicity is not my aim, not nearly so much as it is in verse. In one word, if you would write a series of articles on Coleridge and his surroundings just as if you were writing them in letters, everybody will be delighted, and as you are so *exceptionally* informed on those subjects you may do something memorable – why not a book? – an indispensable addition to Coleridge literature.[8] I shall not be satisfied till I hear you are at work (perhaps you are?). If I can be of any help in the way of commenting on your work as you did on mine in the Browning, do please make use of me. It would really gratify me if you thought my scribbled suggestions could in any way add to the value of your MSS.

I am writing at a table so covered with Shakespeare litter that I can hardly find room to spread my note-paper. I have got *two* plays more to do – *Winter's Tale* (nearly a third done now) and *Henry VIII*,[9] – which with the other two already done, will mean £100, a sum which I have never earned, nor even had, before. Besides this, I am to collaborate with F. A. Marshall, at his *earnest* wish, over a couple plays more; and he promises me *at least* half of what he styles the pittance.[10]

I have a heap more things to say, but I really can spend no more time over this inordinately long letter – for I am torn as it is between the Shakespeare work on the one hand and some imperative practising on the other. Otherwise I would tell you how not long since I robed myself in wondrous garments and descended into the bowels of the earth, and of a new friend who has come unto me, and of many other matters, the which I give over unto silence.

Yours ever
Arthur Symons

Notes

1. Symons had sent Campbell a poem titled 'A Revenge' in November. For Browning's response, see *Memoirs*, p. 28.
2. Symons did eventually change the lines in the published version. See *DN*, p. 14.
3. This and other poems mentioned in the paragraph were all included in *Days and Nights*. The 'Opium' sonnet refers to 'The Opium-Smoker'.

4. Robert Herrick (1591–1674), the Cavalier poet.
5. From 1887 to 1889 Wilde was editor of *Woman's World*. Symons's poem, 'Charity', appeared in the Sep. 1888 issue, p. 9.
6. Alois Leonhard Brandl (1855–1940), German scholar and philologist, author of *Samuel Taylor Coleridge und die englische Romantik* (Berlin, 1886; English trans. 1887). See Campbell's unsigned review of *Samuel Taylor Coleridge and the English Romantic School* in the *Athenaeum*, 18 June 1887, pp. 791–4. See also Brandl's response to Campbell's unfavourable review, 'Prof. Brandl's Life of Coleridge', ibid., 2 July 1887, p. 20, and Campbell's response to Brandl's letter, ibid., pp. 20–1.
7. Biographer, short-story writer, and art critic (1844–1921), who also published *Memories: A Book of Reminiscences, Social and Literary* (1912).
8. Campbell later published *Samuel Taylor Coleridge: A Narrative of the Events of His Life* (1894).
9. For the 'Henry Irving Shakespeare', Symons edited and wrote introductions for the following volumes: *Twelfth Night* (1888), *Antony and Cleopatra* (1889), *Macbeth* (1889), *Measure for Measure* (1889), *The Winter's Tale* (1889), *Henry VIII* (1890). Introductions for these six plays rptd in *STL* and *SED*.
10. Francis ('Frank') Albert Marshall (1840–89), playwright and critic, was the general editor of the 'Henry Irving Shakespeare'. When Marshall died, Symons wrote to Campbell (MS., 20 Jan. 1890, BL): 'His death is a real loss to me: the man attracted me, and I used to like going there and getting his witty letters. He was always very kind to me, and used to plan that we would someday edit together a superb edition of the Elizabethan dramatists.'

13   To James Dykes Campbell
   (MS., BL)

2 January 1888   Coton Road

My dear Mr. Campbell

I am very much in your debt, but Xmas predisposes one to postponement, and I hardly think I shall apologise very profoundly. Please thank Mrs. Campbell for her very kind note, a sentence of which, about Pater, set me in a state of great exaltation, from which I am but slowly recovering. Pater to have written a review of my book, and *such* a review![1] Why did he never tell me? Do you know, when I read that review first I said to myself, "This is rather nicely written: I wonder who wrote it? Evidently one of Pater's disciples." The thought never occurred to me for a moment that he had done it himself. Is he accustomed to write reviews there, or anywhere, or was this exceptional? I sincerely hope he is not condemned to much of that sort of work. As it was, it was exquisitely characteristic that the notice should come out just precisely a year after the publication of the book!

I shall hope to hear from you your impressions of the man at a closer view: his outward man you have sketched for me, but the inner?

To recur to your letter, – thanks for giving some thought to the end of the "Revenge", but I don't think your suggestion in this case quite intense enough to be satisfactory, while I quite agree with you in being doubtful as to my suggestion. Let it rest so for the present, and if either of us thinks of anything *really* better, it – my reading, that is – shall be discarded in the twinkling of an eye.

I suppose you have received my fair friend Bell[2] (no better than she should be, poor girl!) and seen the slight alterations. "Charlie" was preferred to "Robert" on the ground (which had never occurred to me) that such a name would inevitably become "Bob" and nothing else. I think you might, if you would be so kind, send on the magazine to Havelock Ellis (8 St. Alban's Place, Blackburn) who will return it to me – it is my only copy.

Fotheringham's Browning essays[3] I have not seen; indeed I am reading no English now – chiefly the extraordinary books of Monsieur le Comte de Villiers de l'Isle Adam, about which I want to write for Oscar Wilde.[4] His *Contes cruels* [1883] is one of the most remarkable collections of tales I have ever come across: you ought to read it: I feel quite ashamed to have known so little of the man for so long. I hope my article – if I can write it – will make him better known to a few people in England. Now that so much French rubbish is being translated I should like to see those *Contes cruels* taken in hand for a change. I think I shall suggest it – *after* my article – to Vizetelly. But perhaps they are not indecent enough for him.[5]

I think you are too hard on Saintsbury,[6] who is of course not a profound critic nor a pattern pedagogue. What, by the way, of his *Borrow* article?[7] I, who am a fervent Borrovian, thought it capital in its way as a light popular resumé of Borrow's work. Why do you call it an "awful exhibition"?

What do you think were the last words said to me last year? I met a woman in the street: "Are the public-houses open, gaffer?" she said. (gaffer is a term used here actually in *respect* – respectful familiarity, one might say.) I thought that was rather picturesque. – A wretched thaw to-day – skating, which was possible yesterday, is out of the question to-day.

I wish you and Mrs. Campbell the best of all wishes for the New Year.

Sincerely yours
Arthur Symons

Notes

1. See Pater's unsigned review of Symons's *Introduction to the Study of Browning* in the *Guardian*, 42 (1887) 1709–10; rptd in *Essays from 'The Guardian'* (1910).
2. 'Bell in Camp' was published in a magazine devoted to the humanities as well as to

theology and philosophy: *Time*, vii, n.s. (Jan. 1888) 69–71; rptd in *DN*.

3. James Fotheringham, *Studies in the Poetry of Robert Browning* (1887).

4. Philippe Auguste Mathias, Comte de Villiers de l'Isle Adam (1838–89), French Symbolist author, best known for his play *Axël* (1890). Symons's article on him appeared in *Woman's World*, 2 (Oct. 1889) 657–60. Wilde, who had asked Symons to write the article, was by then no longer editor.

5. Henry Vizetelly (1820–94), writer, translator, and publisher of Zola's novels, then considered indecent. Despite the tone of Symons's remark, Symons signed a petition, along with such figures as Thomas Hardy, John Addington Symonds, and Havelock Ellis, for Vizetelly's release from Holloway Gaol, where he had been sentenced for publishing Zola's *La Terre*. See 'Voices for Vizetelly's Release', *Star*, 30 July 1889, p. 2.

6. George Saintsbury (1845–1933), critic and Professor of English, Edinburgh University, 1895–1916. For Symons's later opinion of Saintsbury, see Letter 36, n. 3.

7. 'George Borrow', *Macmillan's Magazine*, 53 (1886) 170–83; rptd in *The Collected Essays and Papers of George Saintsbury, 1875–1920* (1923) vol. ii, pp. 53–81. Borrow (1803–81) is known for his semi-fictional accounts of his wanderings, *Lavengro* (1851) and *Romany Rye* (1857).

14   To James Dykes Campbell
(MS., BL)

3 April 1888   Coton Road

My dear Mr. Campbell

It is almost cruel of you to tell me what I lost by not coming to London. If that friend of mine is not hauled over the coals the next time I see him – well, it will be rather singular! But though I missed for the present Pater and [Theodore] Watts I saw last Sunday a greater man than either, and one whose chances of being seen are, alas, rapidly diminishing – John H. Card. Newman.[1] I heard that on Easter Sunday there was some faint chance of his preaching at the Oratory at Birmingham, and a certainty of his at least being present if his health could possibly allow of it. On reaching the church I found that he was not to preach, but would be present, and I was fortunate enough to get a seat in full view of the Cardinal's overcanopied chair – a privilege shared by only a *very* small proportion of those present. So there for two hours I sat and watched him. He was painfully bowed and weak, and shaken by a cough – a handkerchief scarcely ever out of his hands, and when he read a few sentences there was at first a cough between each word. His voice got better though, and it struck me as a rather curious one. The best, because the nearest sight I got of his face, was when at the close he passed down the aisle, supported on either side, and blessing the people as he went. For all his 87 years it was a splendid face – I think I have never on the whole seen a finer – still full of power and the remains of a vivid energy. As he looked then, the portraits one sees were too mild and smiling; but it was, save for a moment at one other time, the only flash of the old fire. The musical part of the service was in the hands of a good – scarcely an excellent – choir, and an admirable orchestra (including even a drum!). And to my ecstasy the setting of the mass selected for that morning was Beethoven's in C. – every note of which I knew, or at least could recognise – from repeated piano-playing: one of the grandest things even Beethoven ever wrote.

I am glad to hear you have got through Mrs. Sandford's proofs[2] and that you are going into retirement for a bit at Hastings. Indeed, I have my own reasons for this, as – heartless as I am! – I shall perhaps be asking a little favour of you when you get domiciled in quiet by the sea.

I sent a copy of my Day book, as you appropriately name it, to Halliwell-Phillipps;[3] he once edited [Day's] *Humour out of Breath* and I thought the volume would perhaps interest him. I got in return the most genial of little notes ("It is most good of you thinking of an old fellow like me") and a pretty little book about his Shakespeare rarities.[4]

Don't forget, by the way, to glance through those two plays – they are really so attractive.

I have been hearing bad news from two of my friends of late. One,[5] a friend of seven years' standing (quite 'old' to me) is obliged to vacate the editorship of the *Salisbury Journal* to make room for the son of a proprietor. This comes at a time when he is specially pressed – and wanting still better paying work. His father has for 20 years been carrying on a lawsuit in America, involving all his fortune, some £30,000: the case was decided in his favour, but on being carried to another court the judgment was reversed by a judge who had a bitter enmity against the master in Chancery. This means simply ruin, and there seems to have been no real doubt as to the right. Of course Osborne will now have to help his father, as well as maintain his own household, and it does seem very cruel. I do not doubt he will get a good position, for he is an excellent journalist, and his testimonials – from employers, and such men as Dr. Garnett – are simply as good as good can be. I have written a few lines myself which will be printed with the other weightier ones,[6] and I wrote to Mr. Ireland, but he has, naturally enough, no vacancy. Then a note from Havelock Ellis's mother or sister tells me this morning that Ellis is down with the scarlet fever. I have offered to do what I can in the way of correcting proofs and the like for the 'Mermaid' volumes that are due; but it is of course very hampering for him, besides the other considerations.

For us, we have a certain amount of anxiety as to where we shall be in less than six months' time. I suppose you know that my father is a Wesleyan Minister, and that by the unevadable laws of the Connexion no minister may stay in one circuit longer than 3 years. Assignment to another place is done usually by invitation, and we have not yet got any invitation that we care to accept. What we want is to get in a London suburb, or in some small town near London; but of course these are just the most attractive places to so many, and my father is getting an old man. There seemed at one time to be a chance of Hertford and I daresay we should have accepted, but the chance seems to have gone by. Should we be set down to some out of the way place I don't know what I shall do. It is getting more and impossible to exist so far from London.

To turn to cheerfuller matters, I saw on Monday a capital review of Canon Ainger's ed. of Lamb's letters in the *Manchester Guardian*.[7] That is a book I really think I must get, for those letters are the most purely enjoyable reading, I think, in existence; and now at last they are worthily edited.

Shall you be getting the new edition of Browning? If so I wish you would lend me the first vol. when it is out, as I should like to see if R.B. has spoilt *Pauline*.[8]

Sincerely yours
Arthur Symons

Notes

1. John Henry Newman (1801–90), Anglican churchman, author, and theologian, was, in 1833, one of the founders of the Oxford Movement, designed to revive the Church of England by introducing certain Roman Catholic rituals and doctrines. In 1845, he converted to Roman Catholicism, becoming a cardinal in 1879.
2. Mrs. Margaret E. Sandford's *Thomas Poole and His Friends*, 2 vols (1888). Poole (1765–1837) had been one of Coleridge's friends.
3. James Orchard Halliwell-Phillipps (1820–89), lexicographer, Shakespeare scholar, and editor of Shakespeare's plays (1853–65), published more than a dozen books and pamphlets on Shakespeare's life and work as well as dictionaries of archaic and provincial words and old English plays.
4. Halliwell-Phillips's *Brief Notices of a Small Number of Shakespeare Rarities* (1885).
5. Churchill Osborne.
6. Symons' testimonial letter on Osborne's behalf, along with others that supported his application for appointment as Secretary of the Reform Club, is printed in *Secretaryship of the Reform Club: Copies of Mr. C. C. Osborne's Testimonials* (1888), a rare copy of which is in the British Library. Osborne did not obtain the position, but by the end of the year he accepted the secretaryship to the Baroness Angela Burdett-Coutts (1814–1906), a position that lasted until 1898.
7. *The Letters of Charles Lamb* (1888), ed. Alfred A. Ainger (1837–1904), churchman, critic, and editor. See 'Books of the Week', *Manchester Guardian*, 2 Apr. 1888, p. 7.
8. *The Poetical Works of Robert Browning*, 17 vols (1888–94); *Pauline: A Fragment of a Confession* (1833: rev. in 1867 and 1888).

15   To James Dykes Campbell
(MS., BL)

8 [August] 1888[1]   Coton Road

My dear Mr. Campbell

The address on the outside of this envelope is I *believe* what you gave me as yours for the present, but your last letter is out of reach in some box and I have but a vague recollection of the precise form of said address. I hope it is right, for I wanted to give you mine (for about a month to come) in case you should have a spare half-hour to spend on me. It is

> Emma Place
> Bodmin
> Cornwall.

We leave to-morrow, and spend Wednesday night at Plymouth. You will be glad to hear that my cousin is decidedly better – we are thus relieved of that impending cloud. Buckingham too is confirmed.[2]

I was in London yesterday, and spent an hour with Pater. He has the MS. of my poems [*Days and Nights*], and his judgment is wonderfully flattering. He considers it needless to give any further attention to them (except to the arrangement) before the final touches on the proofs – which he has asked me to send him. So after all I shall not need to trouble you with any further consideration of them until they are in print.

This was my first sight of Pater. He is a curious personage – not at all unlike what one would expect him to be – a little difficult to talk with on account of his excessive complaisance, and the dainty way in which he holds an opinion, making it seem quite gross and rude to have ever ventured a difference. Nothing could have been kinder than his manner, or more flattering than his opinions about my pieces. I do honestly think he exaggerates their merit – and that is a strange thing for an author to say of his own bantlings. And he professes that he "never reads" modern poetry. He told me some interesting things about his ways of work, and some evidences of them in his study were significant. I was glad to hear that he intends to bring out a volume of collected essays on English writers – the Coleridge, Wordsworth, Lamb, Shakespeare and other papers.[3]

I have just room to say that I hope you will enjoy your Western holiday, and have at least endurable weather.

Sincerely yours
Arthur Symons

Notes

1. Symons erroneously wrote 'July 8, 1888', but he had met Pater on 7 Aug. 1888.
2. Symons's father had been assigned to Buckingham.
3. Walter Pater, *Appreciations: With an Essay on Style* (1889).

16   To James Dykes Campbell
    (MS., BL)

21, Chandos Road

11 December 1888   Buckingham

My dear Mr. Campbell

I am glad to have your opinion as to author's copies, etc. I will leave out W.M.R. and A.L.[1] and make the list 20. As for private friends I am much inclined to leave that to Macmillan's own generosity,[2] as I have made so many requirements. The last demand I have made (and it has been granted) is that the size of the vol. shall be Crown 8vo instead of Fcap 8vo. I found that with such thick paper the book would look quite stumpy in the smaller size, and Pater strongly approved of the wider margin.

I am very sorry I was not able to be one of the "happy little party" that Thursday. But perhaps it was best – as they were "all very clever bright people" and *I* am such a very stupid dull person!

One day last week I spent some hours very pleasantly with Pater at Oxford – lunched in his rooms, and when we had done our "business" (concerning the poems) went with him all about the place. You would never imagine what a cicerone – almost bustling – he can be! I like him much better than I did on the first meeting – we met more as friends, naturally, and I was less awed, so much less, indeed, as to discover in him an unsuspected and most charming *simplicity*. So you see I am beginning to peep behind the mask. He could not have been kinder, and, as he confessed, quite tired himself in trotting me over Oxford. I took over those of your notes on the proofs about which I was undecided, and he seemed quite struck by some of the things you had said – so very "thoughtful", his word was. I find he is working into his later essay on Coleridge some bits of the earlier one – which, however, he rightly disowns as it stands. The book of essays (some of those old *Fortnightly* ones, etc) he hopes to bring out in the summer, and he is writing a fresh Shakespeare one, on the historical plays.[3] I am glad to find that "Gaston de Latour," as published, is only Part I (a fourth) of the whole thing, on which he is still engaged.[4]

You know how ill Vernon Lee is.[5] Pater told me she is just starting for a voyage to Tangiers. Apropos, the British weekly "article" turns out to be a mere small paragraph.

I spotted "Persons from Porlock" as Lang's[6] – but it seems to me poor enough. In an American paper just come I see that A.L. has an article on "Esoteric Browningism" in the November number of the *Forum*. I should be curious to see it – specially to see if *I* am offered up as part of the sacrifice.[7]

I saw that review of Thomas Poole,[8] and was very glad to see it – for your sake, and also for the sake of the writer of that letter about "Sar' Ellen"[?] – you remember that unfortunate schoolgirl![9]

I am pleased to hear from Sarrazin that Harry Quilter (to whom I sent him when he was in England) has quite taken him up. Q. is going to have S's forthcoming vol. of essays on English poets translated, to appear at the same as the French ed.; and has promised also to print his essay on Browning in the *Universal Review*.[10] This reminds me of my grievance. It was some time in October that I sent 'Arry my paper on Ibsen, and I specially asked him to return it at once if he did not wish to use it. I have never heard a word, tho' some weeks back I wrote again and asked if I was to consider the article accepted. I even enclosed a stamp. But no reply. Would you take it for granted that he means to print it? It is very uncivil in any case, and most vexatious when one has no copy of one's article. I hardly like to write again, for fear of exasperating a man who may be useful to me.[11] Pater told me that H.Q. had written asking him to contribute, but he "didn't like the way he wrote."

I have just had a very interesting well-written letter from Mathilde Blind.[12] She has been staying at Tunbridge Wells. I am looking out for a letter from Michael Field, to whom I wrote in a wickedly teasing way, pretending I had revealed the whole awful secret[13] when I got back to your house after seeing her.

You will read with delight the scarcely too severe onslaught upon the Richard Jefferies myth in last week's *Athenaeum*. I could almost swear it is written by George Moore, who I know writes for Maccoll.[14]

Have you seen the extraordinary printer's freak in to-day's *Daily News* – among the book reviews in the 2nd col? There is a word (absolutely without sense too) printed upside down, a total blank, and at least one stop out of place in a rather laughable way.

Now I must try to stay at home and really work. These proofs have thrown me off all *work* and I have been doing nothing except doze over them for weeks and weeks.

Yours ever
A.S.

Notes

1. William Michael Rossetti (1829–1919), critic and biographer, the brother of Dante Gabriel Rossetti; Andrew Lang (1844–1912), poet, critic, and folklorist.
2. George Macmillan (1855–1936), publisher, became a partner in the family publishing business in 1879 and subsequently its director. In December, Symons met Macmillan while in London: see Letter 17.
3. See Walter Pater's *Appreciations: With an Essay on Style* (1889). The essay on Coleridge in *Appreciations* is an amalgam of a revised version of 'Coleridge's Writings', *Westminster Review*, 85 (Jan. 1866) 106–32, and the introduction to selected poems of Coleridge in *The English Poets*, ed. T. H. Ward (1880) vol. IV, pp. 102–14.
4. Pater's *Gaston de Latour* was never completed. The first five chapters appeared in *MM*, 58 (1888) 152–60, 222–9, 258–66, 393–400, 472–80; part of ch. 7, 'Giordano Bruno', appeared in *FR*, 52 (1889) 234–44. *Gaston de Latour: An Unfinished Romance* appeared in 1896.
5. Pseudonym of Violet Paget (1856–1935), aesthetician, novelist, critic, and disciple of Walter Pater. In a letter to J. Dykes Campbell on 4 October 1886 (MS., BL), Symons wrote of her: 'I admire her vastly, and when I wrote the introduction to *Venus and Adonis* imitated her style so conscientiously as to make Dr. Furnivall swear – alas! at her.'
6. Andrew Lang, 'Persons from Porlock', *SR*, 66 (1888) 665–6.
7. Lang's 'Esoteric Browningism', *Forum*, 6 (1888) 300–10, does not mention Symons.
8. An allusion to Mrs H. Sandford's book (see Letter 14, n.2), reviewed in the *Athenaeum*, 29 Dec. 1888, pp. 871–3.
9. Unidentified.
10. Harry Quilter (1851–1907) was founder and editor of the *Universal Review*, 1888–90. Sarrazin's *La Renaissance de la poésie anglaise, 1798–1889* (Paris, 1889) did not appear in translation. See Sarrazin's 'Robert Browning', *Universal Review*, 3 (1889) 230–46. Gabriel Sarrazin (b. 1853), French critic, who introduced the Pre-Raphaelites to French readers.
11. Symons's article, 'Henrik Ibsen', appeared in the *Universal Review*, 3 (15 Apr. 1889) 567–74.
12. Poet and biographer (1841–96), whom Ernest Rhys, in *Everyman Remembers* (1931), quotes as saying that Symons was 'the coming poet, the Poet of the New Time, for whom we were all looking' (p. 111). In a letter to Rhoda Bowser, later Symons's wife, Symons wrote in 1899: 'I never knew [Mathilde Blind] until she was over 40; her face was the most emotional, but the most worn and haggard and furrowed I have ever seen. She was very good to me and very fond of me, and I, as usual, very ungrateful' (MS., postmarked 9 Oct. 1899, Columbia). Symons edited *The Poetical Works of Mathilde Blind* (1900), in the Preface of which he states that he had been appointed her literary executor with Ludwig Mond (1839–1909), industrialist and art collector.
13. Presumably the 'secret' of their identity.
14. The 'onslaught' on Jefferies (1848–87), the novelist and naturalist, occurred in an unsigned review of Walter Besant's *The Eulogy of Richard Jefferies* (1888) in the *Athenaeum*, 8 Dec. 1888, pp. 765–6, which concludes: 'To bleat about heroism is not the way to make heroes; and it may be that Jefferies, had his environment been less fluent and sonorous, would have been something more heroic than he was.' George Moore (1852–1933), Irish man of letters, was apparently not the author of the review: it is not listed in Edwin Gilcher's *A Bibliography of George Moore* (DeKalb, Ill., 1970). Norman Maccoll (1843–1904) was editor of the *Athenaeum*, 1871–1900. See Symons's 'Richard Jefferies' in *STL*. Earlier, Symons had described Moore's *Confessions of a Young Man* (1888) in a letter to J. Dykes Campbell as 'a shallow, brilliant, trenchant, acute, impertinent book, with a portrait of the man which interests by its commonplaceness, its air of sincerity, its heavy solemn cavalry-captain sort of look' (MS., 14 Apr. 1888, BL).

17 To Churchill Osborne
(MS., Princeton)

12 December 1888   21, Chandos Road

My dear Churchill

I have not liked to bother you with writing, but when you have a little time I should very much like to know how you are getting on – if you are better, and if Mrs. Osborne is well on the way of recovery too. I have heard a little news of you from Veitch, and was exceedingly glad to learn that he had been down at Salisbury doing editorial duty for you. That must have been a great relief and comfort. I am sorry *Dives* hasn't done better with the reviews – I don't know if the public has rendered it more justice. The only decent review I saw was in the *Spectator* – which thinks Leith Derwent is a woman![1]

I am beginning to wonder now what luck *my* book [*Days and Nights*] will have. I have not yet done with the proofs, and shall probably send R. & R. Clark into a lunatic asylum before I have finished my corrections. I was in London the other day, and paid a visit to Mr. Geo[rge] Macmillan, who is an extremely nice man, a gentleman as well as a publisher, and not at all rigid in his own ideas. So I am to have everything my own way – paper, binding and shape are all selected by me. The paper and binding will be similar to those used in Pater's books – a sort which was prepared under his personal supervision and which I think very charming. The vol. will be as thick as Swinburne's *Songs before Sunrise* [1871] or Rossetti's *Poems* [1870], though not containing so many pages.

I have paid some agreeable visits to London and elsewhere of late. I spent a very delightful afternoon some weeks ago at "Michael Field's," the mystery of whose personality I am not permitted to reveal. I saw Garnett too at the British Museum, and he spoke very kindly of you. The other day I lunched with Pater at Brasenose College, of which he is Fellow and Tutor, and spent the afternoon going about Oxford with him. He is the kindest-hearted of men, and most simple and genial when one has got through the veil or mask of formal politeness and rather forbidding gravity which he ordinarily wears. I saw in London too the ever-vivacious Dr. Furnivall, who is as brisk, light-hearted and vigorous as ever. His last argument is to show that Shakespeare was *not* born at "Shakespeare's Birthplace," and he detailed it to Dykes Campbell and me with infinite detail and equal assurance.

I suppose you know that after all the new editor of the *St. James's Gazette* is Low, the former sub-editor. I learnt this from Campbell, who had it from Greenwood himself.[2] I hope therefore that Greenwood's absence will not make any difference to your position on the paper.[3]

My father and mother and my sister all wish to be very kindly remembered to Mrs. Osborne and yourself, and join with me in hoping for some news from you soon, and good news.

Very sincerely yours
Arthur Symons

Notes

1. The reviewer of *A Daughter of Dives*, Leith Derwent's novel, stated in the *Spectator*, 61 (1888) 1476, that it was 'the cleverest work she has yet produced'.
2. Sidney Low (1857–1932), editor of the *St James's Gazette*, 1888–97; Frederick Greenwood (1830–1909), author and journalist, was editor of the *St James's Gazette*, 1880–8.
3. What Osborne's 'position' was on the *St James's Gazette* is unclear, but the change in editors may have been a decisive factor in his acceptance of the Baroness Burdett-Coutts's offer to be her secretary.

18 To Remy de Gourmont[1]
(MS., Castex)

16 January 1889   21, Chandos Road

Dear Sir

I am much obliged to you for your kind and most interesting letter. I did indeed write to M. de Villiers, but it was not for permission to translate any of his works: it was for information respecting them. As you know, I have written an article on Villiers de l'Isle Adam which is to appear in the *Woman's World*.[2] Before writing it I wished if possible to read some of those early and now almost inaccessible works – such as *Isis* [1862], etc. – and I ventured to ask M. de Villiers if he could lend me any of them.[3] Not receiving any answer, and not being able to meet with these works anywhere, I had to write the article without consulting them. It occurs to me that perhaps you may have any of them, and that you might be willing to lend them to me for a short time. I would of course take the utmost care of them and would return them as quickly as possible. I am still anxious to make some reference to these early works, and as the article is not yet in print I should have no difficulty in getting it back and re-writing it.

The books that I have – those on which I have founded my study – are the *Contes cruels* [1883], *L'Ève future* [1886], *La Révolte* [1870], *L'Amour suprême* [1886] and *Tribulat Bonhomet* [1887]. The one I prefer *infinitely* to all the others is the volume of *Contes cruels*. I know nothing in any language more perfect, more delicate in touch, more subtle in texture, more exquisite in charm, than some of these tales. As for the later work, I admire it less.

Though, as I have said, I did not write to M. de Villiers in reference to a translation, I will confess to you that I had always intended to make an attempt, after the appearance of my essay, to induce Vizetelly – the publisher who has translated Zola – to publish a translation of the *Contes cruels*. I could not undertake to do this myself, as I am far too busy; but I might perhaps *revise* such a translation, if any suitable translator and publisher could be found. Whether Vizetelly will consent is of course very doubtful, and I do not wish to say anything to him until my essay has appeared. But now that I have, through you, the assurance that M. de Villiers would not object to a translation if I could find a translator likely to do the work well, I will certainly make the attempt to induce Vizetelly to undertake the matter.

I thank you sincerely for the very kind words you have said about my work. For my part I take an immense interest in contemporary French literature, and I am always glad to hear of the study of our writers in France. In the modern world there have only been two great literatures – yours and ours – and I think there is every reason why we should study each other. I hope that my brief article may do something to awaken interest among our readers in one of the most remarkable writers of the day.

You may perhaps have learnt from Sarrazin that I am about to publish a volume of poems. One of the pieces contained in the volume is a translation of the delicious little poem of Villiers called "L'Aveu"[4] – you will remember it, in the *Contes cruels*. I had wished to send a copy of the volume to M. de Villiers, but, not being sure of his address, should not have done so had I not heard from you. Perhaps you will be good enough either to tell me at what address the book will be certain to reach him, or to take charge of a copy on his account and see that it comes safely into his hands?

> Believe me, dear Sir
> Yours sincerely
> Arthur Symons

Notes

1. Printed, with several errors in transcription, in Roger Lhombreaud, *Arthur Symons: A Critical Biography* (1963) pp. 46–8. Remy de Gourmont, French critic (1858–1914), prominent in the Symbolist Movement, who, as a prolific contributor to the *Mercure de France*, was a leading theoretician. T. S. Eliot referred to him as 'the critical consciousness of a generation' (*The Sacred Wood*, 1920, p. 44).
2. See Letter 13, n. 4.
3. Symons wrote to Villiers on 11 Jan. 1888 (MS., Castex): 'I am studying your works with intense interest and delight, and am hoping to write on them a critical study in which I shall try to introduce them to a wider public in England.' When Villiers did

not respond, Gourmont wrote to him on behalf of Symons, 'jeune homme de grand talent'. See Alan William Raitt, *Villiers de l'Isle Adam et le Mouvement Symboliste* (Paris, 1965) p. 316.
4. See 'Confession', *DN*, p. 168.

19   To James Dykes Campbell
(MS., BL)

24 March [1889]   21, Chandos Road

My dear Mr. Campbell
   Have you seen Pater's review in last night's *Pall Mall*? I expected something good, but not anything so good as that. It is a review that ought to make the fortune of the book.[1] I only hope that some of the adversaries of the *P.M.G.* won't say the book is bad simply because the *P.M.G.* says it is good.
   The review is simply ideal, and in every way. As a piece of writing there is no one but Pater who could have done it. What a magnificent advertisement the last sentence or two will make, if M[acmillan] and Co. will only put it in their list, as I daresay they will. After this, all the reviews will seem tame, but I sincerely hope they may follow on the same lines. At all events, after such praise, and so deliberately worded, in so widely read a paper, there will be no likelihood of the book getting *overlooked* – and that is a main point.

                                                     Yours ever
                                                     AS

Note

1. Walter Pater, 'A Poet With Something to Say', *PMG*, 23 Mar. 1889, p. 3, which concludes: 'The finer pieces of this volume [*Days and Nights*], certainly, any poet of our day might be glad to own, for their substance, their dramatic hold on life, their fine scholarship; and they have this eminent merit, among many fine qualities of style – readers need fear no difficulty in them. In this new poet the rich poetic vintage of our time has run clear at last.' Pater's review was reprinted in *Sketches and Reviews* (New York, 1919).

20 To Michael Field
(MS., BL)

5 April 1889   21, Chandos Road

Dear Miss Bradley

Pater's review [of *Days and Nights*] is now chez Ellis: he will send it on to you. Meanwhile I enclose something else which you may care to see of his: he sent it to me a few days ago. It is from *Scribner's Magazine*. It seems to me a very original handling of a theme difficult to say anything fresh about.[1] In writing him yesterday, by the way, I enclosed one of the *Long Ago* leaflets.[2]

I send the *Contes cruels*, which I deliberately think the most wonderful volume of short stories known to me in any language. I feel towards certain of them much as you feel towards the work of Pierre Loti:[3] – I wish Oscar Wilde would bring out my article:[4] it has been waiting partly, I think, for a portrait which is to accompany it, and with which, I hear from France, Villiers is much pleased. I could tell you a lot of stories about the man, who is as extraordinary as his works. He claims to be, and probably is, the head of the family of Villiers de l'Isle Adam, which is one of the very oldest in France, and much of his life he has lived almost on charity. Whenever he got a little money he would go and stay with his friend, Wagner. At one time he would be dining with the Czar; then you would meet him in the lowest of Parisian cafés, hobnobbing with its habitués and dashing off a story in the midst of the clatter. He is deeply read in all occult literature, a magnificent pianist, takes opium, talks with a studied extravagance and in epigrams that often bite – and, in short, is himself one of the bizarre heroes of his own books. His best friends rarely know his address, and as one of them wrote me the other day: "Il oublierait aussi de répondre à un editeur qui lui offrirait cent mille francs de son prochain livre qu'a une simple demande de renseignement."

In correcting the proofs I hope you won't forget to scrutinize every word and every stop by as many pairs of eyes as the household will willingly provide, and the same with every fresh proof. On even a final proof there are almost sure to be errors. Nothing is more common than for one error to be made in the process of shifting the type to correct another. I read my proofs so many times over that I got quite to hate the sight of them.

Sincerely yours
Arthur Symons

Notes

1. Walter Pater, 'Shakespeare's English Kings', *Scribner's Magazine*, 5 (1889) 506–12; rptd in *Appreciations*.
2. In a letter to J. Dykes Campbell of 24 Feb. 1889 (MS., BL), Symons writes: 'I hear today from Michael Field that her book – "Long Ago: a series of lyrics expanded from the fragments of Sappho" – is to be got up in a very pretty way, frontispiece from a Sapphic vase at Athens, head of Sappho in gold on the cover, Greek headings in red, etc. Only 100 copies are to be printed. The attempt is unparalleled for audacity: may it in some measure succeed.'
3. Pseudonym of Julien Viaud (1850–1923), French novelist and author of travel books.
4. See Letter 13, n. 4.

21   To William Holman Hunt[1]
(MS., Hart-Davis)

8 May 1889   21, Chandos Road

Dear Mr. Hunt

I don't know whether you heard from Dr. Furnivall that I have just been bringing out a volume of poems. Will you accept a copy from me? I should so much like you to see my work – whether you will approve of my principle of art I scarcely know, but I shall be very proud if you should at all care for any of the pieces. While you were, I think, out of the room on Sunday, Mrs. Hunt, Dr. Furnivall and I were discussing Sim's ballads,[2] and Dr. Furnivall – who spares no one – was cruel enough to say that some of the things in my book were just of the same kind. I vehemently protested, for I think that there is a quite radical difference, and nothing distresses me so much as a comparison of that sort. I so much wish Mrs. Hunt would be good enough to read "The Knife-Thrower," "Margery of the Fens" and "Red Bredbury's End" (poems written in the ballad measure) and then give judgment for or against.

I am sending you the book through my publishers.

Very truly yours
Arthur Symons

I saw on Monday at one of the galleries a wonderful little picture of yours called "Sorrow."[3] I was particularly struck with the reticence – so rare and so priceless a thing in all kinds of art – in the representation of what really did affect one as intense grief. The expression was all inward, as the deepest expression always is. Near it I saw a portrait of Mrs. Hunt, which I recognized from a distance as a very good likeness, though scarcely, I thought, adequate.[4]

Notes

1. Painter (1827–1910) and original member of the Pre-Raphaelite Brotherhood, established in 1848. As artist and man – Symons told Michael Field – Hunt was 'incomparable' (MS., 19 May 1889, BL).
2. George Robert Sims (1847–1922), writer of popular ballads and collaborator with Robert Buchanan on several plays. Marion Edith Hunt, née Waugh (d. 1931), sister of Hunt's first wife, Fanny (who died in childbirth in 1866), married him in 1875. The poet and painter William Bell Scott, a mutual friend, said that Edith, who was buried beside her husband in Westminster Abbey, was Hunt's 'salvation by the amiability and helpfulness of the noblest of women' (quoted in A. C. Gissing, *William Holman Hunt* [1936] p. 183).
3. Exhibited at the New Gallery's Summer Exhibition, which opened on 2 May.
4. Mrs Hunt's portrait was painted by Mrs Henry Merritt (1844–1930), an American who had settled in London in 1871.

22   To James Dykes Campbell

(MS., BL)

15 June 1889   21, Chandos Road

My dear Campbell

I was very glad to get your letter of the 5th and to hear how nicely all your arrangements seemed to be going, particularly about Mrs. Campbell. I hope they are going on as well as you expected, and that the nurse etc proves the treasure you anticipated. Since your letter came I have been one day to Oxford, to see Pater and a picture-exhibn. and have since been spending five crowded but delightful days in London, from Friday to Tuesday. I went up to see Ibsen's play[1] and to see Sarrazin, who is again in England, accompanied by a literary friend Antonin Bunand,[2] who – alas for me! – doesn't know a word of English. They are both excellent fellows, and full of information about French literature – very valuable to me. They almost *live* at Madox Brown's, [3] where Miss Blind has been taking them in charge, and while I was up I too was there a great deal. Miss Blind was kind enough to introduce me to the Wm. Rossettis, where we went one afternoon. Quite a crowd of people there – the Miss Ferraris[4] sang some Abruzzi popular songs – I was introduced to "Mrs. [Augusta] Webster's husband"[5] (poor man, to have such a title – and such a nice old fellow too) and saw Amy Levy,[6] who is getting noted for her stories of Jewish life. I liked Mrs. better than Mr. Rossetti, as far as first impressions go. Does he always, I wonder, talk in that cool critical way, seeing the seamy side of all fine reputations, and gazing abstractedly across the room as he talks? But I was extremely interested to see him, and very pleased with the way he spoke of my article about Christina.[7] I hope some day he will take me to see her.

I have made one or two other acquaintances. On Sunday Miss Blind, Sarrazin, Bunand and I lunched with the eminent *Mrs. Mona Caird*,[8] and then all went down, a jolly (and very peculiar-*looking*) party, to Kew! We didn't discuss marriage *all* the time. No Mr. Caird was visible. Sir James[9] turned up, and was left behind with the little boy. About 10 or 11 we all turned up at Wm. Sharp's and there, to my great delight, I met Mrs. Meynell.[10] Do you know her little vol. of *Preludes*, published in 1875 when she was Alice Thompson? It is some of the most truly poetical poetry any woman has ever written. You can fancy how prepared I was to meet the writer of it, and my enthusiasm seemed to please her very much. She asked me to come to see her when I am in town, and gave me her address. There is something pathetically weary and harassed about her, but she talks really like a poet. Graham Tomson[11] was there too, in an antique peplum of red, looking very handsome, but I was only introduced to her husband (he is No. 2 and they both look about three and twenty) – *not* a fascinating person, which makes Bunand anticipate the chance of some day offering himself as 'le troisième'!

I lunched with Frank Marshall one day and dined with Madox Brown the same evening, where I met Mrs Hueffer.[12] Ada Marshall (la Cavendish)[13] is both handsomer and more interesting than I thought – I had more talk with her this time, and saw her better. She admired "Anactoria" and "The Leper"[14] over her cigarette – which was at least interesting. And she admired Red Bredbury and the Revenge[15] – which was admirable. Both they and Mme. Petrici,[16] whom you probably know as an attachée of the Rossettis, talked of reciting some of my poems.

Then, best by far of all, I spent a good part of Monday with Olive Schreiner, at her chambers in that big block of Ladies' Chambers in Chenies Street.[17] You cannot imagine what a wonderful woman she is: the *African Farm* + all the living personality which that gives only through the medium of print. I never had such a talk in my life – literally, both as regards quality and quantity! And it was nearly all about herself – just the most interesting subject, and the most difficult, generally, to get at.

What have you been doing this week? Have you seen [James Russell] Lowell, who I hear is in England? If so, I envy you.

Sincerely yours
Arthur Symons

My *P.M.G.* review has not appeared yet.[18] Maccoll has sent me Mrs. Woods' poems for review.[19]

Isn't Amelie Rives (Mrs. Chanler) also in England?[20] Some sonnets of hers are really extremely fine.

Notes

1. Henrik Ibsen, *A Doll's House*, translated by William Archer (1856–1924), Scottish drama critic and champion of Ibsen, opened on 7 June 1889 at the Novelty Theatre. See Symons's review, 'Ibsen on the Stage', *Scottish Art Review*, 2 (July 1889) 40.
2. French critic, author of *Petits lundis: notes de critique* (Paris, 1890).
3. Ford Madox Brown (1821–93), painter and poet, was associated with the Pre-Raphaelite Brotherhood.
4. The Countesses Augusta and Ernesta Ferrari d'Occhieppo, singers of popular songs.
5. Augusta Webster (1837–94), playwright and poet, who published several volumes of verse under the name of 'Cecil Home'.
6. Author and feminist (1862–89), who contributed stories and articles to *Woman's World* during Oscar Wilde's editorship. In Sep. 1889, she committed suicide; see Letter 23.
7. Arthur Symons, 'Miss Rossetti's Poetry', *LQR*, 68 (July 1887) 338–50; rptd in *STL*.
8. Author (d. 1932), who achieved notoriety for her articles, 'Marriage', *Westminster Review*, 130 (1888) 186–201, and 'Ideal Marriage', *ibid.*, pp. 617–36. They provoked considerable controversy on p. 5 of the *Daily Telegraph* between 10 Aug. 1888, and 29 Sept. 1888, under the heading 'Is Marriage a Failure?'
9. Unidentified.
10. Alice Meynell (1847–1922), poet and critic, who in 1877 married Wilfrid Meynell (1852–1948), editor and author, an admirer of her first volume of verse, *Preludes* (1875). Both are noted for their rescue of the self-destructive poet Francis Thompson (1859–1907). In 1895, the poet Coventry Patmore proposed Mrs. Meynell as the new poet laureate to succeed Tennyson.
11. Poet, critic, journalist (1863–1911), and onetime wife of Arthur Tomson, the artist, whom she left for H. B. Marriott Watson (1863–1921), the New Zealand journalist.
12. Mrs. Catherine Hueffer, wife of Dr. Francis Hueffer (1845–89), music critic of *The Times*. She was the mother of Ford Madox Hueffer (he later changed his surname to 'Ford'), the novelist (1873–1939).
13. Actress (1847–95), who made her *début* in 1865, and achieved moderate success in both the United States and England.
14. Poems by Swinburne, included in *Poems and Ballads* (1866).
15. An allusion to two poems in *Days and Nights*.
16. According to William M. Rossetti, Mme. Petrici knew his wife 'extremely well, and often relieved some hour of depression by lively and pointed talk' (*Some Reminiscences*, [1906], vol. II, p. 492).
17. For Symons's account of that meeting, see S. C. Cronwright-Schreiner, *The Life of Olive Schreiner* (1924) pp. 184–90.
18. Unsigned review of William Sharp's *American Sonnets* and William D. Lighthall's *Songs of the Great Dominion* in *PMG*, 18 July 1889, p. 3.
19. See Symons's unsigned review of *Lyrics and Ballads* by Mrs. Margaret Woods (1856–1945), poet and novelist, in the *Athenaeum*, 3 Aug. 1889, pp. 157–8.
20. Amélie (Rives) Chanler, pseudonym of Princess Troubetskoy (1863–1945), American playwright, novelist, and poet, about whom Symons wrote to J. D. Campbell on 1 Sep. 1889 (MS., BL): 'she has power, tho' undisciplined, and if you had seen her portrait you would want to meet her too!'

23 To James Dykes Campbell
(MS., BL)

[mid-September 1889]

My dear Campbell

Have you heard? – Amy Levy has killed herself[1] – with charcoal fumes. I have only heard that, and that she "wanted to be happy." She was only 27. I can not tell you how sorry I am. I never knew her – only once saw her – but Miss Schreiner was very anxious for us to meet, as she thought we should like each other. It will be a great blow to O[live] S[chreiner], who thought her the most fascinating girl she had met in England! I know how sorry you will be. Don't mention anything of this to anyone, unless it becomes generally known.

Yours
A.S.

Note

1. In her final letter to Olive Schreiner, Amy Levy wrote: 'you care for science and art and helping your fellow-men, therefore life is worth living to you; to me it is worth nothing'. See *Letters of Olive Schreiner*, ed. S. C. Cronwright-Schreiner (1924) p. 207; 'Death of a Jewish Authoress', *PMG*, 14 Sep. 1889, p. 5.

24 To James Dykes Campbell
(MS., BL)

6 October 1889   21, Chandos Road

My dear Campbell

I have only now found time to write to you though I have been back in England since the Saturday before last. Ellis and I only spent eight days in Paris, confining ourselves chiefly to the Exhibition,[1] as we intend to go over again, perhaps after Xmas and really live in Paris for awhile. As might have been expected, everybody was out of town, or engaged somehow (Verlaine[2] in the hospital!) and we only made three calls. At Sarrazin's I met Jules Case,[3] one of the most rising novelists – a very impressive looking man, something like a younger Daudet.[4] But as for Paris, I was truly enchanted, and felt, as I expected to, that I never wished to come away again. Our hotel was in the Rue de Choiseul, turning out of the Boulevard des Italiens, and that Boulevard was something unforgettable. On Sunday night I patrolled it from 9 to 12, taking what Baudelaire calls a "bath of multitude." The results of the elections were being announced on a "transparency" outside the Gaulois as fast as they arrived, and the crowds there made it impossible for the buses to pass. I had the delight of observing the humours of a French crowd.[5]

Besides the Exhibition (we did *not* go up the Eiffel Tower, though I have a sort of recollection of having seen it about somewhere) we went several times to the Louvre, twice to Notre Dame (once on the towers) to the Morgue[6] of course when we were in the neighbourhood, to one or two theatres etc, including the Montagnes Russes, which has already given me the material for a poem,[7] to the Latin Quarter, besides the various places one saw from omnibuses and in walking. It was a great pleasure to visit the shop of Léon Vanier, the "Decadent" publisher,[8] where we saw photographs of Verlaine, Villiers etc., and bought some books and papers. Of course there was a cat in the establishment – most meditative, mysterious, truculent, and altogether entirely decadent! The Exhibition you have probably heard quite enough of already. It really is magnificent – on every side. We spent our time largely in the Beaux Arts and the Rue de Caire. The latter is delightful – it tempted us into a number of purchases, notably a pair of white and gold burnouses with gorgeous sashes, which will make the most effective (and indeed most comfortable) dressing-gowns. We visited I think every one of the Arab entertainments, and are now competent to instruct all and sundry on the whole form and order of the Danse du Ventre – really a most wonderful performance, unlike anything European bodies have ever achieved. We saw too the Javanese dancers,[9] who have a special cachet of their own. It has been like making a tour of the world, not merely going to Paris.

Altogether our trip has been voted an entire success. We went by the Calais night-service – rather rough going, basins plentiful, smooth enough returning, and no basins visible. Ellis endured it in patience and certainly did not enjoy himself. I did enjoy myself, back by the stern, watching the racing froth. But the long slow journey to Paris was wretched, and so the return journey from Dover to London. We got to London, I think, about 8, on Saturday morning, very much astonished to find everybody talking English, and very much disgusted with English fare!

You may have seen from the *P.M.G.* that Olive Schreiner has left England for the Cape.[10] I knew, long ago, that she was going, but was not at liberty to mention it, as she did not wish people to know, dreading farewell calls and letters. She is going to a lonely place right at the very edge of the Cape, where she will be in perfect solitude but for the old people she is to lodge with. And how long she will stay there not even she herself has the least idea.

How are things going at West Hill? As they should, I hope.

Very sincerely

Arthur Symons

Do you know the name of Sir Chas. Murray, K.C.B.?[11] He wrote to me in reference to Villiers.

Notes

1. The Exhibition commemorated the centenary of the French Revolution.
2. Paul Verlaine (1844–96), a profound influence on Symons, who wrote many reviews and articles on him, translated a number of his poems (see *KH*), and, in November 1893, helped to arrange his lecture tour in England. On his second trip to Paris with Ellis, Symons met Verlaine on 29 April 1890. See Beckson, pp. 54–5.
3. French novelist and dramatist (b. 1856).
4. Alphonse Daudet (1840–97), French novelist, best known for his stories of Provençal life in *Lettres de mon moulin* (1869) and for his naturalistic novels.
5. Symons and Ellis were in Paris at the time of the crucial elections to the Chamber of Deputies on 22 September, in which the Republicans won a decisive victory.
6. In Karl Baedeker's *Paris and Environs*, 10th rev. edn (Leipzig, 1891), the Morgue, at the southeast end of the Ile de la Cité, is described as 'a small building, re-erected in 1864, where the bodies of unknown persons who have perished in the river or otherwise are exposed to view. They are placed on marble slabs, kept cool by a constant flow of water and are exhibited in the clothes in which they were found. . . . The bodies brought number about 800 annually, one-seventh being those of women. The painful scene attracts many spectators, chiefly of the lower orders' (p. 224). See Symons's poem 'At the Morgue' in *KH*.
7. One of the many *cafés chantant* in Paris, the Montagnes Russes was located on the Boulevard des Capuchines. As described by Baedeker, the music and singing were 'never of a high class, while the audience is of a very mixed character' (*Paris and Environs*, p. 33). Which poem may have been inspired by this café remains unknown.
8. French publisher and editor (1847–96), who published the works of Verlaine and other French Decadents and Symbolists.
9. Symons later wrote one of his finest poems, 'Javanese Dancers' (included in *Silhouettes*, 1892), inspired by this performance.
10. Reported in 'Today's Tittle-Tattle', *PMG*, 4 Oct. 1889, p. 6. In November, Schreiner returned to South Africa after an absence of eight and a half years, emotionally drained after her unsatisfactory relationship with Karl Pearson (a professor of mathematics at University College, London), convinced of her failure as a writer, and worried over her chronic asthma.
11. Sir Charles Augustus Murray (1806–95), diplomat and author.

2

Achievement and Dissipation: 1890–6

In the spring of 1890, Symons, with Havelock Ellis, was in Paris for a second visit, where he met most of the leading writers and artists. These months, Ellis later wrote, 'the climax of the whole early part of my life', were passed 'pleasantly and instructively'.[1] The two, spending much time in the cafés along the Boulevard St Michel and in the literary salons, met such figures as Huysmans, Remy de Gourmont, Taine, Mallarmé, Maeterlinck, Moréas, and Verlaine, though they missed Zola, whom they had hoped to meet. A confirmed Francophile, Symons wrote to Campbell on May 25: 'I am by this time getting so Parisian that the thought of London fills me with horror.'[2]

Early in June, however, he returned to London to resume his life as a literary journalist. In August, he was asked by J. S. Cotton, editor of the *Academy*, to take over his post during his holiday – the first such opportunity for gainful employment. At this time, he became associated with the Rhymers' Club (or the 'Rhymsters' Club', as some members called it), which had been founded early in 1890 by Yeats, Rhys, and other young poets. Though he did not take the club seriously (he rarely mentions it in his letters), he did contribute to its two anthologies; it also extended his circle of friends to include, besides Yeats, Ernest Dowson, Lionel Johnson, and John Davidson, among others in the club.

In January 1891, Symons moved into a flat in Fountain Court, The Temple, which he occupied for ten years. Nearby, in King's Bench Walk, lived George Moore, whom he had met in Paris and who became a close friend. Recalling that time in The Temple, Symons wrote in his dedication to Moore in *Studies in Two Literatures* (1897):

Do you remember, at the time when we were both living in the Temple, and our talks used to begin with midnight and go on until the first glimmerings of dawn shivered among the trees, your trees and mine; do you remember how often we have discussed, well, I suppose everything which I speak of in these studies in the two literatures which we both chiefly care for?

Also not far away from Fountain Court was Herbert Horne, editor of the *Century Guild Hobby Horse*, poet and art historian, with whom Symons made occasional trips to the Continent.

At about this time, Symons became acquainted with Katherine Willard, a young American girl interested in an operatic career. Symons's letters to her reveal a growing attachment, bordering on a love affair but cooling in the mid-1890s, apparently the result of her uncertainty about Symons's Bohemian tendencies. He dedicated two poems and his second volume of verse, *Silhouettes* (1892), to her. Her brother, Frank, a professional tramp who wrote under the name of 'Josiah Flynt', became a close friend and on occasion stayed at Fountain Court.

In the spring of 1891, Symons embarked on another trip to the Continent with Ellis, this time to Spain, returning in May. In July, he left for Germany to visit the Willards (Katherine's mother conducted a school in Berlin for American girls), a journey perhaps suggested by Mrs Willard in order to see whom her daughter had been corresponding with. In his posthumously published memoirs, Frank Willard wrote of Symons's visit: 'He had spent a month with me in my home in Berlin, where, as usual, he dug all over the city, for impressions and sensations – "impreshuns" and "sensashuns" was the way they were finally called in my household.'[3]

Late in 1891, Symons was at work on his first play, *The Minister's Call*, based on a story by Frank Harris. Uncertain of the structural problems in writing for the stage, Symons turned to George Moore for help, and the two spent many hours restructuring Symons's first dramatic effort. Indeed, Symons attempted, without success, to persuade Moore that his name should appear as co-author, but Moore refused.[4] The play, produced for one performance by the Independent Theatre in March 1892, was received with a disappointing array of praise and condemnation.

Symons's letters to Rhys during this time reveal how he had been able to free himself from his pious family background, how involved and exhilarated he was with his literary and theatrical life in London. He was now a regular critic of ballet and music-halls for the *Star* (Yeats, in an article on the Rhymers, referred to him as 'a scholar in music-halls'),[5] extending his nightly visits to his favourite public house, the Crown near Leicester Square, where Symons frequented the Empire and Alhambra Theatres, and the more respectable Café Royal in Regent Street. His letters delight in telling Rhys of his frenzied pursuit of ballet girls or of his parties at Fountain Court. But Symons was at the same time seriously using the imagery of the music-hall in his verse – in short, heightening the triviality of passing pleasures with the secondary dancers of the *corps de ballet* into the meaningful, symbolic design of art.

In May 1892, Symons returned to Paris for a month to renew his friendships with Verlaine, Mallarmé, and Remy de Gourmont. Shortly after his return to London, he received word from John Addington Symonds that he was planning a trip to England (Symons had first met him in London in 1889). In June, Symonds wrote: 'You are so good to me, and so understanding of the real man who has "never spoken out" yet, that I should like to tell you some things about myself which cannot well be written.'[6] Wrote Symons later: 'On his arrival in London [in July], Symonds asked me to lunch with him. His exquisite charm and innate courtesy soon put me at ease. . . . We had much in common; and yet with what singular differences!'[7]

Symons invited him and Ernest Dowson to Fountain Court to have tea and haschisch with ballet dancers from the Empire, then took him in the evening to see them dance. This was the last time that Symons saw Symonds, for he died in the following year; Pater followed in 1894. Symons felt both losses deeply.

In November 1893, two events occurred which made Symons's name, in the public mind, synonymous with Decadence in literature: the publication of his article 'The Decadent Movement in Literature'[8] and the visit of Verlaine to England, a lecture tour arranged by Symons and the artist William Rothenstein. The article established Symons as a spokesman and champion of the Decadence (which he called 'a beautiful and interesting disease' and which discussed such figures as Verlaine, Huysmans, Maeterlinck, and Mallarmé, 'the prophet and pontiff of the movement, the mystical and theoretical leader of the great emancipation'). When Verlaine, who stayed at Fountain Court during his visit, lectured at Barnard's Inn, Holborn, on 21 November, Symons escorted the lame poet to the platform.

In 1894, literary London was anticipating the publication of a new periodical, the *Yellow Book*, edited by Henry Harland, the American novelist, and by Aubrey Beardsley, the young artist whom Symons had met in the previous year. Symons wrote to Verlaine in February that he was contributing a poem somewhat daring for an English review.[9] When the first issue appeared in April, Symons's poem, 'Stella Maris', was singled out, in the furor that followed, by outraged critics who were offended by its candid description of 'the Juliet of a Night'. In the second number in July, Philip G. Hamerton, in a critique of the first number (an attempt, apparently, on the part of the *Yellow Book* to publicise its own daring), wrote:

I regret the publication of 'Stella Maris', by Mr. Arthur Symons; the choice of the title is in itself offensive. It is taken from one of the most beautiful hymns to the Holy Virgin (Ave, maris stella!), and applied to a London street-walker, as a star in the dark sea of urban life. We know that the younger poets make art independent of morals, and certainly the two have no necessary connection; but why should poetic art be employed to celebrate common fornication?[10]

Though pleased with the attention given to his poem, Symons published only one more poem in a subsequent issue of the *Yellow Book*.

In March 1894, Symons, on a tour of Italy, met Henry James, whom he characterised as 'the exquisite, complex, perverse, unpassionate, subtle, cruel novelist, a continental American who was in love with England'.[11] And, in company with Ellis, he met Horatio Brown, friend and biographer of Symonds. But aside from these new contacts, Italy, particularly Venice, had a profound effect upon him:

> Only to live, only to be
> In Venice, is enough for me.[12]

On his way back to London, he stopped in Paris to visit the ailing Verlaine and saw, to his delight, the comic *diseuse* Yvette Guilbert. When she visited London in December, Symons met her and was enchanted. Writing over thirty years after the event, Mme Guilbert (underestimating Symons's age, for he was twenty-nine at their first meeting) recalled her first impression:

> Quite young, twenty-four or five, fair hair plastered on his temples, a narrow thin face, pale skin, rather pink on the cheek-bones, thick, rather sensual, very red lips, wet and shiny; restless, darting eyes, now looking blue, now black, eyelids and lashes that beat wildly like the wings of a frightened bird.[13]

In May 1895, Symons's third volume of verse, *London Nights*, was published by Leonard Smithers, a man of cultivated tastes who conducted a lucrative business in erotica and whom Symons characterised as 'my cynical publisher, Smithers, with the diabolical monocle'.[14] As Symons later wrote in his Preface to the second edition (1897), the book was received with 'a singular unanimity of abuse'. The reviewer for the *Pall Mall Gazette*, for example, called Symons 'a very dirty-minded man' (see Letter 57, n. 2), but without adequate funds, Symons could not press for a libel suit.

The Wilde disaster in the spring of that year had little direct effect on Symons. Never on intimate terms with Wilde, he now thought more highly of Wilde as a writer than he had in the 1880s, when he referred to him in a letter to Osborne as a 'flighty-brained enthusiast and *poseur*'.[15] Since a number of Wilde's acquaintances sought the refuge of Dieppe during the trials and during the period following his fall, Symons was attracted to this favourite resort of English tourists in France. He spent the summer of 1895 with the artist Charles Conder and Beardsley, who had been dismissed from the *Yellow Book* principally because he had illustrated Wilde's Decadent play *Salome*. When Smithers offered Symons the editorship of a new journal to rival the *Yellow Book*, Beardsley became its principal illustrator. In Dieppe, Symons and Beardsley planned the first number.

The publication of the *Savoy* in January 1896, heralded a formidable rival to the *Yellow Book*. Containing contributions by Yeats, Shaw, Ellis, Dowson, Beerbohm, and graced by Beardsley's illustrations and designs, the *Savoy* was a high point in Symons's career, but the triumph was brief, for sales began to drop after the third number in July, when the *Savoy*, begun as a quarterly, now began to appear monthly. By September, Smithers decided to end the periodical with the December issue, which was to be entirely written by Symons and illustrated by Beardsley, now quite ill. Letters from the artist to Smithers reveal a hostility towards Symons which made work on the publication difficult,[16] though this was only one reason among others (mostly financial) that accounted for its death.

While editing the *Savoy*, Symons had managed, in August, to go on holiday with Yeats to Ireland, a significant trip which resulted not only in poems and essays on the experience but also in a stronger conception of himself as a Celt.[17] They met Edward Martyn, a wealthy landowner and playwright interested in the Irish Literary Renaissance who later dedicated three plays to them. Symons also met Lady Gregory, later Yeats's patron, for whom he developed a distaste after his breakdown.

Though 1896 had placed Symons at the forefront of the *avant-garde*, he suffered deeply that year the death of Verlaine, the marriage of the ballet-dancer named Lydia, whom he had loved, and the death of his mother (also named Lydia).[18] The high-spirited Symons, as he had revealed himself in letters to Rhys in earlier years, became more restrained, more restless as the decade wore on.

Notes

1. See Havelock Ellis, *My Life* (1939; 1967 ed. Alan Hull Walton) pp. 203–10.
2. See Letter 29. From Switzerland, John Addington Symonds wrote to Symons (MS., 18 June 1890, Brown University): 'I congratulate you on the good time you have had at Paris. It is the duty of human soul to give itself good times, and to get the most it can out of them. This philosophy of life is the reverse of the Calvinistic. But I believe that it is just, and squares with the nature of man. But we must have enough of the theologian left in us to know that we have to use our opportunities for labour. I expect to see the results of your experience at Paris in literature very shortly.'
3. 'Josiah Flynt', *My Life* (New York, 1908) p. 186.
4. Arthur Symons, 'Frank Harris', MS., Princeton: see Letter 41, n. 1.
5. 'The Rhymers' Club', in Yeats's *Letters to the New Island*, ed. Horace Reynolds (Cambridge, Mass., 1934) p. 144.

6. *The Letters of John Addington Symonds, 1885–1893*, vol. III, ed. Herbert M. Schueller and Robert L. Peters (Detroit, 1969) p. 691.
7. Arthur Symons, 'A Study of John Addington Symonds', *FR*, 115, n.s. (Feb. 1924) 229; rptd in *Memoirs*. Erroneously, Symons says that he first met Symonds in 1892 after six years of correspondence.
8. See Introduction, n. 9.
9. See Letter 51.
10. Philip Gilbert Hamerton, 'The Yellow Book: A Criticism of Volume I', *Yellow Book*, 2 (1894) 181.
11. *Memoirs*, p. 43.
12. From 'III. On the Zattere', one of a series of poems entitled 'Intermezzo: Venetian Nights', in *LN*.
13. Yvette Guilbert, *The Song of My Life* (1929) p. 313.
14. 'Charles Conder', *Memoirs*, p. 183.
15. Letter dated 4 Oct. 1887 (MS., Princeton) to C. Churchill Osborne.
16. See *The Letters of Aubrey Beardsley*, eds Henry Maas, J. L. Duncan and W. G. Good (Rutherford, NJ, 1970) pp. 165 and 223.
17. See Symons's essays, 'From a Castle in Ireland', 'In Sligo: Rosses Point and Glencar', and 'The Isles of Aran', *Savoy*, nos 6, 7, and 8 (Oct., Nov., and Dec., 1896).
18. In an unpublished sonnet, dated 14 Apr. 1938 (MS., Princeton), Symons identifies the young ballet dancer with his mother in a revealing line: 'My mother's name was Lydia; hers was Lydia.'

25 To Michael Field
(MS., BL)

5 January 1890   21, Chandos Road

Dear Miss Bradley

I was wondering if I should see Michael Field at the Abbey last Tuesday.[1] I did not see him: was he there? The distressing thing of these national funerals is that they almost cover up, for the time, even from one's own mind, the real presence of the loss, by the cold contact with all that is unsympathetic in people and things about me. It is almost grotesque, that the only person I saw who was visibly affected was – Browning's publisher.[2] The commonplace little son was smiling just when I happened to see him.

Historically, one of the most interesting people there was Ernest Coleridge, the grandson of the poet – S.T.C.'s only surviving lineal descendant.[3] His presence seemed in a sense to link two generations of English poetry, and it interested me not a little to be introduced to him after the service.

You have of course seen the birthday letter of Browning's to Tennyson which has recently been published.[4] On Wednesday, when I was talking with Cotton[5] at the *Academy* office (where I heard tidings of you) Theodore Watts came in, and some reference being made to that letter, he told how he had just been visiting Tennyson, and how Tennyson had showed him the letter, and how he had said, stroking it tenderly with his hand, "How kind, how good of such a *great* man to write to me like that." On my part, I remember well in what deeply moved tone Browning spoke to me, four days before he left England for the last time, of a birthday letter *he* had had from Tennyson: "it was too *sacred* to show to anyone – it was inexpressibly kind – no one would believe what a letter I have had from Tennyson!"

Do read Wilfred Meynell's paper in the *Athenaeum* – so acute, so sympathetic. The "poems" referred to are the *Preludes* [1875] of Alice Thompson (Lady Butler's sister), now Mrs. Meynell, about which I once told you.[6]

Sincerely yours
Arthur Symons

Notes

1. Browning, who had died in Venice on 12 Dec. 1889, was buried in the Poets' Corner of Westminster Abbey on 31 December. See Michael Field's poem, 'The Burial of Robert Browning', *Spectator*, 63 (1889) 923; Symons's poem, 'Dead in Venice: December 12, 1889', *Athenaeum*, 21 Dec. 1889, p. 860.

2. George Murray Smith (1824–1901), Browning's publisher and founder of the *Dictionary of National Biography*, 1882, was a pallbearer.
3. Ernest Hartley Coleridge (1846–1920) poet, biographer, and editor of *The Poetical Works of Samuel Taylor Coleridge*, 2 vols (Oxford, 1912).
4. The letter, written on 5 Aug. 1889, the eve of Tennyson's birthday, appeared in 'Notes and News', *Academy*, 37 (1890) 8.
5. James Sutherland Cotton (1847–1918), editor of the *Academy*, 1881–96. John Addington Symonds had given Symons a letter of introduction to Cotton. See Phyllis Grosskurth, *The Woeful Victorian: A Biography of John Addington Symonds* (1961) p. 223n.
6. Wilfred Meynell wrote: 'I sent Browning in 1878 a book of poetry which had won my heart before I knew its author.' See 'The "Detachment" of Browning', *Athenaeum*, 4 Jan. 1890, pp. 18–19; see also Letter 22, n. 10. Lady Elizabeth Butler, née Thompson (1846–1933), a popular painter, was Alice's older sister, who, in 1897, married Sir William Francis Butler (1838–1910), appointed High Commissioner in South Africa in 1898 but forced to resign the following year because of his opposition to the Boer War.

26　To James Dykes Campbell

(MS., BL)

5 January 1890   21, Chandos Road

My dear Campbell

I have been busy, ever since I came home, over a review of Browning's *Asolando* for the *Academy*,[1] which, you see, I am after all to do. I called on Cotton when I was in town – on Wednesday morning – and tho' no copy of the book has been sent him (thro' some quarrel with [George Murray] Smith I believe) he told me I might review it if I liked. I wrote, somehow, with a great deal of difficulty, but I think the thing will do pretty well. I shall send you a copy of the proof, when I get some. – While I was talking with Cotton, there was a knock at the door. "Damn!" said the able editor with a stamp of his foot; and then "Come in!" Whereat the oddest little man did come in – like an owl in bad human circumstances, I thought, and was greeted rapturously with "Oh, my dear fellow, come in, I'm awfully glad to see you." And the next moment I was introduced to – Theodore Watts! He certainly talked very interestingly – about Browning, etc. And here is a bit that will interest you. Watts has just been visiting Tennyson, and T. showed him that birthday letter of Browning's which has since been printed, and, says Watts, he kept on *stroking* the letter as it lay on his knee and saying "It's so good, so kind, of such a *great* man to write to me like that." Isn't that a pretty parallel with Browning's words to you and me about the letter he had had from Tennyson on *his* birthday, and which he said was too sacred to show to anyone?

Is not that a charming paper of Wilfrid Meynell's in the *Athenaeum* about R[obert] B[rowning]? I should like much to know what you think of his view of things. You know Meynell's wife (the writer of the "book of poems" he refers to) is a sister of Lady Butler.

You were right as to Pater's view of the *Athenaeum* notice: he had only the barest possible suspicion that it might have been done by me, and sent it simply as something I should be interested to see.[2] Do you know If Palgrave[3] writes in the *Spectator*? Pater guesses that he might have written the review of *Appreciations* – an interesting one from the very independence of its attitude.[4] The old enemy of *Blackwood's* is at him again this month – in a style and tone which would be impertinent if applied to, say, Oscar Wilde.[5]

Miss Pater[6] was enquiring very kindly after Mrs. Campbell. I was glad to be able to give some rather better news.

Do you imagine that Browning has left behind him much unpublished verse? Some people have that impression: I should not have supposed so.

Probably you have seen in the *Daily News* that *Dr*. Dykes Campbell was present at the funeral. Any relation?[7]

Yours ever

Arthur Symons

Notes

1. See Symons's review, 'Browning's Last Poems', *Academy*, 37 (11 Jan. 1890) 19–20.
2. See Symons's unsigned review of Pater's *Appreciations*, *Athenaeum*, 14 Dec. 1889, pp. 813–14.
3. Sir Francis Turner Palgrave (1824–97), poet and anthologist, best-known for his collection, *The Golden Treasury* (1861), was Professor of Poetry at Oxford, 1885–95.
4. See the unsigned review, 'Mr. Pater's Essays', *Spectator* 63 (1889) 887–8. The identity of the author remains unknown.
5. The anonymous review of Pater's *Appreciations*, which appeared in *Blackwood's Edinburgh Magazine*, 147 (1890) 140–5, was written by Margaret Oliphant (1828–97), novelist and writer on historical subjects, who was a frequent contributor to *Blackwood's*. The review begins: 'we have here a specimen of a critic who is of the most cultured and esoteric type; one of those who demand a special audience, and almost a special education in order to understand and enter into the strain of thought which is almost too superfine for human nature's daily food'.
6. Pater had two sisters: Hester Maria (1837–1922) and Clara Ann (1841–1910). Symons is presumably referring to the elder sister.
7. See 'The Burial of Robert Browning', *Daily News*, 1 Jan. 1890, p. 3.

27   To James Dykes Campbell
   (MS., BL)

                                                      Hôtel Corneille
                                                      Rue Corneille
16 April 1890   Paris

My dear Campbell
   Ever since I came here I have been so full of work and pleasure
(chiefly the latter) that I really haven't had a moment to write a letter. I
must however tell you something of what I am doing and seeing.
   First of all, Ellis and I have found very comfortable rooms here, in a
hotel which seems to be very well known in Paris, and which is cheap
as well as comfortable. The side of the Odéon faces the front of the
hotel: five minutes' walk takes us to the Luxembourg gardens and also
to an omnibus centre. As you see we are en plein quartier Latin, close
to the Boul' Mich' – the most attractive neighbourhood I think in Paris.
As for our doings and seeings, I really don't know where to begin or
how I am likely to end. This is something like our theatre list: Français
(Augier's *Gabrielle*, Pailleran's *Étincelle*, Dumas' *Demi-Monde*), Odéon
(*Méd. Malgré Lui* and Hénnique's *Amour*), Porte St. Martin (Sarah in
Jeanne d'Arc), Palais Royal (Meilhac and Halévy's *Le Roi Candaule* and
Blum and Toché's *Les Miettes de l'Année*),[1] Folies-Bergère, Montagnes
Russes, Nouveau Cirque (Lamoureux concert and that Passion-play
about which you have no doubt heard), Châtelet (Berlioz's *Faust* and
Romeo and Juliette), Op. Comique (Concert Spirituel), Eden-Théâtre
(*Orphée aux Enfers*). Add café's unlimited, flânerie in general, the Foire
au pain d'épices,[2] Easter services at Notre-Dame, a lecture by Catulle
Mendès,[3] and a good amount of déjeuners, dîners, and promenades
with friends – and you have *something* of what we have been doing. As
yet, the people we have met have been as a rule the younger and less
known men, but tomorrow week I am to be presented to Mme. Adam,[4]
at a great reception (I am already in treaty with the sub-editor of the
Nouvelle Revue in reference to an article on Pater, which if accepted will
make me only the 3rd Englishman, H[erbert] Spencer and Sir Ch[arles]
Dilke being the others, who have had articles there)[5] – also, when he
returns to Paris, to Zola, to Renan, to Huysmans, to Coppée[6] (unless,
as I fear, he has left for Italy), and no doubt to others who are not yet
arranged for. On Friday I am to meet Henry Gréville at Charles Dyer's
(Geo. Macmillan introduced me to Dyer, whose brother has married G.
M's sister).[7] I am to meet Verlaine (dans les vignes du Seigneur) soon,
also the marvellous Mallarmé.[8] I have already made the acquaintance
of Odilon Redon,[9] a painter who is positively a French Blake. I am
hoping to write an article on him for the *Art Review* and to get some of

his designs reproduced there.[10] I am not forgetting England and have contrived to excite in some of my French friends so much interest in Meredith and Pater that they are talking of translating some of their works. I wrote to Pater yesterday, conveying an offer to translate the *Imaginary Portraits*.[11]

The hour of déjeuner is at hand, and I must go out and meet Ellis at our usual restaurant in the Boul. St. Michel. I shall never be able to settle down to English cookery again!

More another time. Tell me how things are going with the poor folks who are condemned to live in England – terrible banishment from the earthly paradise! I hope you will be able to give me very good news of Mrs. Campbell.

Ever yours
Arthur Symons

Notes

1. *Gabrielle* (1849) by Émile Augier (1820–89); *L'Étincelle* (1879) by Edouard Pailleron (1834–99); *Le demi-monde* (1855) by Alexander Dumas *fils* (1824–95); *Le Médicin malgré lui* (1666) by Molière (1622–73); *Jacques Damour* (1887) by Léon Hénnique (1851–1935); Sarah Bernhardt (1844–1923), French actress in *Jeanne d'Arc* (1869) by Jules Barbier (1825–1901); *Le Roi Candaule* (1873) by Henri Meilhac (1831–97) and Ludovic Halévy (1834–1908); *Les Miettes de l'année* (1890) by Ernest Blum (1836–1907), and Raul Toché (1850–95).
2. See Symons's 'The Gingerbread Fair at Vincennes: A Colour Study', *Savoy*, no. 4 (Aug. 1896) 79–84; rptd in *CSP*.
3. French poet and novelist (1843–1909), associated with the Parnassians as a poet and later with the Decadents as a novelist.
4. Mme Juliette Adam (1836–1936), French novelist and writer on politics, was a founder of *La Nouvelle Revue* in 1879 and a regular contributor.
5. Despite his enthusiasm, Symons published nothing in the journal. Sir Charles Dilke (1843–1911), statesman and leader of the Liberal Party.
6. Ernest Renan (1823–92), French Philosopher and author; François Coppée (1842–1908), French playwright and Parnassian poet; Joris-Karl Huysmans (1848–1907), French novelist, best known for *A Rebours* (1884). On one visit to Huysmans, Symons wrote that he found him lying 'indifferently on the sofa, with the air of one perfectly resigned to the boredom of life'. See Symons's 'Joris-Karl Huysmans' in *FSC*; 'Huysmans as a Symbolist' in *SML*.
7. 'Henry Gréville', the pseudonym of Mme Alice Marie Celeste Durand (1842–1902), French novelist; G. Gifford Dyer, Charles's brother, was a painter who had settled in Paris.
8. Stéphane Mallarmé (1842–98), French Symbolist poet best known for his 'Herodiade' (1869) and 'Prélude à l'après-midi d'un faune' (1876), which inspired the musical setting by Debussy. Symons and Havelock Ellis soon met Mallarmé on one of his Tuesdays in his rue de Rome flat. Symons later translated his poems: see Letter 62, n. 8.
9. French painter and etcher (1840–1916), a friend of Mallarmé and other Symbolist writers, with whom his work is associated.
10. Symons was the first critic to publish an article on Redon in England: see 'A French Blake: Odilon Redon', *Art Review*, 1 (July 1890) 206–7; rev., rptd in *CSP* and *FTTR*.
11. Pater's work was translated by George Khnopff as *Portraits imaginaires* (Paris, 1899), with an introduction by Symons, previously published in the *Savoy*, no. 8 (Dec. 1896) as 'Walter Pater: Some Characteristics'.

28   To George Macmillan
   (MS., BL)

10 May 1890   Hôtel Corneille

Dear Mr. Macmillan

   Mrs. Dyer has just told me that you are afraid I did not succeed in finding his address. I ought to have written before to tell you how easily I found it, and how exceedingly kind the Dyers have been, but this delightfully demoralising Paris fills my days and nights too full – too full. One never finds a moment in which to sit down and write a letter.

   I like the Dyers, all three, extremely, and I have spent some pleasant hours at the house and the atelier. I like very much the pictures of his that I have seen – there is something in them at once conscientious and personal – a poetic way of receiving impressions and a skilful minuteness in rendering them. And yesterday I heard Miss Dyer play – for the first time. You have not heard her, have you? I was quite astonished at her fine clear masterly handling of the instrument.

   Has Mr. Pater said anything to you of an offer made by a friend of mine here, Charles Morice,[1] a rather well-known literary man, who would like to translate the *Imaginary Portraits*? He thinks that Perrin (Librairies Académique Didier) would publish the translation. I wrote to Mr. Pater, but have had no reply. It seems to me that his work would strongly interest the French public. I have proposed to Mme. Adam that I should write an article on Pater for the *Nouvelle Revue*: I don't know yet whether she will accept.[2] I should be glad to know what you yourself think of the proposed translation, and wish you would find out Mr. Pater's view of it, if you are seeing him any day.

   My French friends are very kind in introducing me to the people I want to meet. Yesterday I called on Leconte de Lisle.[3] I reminded him of the copy of my poems [*Days and Nights*] that I had sent him. He said he did not remember it at all – thought he could not have received it. While he spoke I caught sight of the book in a book case close to my elbow. I returned to point it out to him. He took it out, spoke very admiringly of the get-up of the volume, and explained as he turned over its uncut pages, that he knew nothing of English, and could not even make anything out of my translations of his own poems.[4] He is a charming old man.

                                        Believe me
                                        Very truly yours
                                        Arthur Symons

Notes

1. French Symbolist poet and critic (1861–1919), whose book on Symbolism, *La Littérature de tout à l'heure* (Paris, 1889), which stressed the need for vagueness in poetry expressive of great thoughts, Symons described as 'almost the revelation of a new Gospel' (*Mes Souvenirs* [1929] p. 3). Symons was indebted to Morice for an introduction to Verlaine.
2. The proposal was not taken up by Mme Adam. However, Macmillan consented to a translation of *Imaginary Portraits*. See Letter 27, n. 11.
3. Charles Leconte de Lisle (1818–94), French Parnassian poet and member of the French Academy.
4. See 'Requies (From Leconte de Lisle)' and 'Symphony (From Leconte de Lisle)' in *DN*.

29 To James Dykes Campbell

(MS., BL)

25 May 1890   Hôtel Corneille

My dear Campbell

I must quote a sentence of J[ohn] A[ddington] S[ymonds], written from Venice, and apply it to myself at Paris: "The place makes me exceedingly lazy, and annihilates the moral sense." He adds: "Both of which effects seem to me good, if one does not have too much of them."[1] Thus it is that you have had no answer to your last letter – nor indeed would have had one now, but for an appalling thunder-storm, which has driven me back drenched, with a broken umbrella and a streaked silk hat, when I was on the way to the other end of Paris, with some album verses in my pocket written "by special request" of a most charming and accomplished mademoiselle.

I am by this time getting so Parisian that the thought of London fills me with horror. I am contemplating permanent residence here; have forgotten *most* of my English (though I can still write it fairly well) and have begun to write in French for the "public prints." I have been to the Moulin Rouge, the Chat Noir, La Cigale, etc., I have called on M. Antoine of the Théâtre-Libre[2] and secured two places for Ibsen's *Revenants*[3] on Friday week, I have visited Renan and Coppée and Leconte de Lisle, I have seen Taine[4] and Dumas, I have met some more decadent poets, I have been to at homes and soirées from which I have returned at hours varying onwards to 3.30 a.m. – enfin, I have spent as few hours in my hotel as one could well manage to spend, and if I have written anything it has been by a special dispensation of a merciful Providence. To-day has been rather unlucky – besides the contretemps of this afternoon I went to Bourget's[5] in the morning and found he was out of town for a couple of days. Tonight I am going to see Mrs. Moulton,[6] who has just arrived from Rome: perhaps *she* will be out too.

What thousands of things I could tell you! If you are at St. Leonards when I return (in about a fortnight *probably*) I should greatly like to stay a night on my way home and tell you a few of my experiences.

Best regards to Mrs. Campbell and yourself from

Yours ever
Arthur Symons

Notes

1. Letter dated 13 May 1890 (MS., Brown University).
2. André Antoine (1858–1943), French actor, producer, and manager, who in 1887 founded the Théâtre-Libre for the presentation of the new naturalistic drama.
3. See Symons's unsigned review, 'Ibsen's "Ghosts" at the Théâtre-Libre', *PMG*, 5 June 1890, p. 3.
4. Hippolyte-Adolphe Taine (1828–93), French critic, historian, and member of the French Academy.
5. Paul Bourget (1852–1935), French author of more than sixty novels and theorist of Decadence in his *Essais de Psychologie contemporaine* (Paris, 1885).
6. American poet and journalist (1835–1908), who was one of Symons's close friends. To J. Dykes Campbell, he described her as 'plump, but nice-looking, with a very *comfortable* manner, a fluent amicable voice, and vivacious eyes that she nearly shuts while she is talking' (MS., n. d. BL).

30   To Katherine Willard[1]
(MS., Baldwin)

3, Holly Place
Hampstead, N.W.

20 November 1890

Dear Miss Willard

So it is signed and sealed then, our pact of friendship. Certainly on my part it was done long ago, but how good of you to do your part too – for sometimes that doesn't happen. Thank heaven that you are *not* what you call "properly conventional" – for conventions were invented for our unhappiness, no doubt by the powers of darkness. To make a friend is for me the one thing worth doing: how those people exist who go through the world bowing to their acquaintances, and asking them to tea at a certain hour on a certain day, I can't possibly imagine. For my part, I cannot do it, and I certainly could not do it with you. One doesn't forget such meetings. At least, I never dreamed that you would care at all to remember me, but I should not have forgotten you. I wonder if you would be surprised if you knew quite how much pleasure your letters have given me. Curiously enough, I always have a sort of feeling that the people I care for won't care for me, and it comes as the most delightful of surprises when, once upon a time, they do. So thanks, and thanks again, for giving me this delightful surprise.

For about a week past I have been absorbed by Mrs. Langtry's revival of *Antony and Cleopatra*[2] – my favourite play in Shakespeare – at the Princess's. I am doing an introduction to the book of the play,[3] and that has given me an excuse for going behind the scenes. One night I went to a rehearsal at six and came away at half past three in the morning![4] I have never seen so much of the ins and outs of theatres before, and it interests me immensely. The ballet-master is a perfect discovery – quite a genius in his way, and wonderfully comic. I have had long talks with him about his methods and his triumphs. Then of course I have seen a great deal of Mrs. Langtry, who is very charming, and an indefatigable worker as manageress and actress. She is never more beautiful than in her most negligée costumes, and when she is least thinking about effect. The play is mounted with a magnificence quite unheard of. Wingfield,[5] who has done it, tells me he is perfectly happy, for he has "beat the record."

With all you say about Mrs. Tree I can agree entirely. She is a misfortune, artistically, to her husband.[6] I will certainly do your bidding, go to the play, tell you exactly how it goes, in my opinion, and send you some press-notices. I have not had a chance of calling at the Hendersons[7] again, since I told you. I hope I may manage it again soon.

I have been to the opera 7 or 8 times, to Sarasate's two concerts and to one of Paderewski's.[8] Lago[9] has brought out a wonderful singer, Giulia Ravogli, who made a special sensation in Gluck's *Orfeo* – that adorable opera.[10] Her voice has richness, compass, and, above all, passion.

Don't – please, talk about wanting to write better letters than you already write. I wouldn't wish a word of them altered. Only, let me have them as often as possible and as long as possible.

Always your friend
Arthur Symons

Notes

1. Katherine Willard (1866–1932) was the niece of Frances Willard (1839–98), a founder of the Woman's Christian Temperance Union. In the early 1880s, her mother established a school for American girls in Berlin, where Katherine studied to become a singer. In 1895, she married William Woodward Baldwin (1862–1954), who had been Assistant Secretary of State, 1893–5, in Grover Cleveland's administration.
2. Lillie Langtry (1852–1929), the actress, appeared in *Antony and Cleopatra*, which opened on 21 Nov. at the Princess's Theatre.
3. Symons had already written an introduction to *Antony and Cleopatra* for the Henry Irving Shakespeare edition, published in May 1889; introduction rptd in *SED*. What he is referring to here is unknown.
4. It was perhaps at this rehearsal that Symons composed the following poem (MS.,

Folger Shakespeare Library), 'To Mrs. Langtry as Cleopatra (Written during Rehearsal, Nov. 16th)':

> I would that Shakespeare could behold in you,
>   As I, the Cleopatra of his dreams;
>   For I have known, this deathless night, meseems,
> A joy the soul of Shakespeare never knew.
>
> Ah, could he see you, serpent of old Nile, –
>   The rapturous languor of your witching eyes,
> The sweet malicious magic of your smile –
>   The heart of Shakespeare were with Antony's!

5. Lewis Strange Wingfield (1842–91), producer and adapter of plays.
6. Herbert Beerbohm Tree (1853–1917), half-brother of the writer and caricaturist Max Beerbohm (1872–1956), is best remembered for his Shakespearean roles and for his management of the Haymarket Theatre, 1887–97, and Her (later His) Majesty's Theatre, 1897–1917. His wife, Maud Tree (1863–1937) appeared on stage with him many times; opinions differ on her success as an actress. See Hesketh Pearson, *Beerbohm Tree: His Life and Laughter* (1956) p. 75.
7. Isaac Henderson (1850–1909), American playwright and novelist, best known for his popular play, *The Mummy and the Humming Bird* (1909).
8. Pablo Sarasate (1844–1908), Spanish violinist. See Symons's 'Sarasate: An Appreciation', *Illustrated London News*, 99 (21 November 1891) 658. Ignace Jan Paderewski (1860–1941), Polish pianist, composer, and later statesman.
9. Italian theatrical manager at Covent Garden in the 1880s.
10. For a review of Giulia Ravogli's performance in *Orfeo* at Covent Garden on 12 Nov. 1890, see George Bernard Shaw, *Music in London: 1890–1894* (1952) vol. I, pp. 86–7.

31   To Katherine Willard
   (MS., Baldwin)

5 February 1891

Fountain Court
The Temple

My dear Friend

Best of thanks for the best of letters! I re-read it sitting before the fire in a carpetless and curtainless and table-less room at the above address – the most charming locality, and also the most convenient, to my mind, in London – where I have at last succeeded in getting chambers.[1] You know the Temple is supposed to be used only by lawyers, but as a matter of fact other people do sometimes live here. It is an oasis in the heart of London – quietest spot in all the great city, yet with the roar of the Strand only just out of hearing. Fountain Court is charming. There really is a fountain, and there are trees, and picturesque buildings and large stone steps, all about – a broad open space in front. My two rooms are at the top, looking down on the fountain. This is the realization of a dream. – I am now at last a householder, with an establishment of my own, with my own funiture. Or at least this is coming. An old oak table that a friend is sending me from the country has somehow not yet come, and my ink-pot at this moment is resting on a portmanteau at my side! then my aesthetic curtains, which another kind friend has been making up for me, are here indeed, but with nothing to hang them to! A nice old bureau is undergoing repair, bookshelves are a-making – so you see some of the troubles incident to the first realization of one's dreams! I want to make the place look very pretty, and I hope I shall in course of time.

Most of my time, as you may imagine, is taken up with all sorts of new and formidable arrangements. At the same time I have a most important article on a contemporary French poet to do,[2] and at the earliest moment possible – not to speak of my ordinary journalistic work – book reviewing for a lot of papers, to which I have just added music-reviewing.[3] And I have a new volume of poems (how do you like the name – *Silhouettes*?) just on the verge of publication. I fear I am boring you with all this chatter about myself. But at all events it will show you that if I have not answered some of your questions sooner, and don't write now all I should like to, I have some excuse for it.

Some day I shall have a lot of things to say to you about Olive Schreiner and her work, if you care to hear them, but I shall leave that for another day. I think you are very right in what you say of her: it *is* curious how absorbing her personal influence is. She is the most magnetic woman in the world.

Meredith's novels are published in a very decent edition by Chapman and Hall, Henrietta St., Covent Garden – 10 vols at 3/6 each. – How nice it is to find that you share so fully my enthusiasm for O.S. and G.M. It isn't everybody who does. Someone said to me lately, "I knew you must have written the review of *Dreams* in the *Athenaeum*, because no one else would have praised it so much!"[4] And in the *Academy* I see someone is lashing at me because of what I have just been writing about Meredith.[5] In many things I don't mind whether a friend exactly shares one's tastes and preferences, but in a matter so intimate to me as this it does give one a closer feeling of kinship.

And you wonder why we are such good friends. Why wonder? Why should we *not*? I certainly do not "form my friendships by the almanac." How malign you are in insinuating that "possibly I couldn't help" etc.! If you have any power of divination you must have known perfectly well, on that night of our second meeting, that I was simply in an agony of suspense lest the hour – the one chance – should go by without – well, without striking.

How delightful to hear that you will be in London this summer. That *is* something to look forward to. I hope you will come in June, as you think, for I expect I shall go to Spain in the spring, with a friend

[Havelock Ellis] – indeed rather soon, and shall not be back till I don't know what part of May. – How delightful to be able to offer you a cup of tea in this my own domain, where you will ere then, I hope, be presiding in counterfeit! When is that long expected photograph coming? Write your name on it, please, when you send it. And – possibly – by that time I may have met Meredith – who knows? – may have got his likeness for you, or – who knows? – might even be able to take you to see him. These are dreams – but dreams sometimes come true.[6]

It is very kind of you to wish to have my own photograph. You shall have the first good one I can get. I have already had two appointments with Hollyer,[7] both stopped on account of the weather. I don't quite know when I shall get it done. At present I have nothing good. I have taken years to make up my mind to face the ordeal, but I really mean to do it soon.

"The Opium-Smoker"[8] shall be duly copied when I can unearth the book. I don't like to do it from memory, as I am not quite sure of a word or two.

I shall be so glad to see your brother when he comes.[9] Pray send him to me if he is willing to do me that kindness. Tell me something about him. When is he to come to London? Of course I may be in Spain, just when he comes. But it is far from certain.

I will finish with the pretty Italian formula, which to me is a very real wish and feeling –

Scrivetemi presto e vogliatemi bene

      dev. mo vostro

                        Arthur Symons

Notes

1. Symons lived in Fountain Court until his marriage in 1901.
2. Symons's 'Théodore de Banville', *MM*, 64 (May 1891) 56–60; rptd in *STL*.
3. Symons contributed some music reviews to the *Illustrated London News* in Nov. 1891 and Jan. 1892.
4. See Symons's unsigned review of Olive Schreiner's *Dreams* in the *Athenaeum*, 10 Jan. 1891, pp. 46–7.
5. Symons had reviewed Richard Le Gallienne's *George Meredith: Some Characteristics* in the *Academy*, 39 (24 Jan. 1891) 81–2. In the following issue, William Watson (1858–1935), poet, critic, and knighted in 1917, criticised Symons in a letter to the editor for his berating of the public's neglect of Meredith. See 'Mr. George Meredith and His Critics', *Academy*, 39 (31 Jan. 1891) 113.
6. Symons's dream of meeting Meredith never materialised. In later years Symons wrote: 'I never met George Meredith: I was fated never to meet him. I might have met him at Robert Browning's funeral [31 Dec. 1889] in Westminster Abbey. . . . After the ceremony was over and we had found way into the street, we were told that Meredith had left the Abbey five minutes before'. See 'George Meredith: With Some Unpublished Letters', *FR*, 119 (1 Jan. 1923) 50.
7. Frederick Hollyer (1834–1939), the well-known photographer.
8. Published in *Days and Nights* (1889).

9. Josiah Flynt Willard (1869–1907), called 'Frank' by family and friends, was a novelist and vagabond who published under the name of 'Josiah Flynt'. In an introduction to Willard's autobiography, *My Life* (New York, 1908), Symons describes him as 'a little, thin, white, shriveled creature, with determined eyes and tight lips, taciturn and self-composed' (p. xi).

32   To Ernest Rhys
(MS., Princeton)

7 February 1891   Fountain Court

My dear Rhys
     A line to tell you that I am now settled at the above most delightful of abodes, and – more important – to say how extremely I like and admire "Julius Roy,"[1] which convinces me that just that is your line in literature. Nothing you have yet published, nothing I have seen of yours, is within miles of it. It does, adequately and admirably, what I have always imagined you might do, hoped you would do. I am very glad the sonnets are coming out in the *P.M.G.*[2] and will send you the number, if I don't by any chance miss it, when they appear.
     By the way I was telling George Moore about your story an hour or two ago, and he was much struck by the name "Julius Roy."
     Greenwood has asked me for some poems for the *Anti-Jacobin*, and I have already done a couple of reviews for him (not appeared yet).[3] I have corrected proofs of a poem and a Villiers translation for *Black and White*[4] and done a couple of articles for Shorter[5] (one a review of music).
     On coming in I find a note from Yeats announcing the next Rhymesters.[6] Come and join us! Ellis has quite taken to them: he says the last was quite brilliant, with Oscar Wilde, Dorian Gray,[7] etc. I slept at the Ellis's part of this week – have only been here two nights. Furniture is arriving. I am writing on a jolly old oak table, and I have an old oak bureau which my laundress admires as much as I do – a great compliment. 'Tis indeed handsome, and will prove of infinite value for storing all manner of things – as well as for a writing table. Bookshelves are making.
     Ellis and I are still set on Spain if possible.[8] We are trying to get magazines and papers to take articles. Neither of us has any ready money!
     New environment very inspiring. I walk by the fountain, under the trees, after midnight and write verses.
     Glad you are in pleasant quarters in Llangollen. Remember me graciously to Her Grace[9] and believe me your ever
                                                            Arthur Symons

Notes

1. Ernest Rhys, 'The Romance of Julius Roy', a group of thirteen poems, later included in Rhys's *London Rose and Other Poems* (1894).
2. Rhys's 'The Great Cockney Tragedy', *PMG*, 17 Feb. 1891, p. 2.
3. See Symons's unsigned review of Kipling's *The Light that Failed* in *Anti-Jacobin*, 11 April 1891, pp. 264–5; and an unsigned article, 'Mr. Henry Jones and the Drama', *ibid.*, 18 Sep. 1891, pp. 815–16.
4. See Symons's translation of Villiers de l'Isle Adam's 'The Secret of Ancient Music', *Black and White*, 1 (1891) 60; the poem 'In Winter', *ibid.*, p. 86, later included in *Silhouettes* (1892).
5. Clement King Shorter (1857–1926), author and editor of the *London Illustrated News*, 1891–1900, in which Symons published 'Villiers de l'Isle Adam' on 24 Jan. 1891, p. 118.
6. An early name of the Rhymers' Club, founded by W. B. Yeats and Ernest Rhys early in 1890, met as late as 1896, and included poets such as Ernest Dowson, John Davidson, Lionel Johnson, John Todhunter, T. W. Rolleston, Richard Le Gallienne, and Symons – a Celt-dominated club without rules for membership and with only an 'Honorary Secretary', G. A. Greene. Symons later wrote that the Rhymers (who published anthologies of their verse in 1892 and 1894) 'recited their own verses to one another with a desperate and ineffectual attempt to get into key with the Latin Quarter'. See Symons, *SPV*, p. 263; Yeats, 'The Rhymers' Club', *Letters to the New Island* (1934); Karl Beckson, 'Yeats and the Rhymers Club', *Yeats Studies*, no. 1 (1971) 20–41.
7. John Gray (1866–1934), poet and later a Roman Catholic priest, best known for *Silverpoints* (1893), noted for its extraordinary design by Charles Ricketts. The oft-repeated story that Wilde's novel, *The Picture of Dorian Gray* (1890) was inspired by John Gray (who threatened to sue the *Star* for such an allegation) may have a basis in fact, since evidence exists that Wilde and Gray apparently met in 1889. See Ruth Z. Temple, 'The Other Choice: The Worlds of John Gray, Poet and Priest', *Bulletin of Research in the Humanities*, 84 (Spring 1981) 25, n. 28.
8. See Letter 33.
9. Grace Little (1865–1929), poet and later anthologist of children's literature. Because of 'her hunting propensities', Rhys, who married her on 5 Jan. 1891, called her 'Her Grace' or 'Diana'. See Ernest Rhys, *Everyman Remembers* (1931) pp. 165–76.

33   To Katherine Willard
(MS., Baldwin)

20 February 1891   Fountain Court

So you too, dear Friend, are setting off on your travels! May you have every sort of success and happiness, and don't – oh, by all means, don't miss that little visit to London. For my part, I have had to abandon the too seductive programme for Spain, as I found it absolutely impossible to afford it, after all my expenses in taking these rooms and furnishing them. So Ellis and I have decided to modify our plans, and so plan a

shorter trip which will only cost half as much. We intend to visit the
Provençal country on our way, see Mistral, the great Provençal poet,
who has asked me to come and see him, then go on to Spain, and be at
Barcelona by the 1st of May, when there is to be a great Socialist
demonstration – perhaps a revolution – at all events a big row! You will
read perhaps in the papers that the rebels were led by two young
Englishmen mounted on mules, who gave eloquent speeches in excellent
English. Then you will read that we were thrown into prison, endured
great sufferings, and finally escaped through the devotion of a young
Gipsy (you know I take a great interest in the Gipsies, and know their
language a little). So look out for stirring events.

It has come!! The photograph has come!! I dropped this letter to go
out to a literary lunch; then I went to call on a friend of mine, a novelist
[George Moore], who lives in the Temple (he has promised to have his
unused piano tuned for me, and then I shall go and play Chopin to
him); and it was not till 5 o'clock that I got back here. Something was
lying on a chair – I went up to it, carelessly enough – and I saw the
word Photograph! I reverently unwrapped it, sitting in my easy chair
before the fire – I like, in these moments, to arrange everything, so as
to be perfectly at ease, and ready to receive impressions – and then, not
it, but *you* flashed out upon me. I cannot tell you how much I like the
picture, how delighted I am to have it, how I thank you for it. I have
put you where I can see you as I write, and you are looking down, not,
alas, at me, but just past me; in a moment I know you will smile – just
in a moment. Meanwhile you dream – of what? – vague, exquisite
dreams, coming and going in the magic light that glimmers between
your eyelashes. A magical face with the light of happy dreams upon
it – that is what I see before me, and it is happiness to see it.

I am getting quite lyrical, and I ought to be writing mere prose!

Well, since writing this I have been to a concert, a Hallé[1] concert,
where I have heard Wagner, the [Beethoven] *Pastoral Symphony*, Mozart,
Liszt. As I walked back through the misty night fancies began to mingle,
fancies of music and a face – the face I am looking at now – and I walked
up and down the deserted lengths of Trafalgar Square, a certain
monotonous rhythm going over in my head. It beat itself out into a little
piece called "Music and Memory," which shall go to you with this – it
is all I can do to thank you for your gift. If it seems to me good enough
to publish in my new volume, when the time comes, may I dedicate it
to you by your initials?[2]

Meanwhile, I am sending you my book of poems [*Days and Nights*],
which I have been rather wanting you to see, but scarcely liked to
impose upon you under ordinary conditions. On a sea-voyage one reads
anything, and this is just for you to read at sea. Will you? if you have
nothing more amusing to do. You will find a lot of imitative work in

the book: I had certainly not "found myself" when that was published: but I hope there is "a little good grain too." The excessive pessimism of the book is one of the signs of youth, and of the influence of certain writers – not really a personal expression. The book of *Silhouettes* which I am about to publish – in some ways slighter – will be at least much more personal, more my own, and so of more real interest. Ah, what hopes I have of this new book – and how they will come tumbling down about me, I suppose. Well, one has to accustom oneself to all that. The one thing is to know whether or not one has done good work. And how can we ever tell? At times I feel a bit elated, and I say to myself "Well, I *have* done something worth doing!" And then I feel horribly depressed, and envy every creature who isn't myself, and nothing seems worth doing any more. But of course I go on, writing just what "the spirit moves one" to write, and setting against the indifference or the depreciation of Smith or Brown something that Pater has said or Meredith has written to me. There are the consolations!

– And here is a lot of tiresome rubbish that I have been chattering to you. Don't punish me too severely – overlook the fault, even. Write to me while you are away – give me news of yourself and your doings. The concerts – what and where are they to be? And will you really send me something for my new home? How good you are. I shall prize indeed anything that comes from you. Send anything – but do send something! You see I take you at your word in the most grasping way!

Very curious, after what I have just been writing, a letter has come from Marie Corelli,[3] saying she is sending me one of her novels as "a tribute of" etc. etc.! There is also a letter from a woman who is angry with me, I don't know why – a voluminous letter, I feel, so I shall not open it to-night, as I want no dreams.

Perhaps I shall dream tonight, but only of a face that signs itself to music.

> Always your friend
> Arthur Symons

Notes

1. Sir Charles Hallé (1819–95), German-born English pianist, conductor, and founder of the Hallé Orchestra in Manchester in 1857. He was knighted in 1888.
2. Symons's 'Music and Memory', dedicated to 'K.W.', appeared in *Silhouettes* (1892).
3. Pseudonym of Mary Mackay (1855–1924), who published over thirty novels, the best known of which is *Barabbas* (1893). She probably sent Symons her sensationally popular *Wormwood* (1890), set in Parisian absinthe dens, presumably because she thought it would particularly interest him. See Brian Masters, *Now Barabbas Was a Rotter: The Extraordinary Life of Marie Corelli* (1978) pp. 99–102.

34 To Louise Chandler Moulton
(MS., Congress)

8 March 1891   Fountain Court

Dear Mrs. Moulton

Since I saw you last – at Lady Seton's,[1] last summer – I have written fewer letters than I ever wrote in my life before. You will readily believe me – for I have not even written to you. I find living in London cuts off one's inclination to write letters. I have been doing quite a lot of every kind of work and every kind of amusement – which of course is more serious. My editorship of the *Academy* was over I think before you left. Since then I have been doing all sorts of things, and going to all sorts of amusing places – from Mrs. Langtry's rehearsals to Madame Blavatsky's receptions.[2] That Chicago affair turned out badly, I don't know how or why. I sent them a lot of letters, which I am sure were by no means bad: at last, as they never so much as acknowledged them and I had no chance of seeing the paper, I left off sending. Then, at two long intervals, they sent me a beggarly little portion of money – not more than £1 a letter. I have never even seen one of the papers.[3]

Then Sir F. Broome's introduction to the *Times*[4] has never borne fruit, though it still may, in the future. On the other hand I am on the staff of the two new weeklies – the *Anti-Jacobin* of F. Greenwood, and *Black and White*. And I now write for the *St. James's [Gazette]* as well as the *Pall Mall*. So that I can get a fair amount of work if I like to do it.

I wonder if you saw a little poem of mine in the *Athenaeum* of a week or two since?[5] It is to be the end-piece of my volume of *Silhouettes* (don't you like that title?) which I think will be a great advance on *Days and Nights*. It seems to me that I have found myself – myself of the moment – in these later poems, and that they are at all events quite sincere transcripts of moods and memories, faces and places – treated, too, in a much freer rhythm, and with more colour. So much for my opinion of myself!

I see a great deal of George Moore now that I am living so near him. As you see, I have taken chambers in the Temple, and I find it suits me far better than living at such a distance as Hampstead. Then of course the Temple is quite the quietest place in all London – splendid for working in. And my rooms – among the tree-tops – look out on the fountain. I think myself very lucky to have got them – and at so reasonable a rent.

In the middle of April I am going for a little trip with Ellis – to Paris for a few days, then on to Provence, to see Mistral (who has long ago asked me to come and see him) and to visit Avignon, Arles, etc., Marseille for a collection of pictures by Gustave Moreau;[6] then over the

Pyrénées into Spain. What a background for poems – all that!

Yesterday I met two of the people whom I originally met chez vous – Graham Tomson at a Private View, and Violet Hunt[7] at Raffalovich's.[8] I went to see Mrs. Tomson lately, and had a charming talk with her. What a nice woman she seems to be! I am sorry I have hitherto seen so little of her.

Miss Willard – the third person I met that same afternoon at your rooms – is in America now, or should be, by this time. Her brother is now in London – a curious and interesting young fellow.

I hope if you write you will make your letter as strictly autobiographical as I have made mine. I should like to have news of you, and to know when you will be in England again. Not, I hope and trust, while I am away.

With best regards.

Very sincerely yours
Arthur Symons

Notes

1. Helen Hamilton Seton (1836–1922), who, in 1886, married Sir Bruce Maxwell, a principal clerk in the War Office.
2. Helen Petrovna Blavatsky (1831–1901), Russian-born spiritualist, who, in 1875, founded the Theosophical Society in New York and a branch in London three years later. Of her many works, *Isis Unveiled* (1877) and *The Secret Domain* (1888–9) are best known.
3. Symons had four literary letters published by the *Chicago Tribune*, one signed and titled 'London's Latest Hero' (on Kipling, Michael Field, Wilde, and Whistler), 5 Oct. 1890, p. 25; the remainder unsigned: 'London's Latest Drama' (on Herman C. Merivale's *Ravenswood*), 12 Oct. 1890, p. 34; 'Exposition of Ruskin' (principally on Edward T. Cook's *Studies in Ruskin*), 2 Nov. 1890, p. 15; 'Poetry for a Shilling', 23 Nov. 1890, p. 14.
4. Sir Frederick Napier Broome (1842–96), Canadian-born poet and later colonial governor in Australia, was an art critic and reviewer for *The Times*.
5. Symons's 'For a Picture of Watteau', *Athenaeum*, 21 Feb. 1891, pp. 247–8; rptd in *Silhouettes* (1892).
6. French painter (1826–98) of erotic subjects, associated with late-nineteenth-century Decadence in art.
7. Novelist, short-story writer, and biographer (1862–1942), who, from 1908 to 1915, had an intimate relationship with the novelist and editor of the *English Review*, Ford Madox Ford (1873–1939), the affair described – much to Ford's discomfort – in Hunt's memoir, *The Flurried Years* (1926). See Arthur Mizener, *The Saddest Story: A Biography of Ford Madox Ford* (New York, 1971) pp. 176–9; 280–4.
8. Marc-André Raffalovich (1864–1934), Russian–Jewish poet, novelist, playwright, and critic who lived in Paris until 1882, when he emigrated to London. In November 1892, Symons introduced Raffalovich to John Gray in his rooms at Fountain Court. See Brocard Sewell, *In the Dorian Mode: A Life of John Gray, 1866–1934* (Padstow, Cornwall, 1983) pp. 30–1. When John Gray, after having been ordained a priest, was assigned to Edinburgh in 1902, Raffalovich moved to remain near his friend.

35   To Katherine Willard
  (MS., Baldwin)

20 May 1891   Fountain Court

"Don't think, please, that I am an utterly mannerless, ungrateful person" because I have not answered your letter from Spain. I had left London a week before you posted it, and only found it, with a crowd of other letters, on my return to town. I just called at the Temple to see what had come for me while I was away, and then set off for a visit in the country, where I am still staying. I put my permanent address at the head of this sheet, as I may be back any day.

Your letter, I assure you, was well read and re-read as I whizzed along on my two hours' journey in the train. Most of it pleased me immensely – one thing didn't. You are not coming to London! That is indeed a disappointment. I had been looking forward so much to seeing you. It is ridiculous, when I really consider it, how little I have seen of you in person! Your brother seems to have an idea that I know every thing about you and the family generally. I wish I did. And indeed I am getting to know a good deal. It was with a good deal of curiosity that I went to call at Great Ormond Street, where the card dropped in at my letter-box told me I should find Mr. Frank Willard. The first thing I saw when I sat down were some photographs, awfully bad, but just recognizable, with one of your mother, yourself looking like Olive Schreiner in the background. And then I heard all about "Puss." What a charming sobriquet! It took my fancy greatly. You must be very popular at home to get such a name. – Well, I really like Frank very much. What a lot he has gone through – how rich he is in the one thing I for one care to be rich in, manifold experiences. I think he has a wonderfully original temperament, and that he will do much, in one way or another. I don't know whether you have heard of our wanderings by night, our studies of the ins and outs of London. They were very delightful to me, and I was glad of so sympathetic a companion. He and I have many curiosities in common. Do you know, I have no interest in what is proper, regular, conventionally virtuous. I am attracted by everything that is unusual, Bohemian, eccentric: I like to go to queer places, to know strange people. And I like contrast, variety. It used to amuse me to go to see Mme. Blavatsky, and it would satisfy my sense of the piquant to call next day on Cardinal Manning,[1] and then, leaving the arch-episcopal palace with a volume of sermons, drop the book, with the portrait of an actress between the leaves, in the garret of a friend whom I was taking to the open-air ballet at the Crystal Palace. And I like to be all things to all men: to talk about books to a man who cares about books, about horses to a man who cares about horses. More and more do I care about life, about experiences, less and less about books. You know what Walt Whitman says: "Books made out of books pass away."[2] I mean to write no more books made out of books – in poetry, at all events.

You indeed make me happy by what you say about my poems. I wonder what you will think of the new ones, which I think are so much better – so much more personal – all really *lived*. You may imagine I have not come home from Provence and Spain without some impressions in verse. Ah, what a delightful time we had, Ellis and I, as we went from Lyon to Avignon, then through Tarascon to Arles, then on to Marseille, to Montpellier and Perpignan, then to Barcelona, to Zaragoza, to Madrid, to Burgos, and back by Bayonne and Bordeaux to Paris. At Avignon, so delightful a place that we wanted to go and live there (a sentiment we repeated at Marseille and at Barcelona) we made some charming friends, the old Provençal poet Roumanille and his daughters.[3] And how new and wonderful Spain was to me. We saw much, and I think we have gained much.

I think it a pity that you don't care more about "singing for money and the public." Why not be proud to live by one's art?

Your brother told me that you thought of being photographed again by the people who did the portrait you sent me. If so, please send me the result. Charming as that one is, something more is wanted to do you justice. Meanwhile, as I was taken by Hollyer just before I went away, I am at last able to send you a portrait of myself, which is at all events not so bad as all the others I have had taken during the course of my life.

So you are no more "an engaged girl."[4] So much the better! I do most entirely agree with you that the phantom of "Duty," in such matters, is merely something to be disregarded. I confess I have a horror of the word – so often is it used to represent interference with natural instincts, which are really one's only safe guides.

But how tiresome that you are not coming to London. When shall we two meet again?

Always your friend
Arthur Symons

Notes

1. Cardinal Henry Edward Manning (1808–92), author and churchman, was initially ordained in the Anglican Church in 1832, but followed Newman into the Roman communion in 1851. In 1875, he was created a cardinal.
2. Symons was quoting from memory. Whitman wrote: 'The poems distilled from other poems will probably pass away'. See Walt Whitman's Preface to his *Leaves of Grass: The First (1855) Edition*, ed. Malcolm Cowley (New York, 1959) p. 23.
3. Joseph Roumanille (1829–94), Provençal poet and playwright, leader of the Félibrige, a

group of poets interested in restoring Provençal as a literary language. One of Roumanille's daughters married the French poet and diplomat Jules Boissière (1863–97). See Letter 74.
4. Katherine Willard had informed Symons of her engagement in Oct. 1890, at which time he wrote (MS., 31 Oct. 1890, Baldwin): 'You have certainly a startling piece of news for me. And you expect me to be "very glad for you." Well, you can't expect me to congratulate *you*, but I must and do congratulate the man, whoever he is. I ought to be glad, however, for anything that makes you happy. How otherwise can one really care for people than by wishing that, and that only?'

36   To Edmund Gosse[1]
(MS., Leeds)

[29 June 1891][2]   Fountain Court

My dear Gosse

I was extremely surprised by the way in which you seemed to look at my review of Saintsbury in the *Athenaeum*.[3] It seems to me so scrupulously accurate. Indeed I don't see that I have said anything substantially different from what I have heard you yourself say in conversation. Compared with the view which everyone I know takes of Saintsbury's work, I think mine is lenient rather than otherwise. I am certainly obliged to defend him against my friends. People as different as Dykes Campbell and George Moore can see absolutely no merit in his work whatever. I can. But I never even heard of anybody who considered him a great critic. Surely then what I have said is absolutely true.

Of course I am quite aware that no one likes to be told he is not a great critic, so I should be sorry for Saintsbury to know I wrote the article. The more so, as I have no doubt he would recognize that what I say is perfectly true.

I don't know whether you have heard that Shaw is bringing out with Walter Scott a little book about Ibsen.[4] I see in a paper to-day that Hedda Gabler Robins is to act in Robert Buchanan and Sims's new melodrama.[5] I wonder how she will like that after Ibsen!

Very sincerely yours
Arthur Symons

Notes

1. Poet, critic, biographer, and translator (1849–1928), best known for his autobiographical *Father and Son* and *Ibsen*, both published in 1907. While pursuing a distinguished literary career, which included translations of Ibsen and essays on the French Symbolists, he was an assistant librarian in the British Museum in 1867, a translator at the Board of Trade in 1874, and Librarian of the House of Lords, 1904–14. He was knighted in 1925.

2. The date appears on the letter, apparently written by Gosse when he received it.
3. Symons had written that Saintsbury's criticism had 'high second-rate quality. It is the very best kind of review work, and it fulfills its purpose in giving a clear idea of the general characteristics of every author dealt with – a perfectly clear outline without any of the irregularities which trouble the design of those who go deeper into things'. Symons wrote to J. D. Campbell on 28 June 1891 (MS., BL): 'Have you seen my Saintsbury review in yesterday's *Athenaeum*? Please don't tell anybody it is mine, for no doubt he will be furious. Gosse to-day seemed quite offended about it – talked about "refinement of cruelty" and the like in a very absurd way. I think I have been scrupulously just.' See Symons's review of Saintsbury's *Essays in English Literature* in the *Athenaeum*, 27 June 1891, p. 819.
4. Shaw's *The Quintessence of Ibsenism* (1890), published by Walter Scott Publishing Co.
5. Elizabeth Robins (1862–1952), American actress and novelist (who wrote under the pseudonym 'C. E. Raimond'), achieved fame in Ibsen's plays, hence Symons's allusion to one of her notably successful roles. *The Trumpet Call*, by Buchanan and Sims, opened on 1 Aug. 1891, with Mrs Patrick Campbell (1865–1940) as co-star. See Margot Peters, *Mrs. Pat: The Life of Mrs. Patrick Campbell* (New York, 1984) pp. 62–4.

37   To Ernest Rhys
(MS., BL)

9 September 1891   Fountain Court

My dear Rhys

I have just found your letter on my return from my third visit this year. Thanks for it and for your sombre and striking sonnets, to which I wish all good luck. Jack Yeats's drawings are certainly powerful.[1]

Yes, true enough, I have been in Provence and Spain – in the Spring; and a wonderful trip it was. But since then I have had another trip, of which you can scarcely have heard, – namely to – Berlin! I had nearly two months there, and only got back a fortnight ago, half of which time has been spent down at St. Leonards with the Campbells. Two of Lady Ellis's little girls were staying there too, and we had great fun together: one of them, aged five, proposes matrimony![2]

But it is Ellis, not I, who is to be married. Have you heard that he is engaged to Edith Lees?[3]

If I told you all the stories of my adventures I should never stop, so don't let me begin. But, to make your mouth water, let me just allude to hours among the Velasquez at Madrid, with the doyen of the Félibrige at Avignon,[4] among the women of Arles; to a visit to the dressing-room of a great singer at Berlin, to a night in a bathing-machine at Havre, to days and nights on board an ocean liner with the beautiful Katherine Willard.[5] I might tell you strange tales indeed, of Gisella Bekeffy,[6] the fair Hungarian, of the yet fairer German Emmy.[7] But of these things you will some day read in verse. Of my time at Berlin the first half was spent with Frank Willard – no one else in the house. We employed much of the time in social studies, and are prepared to write a scientific work in large 8$^{vo.}$ on "The Cafés of Berlin from 10:30 P.M. to 6 A.M., sociologically considered. With Portraits and Autographs." Then the family returned, and we turned over a new leaf – gladly enough. Imagine me going out shopping, going to church, going to opera, superintending and aiding in packing and unpacking, playing and singing Wagner in the evenings – with Kate the Queen. On all this I need say nothing: you will know without my saying. Then K., F., and I all started together, they for America, I for England via Havre.[8] K. is going out for 9 months to sing in a church in Baltimore – an awfully good engagement. Even many of her friends suppose she is going out to be married – the fact of course being (do you know?) that the engagement was broken off six months ago.

Don't ask me for literary news. Let me rather tell you of a Spanish music-hall, a German Hamlet.[9] But there is great news – Ada Rehan is here, and my stall-ticket for to-night (the first performance) is in my pocket.[10] I am expecting to hear from her, appointing a meeting. To-morrow I go to meet Gladys Vane[11] (who has been in Berlin!!). I am writing a one-[12] [Incomplete]

Notes

1. Irish painter, illustrator, and author (1871–1957), the brother of William Butler Yeats. Jack Yeats had illustrated Rhys's volume of poems, *The Great Cockney Tragedy* (1891).
2. Lady Ellis (d. 1940), née Kathleen Robert Mitchell, whose home near Ham Symons used to visit.
3. At the time of this letter, Ellis was prepared to marry Edith Lees (1851–1916) after having discussed with her the kind of relationship he expected they would share – a union of souls as well as bodies, absolute freedom for both partners to pursue their separate interests, and no children. After a trial period of living together, they set 19 Dec. 1891 for their wedding. See Havelock Ellis, *My Life* (1939; 1967 ed. Alan Hull Walton) pp. 327–8.
4. See Letter 35, n. 3.
5. Symons had returned after two months in Germany, via Le Havre; Katherine and her brother, Frank, continued from Le Havre to America (she had a nine-month singing engagement in a Baltimore church; he hoped to interest a publisher in stories about tramps).
6. Symons and Frank Willard had met her in a Berlin café. See Arthur Symons, *Wanderings* (1931) p. 136.
7. Emmy Dobschin, a twenty-year-old Polish girl whom Symons and Frank Willard met in a Berlin dancing-hall: 'the most unsophisticated animal I ever saw, unspoilt, with immense high spirits, a fresh innocent face' (*Wanderings*, p. 136). She is the subject of 'Emmy' in *Silhouettes* (1892).
8. For Frank Willard's account of the Havre episode, when Symons found himself short of funds, see 'Josiah Flynt', *My Life* (New York, 1908) pp. 186–9, and Symons's account in *Memoirs*, pp. 165–6.
9. See Symons's 'A Spanish Music-Hall', *FR*, 51, n.s. (May 1892) 716–22; rptd in *CSI*. Symons reviewed the performance of Josef Kainz (1858–1910), a Hungarian-born actor, in 'A German Hamlet', *Illustrated London News*, 99 (31 Oct. 1891) 567.

10. Irish-born American actress (1860–1916), the leading member of Augustine Daly's company from 1879 to 1899. She was currently appearing at the Lyceum Theatre in *The Last Word*, an adaptation by Daly from a German play by Franz Schönthan (1849–1912).
11. A fifteen-year-old actress and musician whom Symons describes in his unpublished 'Unspiritual Adventures' (MS., Princeton). He first met her on 24 July 1889, in a rooming house for theatre people in Arundal Street, where she had gone to take rooms. She was 'certainly pretty, though not of a refined type – full, round face, saucy expression, with capabilities of sweetness and coarseness'. It was not long before Symons made love to her.
12. Probably the one-act play, *The Minister's Call*. See Letter 41 and n. 1.

38   To James Dykes Campbell
(MS., BL)

Sunday
[late September 1891]   [Fountain Court]

My dear Campbell
    First of all – or I shall certainly forget it in more interesting matters – I am going to follow your advice and open an account at Twining's[1] next door here. Tell me, for I forget, is it not necessary to be introduced by somebody? Whom had I better victimise?
    Now let me tell you that I have seen the divine Ada [Rehan] (a brilliant black maid-servant appropriately led me upstairs) and I had a delightful time, and anticipate many more, for we are already the best of friends. Almost before the door was opened she was at it, holding out her hand, and in five minutes I was talking away with her – about our personal tastes and idiosyncrasies – as if we were old acquaintances. She is indeed the same woman off the stage that she is on – full of excited life, giving the same sensation of exhilarating force. She looked such a big creature in her long loose grey peignoir. I enjoyed my talk immensely. She told me about her little adventures, and I told her about mine. We sympathized over Sarah Bernhardt[2] and Réjane,[3] and she described a supper at Irving's[4] – Sarah, exhausted by her performance, drinking several glasses of champagne and then talking as brilliantly as she had acted; Ellen Terry,[5] who had been to see her, utterly knocked up by the excitement – "wilted," as Miss Rehan expressed it. She told me characteristically how, when she is acting, if those about her hang fire, she likes to move about among them and wake them up. All the excitement she expresses is really felt. And then, when the curtain is down, all the steam goes out of her, and she is fit for nothing. – She shook hands several times in saying good-bye, and told me the time

when she is generally at home. I never met an actress whom I liked so much as a woman – who was so womanly, so nice and unassuming.

Henry James's play was lamentable.[6] It has the combined qualities of a mild farce, high-falutin French drama of an extinct school, and an Adelphi melodrama of the present.[7] That is what I am now saying, in other words, for the *Academy*.

Yours ever
Arthur Symons

Notes

1. The tea and coffee shop located for over 200 years in the Strand.
2. The noted French actress whom Symons had first seen on the stage in London in 1889 and in Paris in 1890 (see Letter 27, n. 1). He regarded her as 'the greatest actress in the world'. See Symons's 'Sarah Bernhardt' in *PAM* and 'The Importance of Sarah Bernhardt' in *Eleonora Duse* (1926).
3. Stage name of the French actress Gabrielle Réju (1857–1920), whose most notable role was in Victorien Sardou's *Madame Sans-Gêne* (1893). See Symons's 'Recollections of Réjane' in *DP*.
4. Sir Henry Irving, né John Henry Brodribb (1838–1905), actor and manager of the Lyceum Theatre, 1878–1902, notable for his Shakespearean productions. Symons regarded him as 'the only actor on the English stage who has a touch of genius'. See Symons's 'Sir Henry Irving' in *PAM*.
5. The acclaimed actress (1847–1928), who, in 1864 at the age of sixteen, married the painter G. F. Watts, a marriage soon dissolved. She had two children – Gordon and Edith Craig – with the architect and theatrical designer E. W. Godwin. During Henry Irving's management of the Lyceum, she was his leading actress.
6. *The American*, based on James's own novel of the same title, was produced in London on 26 September 1891 with Elizabeth Robins in a leading role. Most of the critics agreed with Symons: see his review, '"The American" at the Opéra Comique', *Academy*, 40 (3 Oct. 1891) 291–2.
7. The Adelphi Theatre was noted for staging popular melodramas.

39   To the Editor of the *Star*
(19 October 1891, p. 2)

Sir, – As an aficionado of the music halls, allow me to express my feelings of pleasure at "Spectator's" second visit to the Pavilion, and his admirable eulogy of Miss Jenny Hill.[1] But may I also be allowed to protest, in the most convinced way, against his rash assumption that "nothing is so much like one music-hall as another music-hall – that the difference between the Pavilion and the Trocadero, between the Tivoli and the Royal, is doubtless only that 'twixt Tweedledum and Tweedledee"? To a discriminating amateur, each music-hall has its cachet, as definitely as each music-hall artist worthy of the name; one could no more mistake the programme of the Royal for that of the Tivoli than one could mistake Miss Marie Lloyd for Miss Katie Lawrence.[2] To thoroughly understand this very serious question it is necessary to visit the Paragon as well as the Pavilion, Collins's as well as the Canterbury. You will find a queer kind of unity in the midst of all this seemingly casual variety, and in time – if you think it worth the time – you will come to understand the personality of the music-halls. For instance, take the Metropolitan, in Edgware Road – not what is advertised as "a fashionable lounge," but a house which gives you good value for your money. The audience is composed of the people who throng the pavement from the Marble Arch to the Harrow Road on Saturday nights and Sunday afternoons. To suit their tastes, the entertainment at the Metropolitan is full of movement and go, somewhat rollicksome, with a distinct element of horse-play. It is not overdone, but there it unmistakably is. To note one significant fact – nowhere do you hear the heels of the dancers tap the boards so audibly. Go from the Metropolitan to Gatti's at Charing Cross, a house which I choose as being somewhat of the same character, in a way. High spirits have given place to something like sentimentality, with a more conventional kind of farce in the comic songs and dances. Both are houses where the audience joins in the refrains – a detail which of itself distinguishes them from places like the Pavilion, where it is only on occasion (as in Miss Jenny Valmore's song) that the audience condescends to do something for its own amusement. In this, as in all else, fashions vary, and so, though a silent audience is in general more what is called "respectable" than a singing audience down East at the Paragon even the four-penny gallery does not take up the refrains – perhaps because it is tired out, and in no mood for song.

"Spectator" is rightly enthusiastic over Miss Jenny Hill. But Miss Jenny Hill is not the only lady on the music-hall stage who is worth hearing and seeing. There is Miss Katie Lawrence, for instance, who is the incarnation of the most perfectly artistic vulgarity – a true artist, a child of nature. At present she is at Gatti's, and the atmosphere does not suit her; she should be seen, as I used to see her, at the Metropolitan, where her gaminerie was just in its element. She has a manner of her own, both in singing and dancing, which is quite unique – a staccato manner, one might call it, which is full of surprises in its violent and vivid spontaneity. She dances with an abandonment that one rarely sees on the English stage. To surpass her in this particular quality one must go to Mdlle. Larine, who has risen from a Clichy music-hall to the Parisian celebrity of the Palais Royal; one must go to Isabel Santos and see the Baile Sevillañas at the Alcazar Español in Barcelona,[3] – Yours, &c.,

Arthur Symons

Notes

1. 'Spectator': pseudonym of Arthur Bingham Walkley (1855–1926), dramatic critic of the *Star*, 1888–1900, and *The Times*, 1900–26. For his comments on Jenny Hill (1850–96), comedienne and first woman to be called the 'Queen of the Halls', see Walkley's 'Actors and Acting: Spectator's Dramatic Notes', *Star*, 17 Oct. 1891, p. 2.
2. Marie Lloyd (1870–1922), the most famous of the music-hall performers of the 1890s. Katie Lawrence (d. 1913), popular singer. See Symons's 'An Artist in Serio-Comedy: Katie Lawrence', *Star*, 26 Mar. 1892, p. 4 (signed 'Silhouette').
3. See Letter 37, n. 9.

40   To Ada Rehan
    (MS., Pennsylvania)

18 November 1891   Fountain Court

Dear Miss Rehan

It was really most kind of you to think of me in all the bustle of your last days here, and to send me the delightful photograph of you as Lady Teazle.[1] It is a perfect likeness, and makes a very pretty picture with its hat and wig and lace. It dominates among my crowd of lesser photographs as it should. How could it but do so?

The play of Shakespeare's that was performed in the Temple in his time was *Twelfth Night*. Middle Temple Hall, where it was given, is just outside my windows, skirting Fountain Court. If the moon were out, I could see it from where I am now writing. *The Comedy of Errors* was given in the Hall at Gray's Inn, and we are not far here from the site – but only the site – of the Globe Theatre. You must not forget, when you are in London again, to let me show you round these places. I hope that will be next year, and not the far-away 1893. We can not do without you in London for a whole year.

I hope you are having (will have had, when this reaches you) a voyage of real rest. I have been glad to hear no such wind as that which howled outside your windows when I saw you last, so I trust you are having a smooth passage. If I come to America before you are here again – and more impossible things might happen – you will let me come and see you, will you not? It would be one of the pleasantest things to look forward to. And if you visit London before I can manage the trip to America that I am anxious to make one of these days,[2] I hope equally that you will let me see you – and more of you than I have seen this time.

                                    Always most truly yours
                                    Arthur Symons

Notes

1. One of Ada Rehan's celebrated roles in Richard Sheridan's *The School for Scandal* (1777).
2. The hoped-for trip to America was never to occur.

41   To Ernest Rhys
    (MS., Princeton)

15 December [1891]   Fountain Court

My dear Rhys
   Probably while you were peacefully writing to me under the shadow
of your own vine and figtree I was chasing a fugitive actress over
London. But no – that was on Sunday, a day of frightful storm. First I
couldn't find the street – then I couldn't find the woman. I mounted to
the topmost flat only to find a fireless room with an open letter on the
table. The chimney had smoked – and I was to follow her elsewhere.
Off I went Northwards, and at last found my lady. After three or four
exciting hours I left her – starving but triumphant. But I am not at the
end of the complication.
   The play[1] which will be given early in January is certain to be a
success – that is the verdict of everyone who has heard it. It will owe a
good deal to George Moore – who gave me the most valuable advice
and assistance. It is curious that he – who has always failed to write a
play – should have been able to help me as he has done over the
construction. It is an argument in favour of the view of some people
that he is better as critic than as creator.
   Your letter has the cheerfulness of Henley's

> "I thank whatever gods may be
> For my unconquerable soul."[2]

But I wish it had been a more jocund cheerfulness. If however
circumstances bring you back to town, I shall be mean enough to be
just a little obliged, after all, to circumstances.
   Thank you for Headlam.[3] I have not yet done him full justice. Review
books are pouring in upon me, and for some days I have been unable
to write a line. To-day, however, I have done a review of a Spanish
novel – *Pepita Jiménez* – for the *P.M.G.*,[4] and I may do part of another
(*Stories after Nature*) for the *Athenaeum*,[5] before going to Requiem given
by the Bach Choir.
   The editor of *Life* sent me copies of the wrong number, and I have

not yet taken the trouble to change them. But I shall send you the thing eventually.[6]

I observe that the first result of the Copyright law[7] is that we are deluged with American short stories. And if they once begin to reprint them, when will there be an end?

I suppose I shall stay in London over Christmas – not being about to get married, like poor Ellis, who looks quite agitated at the prospect. He treats it conversationally as a casual matter.[8]

Shall I send urban or urbane remembrances to you both?

Yours
A.S.

Notes

1. Symons's *The Minister's Call*, performed for the first and only time at the Royalty Theatre by the Independent Theatre Society on 4 March 1892. In 'Frank Harris' (MS., Princeton), Symons describes the genesis of the play: 'After I had read this story [Frank Harris's 'A Modern Idyll'] it occurred to me to turn this rather revolting material into a One Act Play. I mentioned the fact to Harris and to Moore, who urged me to try my hand in a form which was novel to me. Just then I had not the faintest idea of how one begins to write a play, how one constructs it, how one sets one's figures in motion, and how one contrives the final climax. Night after night I went across to Moore's rooms, showing him the fragments I had composed; which he read and commented upon. We ended by collaborating. Moore refused to have his name put beside mine on the play-bill.' The unpublished manuscript of the play remains unlocated. Frank Harris (1856–1931), was an author, journalist, and editor of the *Fortnightly Review*, 1887–94; he is best known for his *Oscar Wilde: His Life and Confessions* (1916) and the sensational *My Life and Loves*, ed. John F. Gallagher (1964).
2. From W. E. Henley's 'Invictus', *A Book of Verses* (1888). Henley (1849–1903) was the editor of the *Scots Observer* (Edinburgh), which became the *National Observer* (London), 1888–94.
3. Probably Walter George Headlam (1866–1908), the classicist, who translated *Fifty Poems of Meleager* (1890).
4. See Symons's review of *Pepita Jiménez* (1874; English trans., 1891) by Juan Valera (1824–1905) in *PMG*, 23 Feb. 1892, p. 3.
5. See Symons's unsigned review of *Stories After Nature* (1822; ed. W. J. Linton, 1891) by Charles Wells (1800–79) in the *Athenaeum*, 16 Jan. 1892, p. 77.
6. What the 'thing' is remains unknown.
7. The American Copyright Law, passed in July 1891, granted protection to foreign authors whose countries already gave similar protection to US authors. The US insisted, however, that copies of books, photographs, chromos or lithographs were not to be imported but were to be made in the US.
8. Symons wrote to Katherine Willard on 30 Aug. 1891 (MS., Baldwin): 'I have seen Ellis, and find he has just got engaged to be married. I wasn't expecting it in the least. The girl is not one I care for. I daresay she may suit him, in a certain sort of way, but I really don't appreciate his taste. For one thing, the girl is quite markedly plain. How a man who really cares for beauty, and wouldn't endure to look at a homely picture on his walls, can endure to look at a homely wife, is what I can't understand. The girl is also one of those "advanced" people, who lecture.'

42   To Katherine Willard
(MS., Baldwin)

21 December 1891 London

> Dear and great patroness, for whom I sing
> The strains that live but in your honouring,
> If I, through you, have written aught of good,
> Receive the homage of my gratitude,
> Receive the homage that would fain express
> Openly its particular blessedness.
> Your name upon my page will ever be
> A light to my delighted memory;
> And, not for me alone a private bliss,
> But the bright page where brightest Katherine is
> Shall blossom forth upon the eager air
> A magic flower of music unaware.
> So my poor verse, though wanting wings to rise,
> With you shall be familiar with the skies.

So, in a somewhat 'antique mode,' I write on receiving your letter this morning, and by this means I thank you for saying yes about the dedication.[1]

What spurs me, in addition to having written these lines, to answer your letter at once, is what you say about going on the stage. Curiously enough, the last time I saw Miss Blind (she has just gone to Egypt, and wanted me to go with her!) she was saying what a good Elsa[2] you would make. You have often thought of trying the operatic stage, have you not? The question seems to me worth considering seriously, and there are so many things to consider. I think there is little doubt that you would succeed on the lyric stage, though no doubt, like everyone else, you would have difficulties at first. And of course to succeed there is to make money. But I really rather shudder at the thought of all you would have to go through. I doubt if you quite realise what the opera bouffe stage is really like. Few people are fonder of the stage than I am, or more interested in everything theatrical, but I don't quite like the idea of seeing you on it. It is not the fact of the acting, but the associations of every kind. People to whom, at present, you would indignantly refuse to be introduced, would be your companions most of your time. I remember your saying once that you entirely approved of Mrs. Cleveland's refusal to receive Ada Rehan.[3] Well, Ada Rehan's reputation, here at least, is one of the best on the stage: I have heard her sneered at for her virtue. In considering a matter of this kind, there is no use in ignoring facts; and the fact certainly is, that the greater part of actresses on every stage are without even pretentions to virtue. On the opera bouffe stage you would be thrown entirely among this kind of people. I confess I don't like to think of the prospect for you. Look at it yourself. I used to think at one time that it was merely a Puritan prejudice to look on actors and actresses as specially immoral people. But now that I have so many opportunities of seeing for myself, I find that it is only the truth. They *are*, as a class, more uniformly immoral than any other class of people. Now for my part I don't know that there is necessarily any particular "contamination" in associating with people whom one doesn't consider models of virtue; but I do think there would be, on your part, a feeling of considerable discomfort and even disgust which would soon make you discontented with your surroundings.

So much I feel bound to say on the negative side, and it is for you to decide how far you would be affected by these considerations. On the other hand there is of course plenty to be said, all of which you have already said for yourself, no doubt – so I won't repeat it. I hope you will write me again about this. It is of the most vivid interest to me. Of course, should you really decide on the experiment, I will do everything in the world I can for you.

I sent you for Christmas Miss Blind's last book of poems[4] – a book which may interest you for other than its poetic quality when I tell you that the later poems, from "Scherzo" onwards some twenty pages, are written about my humble self. Please do not on any account mention this to anyone. I would tell no one but you, for I confess it seems to me rather ridiculous to be sentimentalised over by a middle-aged woman, whom I appreciate as a friend, whom I admire as a writer, but whose demonstrations of affection are a little uncomfortable to me. There are some people whom you always have to be holding at arm's length. She is one. She is really one of the kindest friends I have. I can't tell you how much she has done for me, and how much more she would always be ready to do. But there is always about her a sort of vague demand, which I cannot respond to. She tires me.

I came across something yesterday in a note of Rossetti's quoted in a book I am reviewing for the *Athenaeum*, which just expresses that feeling of impatience which you rebuke in me. "Ambition, i.e. the feeling of pure rage and self-hatred when anyone else does better than you do. This in an ambitious mind leads to envy in the least, but to self-scrutiny on all sides, and that to something if anything can."[5] I really think it is that feeling more than anything else which makes me so anxious to succeed in everything, and for my success to be recognized – which is confirmation to me of my genuine success. And I think Rossetti is right in saying that one ought to feel so.

I was going to a party this evening at Frederick Wedmore's (do you remember meeting him at Mrs. Moulton's?) but such a frightful fog came on that I despaired of getting to Hampstead and back; so I am writing to you instead – "which is far better," as St. Paul observes. Now as for that divan, it will be very good of you if you will help me. It seems to me most unreasonable of you to think of spending so much as three pounds on my behalf: strike an average between that and the "something costing about a shilling" which you told me in Berlin was your intention. Please don't send me any money, which for one thing I shan't know how to spend, but do buy something for me (telling me exactly the cost, and letting me pay my share). The word divan is unhappily quite too big for the very small space at my disposal in the only corner available, but I want to have something that will do to lounge on, as at present I have nothing. Aforesaid space is only about 45 × 19 inches. Now what is wanted is some such arrangement, I fancy, as you have in the drawing-room at Nettelbeckstrasse – something to cover the seat, to fall to the ground, and to nail up against the wall on the two sides: ⌐: That is of course the angle, and the comparative length. A cushion or two would be an advantage. Seat I could get stuffed here. Now I must try to define to you my "tones" of colour. My room is all green and yellow.[6] Walls painted green, carpet a somewhat dimmer green, with a faint tinge of yellow; ceiling papers in light yellow; window-curtains in two shades of light yellow; bookshelves painted to match the walls, and with a great many yellow books;[7] big bureau in brown oak, small table in black oak; piano unfortunately rosewood, and a touch of red in one or two cushions in chairs, mainly in white and black. Green and yellow are the easiest colours to harmonize; mine are a somewhat greyish green and a somewhat vague yellow. Now do you think you can send me over something that can be manipulated into a beautiful and serviceable divanuccio – to give the contemptuous Italian diminutive to my small affair?

It is half past one in the morning: my candles have burnt themselves out, as a gentle hint: I had better give over now, wishing you only every good New Year wish that you would like to see realized.

Your devoted
Arthur Symons

Notes

1. In a letter dated 28 Nov. 1891 (MS., Baldwin), Symons had asked if he might dedicate *Silhouettes* to her.
2. Heroine of Wagner's *Lohengrin* (1850).
3. Mrs Frances Folsom Cleveland (1864–1947), who married Grover Cleveland (1837–1908) in the White House in 1886, held a series of public receptions in January and February 1889, the final months of President Cleveland's first term of office.
4. Mathilde Blind, *Dramas in Miniature* (1891).

5. From Dante G. Rossetti's letter to James Smetham, dated 21 Nov. 1965. See Letter 653 in *Letters of Dante Gabriel Rossetti*, ed. Oswald Doughty and John Robert Wahl (Oxford, 1965) vol. II, p. 581.
6. Favoured colours of the Aesthetes and Decadents.
7. French editions with yellow paper covers.

43   To Austin Dobson[1]
   (MS., London)

Tuesday
[early 1892?]   Fountain Court

Dear Mr. Dobson
   You have done me a real kindness, and one which I especially appreciate, in giving me the book which (you may have heard) I tried to steal. It fulfills a long wish of mine to possess such a volume, and I am only sorry that everybody else cannot have the same good luck. Why don't you publish a similar one in England?[2]
   I have been dipping into the book this morning, on its arrival, when I should have been otherwise employed; and I have met old friends and made new ones. I think you know how much I prize your work. But the worst of you is – as I find this morning – that you make one despair. Here have I been hammering my brains for rhymes for a bevy of little painted, powdered, and bewigged angels, whose wings were brushing by my face last night, as I watched the ballet from behind the scenes at the Empire. What I want is the loan for an hour of your 18th. century box of maquillage things, to which I will add a dash of *rouge chéret*.[3] But though you give me your book, you won't lend me your recipes.

                                    Yours very truly
                                    Arthur Symons

Notes

1. Poet, biographer, and essayist (1840–1921), who was employed in the Board of Trade for almost fifty years, though he regarded writing as his principal profession. Of Dobson's Parnassian *vers de société*, as in *Proverbs in Porcelain* (1877), Symons regarded his having 'finished perfectly a small, beautiful thing: a miniature, a bust, a coin' (see 'Austin Dobson' in *SPV*).
2. Dobson's *Beau Brocade* (Leipzig, 1892), published by Heinemann and Balestier as part of their English Library series.
3. Possibly an allusion to Jules Chéret (1836–1932), French designer and lithographer, whose richly coloured, carefully executed posters were a familiar sight in Paris during the 1890s.

44   To Ernest Rhys
(MS., BL)

26 January 1892   Fountain Court

My dear Rhys

Thanks for the Pears advertisement letter! I thought it was from Katie Lawrence! Here's a sample of my goings on.

10 a.m. awoke by continuous knocking at outer door. "Knock, knock, wake Duncan with thy knocking – I would thou couldst!"[1] Steps recede, afterwards return, I hear a letter dropt in. Curiosity bids me rise. The *St. James's* [*Gazette*] sends me Mrs. Humphry Ward's new three-decker to be done for next day's paper.[2] I dress excitedly. Laundress comes, and the 3 vols come again, and this time gain admittance. I sit down to déjeuner (which I have at 11.30, and so don't need to go out to lunch), begin *David Grieve*, which is 1200 pages of close, close print. Now it befalls that I have left my precious white cane in a restaurant near Victoria the night before. So David accompanies me down to Rampazzi's (isn't it a fine name?). On returning I find a note praying me to send in the review by 5. I read, read, read, desperately read, but the thick volumes hamper the flying mind, and I light my altar candles at 3.30, only then ready to begin my review. When I have written two pages a little demon comes for copy. "Come back at 5, my little demon", I say persuasively and I return to my desk, listening all the while for an expected frou-frou on the stairs. I have done less than half when, at 4, I hear the frou-frou. "Lord, how punctual women are," I sigh in a rapture, as I open the door to – Mary Ansell.[3] It is her first visit and she is accompanied by two little telegraph boys who are showing her the way, and who wait for coppers. They smile with bland sympathy as I cross their hands with browns. Virginia Vanderpump[4] makes one rush at my photographs, another at my books. Mrs. Humphry Ward (née Elsmere) is forgotten – a fairer than Elsmere is here. And she is saying – oh incautious little woman – she is saying as she turns my books over: "I could spend a week in this room!" Well and good, Mary Ansell, well and good. An hour slips by – a knock – it is the little demon again. "Little demon be – chez vous! You'll get no copy from me till after midnight." For another lady is coming presently, and the other lady is going with me to the Alhambra. The stalls burn in my pocket. Another hour of Mary Ansell – then the new ballet – and after that *David Grieve* shall have his column, in which it shall be said that "we will not forestall the interest of the reader" by saying much about the third volume – for reasons that "tis we reviewers know"!

And so runs the world away. Greetings to her Grace.

                                                      Arthur Symons

Notes

1. *Macbeth*, ii.ii.71.
2. Mrs Humphry Ward, née Mary Augusta Arnold (1851–1920), novelist and philanthropist, was the niece of Matthew Arnold. Her novel *Robert Elsmere* (1888) was an extraordinary popular success. For Symons's review of the 'three-decker', *The History of David Grieve*, see 'Mrs Humphry's New Novel', *St James's Gazette*, 24 (23 Jan. 1892) 4–5.
3. Actress and author (1862–1950), who in 1894 married the novelist and playwright James M. Barrie (1860–1937). After their divorce in 1909, she married the playwright and novelist Gilbert Cannan (1884–1955). See Andrew Birkin, *J. M. Barrie and the Lost Boys* (1979) pp. 176–81.
4. The character acted by Mary Ansell in Frank Marshall's *Brighton* (1874), revived on 1 Dec. 1891 at the Criterion Theatre.

45 To Ernest Rhys
(MS., BL)

17 February 1892 Fountain Court

My dear Rhys

A line to say that I will do your bidding with Maclure[1] at my earliest opportunity. I will also enquire after MS. chez *Black and White*.

Delighted to hear that I shall be seeing you so soon. How much news we shall have for one another! Meanwhile, rejoice with me, if you please, over the fact that my *Silhouettes* are formally and finally accepted by Elkin Mathews and John Lane (that is the name of the firm now)[2] and will be out in the Spring. No such good news has come to me for many a day. Rehearsals of *The Minister's Call* are trying to begin, but that is a slow process. I hope next month will see my Huysmans in the *Fortnightly*. Poor dear Huysmans, what will the British public think of him – and of me![3]

If "A Conversation at the Café Royal" goes into *Black and White*,[4] I should rather like you to see it. It is just a little fantasy round a talk with Scaramouch (or John Davidson)[5] and Saint-Just (or John Barlas, the shooter at the House of Commons).[6]

I need scarcely say I have fallen in love with a new dancer. This time it is Minnie Cunningham.[7] She is very pretty, very nice, very young, and *has a Mamma*.

I like your quatrain extremely. Last night I was experimenting after this fashion:

> Madame, en partant pour Cythère,
> Avec nos voeux pour le bateau,

Soyez princesse mais bergère,
Une bergère de Watteau.

But my morning's work was to another strain. Here it is, and here are my best wishes for you both.

A.S.

Notes

1. Probably Samuel McClure (1857–1949), Irish-born American publisher, founder of *McClure's Magazine* (New York) in 1903.
2. John Lane (1854–1925) co-founded with Elkin Mathews the Bodley Head press in 1887, and in 1892 became his partner. In September 1894, while publishing the *Yellow Book*, the partnership was dissolved, Lane retaining the use of the Bodley Head name. For an account of Symons's relationship with the firm, see James G. Nelson, *The Early Nineties: A View from the Bodley Head* (Cambridge, Mass., 1971) *passim*.
3. See Symons's 'Joris-Karl Huysmans', *FR*, 51, n.s. (Mar. 1892) 402–14; rptd, enlarged in *FSC*.
4. See Symons's 'A Conversation at the Café Royal', *VF*, 8 (July 1917) 49; rptd as 'The Café Royal' in *CR*. For a slightly different version, see *Memoirs*, pp. 80–2.
5. Scottish poet and playwright (1857–1909), best known for his *Fleet Street Eclogues* (1893) and his novel *Earl Lavender* (1895), which contains a satire of the Rhymers' Club. Though a member, he refused to contribute to the club's anthologies. Fear of cancer and perhaps despair over his lack of recognition as a writer resulted in suicide. See J. Benjamin Townsend, *John Davidson: Poet of Armageddon* (New Haven, Conn., 1961) pp. 1–28.
6. Scottish poet and Socialist (1860–1914), who published verse as 'Evelyn Douglas', Alleged to have fired a pistol near the Speaker's residence as an expression of contempt for the House of Commons, Barlas was called 'a charming poet and anarchist' by Dowson (*The Letters of Ernest Dowson*, eds Desmond Flower and Henry Maas [1967] p. 225). In later years, he was confined to a mental institution in Scotland.
7. A dancer at the Tivoli Theatre who inspired Symons's poem 'The Primrose Dance: Tivoli' in *London Nights*. The artist Walter Sickert (1860–1942), wishing to paint her, apparently asked Symons to arrange a sitting; in a letter to Herbert Horne, dated 25 May 1892 (MS., Dugdale), Symons wrote: 'I am glad to learn that she has done my bidding and given a sitting to Sickert. She complains a little that he has made her "*too* tall and thin".' See Sickert's painting, *Minnie Cunningham at the Old Bedford*, in Wendy Baron's *Sickert* (1973) p. 31 and Fig. 37.

46 To Ernest Rhys
(Text: Rhys)

Friday, 4 March 1892
The Day of Judgment[1]   Fountain Court

My dear Rhys
Thank you for your kind letter. I shall let off steam once again by writing to you, as I have so often done before.

'And the evening and morning were the First Night.'

It is now a quarter to 5. After a strange night, – which seems to me now like a dream, so wild and whirling was that carnival of fancy dresses, that dancing hubbub, – I woke to find with your letter, a letter from Albert Chevalier[2] (with whom I am to sup at midnight tomorrow) and another from Minnie Cunningham (who is coming to see me 'after the matinée, about 5'). On my way to send a telegram to a lady, offering her a seat for tonight, I find a delightful folio, 1650, 2nd edition, of the *Vulgar Errors*,[3] which I carry home at a cost of 1/6. Then out again, meet my publisher in the street, whom I am going to see; a few minutes after, meet Pierrot of *Le Baiser* – Bernard Gould:[4] we chat beside the photographer in Burlington Arcade. Then the whim takes me to explore Soho, and I consider old furniture in Wardour Street with the eyes of a millionaire, and wander off into absolutely unknown regions. At last I get back to my Court of the Fountain – to find a letter in marvellous French from my friend M. Peticocu, a Roumanian Impresario, the father of the most wonderful contortionist in the world,[5] saying that he has postponed his departure so that he may accept my invitation to dinner on Sunday, or, as he puts it, 'seulement pour avoir l'honeure de étre d'en votre agreable société (*sic*).' And as the gentleman is coming at 5, and I lunch with Raffalovich at 1.45, I pray that a fiery cab horse may be found outside a certain door in Mayfair.

And what shall I do now? Play Berlioz's *Marche au Supplice*? For the Fates themselves don't know what will happen tonight – nor whether one of the contending company of actresses will get into a cab at the last moment, and leave me minus one of our pieces. That infernal Olga![6]

It is 4.30 a.m. and I have just returned from a supper-party – saved, I trust, not damned! Tomorrow and the newspapers! Well, they are fairly favourable. Here are one or two.[7] I am not satisfied of course, but who ever is?

Yours ever
Arthur Symons

I open this again to tell you of a strange girl I met at the Frankaus'[8] last night – an extraordinary looking young Jewess, about 20, with a long lithe body like a snake, a great red dangerous mouth, and enormous dark amber eyes that half shut and then expand like great poisonous flowers. 'Nuffing amuses me,' she said, with her curious childish lisp, 'everyfing bores me. Nuffing ever did amuse me. I have nuffing to amuse me, nobody to be amused with. I don't care for men, women's talk always bores me. What am I to do? I don't know what to do with myself. All I care for is to sleep. Tell me what is there that will give me a new sensation?' And she lay back, and gazed at me through her half-shut lids. I bent down and whispered 'Opium.' Her eyes opened with almost a flash of joy. 'Yes, there is opium. Where can I get it? Am I too old to begin?'

I wonder when I shall meet her again.

Notes

1. Symons's play, *The Minister's Call*, was presented that night.
2. Actor and music-hall performer (1862–1923), who wrote and sang 'coster' songs. See Symons's 'The Costers' Laureate: Mr. Albert Chevalier', *Black and White*, 3 (18 June 1892) 784.
3. *Vulgar Errors* (1646), an inquiry into popular beliefs and superstitions, was written by Sir Thomas Browne (1605–82).
4. The stage name of Bernard Partridge (1862–1945), actor and illustrator for *Punch*, who appeared in Théodore de Banville's *The Kiss* in the Independent Theatre Society programme of plays, including Symons's *The Minister's Call*, at the Royalty Theatre.
5. An allusion to Eugenie Petrescu, the acrobat. See Symons's 'She Walks on Her Hands: The Most Astonishing Contortionist the World Has Ever Seen', *Star*, 5 Mar. 1892, p. 4 (signed 'Silhouette').
6. Possibly Olga Nethersole (c. 1865–1951), actress (whose Spanish ancestry on her mother's side may have particularly attracted Symons). As a result of her work for the improvement of public health, she was made a CBE in 1936.
7. The *Pall Mall Gazette* praised its 'considerable power' (5 Mar. 1892, p. 2), but the *Saturday Review* referred to its 'dullness and stupidity' (12 March 1892, p. 299).
8. Probably Arthur (d. 1904) and Julia Frankau (1864–1916). Mrs Frankau, a popular novelist, wrote under the name of 'Frank Danby'.

47 To Ernest Rhys
(MS., Princeton)

[late July 1892]   Fountain Court

My dear Rhys

I have been so very frivolously busy of late that I have hardly had time to take pen in hand, except to write articles on the "Training of the Contortionist" and the like.[1] But now that we are on the eve of August I want to send you a line to know whether really I might come down in your neighbourhood[2] shortly, and how it is to be managed. I have two pieces of not very easy work that I want to do, besides amusing myself with mountains instead of footlights. Tell me how much you think I could manage the trip for. The most important thing is, I must not throw any fresh expenses on you. But I think we can manage, can we not, without that?

I have received an unexpectedly large cheque lately from the *Athenaeum* – but as I am employing it in giving ballet tea-parties and taking fair coryphées[3] for trips in the country, it is going fast. It is sad you were not here on Tuesday [26 July]. My guests were: of the Empire, Ada and Lizzie Vincent; of the Alhambra, Florrie Hooten, Janet, Martha, Violet, Marie Blandford, Louie Bryant; otherwise, Herbert Horne, Selwyn Image,[4] and – John Addington Symonds![5] I am now on intimate terms with the stage-manager of the Alhambra,[6] and can walk in at the stage-door whenever I like, and stay as long as I like, and do what I please. And editors all over London are willing to take music-hall articles from me, and the *Star* asks me not to confine myself to Saturday. Voila! No more at present from yours ever

                                                                Arthur Symons

Notes

1. See Symons's 'The Training of the Contortionist', *PMG*, 11 Aug. 1892, p. 11.
2. The Rhyses were living near Llangollen, Wales.
3. The *Corps de ballet* of the Empire Theatre.
4. Poet, engraver, and designer of stained glass (1849–1930), associated with Herbert Horne in the Century Guild of Artists and later Slade Professor of Fine Arts, Oxford, 1910–16.
5. For a description of that memorable afternoon, see Symons's 'A Study of John Addington Symonds', *FR*, 115, n.s. (Feb. 1924) 230–1; reptd in *Memoirs*, p. 117. In this memoir, Dowson's presence is mentioned but not Horne's or Image's.
6. John Hollingshead (1827–1904), theatrical manager and stage director at the Alhambra Theatre.

48   To W. B. Yeats[1]
      (MS., Yeats)

9 November 1892   Fountain Court

My dear Yeats

I am afraid you must have thought me very neglectful – and that I was so – in never thanking you for your book.[2] When it came I was away from London, and I did not find it till my return. That is all the excuse I can plead. Since I came back I have been in such a whirl! Let that be a further excuse. But tonight, as I came in (it is already tomorrow morning) I found in my letter-box the enclosed, which might amuse you for a moment – please throw it in the fire as soon as you have read it. It was the review I wrote for the *P.M.G.* at the time: through some accident, it was overlooked; and the new editor[3] has just disinterred it and sent it back to me. I have been very unlucky in regard to your work. Here you see my luck with *Sherman*[4] – the Countess came out while I was away,[5] and I was too late, on my return, to get it from any paper. I was particularly sorry, for I admire it immensely, and I should so like to have said so. It seems to me by far the most genuine and delightful book of poems that has been done by any of the younger men. No one else has the magic that you have – and that is what really counts. I am so glad that Johnson did you justice in the *Academy* – you saw, no doubt, that admirable review?[6]

What are you doing now? I shall send this to your London address, so that it may be forwarded. Have you seen my *Silhouettes*? I should greatly like to know what you think of it. The edition is all sold – which is pleasant enough.

Yours
Arthur Symons

Notes

1. This letter and others from Symons to Yeats included in this volume were previously printed – with occasional errors in transcription – in Bruce Morris, 'Arthur Symons's Letters to W. B. Yeats: 1892–1902', *Yeats Annual No. 5*, ed. Warwick Gould (1987) 46–61.
2. W. B. Yeats, *The Countess Cathleen and Various Legends and Lyrics* (1892),
3. Clement Kinloch-Cooke (1851–1944), biographer and editor, *Pall Mall Gazette*, 1892–3.
4. *John Sherman* (1892), Yeats's novel, published in the Pseudonym Library series by T. Fisher Unwin.
5. Yeats's *The Countess Cathleen* appeared in September, when Symons was in Wales.
6. See Lionel Johnson's signed review in the *Academy*, 42 (1 Oct. 1892) 278–9. Johnson (1867–1902), poet and critic, was, like Symons, a member of the Rhymers' Club. A close friend of Yeats until the mid 1890s, Johnson figures prominently in Yeats's memoirs, particularly in the section titled 'The Tragic Generation' in *The Trembling of the Veil* (1922).

49   To Herbert Horne
(MS., Dugdale)

Saturday Night
[c. March 1893]   Fountain Court

My dear Horne

I'm in a devil of a row and in a devil of a temper, and as I have no one to talk to I must write to someone instead. For the last few nights I have been balancing Cassy and Violet[1] in an unsurpassed way, and have had the most delightful times with both. To-night Cassy spoke to me in such a way that I left her in a rage; and Violet went away without speaking to me. Isn't that very tragic?

I went to the rehearsal[2] – undress, with scenery. On asking Hollingshead's permission to stay and see it, he said "Why of course; aren't you l'enfant de la maison?" which I thought a very pretty designation. I did stay, and had the most amusing time imaginable. Indeed, I fear too amusing for the rigid manners of the corps de ballet. The girls who were not on, you understand, had sought refuge in front, and petticoats and stockings sprawled over all the stalls and lounges. On one of the lounges, by the side of the stalls, lay three ladies (I can't say sat) – Rosie Dean and two others. They were coiled inextricably together, somewhat in the manner of a design by Félicien Rops.[3] I was standing in front of them with great dignity, addressing moral remarks to them, when a fatal remark of Rosie about "a nice young man," in the general, which could have nothing but a particular reference, precipitated me – if only by mere courtesy – upon the too tempting seat, and before I knew it my arms were round her waist, and the group was not less inextricable, but *I* was one of the group. Rosie's funny little legs kicked in the air; she squirmed with delight, shrieked with laughter; and I need not say the Alhambra – respectable institution! – trembled to its foundation. What is more essential, our little ébats were witnessed by far too many spectators.

After the rehearsal I took Minnie and Ada Kelly and Louie Bryant to have some lunch at Gatti's (where, for a minor misfortune, someone stole my best and only umbrella). We were all rather excited, and, once in the street, cigarettes were proposed, Louie had lit hers, and I was just lighting Minnie's off the end of mine, when – of all diabolical things – the supreme Cassy passed! Well, I proposed the Temple; the girls were nothing loth; and when we got to the gates Louis and Minnie excused themselves for half an hour – on I know not what errand citywards – and Ada mounted with me. I should have preferred that it had been Minnie. We lit the fire and made some tea, and the others duly turned up, we all smoked a great deal, Minnie and I played the piano, and the two Kellys seemed, I thought, a little disappointed at the innocence of the proceedings. Their behaviour was, in its fine shades, instructive; one might say, suggestive. After I had landed them at the stage-door, about half past eight, I had some dinner and betook myself to the Empire. Afterwards occurred what I have told you. Cassy hoped I would excuse her plain speaking – which I emphatically did *not*. She spoke rather plainly, and as I did not feel too much in the right, I was naturally very much annoyed. Violet's sentiments on various points I have yet to hear. I hope you will duly appreciate the gravity of the situation, and its many bearings. Here, at all events, is the story which I felt (very absurdly) impelled to tell.

I hope we are all to meet (you and Muriel[4] and Image and I) and have dinner together on Monday. I imagine that he will see you on Sunday and arrange.

Yours
Arthur Symons

Notes

1. Like the other young ladies mentioned in this letter, they were dancers at the Alhambra Theatre. Cassy (whose real name was Josephine Casaboni) is the central figure of Symons's 'Notes on the Sensations of a Lady of the Ballet', *International*, 8 (Apr. 1914) 114–20; rptd in *ER*, 30 (Feb. 1920) 104–20. Symons told Henry-D. Davray (MS., 7 July 1914, Queen's): 'It is a real confession of mine.'
2. At the Alhambra Theatre, whose productions were more elaborate than those of the Empire Theatre and whose dancers generally superior.
3. French painter and illustrator (1833–98), noted for his erotic subject matter.
4. Muriel Broadbent, whose father was a physician, was Herbert Horne's mistress in the 1890s. Within a week after her arrival in London, probably in 1892, Symons met her on the promenade of the Alhambra Theatre, where she plied her trade as a prostitute. He wrote about her in two stories that appeared in the *Savoy*: 'Pages from the Life of Lucy Newcome', no. 2 (Apr. 1896) 147–60; and 'The Childhood of Lucy Newcome', no. 8 (Dec. 1896) 51–61; rptd in *SA*. He also planned 'a novel in chapters à la Goncourt', based on these stories. See Alan Johnson, 'Arthur Symons' "Novel à la Goncourt"', *Journal of Modern Literature*, 9 (1981–2) 50–64, and 'Arthur Symons' "The Life and Adventures of Lucy Newcome": Preface and Text', *English Literature in Transition*, 28 (1985) 332–45.

    Symons later told John Quinn (1870–1924), the American lawyer, art patron, and collector (MS., 6 Mar. 1915, Quinn): 'The actual girl is still alive. Got married about 1899. Her name was Muriel Broadbent – a sensual enough creature – whose favours I shared with her *amant de coeur*.'

50   To Katherine Willard
    (MS., Baldwin)

Carbis Water
Lelant
Cornwall

30 November 1893

My dear Kate

I was glad to hear from you once more on this side, my side, as you say, of the Atlantic. But why didn't you come back via England? Letters are so unsatisfactory, after all; and I have lots of things to talk to you about. Here are one or two of them.

As you see, I am down at the very edge of England, at Carbis Bay, close to St. Ives, where I lived for three years when I was a small boy. I am staying with Havelock Ellis, who has a little cottage down here. You must absolutely come down some time and see this region: there is nothing like it in Europe. It is impossible to describe, for the effect is so big, so terrifying, really, that words become ridiculous, meaningless, when they put on emphasis enough to come near rendering it. On Monday Ellis and I started on a walking tour. We went to Penzance, and then walked all round the coast, and back here again, visiting every sea-coast village and cove, by way of Land's End, Gurnand's Head, Sennen Cove, the Logan Rock, and other places locally famous. We stayed at fishermen's cottages, and had meals in little quiet country inns. And we did plenty of walking, for the path was generally a mere thread between rocks, and on the edge of cliffs, now climbing up one hill and now sliding down another.

Well then, just before I came down here, I had a very amusing time in town. You know Paul Verlaine, the French poet whom I admire so enormously – far and away the greatest living poet, I think, and a man whose life has been very wild and extraordinary, and who is now living in Paris, in the depths of poverty. Well, one or two of us organized a lecture in London, in order to get him a little money, and he came over and stayed with me in the Temple, in the room that used to be Frank's.[1] I never had such a fine time there as during the few days he was with me. He is rather lame, and I had to take him about leaning on my arm, and in four-wheelers. Then we had friends coming in at every hour of the day and night, parties, and all sorts of expeditions. I can't tell you how really charming he was – so simple and childlike and contented with everything – quite astonishing the people who had only heard the terrible legend which has grown up about him, making him out a monster. He wrote his name on my wall just by the crucifix, as a souvenir. The little visit is something to remember, always.[2]

Did I tell you about my plan of going to Venice, this winter? My friend Herbert Horne and I were going in October, but he fell ill, and our trip had to be postponed. We hope to go before very long, however; and we want to visit Padua, Mantua, Verona, Vicenza, Milan, as well as Venice. I expect we shall stay a month or a month and a half. Then I want to stay in Paris on the way back. Couldn't you after all carry out the plan you had some time ago, of spending some time in Paris, and couldn't you manage to fit in the time with mine? Of course I don't know yet when I shall be there, or indeed, for certain, if I shall have the money to stay there; but I hope to be able to do so. Tell me if there is any chance of meeting you there.

I have had a very good offer for my next book of poems [*London Nights*], which is practically ready. If I take the offer, I am sure of £25, which is not bad, for verses, is it? And I think I am doing better work now than I ever did before.

Now there are all my doings and projects: tell me yours. Write to Fountain Court, please. Remember me to the home folk, and remember me unforgettingly yours

Arthur Symons

Notes

1. With William Rothenstein (1872–1945), artist and author, Symons arranged Verlaine's lecture tour in England. Of Verlaine's lecture on contemporary French writers at Barnard's Inn, London, on 21 Nov. 1893, the critic Arthur Waugh (1866–1943) wrote in the New York *Critic*: 'It was a strange little crowd of critics and poets, artists and musicians. . . . M. Verlaine entered, rather late, impeded by an extreme lameness, on the arm of Mr. Arthur Symons, his most active supporter in this country' (9 Dec. 1893, p. 383). Verlaine went on to Oxford and Manchester for identical lectures. See Paul Verlaine, 'My Visit to London', *Savoy*, no. 2 (Apr. 1896) 119–35; Arthur Symons, 'Paul Verlaine in London', in *Memoirs*.
2. When Verlaine left London for Oxford, where he was met by the don Frederick York Powell (1850–1904) at Christ Church, Symons wrote to Rothenstein (MS., n.d., Harvard): 'Verlaine's visit, to me, has been most delightful, and I think we ought all to congratulate ourselves on ourselves for having brought him over, and on our luck in getting him. I hope he will get a decent amount of money in Oxford: the London sum will be, I think, about £30.'

51   To Paul Verlaine
      (MS., Doucet)

12 février 94   Fountain Court

Mon cher maître et ami

Vous êtes trop charmant pour moi: les vers sont délicieux, et je vous en remercie mille fois. Vous n'auriez pu me faire un plus grand plaisir. Maintenant, si on oublie vite mes pauvres vers, au moins on n'oubliera point mon nom – grâce à vous![1]

Mais, mais, il faut absolument évoquer le souvenir des biscuits et du gin de cette nuit vraiment immortelle! C'est un sujet digne de vous, comme dit Browning "a subject made to your hand",[2] et vous pourriez bien écrire quelque chose à la fois drôle et délicate. Il faut absolument ce poème-là!

On fonde en ce moment une nouvelle revue, *The Yellow Book*, une espèce de revue jeune. Je ne sais pas encore s'il y a de l'argent là-dedans, mais si cela tourne à bien je tâcherai de faire entrer quelques vers de vous.[3] Je vous enverrai le premier numéro, où il y aura un poème de moi,[4] un peu osé pour une revue anglaise, dont j'espère bien que vous serez content.

L'adresse de Morton Fullerton:[5] 5 rue Vignon. Si non, toujours Bureau du *Times*, boulevard des Capucines.

Je suis tellement occupé en ce moment que je n'ai pas encore pu acheter les deux revues que vous m'avez demandées. Mais je les enverrai dans un peu. C'est que je traduis *L'Assommoir* de Zola pour un éditeur;[6] et pour finir la besogne à temps, il faut traduire chaque jour douze à quinze pages. Vous voyez bien que cela m'occupe toute la journée.

Merci encore des vers, et tous bons souhaits de la part de votre

Arthur Symons

Notes

1. Two months after his return to France (on 5 Dec.), Verlaine sent Symons a poem titled 'Fountain Court', dedicated to him and naming him in the poem. See Paul Verlaine, *Oeuvres poétiques complètes* (Paris, 1948) p. 429.
2. From Browning's 'A Light Woman' in *Men and Women* (1855).
3. No verse by Verlaine appeared in the *Yellow Book*.
4. Symons's 'Stella Maris', *Yellow Book*, 1 (Apr. 1894) 129–31.
5. American journalist and author (1865–1952), Paris correspondent for *The Times*, 1891–1911.
6. Alexander Teixeira de Mattos (1865–1921), Dutch-born translator educated in England, was editor of the Zola edition issued by the Lutetian Society (London), which published translations at high prices to avoid prosecution on the grounds that public morals were being debased. Symons's translation appeared in 1894.

52 To James Dykes Campbell
(MS., BL)

6 May 1894   Verona

My dear Campbell

Since half way on in March I have been luxuriating in Italy; most of the time in Venice, which I left at the beginning of this week. I have touched at Padua, Vicenza, Mantua, and now Verona, on my way to Milan, and I get back to Paris in less than a fortnight. I shall probably stay there a month, mainly for the sake of doing some work. You can fancy what my first glimpse of Italy has been: you will know more about it when you read "Venice in Easter: Impressions and Sensations" in a future number of *Harper*.[1] I am far too busy absorbing things Italian to write letters to anybody at present; but I wanted just to send you a line from Italy. Just before I left Venice, Henry James was dining with Horne and me, and a certain Capt. Vaughan, who is a lineal descendant of Lord Rochester of ever-blessed memory, at the house of Horatio Brown,[2] and James delivered quite a little lecture on a certain almost ideal biography of S.T.C.,[3] by way of an object lesson to Brown, who has to write a life of Symonds. So your name has not been unheard while I have been away.

I have been spending the morning in that adorable garden which climbs up a hill over Verona, and I don't wonder that Dante was said to loiter there. On the whole, though, I find Verona disappointing (compared with Mantua, for instance); it has been so horribly pulled about and "improved" almost out of existence. But Venice! There is certainly nothing like Venice. I have made a sort of vow to go there every year, if I can. Horne and I have even been discussing which palace we shall buy![4]

England seems infinitely far away, London ways forgotten, only Italy really an actual thing. I meant to do a lot of work here. I have done very little: do you wonder?

Tanti cordiali saluti to Mrs. Campbell and yourself.

Vostro
Arthur Symons

Notes

1. See *Harper's New Monthly Magazine*, 90 (Apr. 1895) 738–51; rptd as 'Venice' in *Cities* (1903), expanded in *Cities of Italy* (1907).
2. Historian and biographer (1854–1926), a friend of John Addington Symonds, later his literary executor and first biographer in *John Addington Symonds: A Biography*, 2 vols (1895). In 1923, Brown was the editor of *Letters and Papers of John Addington Symonds*.
3. James Dykes Campbell's *Samuel Taylor Coleridge* (1894).
4. Nothing came of this, but Horne did purchase a decayed palazzo in Florence in 1912, restored it, and bequeathed it to the city with his art collection. See Ian Fletcher, 'Herbert Horne: The Earlier Phase', *English Miscellany* (Rome), 21 (1970) 155–6.

53   To the Pall Mall Gazette
   (15 October 1894, p. 3)

11 October 1894

Sir

In reading the reports of the recent meeting of the Licensing Committee of the County Council, and, in particular, the evidence on which that body decided to recommend the suppression of the promenade at the

Empire, I have been struck by certain misstatements and misunderstandings in relation to quite definite facts which I am sure must have been made solely through lack of trustworthy information, and not from any but the most well-meaning motives. I think it may be as well to rectify some of these inaccuracies.

We are told that Mrs. Sheldon Amos used words to the effect that the Empire was the worst place of the kind which she knew in civilized countries.[1] Now I cannot of course say how widely Mrs. Amos may have visited music-halls throughout the civilized world; I can only say that her opinion could certainly not be corroborated on evidence in regard to any European country. Without pretending to know all about the music-halls of every continent, I may say that I have made a special study of music-hall entertainments of every kind, and that I have visited music-halls in Paris and throughout France, in Belgium, in Germany, in Italy, and in Spain, and I can only say that, in my opinion, the Empire is, as a place of entertainment, the most genuinely artistic and the most absolutely unobjectionable that I know in any country, and that, as regards the main point to which special objection has been raised – the question of women – it is managed with a discretion which compares very favourably indeed with the policy pursued on the Continent. Take, for instance, the most popular music-hall in Paris, the Casino de Paris. Women are admitted there without payment, as they are at the larger number of Continental halls, expressly for the purpose of plying their trade and drawing visitors to the place; and both they, and some of the performers in the dances, accost visitors who have come merely to see the performance. Now at the Empire no woman is ever admitted without payment. She goes to the box-office like every one else, and pays down her five shillings every time she visits the theatre. As to the stories of men being accosted by women in the promenade at the Empire, my own experience assures me that this is extremely improbable. I have visited the Empire on an average about once a week for the last year or two in my function as critic for several newspapers, and I must say that whenever I have had occasion to stand in the promenade I have never in a single instance been accosted by a woman. That women come to the Empire for the purpose of meeting men, and men for the purpose of meeting women is, of course, obvious. They also go to every other music-hall in London for precisely the same reason; just as in Paris they go to the Madeleine, in Venice to St. Mark's. Vice, unfortunately, cannot be suppressed; it can only be regulated. Turn out the women from the promenade at the Empire, and within three weeks a new rendezvous will have been made at another music-hall, and, while the Empire will have been seriously damaged, for no fault of its own, another hall will have suddenly grown popular, for no merit of its own, and morals will be precisely where they were before, except that the scene of action will have been changed. Here is where the injustice of such a measure as the suppression of the Empire promenade seems to me to lie. The Empire has won its popularity by the excellence of its entertainment. It has made no attempt to draw a "fast" audience; these people have come simply because all London has come. If the Licensing Committee of the County Council had decided to do away with every promenade in every music-hall, I should, at least, have understood the point of view, though I should have failed to see the wisdom of driving these poor women into the open streets, where, for one thing, it would be needless to pay 5s in order to meet them. But to single out the Empire, and the Empire only – that seems to me a grave injustice. – I am, Sir, your obedient servant,

Arthur Symons

Note

1. Mrs Amos, on behalf of the National Vigilance Association, had testified at an annual hearing of the Licensing Committee that she had gone to the Empire Theatre to inspect the promenade. See 'County Council and Licensing', *Era*, 13 Oct. 1894, p. 16.

54   To Edmund Gosse
(MS., Leeds)

26 February 1895   Fountain Court

My dear Gosse
    I write at once, asking for Benson's book.[1]
    I am glad you liked my Montesquiou.[2] I got those stories from José-Maria de Hérédia.[3]
    I met Coulson Kernahan in an A.B.C.D. [*sic*] to-day, and heard from him that Norman Gale has been running amuck at you in the *Literary World*.[4] How very silly of Tudor Tempest – what a tempest in a tea pot it probably is!
    I have just got Mr. Tabb's poems,[5] which look very like the gentleman's name; also an astounding novel by John Davidson, all about flagellation.[6] Shades of Lord Houghton![7] Is the man serious or joking, I wonder? I am sorry to hear that you have had bronchitis: I can meet nobody who hasn't. All my friends are in bed, and I am doing their work. And I have had such a bad cold myself, that I stayed away from my favourite stage-door for one whole night, the longest night on record.
    As for my poems, I still have plots and plans. The refusal of Lane[8]

and Heinemann[9] was to me so inexplicable that I have just had the MS. read by my very fair-minded and judicious friend Selwyn Image, offering to omit anything to which he himself really took exception on the ground of taste and morals. He deliberately advises me to omit nothing, and, for his own part, imagines that it is the extremely *personal* note which has shocked people. Yet there, if there is any value in them, the value must lie.

Yours ever
Arthur Symons

Notes

1. Probably *Limitations* (1895), a novel by Edward Frederick Benson (1867–1940).
2. Count Robert de Montesquiou-Fezensac (1855–1921), French poet and dandy, the presumed model for the character of Des Esseintes in Huysmans's *A Rebours* (1884). Symons had apparently shown Gosse a manuscript of his essay on Montesquiou, which appeared, unsigned, as 'M. de Montesquiou's Verse', *SR*, 80 (16 Nov. 1895) 638–9; rptd as 'The Poet of the Bats' in *CSP*.
3. Cuban-born French Parnassian poet (1842–1905).
4. Coulson Kernahan (1858–1943), author and journalist, for many years literary advisor to Ward, Lock & Co.; 'A.B.C.': a chain of teashops operated by the Aerated Bread Company; Norman Gale (1862–1942), poet and essayist, had published a review of Gosse's *In Russet and Silver* (1894) in which he remarked: 'Yes, we can conscientiously assert that *In Russet and Silver* contains some poetry.' See Gale's 'A Lost Lyre', *Literary World*, 95 (1894) 450.
5. John Tabb (1845–1909), American priest and poet, whose *Poems* (1894) went through seventeen editions.
6. An allusion to Davidson's *The Wonderful Mission of Earl Lavender* (1895), published with a Beardsley frontispiece depicting a woman flagellating a person of indeterminate sex. Symons had apparently not read the novel but drew his conclusion from the illustration.
7. Richard Monkton Milnes (1809–95), created Lord Houghton in 1863, was a poet, politician, and philanthropist, who shared a taste for flagellation with his friend Swinburne.
8. John Davidson, who read the manuscript of *London Nights* for Lane, submitted a report, which, despite reservations, recommended publication: 'Mr. Symons improves much as a craftsman; throughout his new book his dexterity is very notable; but the range remains limited, has, indeed, contracted, until the whole universe appears as an embodiment of desire. . . . Note always that the desire is utterly loveless and unimpassioned – mere and sheer libidinous desire. . . . Here is a man who can write you the most charming lines in the most cold-blooded inferior mood, the subject also being petty and uninteresting in the last degree' (Walpole 685, Walpole Collection, Bodleian Library, Oxford).
9. William Heinemann (1863–1920), publisher who founded his firm in 1890, published Symons's first volume of verse, *Days and Nights* (1889).

55   To Herbert Horne
(MS., Dugdale)

29 April 1895   Fountain Court

My dear Horne

I have given Mrs. Claydon[1] due instructions, and she promises to carry them out.

Your letter is most inspiring, but I *am* sorry Fauvette[2] is fatter. I am afraid she won't make such a pretty living picture any longer in that chaste little room in the rue Duperré. By the way, look out for a chahût-dancer[3] named Folichonnette. I hope to hear soon of Lucette and the nymphs.

For me, I have carried out your wishes in living a quiet and virtuous life.[4] I have been nowhere, seen nothing; in fact, I have stayed in so much that I have broken one of the castors of my sofa and two of the springs of my bed. If M‡[5] tells you that we discussed S-d-my at the Empire, don't believe her. If Rothenstein tells you he saw me in earnest conversation with a small, but comely, person in a remote neighbourhood at a late hour, and that, with his usual fine sense of fitness, he yelled out "Arthur Symons!" don't believe him. If Gilchrist[6] says he ever saw me sitting in the Café Monico, don't believe him. If anybody tells you I have been in two cab collisions, and once narrowly escaped a bad smash – to say nothing of distracting the whole traffic about Temple Bar – don't believe it. I have corrected a few proofs, had dinner every few days, and said my prayers when I didn't forget them.

When do you get back on Thursday? I could meet you at the Monico at 7.30, if you would be there then. If not, I could be in, I expect, any time on Friday.

                                     Yours
                                     Arthur Symons

Notes

1. Possibly the housekeeper at King's Bench Walk, in The Temple, where Horne had rooms.
2. A Parisian dancer. See Symons's 'Fauvette' in *KH*. (Horne was in Paris at this time.)
3. Symons writes that the *chahût* is the 'successor, one might say the renaissance, of the *cancan*'. See Symons's 'Dancers and Dancing' in *CSP*.
4. Symons's facetiousness is a response to the atmosphere created by the arrest on 5 Apr. and the ensuing trial of Oscar Wilde. On 9 Apr., Symons had written to Verlaine (MS., Doucet): 'We can think of nothing here but the Oscar Wilde case.'
5. Symons's symbol for Muriel Broadbent, later a #.
6. Robert Murray Gilchrist (1868–1917), novelist and playwright.

56 To Herbert Horne
(MS., Dugdale)

2, rue de l'Oranger
[postmarked: 4 September 1895]   Dieppe

My dear Horne

Dowson[1] tells me there is some chance of your coming to join the English colony over here,[2] and – of all excellent and admirable things – with M# [Muriel Broadbent]. I only hope it is true. I promise you if you come that you will never return again – like, first, Conder,[3] secondly myself, and thirdly Beardsley,[4] who has determined to stay here, more or less, forever. I meant to stay a week, and am still here, waiting indeed for an answer from the *Century*, to which I offered an article on Dieppe.[5] A letter from Cléo de Mérode[6] (for particulars ask Dowson) makes me desire above all things to go straight to Paris. I think I shall probably go on there, – if my money lasts sufficiently to enable me to ask her out to dinner when I get there! As for England, I have almost forgotten that it exists. I am writing a good deal of verse, translating Verlaine, sitting for my portrait to Jacques Blanche,[7] meeting Baronesses and chahûteuses from Bullier,[8] bathing, lounging about the Casino, and altogether having the most amusing and irresponsible holiday I have had for a long time. I have a thousand things to discuss with you – the Rochester for our magazine[9] among others – and I shall be extremely glad if you are really coming over. If so, let me know and I will take a room for you at the Sandwich, where Dowson stayed. Also two things: *do* bring M#, and *don't* bring Olive (late Mrs. Dowson)![10] I believe she is under the impression that both Conder and I are frantically in love with her. Now that is by no means the case, and she has already got us into some trouble with other more charming persons. So, if there is any talk of her coming over, please prevent it, in the subtlest way that occurs to you. Say we have gone to Paris, or died, or anything you like. Conder is in particular alarm, and so I said I would tell you how things stand, rather than let him write to Dowson, which he rather absurdly talked of doing. Beardsley is waiting for me downstairs, and I hope to be talking with you soon, so au revoir et à bientôt, et à vous.

Arthur Symons

Notes

1. Ernest Dowson (1867–1900), poet and novelist, a member of the Rhymers' Club who, for the last five years of his life, lived mostly in France. With his article on Dowson in the *Savoy* (Aug. 1896), Symons inaugurated the 'Dowson Legend', much disputed among Dowson's friends. See Letter 67 and n. 8; 'Ernest Dowson' in *Memoirs*.
2. Dieppe, a favourite resort of the English at the time, had become a refuge from the

unpleasantness of, and possibly implication in, the trial of Oscar Wilde. See Simona
Pakenham, *Sixty Miles from England: The English at Dieppe, 1814–1914* (1967) pp. 145–
62; William Rothenstein, *Men and Memories, 1872–1900* (1931) pp. 245–52.
3. Charles Conder (1868–1909), artist, famous for his designs on fans and paintings on
silk. See 'Charles Conder' in *Memoirs*.
4. Aubrey Beardsley (1872–98) had recently been fired as illustrator of the *Yellow Book*,
the result of his association with Oscar Wilde. When Symons first met Beardsley in
1893, he told Herbert Horne that the tubercular artist was 'the thinnest young man I
ever saw, rather unpleasant and affected' (MS., postmarked 24 Aug. 1893, Dugdale),
but when Smithers asked Symons to edit a new periodical to rival the *Yellow Book*,
Beardsley was chosen to be its principal illustrator. See *Memoirs*, p. 170.
5. Symons's 'Dieppe: 1895' appeared in the *Savoy*, no. 1 (Jan. 1896) 84–102; rptd in *CSI*.
6. French ballet dancer (1881–1966), who fascinated Symons 'with her slim, natural, and
yet artificial elegance, her little, straight face, so virginal and yet so aware, under the
Madonna-like placidity of those smooth coils of hair, drawn over the ears and curved
along the forehead; De Mérode, who, more than anyone else, sums up Dieppe for
me' ('Dieppe: 1895', p. 102).
7. French artist and author (1861–1942), whose portrait of Symons, mentioned here, is
in the Tate Gallery, London, a bequest of Rhoda Symons.
8. The dancers of the *chahût* from the 'effervescent Bal Bullier of the Quartier Latin'. See
Letter 5, n. 3.
9. Probably an allusion to a proposed article – not accepted – on Lord Rochester for the
Savoy, then in the planning stage. John Wilmot, 2nd Earl of Rochester (1648–80), was
a poet and notorious libertine.
10. A facetious reference, probably, to a former *amour*.

57   To Henry Cust[1]
(MS., Case)

28 November 1895   Fountain Court

Private and Confidential

Dear Sir

I instructed my solicitor to ask for an apology for a review of my book
of poems, *London Nights*, which appeared in the *Pall Mall Gazette* some
time since.[2] I only heard yesterday that you had replied, and that my
solicitor had issued a writ, which was entirely in excess of my instructions. I have immediately instructed him to withdraw the action. I have
no money whatever, and, no matter how confident I may feel of the
strength of my case, I can not possibly fight Mr. Astor's wealth.[3] But I
think if you will reconsider the matter, you will feel that the review in
question altogether overstepped the bounds of literary courtesy and
justice, and was by no means warranted by a book which was manifestly
written with an artistic intention, and an artistic intention only.

Your solicitors will receive formal notice of my withdrawal: I must
ask you to consider the present communication as entirely confidential.

Believe me, yours faithfully

Arthur Symons

Notes

1. Politician and journalist (1861–1917), editor, *Pall Mall Gazette*, 1893–6.
2. On 2 Sep. 1895, p. 4, a review titled 'Pah!' appeared, in which the reviewer said in part:

> Mr. Arthur Symons is a very dirty-minded man, and his mind is reflected in the puddle of his bad verses. It may be that there are other dirty-minded men who will rejoice in the jingle that records the squalid and inexpensive amours of Mr. Symons, but our faith jumps to our hope that such men are not. He informs us in his prologue that his life is like a music-hall, which should bring him a joint-action for libel from every decent institution of the kind in London. By his own showing, his life's more like a pig-sty, and one dull below the ordinary at that. Every woman he pays to meet him, he tells us, is desirous to kiss his lips; our boots too are desirous, but of quite another part of him, for quite another purpose.

3. William Waldorf Astor (1848–1919), American financier, who, after a political career, moved to England in 1890 and acquired several magazines and the *Pall Mall Gazette* (1892–1909). Recognised for his generous contributions to public causes, he was made a baron in 1916 and a viscount in 1917.

58 To W. B. Yeats
(MS., Yeats)

Via della Rosetta
Rome

New Year's Eve, 1896–7

My dear Yeats

I like Rome more and more, and am getting to know it quite well by now, though I am taking it very gradually, letting things come my way rather than going to seek them. My two good Counts[1] drive me about nearly every day, and, in fact, put all Rome at my feet. Primoli took me yesterday to the Villa Medici, of which I have the entrée, and he is going to lend me the key of the little wood there – the loveliest thing in Rome – where I shall go and work at my verse. I have done some already in the gardens of the Villa Borghese, where I have found a deserted avenue of ilexes, with a fountain and a little temple.[2] I am working at my long poem, and have done "Gluttony" and "Lying."[3] I have also filled nearly 60 pages of one of those little 8$^{vo.}$ note-books with notes and impressions of Rome. I shall probably spend the whole winter here. I have just heard from Ellis that Olive Schreiner and her husband are coming here in February. Miss Blind's friends have just come, but I have not seen them yet. And I have already met various people here:

Monsignor Stanley, the Contessa Bazzolini, Mme. Minghetti, and I am to be taken to see Princess Doria,[4] whose portrait I saw and admired so much at Kilcornan.

I am here in the very midst of old Rome. The front of the Pantheon, so severe, so ample, so reticent, so imposing, in a word, so final, gives me so much pleasure that I can scarcely take my eyes off it when I sit here. I go to the window half a dozen times while I am undressing.

I have just got a lot of proofs of my prose book.[5] I am trying to make my notes for the Rome article not merely impressions, but studies in the meaning of things.[6] I intend to introduce my descriptions only by way of illustration. In this way I think I shall do something of some real value.

The sunset to-day, which I saw from the Pincio, was I think the finest I have ever seen, fit to be the end, not merely of the year, but of the world.

Remember me to all my friends. If you see Merrill,[7] give him my address, and say I wish he would send me Louis Le Cardonnel's exact address.[8]

　　　　　　　　　　　　Yours ever
　　　　　　　　　　　　Arthur Symons

Notes

1. Count Florimond Jacques de Basterot (1836–1904), French author of travel books, had inherited an estate in Galway, Ireland, not far from Edward Martyn's Tillyra Castle, where Symons first met him. See Symons's *Cities* (1903) p. 30. The other count was Count Giuseppe Primoli (1851–1925), Italian author and *littérateur*, who was a friend of the Italian actress Eleonora Duse (1859–1924) and her lover, the Italian poet and playwright Gabrielle d'Annunzio (see Letter 91, n. 4). Primoli introduced them to Symons in the mid 1890s at one of his gatherings in his *palazzo* beside the Tiber River. See Philippe Jullian, *D'Annunzio* (New York, 1973) pp. 45–6; Symons, *Memoirs*, pp. 223–33.
2. See Symons's poem 'Villa Borghese' in *KH*.
3. See 'The Dance of the Seven Sins' in *IGE*.
4. Donna Laura Minghetti was the mother of Princess Doria, who had married Prince Bernard von Bülow (1849–1929), German Ambassador to Rome, 1893–97. The other names we have been unable to identify.
5. Arthur Symons, *Studies in Two Literatures* (1897).
6. Arthur Symons, 'Rome', *Cosmopolis*, 7 (Aug. 1897) 323–39. rptd as Part I of 'Rome' in *Cities* (1903) and *Cities of Italy* (1907).
7. Stuart Merrill (1863–1915), American-born French poet and critic who emigrated to France in 1891, published two articles on Symons: 'Arthur Symons', *L'Aube*, Jan. 1897, pp. 151–3, which discusses the *Savoy* and *London Nights*; and 'L'Oeuvre poétique d'Arthur Symons', *L'Antée*, 3 (June 1907) 66–82, a more comprehensive critique.
8. Louis Le Cardonnel (1862–1936), French Symbolist poet.

3

Triumph and Disaster: 1897–1908

In the earlier part of the decade, Symons was at the centre of literary life in London, where, as Pater might have described it, 'the greatest number of vital forces unite in their purest energy'.[1] The *Savoy*, more than the *Yellow Book*, had united those forces brilliantly. Its sudden death revealed, with stunning clarity, that public support for avant-garde literature was non-existent.[2]

As editor of the *Savoy*, Symons had reached his zenith in the world of literary journalism. As a leading figure in the avant-garde, he had given prominence to the work of Yeats and to the French Symbolists, whom he himself had translated. The journal, therefore, was significant in both the personal life of Symons and the literary life of England. From 1897 onwards, he would gradually but progressively find himself isolated from the centre of literary activity.

In December 1896, Symons had left London for a three-month stay in Rome, where he prepared for the press a collection of his previously published essays, *Studies in Two Literatures*, dedicated to George Moore. While there, he met d'Annunzio, whom he believed the greatest figure in Italian letters and whose plays he later translated.

He returned to London in May after visiting Naples (which he abhorred) and Venice (which always fascinated him) to his post as a regular reviewer for the *Athenaeum* and *Saturday Review*. In August, however, he departed for Moscow with Havelock Ellis, who was to attend a medical congress there. Disappointed at not having met Tolstoy, Symons returned to a reviewing post on the *Saturday Review*, then edited by Frank Harris, to which he would contribute, over the next few years, a great many articles on French writers (later revised for *The Symbolist Movement in Literature*) and impressions of places he had visited (later collected in *Cities*).

In the autumn of 1897, Symons was advising George Moore on *Evelyn Innes* and in early 1898 was reading the proofs of the novel,[3] which was dedicated to Symons and Yeats. In the spring of that year, Wilde's *Ballad of Reading Gaol* appeared, which Symons acquired for review. Regarding Wilde's fall as a tragedy for the artist and a victory for the philistines, Symons had written to Smithers, Wilde's publisher, before the *Ballad* appeared:

I see by your advertisement in the *Athenaeum* that you are publishing Wilde's poem. I need scarcely say that if I could do anything that would be of service to Wilde, now that he is making his first attempt to return to literature, I should be only too glad to do it.[4]

Wilde was pleased to learn that Symons had made the offer, and when the review appeared in the *Saturday Review* on 12 March 1898, he wrote to Harris: 'I am greatly touched by Symons's article; it is most admirably phrased, and its mode of approach is artistic and dignified. A thousand thanks to you and to him.'[5]

In the same month, Symons was again saddened by the death of an artist whom he had admired (the deaths of Browning, Pater, Symonds, and Verlaine had moved him deeply). Now it was Beardsley, who died before his twenty-sixth birthday. Though relations between the two had been strained during the editorship of the *Savoy*, Symons wrote a sympathetic appreciation for the May number of the *Fortnightly Review*,[6] which Yeats, in a letter to Lady Gregory, declared a 'masterpiece'.[7] In September, still another admired artist died, one whom he had met several times in Paris and of whom he had written – Mallarmé – whose obituary notice he wrote for the *Fortnightly Review*,[8] not so much a notice but a summing up of his achievement. Symons incorporated it as the central chapter of *The Symbolist Movement in Literature*.

In May 1898, Symons met Rhoda Bowser, to whom he had been introduced by Ernest Rhys's sister, Edith. Miss Bowser, the daughter of a wealthy Newcastle ship-owner and ship-builder, was only twenty-four; Symons was already thirty-three. Her admiration for his poetry and her interest in the arts (she had come to London to study at the Royal Academy of Music) struck a responsive chord in Symons, who took her to concerts and plays. But it was a year or so before he thought of her seriously.

Symons spent most of 1898 and part of the following year in France and Spain, recording in letters and essays his impressions and preparing the manuscript of his next book, *The Symbolist Movement in Literature*. In April he was back in London, but after some work on the book, he left again in August for the continent at the invitation of Count Lützow, a Czech historian, to examine Casanova's unpublished manuscripts at Dux in Bohemia, where he had lived. To his delight, Symons discovered two long-lost chapters of Casanova's *Memoirs* and letters written by one of Casanova's loves. To Rhoda, he wrote on 28 September 1899 (MS., Columbia): 'In one of these castles, I made a discovery which will excite all the literary people in Europe – I found some MSS. which people have been trying in vain to find for half a century. Congratulate me!'

Returning to London that autumn, he spent his time revising *The Symbolist Movement*, writing reviews, and attending soirées given by such prominent figures as Arnold Dolmetsch and Mrs Patrick Campbell. Symons's letters to Rhoda during this period are obviously calculated to impress her with his extensive artistic and social connections. In time, however, she would be offering him advice in the criticism of music, in which, Symons admitted in his dedication to *Studies in the Seven Arts* (1906), she was more knowledgeable: 'You have a far clearer sense than I have of the special qualities, the special limits, of the various arts. . . . You will find then, in this book, much of your own coming back to you.'

When Ernest Dowson died in February 1900, Symons, who was not a close friend, wrote a sympathetic but misleading account of his life (in part a reworking of a previous essay on Dowson published in the *Savoy* [August 1896] with the title 'A Literary Causerie'), which Dowson's friends resented. But as his letters to Rhoda reveal, Symons was in no way attempting to sensationalise Dowson's life; indeed, he was most concerned about the possibility of distortion.

The appearance of *The Symbolist Movement in Literature* in March (delayed because Heinemann had been trying to secure an American publisher but also perhaps because of the Boer War) was heralded by most critics as a major achievement. Yeats wrote an important essay on Symbolism, stimulated by Symons's study, to which Yeats refers as 'a subtle book, which I cannot praise as I would, because it has been dedicated to me'.[9] A letter from Gosse, praising the work in effusive terms, was treasured by Symons throughout his life.[10]

On 6 May Symons proposed to Rhoda in a letter which, curiously, begins as a dialogue between himself and his sister, Anna, on the subject of marriage. Though uncertain, Rhoda accepted, subject to her father's approval. During that summer, Symons attempted, with the help of Gosse and others, to find a steady position but without success. He had to content himself, therefore, with writing occasional articles, reading manuscripts for publishers, and translating Racine. Despite this, Rhoda's father gave his consent in September.

During this time, Symons met Thomas Hardy, who invited him to Max Gate, Dorset, for a weekend in August. Hardy, who had no doubt appreciated Symons's inclusion of Ellis's essay on him in the October number of the *Savoy*, purchased *The Symbolist Movement in Literature* on the day of its appearance and particularly liked *Images of Good and Evil*, Symons's fifth volume of verse.

On 19 January 1901, Symons married Rhoda in Newcastle, and after a brief honeymoon in Paris, moved into a London flat in Maida Vale. Though 'the bloody sweat of those fornicating years in Fountain Court'[11] was at an end, Symons continued to frequent the music-halls as a reviewer for the *Star*. His evenings, formerly spent at the Crown and the Café Royal with the Alhambra dancers and with his literary friends, were now curtailed by an altered pattern of life. He knew that he would have to work hard to support both Rhoda and himself, but he was reluctant to lower the quality of his writing. As he wrote to Rhoda in December 1900 (MS., Columbia), before his marriage:

> I never feel quite sure that you realize all that it means, marrying a man with no more money than I have, or am ever likely to have – for, though I hope to get a little more than I do now, I shall *never* be rich unless I give up trying to do good work.

An opportunity for an assured income arose early that year when Symons was offered the post of drama critic for the *Academy*, but even this would last, he was told, only a few months – until August. During this period, he was involved in numerous other projects: a major critical work on the romantic movement, a translation of d'Annunzio's *Francesca da Rimini* and articles for numerous journals.

Soon after Symons's return from a trip to the Continent, Yeats brought a young Irish writer named James Joyce to his flat in Maida Vale in early December 1902. Symons chatted about some of his friends in the 1890s and played the Good Friday music from Wagner's *Parsifal*. Later, Joyce was amused by Yeats's remark: 'Symons has always had a longing to commit great sin, but he has never been able to get beyond ballet girls.'[12] More important, however, was Symons's promise to find a publisher for Joyce when he had a book of poems ready. This Symons eventually did, after persuading editors to accept individual poems for their journals, assistance that Joyce never forgot.[13]

Symons's contacts with American publishers and critics had been slight before the turn of the century, but in 1903 he began corresponding with Thomas B. Mosher, the American publisher who habitually pirated the works of *fin-de-siècle* authors for the *Bibelot*, a monthly publication which appeared between 1895 and 1914. Symons, hoping for a wider audience as a poet in America, carried on a lengthy correspondence with Mosher, who sought his advice about selections for publication.

In the summer of 1903, Symons left for an extensive stay on the continent – Italy, France, Switzerland – where he gathered material for his next book, *Cities* (1903), dedicated to the Comtesse de la Tour, whom he visited at Puy de Dôme. In March 1904, having written a number of literary studies (which form *Studies in Prose and Verse* [1904]) and many poems, he returned to irregular employment. Again, Symons was forced to engage in editorial projects for which he wrote introductions. At the same time he was writing plays, two of which – *The Fool of the World: A Morality* and *Cleopatra in Judaea* – were given single performances by the English Stage Society.

Since 1902, Symons had developed a friendship with Edward Hutton, novelist and authority on Italian culture, who, like Symons, wrote many travel books. Their relationship was close in those years,[14] Symons offering advice to the younger man and Hutton deepening his friend's interest in Italy.

In the spring of 1906, Symons decided to purchase a seventeenth-century timbered cottage in Wittersham, Kent, and move from his spacious flat in Maida Vale to a small, detached house in St. John's Wood. Publishing widely, Symons felt confident that such a major change in his life could be managed without financial hardship; however, repairs to the cottage amounted to more than twice the expected cost, and after July, when he and Rhoda moved in, references to the bill increase in his letters. To discharge the debt, he had to borrow from relatives and from Gosse, who offered a loan of £100.

In 1906, Symons published *The Fool of the World and Other Poems*, his first volume of verse in five years, and *Studies in Seven Arts*, a collection of previously published essays. In 1907, *Cities of Italy* appeared as well as *William Blake*, one of his most important critical works. But Symons's desire to make his mark in the theatre, either with his own plays or with translations, was destined to continual frustration.

An ominous note sounds in a letter from Symons to the actress Julia Marlowe, who had taken his play, *The Harvesters*, for production in the United States. When nothing came of it, Symons wrote to her on 21 March 1908 (MS., Museum, NY), revealing his deep-seated anxiety:

> All my friends are waiting to see what I can do, and they are only now, on hearing that you have taken my play, beginning to believe in the possibility of my achieving something on the stage. I put in, just to show you the interest that people in America are ready to take, a letter I have just had from Brander Matthews.[15] Destroy it: I don't want it back. Thomas Hardy is equally anxious about it here. The mere mention of your name has its instant effect. So if, after all, this whole structure should tumble about my ears, I should be pretty well obliterated under it.

Shortly thereafter, when he received word that Duse would act in his *Tristan and Iseult* in Rome, Symons excitedly told Hutton (MS., 11 April 1908, Harvard): 'I imagine the splendour of a first dramatic triumph in Rome!' But the planned production failed to materialise. A further disappointment occured when an article on Conrad, whom Symons regarded as the greatest living English novelist, was rejected by several magazines. Judging the article as one of his best, Symons began a correspondence with Conrad, whom he did not meet, however, until 1910.

Despite extensive publishing and regular bi-weekly music reviewing for the *Saturday Review*, Symons declared himself 'penniless' in a letter to Hutton (MS., 11 April, Harvard). Yet he and Rhoda left London in September to spend some time in Venice, their first Continental trip in three years. There, Symons went to the theatres, explored the city, translated Verlaine and Baudelaire, and listened to the songs of the gondoliers.

But something quite strange had entered an article he sent to the *Saturday Review* on Venetian music (which appeared on 17 October). Describing the songs sung in the gondolas, he wrote: 'I remember a beautiful one, really no more than a rattling jig, but sung with conviction, that had a passage which went in one breath to this effect: La ta ta ta ta ta ta ta ta ta ta ta ta ta ta ta.'[16] The journal printed the passage as written. In his *Confessions* (1930), Symons wrote that he regarded the article as a 'document in which my madness is most evident'. However, except for the passage quoted (another 'ta ta ta' passage occurs elsewhere in the article) there is little indication of madness in the account; but his letters at this time, particularly those to Hutton, reveal a disintegrating mind.

On 26 September, Symons, in a state of tension, suddenly left Venice for Bologna, where Rhoda joined him the following day. She became alarmed, however, when Arthur, who was out one night, did not return to the hotel because he had lost his way. He spent the night in a 'miserable little hotel' (as he described it in the *Confessions*), and on the following day, in 'a state of nervous exasperation', he quarrelled with Rhoda, stamping about the room when she complained of his strange behaviour.[17] The next day, after Rhoda's departure for Paris (she had tried to get him on the train), he left for Ferrara, where darkness descended on his mind. According to his own account, written many years later, he wandered about the countryside for several days, sleeping under the open sky or in barns. Given food by peasants, he was driven back to Ferrara by cart. Then, apparently, the 'under-manager' of the hotel where he had been staying authorised him to be locked up in the Castello Veccho, an old doge castle, where he was thrust into a dungeon, manacled hand and foot, and flung to the stone floor.

In London, Rhoda prevailed upon a friend, the Italian ambassador, to locate Arthur. Finally found, he was removed to a rest home in Ferrara, then to another in Bologna. Three weeks later he returned to London, accompanied by two male nurses.

At home, Symons became quite disturbed. Convinced that he was being pursued, he refused to sleep and locked himself and Rhoda in his study. He was consequently sent to a Crowborough sanatorium for several weeks, where he was much calmer, then transferred to Brooke House, Clapton, another private mental home, on 2 November, when he was certified as insane. There he became highly agitated, obsessed with vague fears, and filled with delusions of persecution and grandeur. Rhoda confided to the American critic James Gibbons Huneker (MS., 11 January 1909, Dartmouth) that her husband's doctors had diagnosed his insanity as one generally caused by syphilis:

> My poor, beloved Arthur is in a private asylum close by – I am in lodgings to be near him – there is no hope of recovery; and they can do absolutely nothing for him – they don't even attempt treatment – it is General Paralysis (the doctors say there is no trace of the disease which generally accounts for this malady – and Arthur always told me he never had had it – he would not tell a lie . . . .

Despite the bleak prognosis, Symons did, in fact, improve, and though his career resumed, it was radically different. That his significance as a vital force had ended is suggested in Yeats's remark to Allan Wade after news of Symons's breakdown had reached England: 'Symons has become a classic, overnight.'[18]

Notes

1. From Pater's 'Conclusion' to *Studies in the History of the Renaissance* (1873).
2. In the final issue of the *Savoy*, Symons, in accounting for the demise of the periodical, concluded: 'And then, worst of all, we assumed that there were very many people in the world who really cared for art, and really for art's sake'. See 'A Literary Causerie: By Way of Epilogue', *Savoy*, no. 8 (Dec. 1896) 91–2.
3. See *George Moore in Transition: Letters to T. Fisher Unwin and Lena Milman, 1894–1910*, ed. Helmut Gerber (Detroit, Mich., 1968) pp. 151, 155, 159.
4. Extract quoted in *The Oscar Wilde Collection of John B. Stetson, Jr* (New York, 1920), the catalogue of Mitchell Kennerly, dealer and publisher, Item 408, p. 70.
5. *The Letters of Oscar Wilde*, ed. Rupert Hart-Davis (1962) p. 716.
6. See Letter 62, n. 2.
7. W. B. Yeats, Letter dated 25 Apr. [1898] in *The Letters of W. B. Yeats*, ed. Allan Wade (1954) p. 298.
8. Symons's 'Stéphane Mallarmé', *FR*, 64, n.s. (Nov. 1898) 677–85; rptd in *SML*.
9. See W. B. Yeats, 'The Symbolism of Poetry', *Dome*, 6 (1900) 249–57; rptd in *Ideas of Good and Evil* (1903).
10. See Letter 73.
11. Symons to John Quinn, 9 January 1920 (MS., Quinn).
12. Stanislaus Joyce, *My Brother's Keeper* (New York, 1958) p. 197.
13. For an account of Symons's friendship with Joyce, see Karl Beckson and John M. Munro, 'Letters from Arthur Symons to James Joyce, 1904–1932', *James Joyce Quarterly*, 4 (1967) 91–101.
14. In a letter to Professor Peter Irvine, Edward Hutton wrote on 26 Aug. 1961: 'I do not think Arthur had any closer friend than myself between 1902 and 1908' (quoted in Professor Irvine's 'Arthur Symons: A Biographical Study', unpublished dissertation, Columbia University [1965] p. 141).
15. American author (1852–1929), who was Professor of Dramatic Literature at Columbia University, 1900–24.
16. Arthur Symons, 'Music in Venice', *SR*, 106 (17 Oct. 1908) 480–1. Of Symons' condition, Max Beerbohm wrote to Florence Kahn, American actress and his future wife: 'I only heard yesterday about poor Symons – and was much distressed at reading his article

in the *Saturday* this morning. It is a mystery to me how the article came to be published. Its appearance is cruel to Symons, and very bad for the *Saturday* itself' (from typescript, Beerbohm Collection, Merton College Library, Oxford).

17. Rhoda dates her husband's mental collapse in a letter to Katherine Willard Baldwin (MS., 29 Dec. 1908, Baldwin): 'it happened without the faintest warning on Sept. 28th in Italy'.

18. Allan Wade, 'Arthur Symons', *Times Literary Supplement*, 10 Mar. 1945, p. 115.

59 To Edmund Gosse
(MS., Leeds)

15 January 1898   Fountain Court

My dear Gosse

It was so good of you to give me a part to play in the little comedy of the *Academy*.[1] I saw the paper itself for only two minutes, last night, in the hands of Binyon,[2] the winner's cousin: he tells me that Phillips is really in need of the money, as he is poor with a wife and family. Well, I am happy in having neither a wife nor even a family; though there are many ways in which a "single gentleman" may agreeably spend £100. Of S[tephen] P[hillips] you may have seen my review in the *Saturday*.[3] As for my book I rather agree with the point made by the *Academy*:[4] it is indeed, as Mallarmé said of his *Divagations* [1897]: "un livre comme je ne les aime pas, ceux épars et privés d'architecture." I could hardly have done otherwise, but that is a fault I am particularly anxious not to repeat.

I see you are again praising Loti in what seems to me so inconceivably generous a way.[5] How you will hate the article I shall some day write on that subject![6]

Yours ever
Arthur Symons

Notes

1. Gosse had recommended Symons's *Studies in Two Literatures* for a prize of 100 guineas as the best book of 1897. The prize went to *Poems* by Stephen Phillips (1868–1915). See 'The *Academy*'s Awards to Authors', *Academy*, 53 (8 Jan. 1898) 34.
2. Laurence Binyon (1869–1943), poet, playwright, translator, who, from 1913 to 1932, was an assistant, then Keeper in the Department of Oriental Prints and Drawings in the British Museum. His major work is his translation of Dante's *Divine Comedy*, published between 1933 and 1943.
3. See Symons's unsigned review, 'Mr. Stephen Phillips' Poems', *SR*, 85 (1 Jan. 1898) 21–2.
4. In announcing the awards for 1897, the *Academy* observed that Symons's *Studies in Two Literatures* was a 'thoughtful, graceful work, but it is detached, a series of flutters rather than a steady flight'. See 'Our Awards for 1897', *Academy*, 53 (15 Jan. 1898) 47.
5. Edmund Gosse's 'Current French Literature', *Cosmopolis*, 6 (1897) 638–42.
6. Symons apparently never wrote on Loti.

60 To Edmund Gosse
(MS., BL)

[31 January 1898] Fountain Court

My dear Gosse

I have just read your letter in the *Chronicle* with the most extreme pleasure, not only because of your very kind mention of myself, but because it seems to me a most important protest against that sweeping blindness of the present-day critic to the verse-writers whom he is only able to see anything in because they sing the words of the moment to the moment's tune.[1] One's only confidence is that things always find their level sooner or later. By this time Le Gallienne has found his; yet not so long ago, Le Gallienne asked *The Times* £100 for his elegy on Stevenson, and his request was considered for an evening.[2] Soon Newbolt's drum-taps will die away like the Salvation Army brass band as it turns the corner;[3] but those of us who have ears will still hear Bridges' flute, coming from higher up the Thames than the place where there are barges.[4] But how many are there who have ears to hear?

Yours ever
Arthur Symons

Notes

1. On 29 Jan. the *Daily Chronicle* had printed an account of a lecture by William Archer on 'Some Living Poets', presented before the Society of Women Journalists on 28 Jan. Archer, citing Swinburne and Meredith as the two great living poets of the day, discussed such poets as Yeats, Kipling, and Newbolt, among others. Gosse, in a letter to the editor which appeared on 31 Jan., objected to Archer's failure to mention, among 'the poetic forces of our time', such men as Lionel Johnson, Robert Bridges, and Arthur Symons. Replying to Gosse's letter on 1 Feb., Archer defended himself by stating that his lecture was 'only an hour's desultory gossip on "Some Living Poets"'.
2. Le Gallienne's 'Robert Louis Stevenson: An Elegy', appeared in the *Daily Chronicle* on 25 Dec. 1894; rptd *Robert Louis Stevenson: An Elegy and Other Poems, Mainly Personal* (1895). Stevenson had died on 3 Dec. 1894. Richard Le Gallienne (1866–1947), poet, novelist, essayist, and critic, was a member of the Rhymers' Club and author of memoirs, *The Romantic '90s* (1926), which contains a few passing references to Symons. See Richard Whittington-Egan and Geoffrey Smerdon, *The Quest for the Golden Boy: The Life and Letters of Richard Le Gallienne* (1960).
3. Henry Newbolt (1862–1938), poet, novelist and barrister, is best known for his patriotic verse, as in his immensely popular *Admirals All* (1898), dedicated to Andrew Lang, and *The Island Race* (1899), dedicated to Robert Bridges. In 1915 he was knighted and, having been an official naval historian during the First World War, he published *A Naval History of the War, 1914–18* (1920).
4. Robert Bridges (1844–1930), poet and dramatist, best known for his *Testament of Beauty* (1929). Symons here alludes to Bridges's home at Yattendon, Newbury, in the Thames Valley, far from the commercial traffic of London. Later, Symons wrote that in *Shorter Poems* (1890) Bridges appeared 'to be alone in our time as a writer of purely lyric poetry, poetry which aims at being an "embodied joy," a calm rapture'. See 'Robert Bridges' in *SPV*.

61 To Émile Verhaeren[1]
(MS., Bibliotheque Royale)

[early 1898] Fountain Court

Cher Monsieur Verhaeren

Merci bien de votre lettre. Je travaille à ma traduction[2] avec beaucoup d'enthousiasme. Mon principe est ceci: de traduire la prose en prose et le vers en vers, mais en vers sans rimes, quelques morceaux exceptés, où les strophes, à peu près régulières, demandent la rime: c'est à dire toutes les paroles du Voyant, et la ronde, p. 141. Tout le reste je traduis rythme pour rythme, et presque mot par mot, avec au moins, je crois, le résultat de vous faire parler en d'assez beaux vers anglais! Dites-moi si vous approuvez de cette méthode. Il me semble que cela vous donne un peu l'air "élisabéthain," et surtout par la suppression de la rime, qu'on ne trouve dans le drame de ce temps-là que très rarement, et presque seulement dans certain pièces écrites avant Shakespeare, ou dans les pastorales.

Je tâche en ce moment de procurer vos livres entre *Les Flambeaux noirs* [1890] et *Les Villes tenaculaires* [1895]. J'ai prié Osman Edwards[3] de me les prêter, mais je ne sais si il est à Londres en ce moment. Je l'espère toujours bien à vous.

Arthur Symons

Notes

1. Belgian Symbolist poet, playwright, and critic (1855–1916), whom Symons, in a letter to Mrs Edmund Gosse, called 'quite the finest living writer of French verse' (MS., n.d., Cambridge University).
2. Symons was translating Verhaeren's play *Les Aubes*, published as *The Dawn* (London, 1898; Boston, Mass., 1915). As a dramatist, Verhaeren had achieved – said Symons – 'a melodrama of the spirit, in which there is poetry, but also rhetoric'. See 'Émile Verhaeren' in *DP*.
3. Translator and author (1864–1936), best known as translator and editor of *The Plays of Émile Verhaeren* (1916), which contains Symons's translation of *Les Aubes*. Edwards also contributed to the *Savoy*: a translation of Verhaeren's poem 'Pieusement' in no. 4 (Aug. 1896); and an essay, 'Émile Verhaeren' in no. 7 (Nov. 1896).

62   To W. B. Yeats
   (MS., Yeats)

                                                     Gran Hotel de Rome
11 November 1898   Valencia

My dear Yeats
   Please send cheque to me, c/o British Vice-Consul, 35 Calle San
Fernando, Alicante, Spain. I may leave here any day for Alicante, and
that will be the safest address. Today I have recovered a postcard, and
two books, but not your letter, or the proofs from Oldmeadow.[1] I hope
you will like the Beardsley:[2] of course I haven't seen it.
   Old May[?][3] is a wonderful old person. It is very strange.
   Here, in how different a world, I am often finding myself back in the
Middle Ages. Did I tell you of the "Tribunal of the Waters," when the
peasants meet outside the Cathedral door to decide their differences in
regard to the watering of the lands: six of them, chosen by themselves,
and with their own president, sit on a divan in the open street, inside a
temporary railing, and decide all cases: the pleading and the judgment
take 5 or 10 minutes, and the judgment holds good as law. This has
taken place every Thursday at 11.30 since the time of the Moors, that
is, for about five centuries. Then the other day I attended a Latin
disputation in the Cathedral. It seemed as if nothing had been changed
since the days of Abelard.[4]
   I have just translated a lovely song from Calderón's *Life is a Dream*
[1635],[5] and two or three poignant little pieces from a modern man
Gustavo Becquer,[6] who died in 1870, at the age of 34, and whose work
I am reading with great interest. His verses are the best things that have
ever been done in the Heine style, and his prose stories are often of a
wonderfully poetical fantasy – some of them very like your *Secret Rose*
[1897], more macabre, less philosophical, just as romantic. I think I shall
write something about him.
   Do write about the incomparable Althea,[7] and, among other things,
save the *Dome*. The last number, but for the pictures, is frightful. But
one mustn't say so, for the good Oldmeadow who gives us guineas is
the worst sinner of the lot.
   Don't miss my Mallarmé, and especially the two poems in it.[8]
                                                     Yours ever
                                                     Arthur Symons

   Has the Wind died away, then, among the Reeds?[9]
   I have been to a bull-fight, and written a *horrible* description of it,
theorising [on] the universal instinct of cruelty, and confessing my own
share [in] it. I shall send it, I think, to the *S.R.*[10]

Notes

1. Ernest James Oldmeadow (1867–1949), novelist, editor, and music critic, was a director of the Unicorn Press and editor of the *Dome*, 1897–1900, a journal of the several arts, to which Symons and Yeats contributed.
2. *Aubrey Beardsley* (1898), a volume of prints, to which Symons contributed an introduction, a reprint (with four additional paragraphs at the opening) of a previously published essay: 'Aubrey Beardsley', *FR*, 63, n.s. (May 1898) 752–61. In a letter to Lady Gregory on 25 Apr. 1898, Yeats referred to the latter as a 'masterpiece' (*The Letters of W. B. Yeats*, ed. Allan Wade [1954] p. 298).
3. Unidentified.
4. Peter Abelard (1079–1142), French philosopher, reputed to be the founder of the University of Paris. For further details on the 'Tribune of the Waters' and the Latin disputation in Valencia, see *CSI*, pp. 108–10.
5. The translation from the Spanish dramatist Pedro Calderón de la Barca (1600–81) appeared in the *Dome*, 3, n.s. (June 1899) 160–1. Yeats praised it, along with Symons's translations of Verlaine, Mallarmé, and St John of the Cross, as 'the most accomplished metrical translations of our time' (the *Autobiography of W. B. Yeats* [New York, 1965] p. 214).
6. Spanish Romantic poet (1836–70). Symons's translations of Becquer's *Rimas*, apparently never published, are in a sixty-page typescript in the Symons Papers, Princeton.
7. Althea Gyles (1868–1949), Irish artist and poet. In November 1899, Yeats wrote to Lady Gregory: 'A very unpleasant thing has happened but it is so notorious that there is no use hiding it. Althea Gyles, after despising Symons and Moore for years because of their morals, has ostentatiously taken up with Smithers, a person of so immoral a life that people like Symons and Moore despise him. . . . She seems to me perfectly mad, but is doing beautiful work' (*Letters*, ed. Wade, p. 330). Gyles had designed the covers of Yeats's *The Secret Rose* (1897) and *The Wind among the Reeds* (1899). See Ian Fletcher, 'Poet and Designer: W. B. Yeats and Althea Gyles', *Yeats Studies*, no. 1 (1971) 42–79. In 1904, Symons attempted to find a publisher for Gyles's verse, in which he found 'great merit' (see Letter 89).

    Leonard Smithers (1861–1907), formerly a solicitor in Sheffield, was a publisher and bookseller who established a reputation for dealing in erotica (his partner until 1895, H. S. Nichols, apparently dealt in hard-core pornography). Smithers, who had a cultivated taste for the unusual and daring, published such authors as Dowson, Wilde, Beardsley, and Symons.
8. See Symons's 'Stéphane Mallarmé', *FR*, 64 n.s. (Nov. 1898) 677–86; rptd in *SML*. The two poems mentioned are Symons's translations from Mallarmé's *Poésies*: 'Sea-Wind' and 'Sigh'. See Symons's translations of *Poésies*, selected and edited with notes and a bibliography by Bruce Morris (Edinburgh, 1986).
9. The appearance of Yeats's *The Wind among the Reeds* was delayed by the failure of American printers to send the printed sheets. See Yeats's explanation in his letter to Lady Gregory: *Letters*, ed. Wade, p. 313.
10. See Symons's 'A Bull Fight in Valencia', *SR*, 86 (26 Nov. 1898) 695–6; rptd in *CSI*.

63   To W. B. Yeats
(MS., Yeats)

Grand Hotel de Rome
29 November 1898   Seville

My dear Yeats

The above will be my address, I expect, for some time to come. (Best to put: *Hotel de Roma, Sevilla.*) I got here the day before yesterday, and have a charming room with a balcony, on the second floor, practically the third, looking out on a lively little square planted with palms and orange-trees, with a theatre at the other end. I think I shall work well here. At present I am copying, and touching up, the Villiers for the *Fortnightly.*[1] So far I wrote before dinner: I continue in a café, in a street called "O'Donnell"!²   Will you hand on the enclosed scrap to Martyn³ when you are writing: it may interest him, as it is an advt. of early ecclesiastical music.

I am very much interested in the Moorish music–songs – which one hears in Seville. It has no recognisable tune, the notes are held-on for a long time, and the effect is singularly pathetic – a kind of wail, always ending abruptly. The songs are often obscene, generally of only a few lines, but there is always this queer kind of religious, almost Gregorian, quality, and this strange anguish of the voice. They are accompanied by a monotonous buzzing of the guitar, often by the clapping of hands. The dancers are also accompanied in the same way, half a dozen people sitting in a row and clapping hands in a chorus. I saw an extraordinary pantomimic dance by a man the other night – with an obviously, but not openly, obscene intention; done with great seriousness. I have not yet been across the river to the gipsy dances: I don't know my way about here yet, and it is not quite safe for a stranger to go in to some of these places. But I shall gradually see them all, and take good note of them. They are quite different from anything one can see anywhere else in Europe, being handed down directly from the Moors.

I hear with some concern that the *Saturday* is changing hands.⁴ I wonder if the report is true. They already owe me quite £30. Goodness only knows if I shall ever get it.

You don't tell me how your novel is getting on.⁵ I am anxious to know.

Yours ever
Arthur Symons

Notes

1. Symons's 'Villiers de l'Isle Adam', *FR*, 66, n.s. (Aug. 1899) 553–4; rptd with additions in *SML*.

2. Calling Yeats's attention to an O'Donnell Street in Seville reveals Symons's delight in discovering such an unexpected street name and a reminder to Yeats of his recent conflict with Frank Hugh O'Donnell (1848–1916), politician and Vice-President of the Home Rule Confederation, who had attacked Michael Davitt, founder of the Land League. In his *Memoirs*, ed. Denis Donoghue (1972) Yeats refers to him as the 'Mad Rogue' (p. 115).
3. Edward Martyn (1859–1923), Irish playwright and a founder of the Irish Literary Theatre, was a cousin of George Moore. Symons and Yeats stayed at Martyn's home in Galway, Tillyra Castle, in the summer of 1896.
4. Harold Hodge (1862–1937), journalist and author, became the new editor of the *Saturday Review*, 1898–1913. Frank Harris, who had bought the newspaper in 1894, sold it to Albert Yorke, 6th Earl of Harwicke (1867–1904), lawyer and later Under-Secretary of State for India, 1903–4.
5. Yeats was at work on his autobiographical novel, *The Speckled Bird*, at which he worked from 1896 to 1902, when he abandoned it. See Introduction to *The Speckled Bird*, ed. William H. O'Donnell (Toronto, 1976), which contains Yeats's four versions.

64   To W. B. Yeats
   (MS., Yeats)

9 January 1899

Hotel Hernan Cortes
Caleta, Malaga

My dear Yeats

I was very glad to hear from you yesterday. You will already find a letter, explaining how impossible it would be for me to write on the Spanish drama, and suggesting Fitzmaurice-Kelly.[1] I shall not be back till the beginning of May: I hope you will be in London as soon as the plays are over.[2] By the way, an English dramatic critic has turned up here, J. F. Nisbet,[3] of the *Times* and *Referee*, and I am going to try and pump light into him on the subject of the Irish Literary Theatre. He is ill, so will probably be meek and receptive.

I may be going on to Granada almost anytime. I have finished my long article on Seville, and am offering it to the *Fortnightly*.[4]

I am very glad your *Poems* are going to be at last decently covered.[5] I thought your poem in the *Dome*[6] by no means one of your best things – a little vague, and, for you, a little ordinary. Nor did the prose seem to me up to your level.[7] I hope I shall get the *Wind among the Reeds* from somewhere.[8] I failed to get Martyn's plays,[9] for Max had already had a cheap sneer at them by the time my letter reached the office.[10] I am sorry.

I should like to see you and talk over many things. Do be in London in the latter half of May. I have done the whole of my *Symbolist Movement* except the Introduction, which is difficult, and very important. I don't intend to do that till I get back, and should like to talk it over with you.

I want also to dedicate the book to you in my usual form of a prefatory letter.[11]

Yours ever
Arthur Symons

Notes

1. James Fitzmaurice-Kelly (1858–1923), author of *A History of Spanish Literature* (1898), who contributed an article on Spanish literature to the *Encyclopaedia Britannica*, 10th edn (1902) vol. 3, pp. 762–6.
2. After many difficulties, the Irish Literary Theatre presented its first plays, Yeats's *The Countess Cathleen* and Martyn's *The Heather Field*, in the Antient Concert Rooms, Dublin, in May. At the time of Symons's letter, Yeats was busily engaged in the organisational problems of the venture. See Lady Gregory's *Our Irish Theatre* (1913) pp. 6–25.
3. Drama critic (1851–99), whose most notable book was *The Insanity of Genius* (1891).
4. Arthur Symons, 'Painters of Seville', *FR*, 69 (Jan. 1901) 48–60; rptd in *CSI*. 'Seville' appeared in *Harper's Monthly Magazine*, 102 (Mar. 1901) 497–504; rptd in *Cities* and *CSI*. Which article Symons is referring to is unclear.
5. For his 1899 edition of *Poems*, which had first appeared in 1895, Yeats told Lady Gregory: 'I am abolishing the old cover which tries me by its facile meaninglessness and trying to get one of Althea Gyles's put in its place' (*The Letters of W. B. Yeats*, ed. Allan Wade [1954] p. 313). Gyles's remained through many printings to 1927.
6. W. B. Yeats, 'Aedh Pleads with the Elemental Powers', *Dome*, 1 (Dec. 1898), 238; rptd as 'The Poet Pleads with the Elemental Powers', *The Wind among the Reeds* (1899).
7. Yeats on Althea Gyles: 'A Symbolic Artist and the Coming of Symbolic Art', *Dome*, 1 (Dec. 1898) 233–7; rptd in *Uncollected Prose by W. B. Yeats*, eds John P. Frayne and Colton Johnson, vol. II (1975).
8. Symons's review of *The Wind among the Reeds* and *Poems* appeared as 'Mr. Yeats as a Lyric Poet', *SR*, 87 (6 May 1899) 553–4; rptd as Part I of 'Mr. W. B. Yeats' in *SPV*.
9. Edward Martyn, *The Heather Field* (1899) and *Maeve* (1899), dedicated to Yeats, Moore, and Symons.
10. Max Beerbohm had become the drama critic of the *Saturday Review* in May 1898, replacing Shaw. For his reviews of Martyn's *The Heather Field* (about which he changed his mind after seeing the Dublin production) and Yeats's *The Countess Cathleen*, see 'Pat and Sandy', *SR*, 67 (1899) 106–8; and 'In Dublin', ibid., p. 587; both rptd in *More Theatres, 1898–1903* (1969).
11. Symons sent Yeats a draft of his dedication to *The Symbolist Movement in Literature*. When Yeats suggested revisions, Symons later wrote: 'I corrected my dedication as you suggested, and indeed a little more. I hope you will like the whole book' (MS., n. d., Yeats).

65 To W. B. Yeats
   (MS., Yeats)

[mid June 1899]   Fountain Court

My dear Yeats

   Will you thank Lady Gregory for me most heartily for her kind invitation.[1] I wish I could think there were much chance of my being able to accept it. But I am afraid it is hardly possible. I should immensely like to be with you, especially as you would be invaluable to me in the work I am doing now – finishing the *Symbolist* book, of which proofs have begun to come to-day. And it would altogether be most enjoyable. But at the same time I am tied to London, except for a few days now and then, at all events for the present: I have to be near my books, and, besides the Symbolist one, a lot of things sketched out in Spain can only be done here. Then I have already promised to go down to Wales for a short while with Rhys. August you say would not do; and indeed a part of that month I am already booked for Bayreuth. So I fear there will be no chance.

I have of course heard all about everything. I met your 2nd Demon one night by chance, and heard his version of things.[2] Your little pamphlet with Unwin just reached me.[3] I will not write you a long letter now, for, after dining out almost every night since I got back, or since you left, rather, and going to concerts and the opera, and going through an extraordinarily charming experience on my own account, of which you shall hear another time, I have just replunged into work. I have rewritten the Laforgue essay, and am in all haste to start on the Rimbaud; and I am even contemplating a new essay on Huysmans – besides the Introduction, and some enlarging of the Villiers. And the book should appear in September![4]

I am more glad to hear you are going on with the *Shadowy Waters*[5] than of anything else you could tell me.

Yours ever,
Arthur Symons

Davray[6] stayed with me a couple of days lately. Send him the new edition of *Poems*. I think it is worth while. Heredia has just been made editor of *Le Journal*, and has asked Davray to help him. So he at once reaches a much wider public.

I think you will still get that £2 from the *Saturday* if you write to J. F. Runciman,[7] 1 Nassau House, Shaftesbury Avenue, W., and tell him that you had 2 poems in the *S.R.*, that you received £3 for one (for which they have your receipt) and that the £2 is owed you for the other. He thought there was only one.[8]

Notes

1. The invitation was probably to spend the summer at Coole Park, Lady Gregory's estate in Galway. Lady Isabella Augusta Gregory (1859–1932), Irish author, a friend and patron of Yeats, was a founder of the Abbey Theatre. Symons and Yeats had met her during their holiday in 1896 at Tillyra Castle, Edward Martyn's home (Yeats had previously been introduced to her at a literary function). John Butler Yeats's report that Symons always disliked Lady Gregory, whom he allegedly called 'Strega' (Italian

for 'witch') after 'her terrible eye' first fell upon Yeats (the result being a loss to lyrical poetry), seems to have little basis in fact, though after Symons's breakdown in 1908 his attitude towards her changed noticeably. See *J. B. Yeats: Letters to his Son W. B. Yeats and Others, 1869–1922*, ed. Joseph Hone (New York, 1946) p. 151; Beckson, p. 278.

2. Trevor Lowe, an English actor, had played the role of the Second Demon Merchant in Yeats's *The Countess Cathleen*, produced at the Antient Concert Rooms in Dublin on the evening of 8 May 1899. Fearing a disturbance by those incited by attacks on the play by the 'Mad Rogue' (Frank Hugh O'Donnell, who declared it 'anti-Catholic'), Yeats brought in the police.

3. *Literary Ideals in Ireland* (1899), containing essays by Yeats, A.E. (pseudonym of the Irish mystic and poet George Russell [1867–1935]), and lesser known figures.

4. *The Symbolist Movement in Literature* and *Images of Good and Evil* were delayed because Heinemann had been trying to arrange for simultaneous publication in the United States. The Boer War was probably an additoinal factor that delayed release of both books: the former appeared, finally, on 5 March 1900; the latter in May.

5. Yeats had begun work on this play in 1894. For his evaluation of its progress, see *The Letters of W. B. Yeats*, ed. Allan Wade (1954) pp. 320–1. The play was published in 1900; drafts of the work appear in *Druid Craft: The Writing of 'The Shadowy Waters'*, ed. Michael J. Sidnell, George P. Mayhew, and David R. Clark (Amherst, Mass., 1971).

6. Henry-D. Davray (1873–1944), French translator and journalist, who was the principal reviewer for *Mercure de France* of books in English.

7. Music critic (1866–1916), who was Frank Harris's assistant editor on the *Saturday Review*.

8. Yeats's poems were 'The Valley of Lovers', *SR*, 83 (1897) 36, rptd as 'Aedh tells of a Valley Full of Lovers', in *The Wind among the Reeds* (1899); and 'Song', *SR*, 84 (1897) 82, rptd as 'The Poet pleads with his Friend for old Friends', ibid.

66   To Rhoda Bowser
(MS., Columbia)

Thursday
[29 June 1899]   Fountain Court

My dear Rhoda

I don't know whether to address you at Newbiggen or Newcastle. Does it matter which?

I have now corrected all the proofs of my poems, and most of the proofs of the prose,[1] but I have still that infernal Introduction to do![2] I can't get away from people and things. Last night the Masque at the Guildhall – a lovely thing.[3] After all I forgot even to notice the drummer-boy's costume. May Morris[4] looked splendid in Byzantine costume; Hélène Dometsch[5] delicious as a boy. Then I have gone wild over a new Spanish dancer – La belle Guerrero.[6] She is quite a splendid creature: I go to see her every night I am free. Carefully as she is looked after (by M. Chocolat Menier!)[7] I have had the chance of talking a little Spanish with her: she is, as they all are in Spain, very nice and simple. I wish you were here to go and see her dance. Then I have been writing the songs for the Indian drama *Sâkuntalâ*[8] for Dolmetsch to set to music. It is to be given in the Botanic Garden on Monday.[9] Then all kinds of people are asking me to do all sorts of things – from criticising MS. volumes of verse, dedicated to their husbands, to going down into the country from Saturday to Monday. How on earth am I to do this Introduction, which requires complete absorption? I must do it here, on account of having all my books at hand. Next week I must really try to turn over some kind of new leaf – such as "sporting my oak,"[10] perhaps, and not being at home to anybody. The worst of it is, that, as it is, I come back unsatisfied every night. I envy you if you can find "mad gaiety" at command. I can't. I wish I could. But I am too horribly critical.

In a week or two I expect to join Ernest Rhys in Wales for a week or fortnight, to go round the South coast, visiting Milford Haven, which I haven't seen since I was born there. Then I hope to join the Comtesse de La Tour[11] at Bayreuth about the middle of August. Whether I shall go on after that to Bohemia is doubtful, though the Lützows have invited me again.[12] I want to come back to London again for the autumn, and then, if I can, go to Rome and after that to Sicily. There is even some faint chance of Greece in the spring – but very faint, so far. I am not making much money just now, and these things require money.

Tell me what you are doing, and going to do. I ought to say good-night: it is very late, but I am in no mood for sleep, so I shall play Wagner instead of going to bed.

Duerme bien, querida.

AS

No, I shall not play Wagner, I shall read Pater.

Notes

1. 'Poems': *Images of Good and Evil*; 'prose': *The Symbolist Movement in Literature*.
2. When he completed it, Symons wrote to Yeats (MS., n. d., Yeats): 'I have made the Introduction rather short, but I think it is sustained at a rather high note though, which can't be done if one develops details.'
3. The masque, titled *Beauty's Awakening: A Masque of Winter and of Spring* (published in 1899) and presented before the Lord Mayor, Sheriffs, Aldermen, and Common Council at the Guildhall, was 'designed and contrived by the members of the Art Workers Guild'. Scenes, properties, costumes, and dances were written and designed by a committee (including Selwyn Image), the chairman of which was Walter Crane (1845–1915), illustrator and author; the music for the masque was composed by Arnold Dolmetsch (1858–1940), who devoted his life to the revival of medieval and Renaissance music and its instruments. Symons, who first became interested in Dolmetsch in the mid 1890s, attended his concerts at his home near Bedford Square. See Symons's 'A Reflection at a Dolmetsch Concert' in *PAM* and Margaret Campbell, *Dolmetsch: The Man and His Work* (1975) pp. 120, 122, 128.
4. Author (1862–1938), the daughter of William Morris (1834–96), about whom she wrote *William Morris, Artist, Writer, Socialist* (1936).
5. Musician (1880–1924), the daughter of Arnold Dolmetsch by his first wife and an accomplished performer on the viola da gamba.

6. Rosario Guerrero, Spanish ballerina at the Alhambra Theatre.
7. A facetious allusion, apparently, to her black attendant, after Jean-Antoine Menier, who devised a process for the manufacture of chocolate.
8. A Sanskrit drama by Kālidāsa (fl. 5 AD). The manuscript of one song is in the Dolmetsch Library, Haslemere, Surrey.
9. Symons wrote to Rhoda (MS. postmarked 27 May 1899, Columbia): 'I am to play an Indian drum, also a bell, am to wear a costume of white and gold, and to make-up dark!! It will be "positively my first appearance on any stage!"' *Sákuntalā*, performed on 3 July in the Conservatory of the Botanical Gardens in Regents Park, was produced by William Poel (1852–1934), scholar, actor, and theatre manager, the founder of the Elizabethan Stage Society. For an account of the performance, see Campbell, *Dolmetsch*, p. 133.
10. A university colloquialism, associated with Oxford, as defined by the *Oxford English Dictionary*: 'to shut the outer door of one's rooms as a sign that one is engaged'.
11. La Comtesse Victor Sallier de la Tour (1852–1912), to whose fourteenth-century chateau near Puy de Dôme in southern France she invited Symons and other writers. Symons, who stayed at the Chateau in 1898, found the Comtesse 'the best of companions' (MS., 16 Sep. 1898, Yeats).
12. During part of August and September, Symons was the guest of Count Franz von Lützow (1849–1916), Czech author and historian, at Zambach in Bohemia. Symons wrote to Rhoda (MS., 11 Sep. 1899, Columbia): 'the Lützows couldn't be nicer, nor their place, a 17th century monastery. . . . I enjoy an easy reputation in this country as a great English poet, and have to write my name in the Visitors' Book of Countesses whose names I can't pronounce.'

67   To Rhoda Bowser
(MS., Columbia)

Monday night
[12 February 1900]   Fountain Court

I *am* content, Rhoda, *now*. You give me new strength, patience, the desire and the power of work.[1] Be assured, the Byron shall be one of the best things I have ever done.[2] I have been thinking about him hard, all to-day, and every time I have thought of you it has been a spur to me, not a distraction – as it is when I am uncertain and troubled. You don't know what you do for me when you write to me like that; or, yes, I think by now you *do* know. I have been living and working for so many years, without a single day passing (no matter where I was) in which I have not felt, some time in the day, a sense of the utter futility of all I was doing – I cannot even explain to you what I mean, but you will understand some of it at least – that now, well, – need I go on?

On Saturday, when you were sledging (I have been rejoicing in this weather for you) I was either sitting in the smoke-room of the Savoy, thinking of you while I talked literature with a man who professes to care a good deal for my work, or else, later on, re-writing the "tiger" poem,[3] which I am enlarging and improving, as you will see in time.

So we were not so far apart, you see. And then on Sunday, just before I had to dress for dinner I wrote the enclosed, which I am inclined to think, as a poem, the best thing I have ever written about you. I wonder what you will think? It was suggested by a sudden memory of your face, once, when it had so exactly the look of Rossetti's Beata Beatrix that I was startled. I shall never forget that look.[4] – After dinner there was Bach and Brahms. I now *always* think of you, all the time, without being able to help it, during music.

Have you a particular selection from Browning – the 1st series published by Smith and Elder?[5] If not, please tell me, and I will send it to you – don't get it yourself. But I want you to read some of those poems, perhaps "Pippa Passes." You may have looked at them hastily, and been put off by a certain lack of music – but if you read them now I am almost sure you will see exactly what is so wonderful in Browning – a quality as human as Ibsen, and more noble, more passionate.

Some day I will lend you Dowson's book,[6] and tell you all about him – but I may have to send my copy to Archer, as I am trying to interest him in the subject. Lane has already agreed to put in his portrait if I can get Archer to agree.[7] Dowson has had a miserable life every way: hereditary craving for drink, an insane mother who committed suicide, debauchery of the vulgarest kind, united with an almost crazily ideal affection for a very young girl, the daughter of a Polish inn-keeper in Soho – his whole story is as strange and sordid a romance as I know.[8]

It is your "big dance" tomorrow, isn't it? I hope you will thoroughly enjoy it.

Anna[9] came in to-day (to mend my clothes – which are getting horribly shabby!) and told me she had seen your "Turkish delight" breaking into his own shop, with a little crowd at his heels! He had forgotten his latchkey apparently, and so had to attack his own defences.

When I feel miserable, or doubtful, or anything but what I should, I shall read your letter over again. May I? as if, always, you were just saying it?

Yours
Arthur

Notes

1. Symons's recurrent doubts concerning his career as a writer and Rhoda's encouragement are a major theme in their correspondence.
2. See Symons's 'Lord Byron', *QR*, 192 (July 1900) 25–44; rptd in *RMEP*.
3. This seems not to have been published.
4. See Symons's 'Beata Beatrix' in *The Loom of Dreams* (1901). Rossetti's painting of the same name was completed in 1863.
5. *A Selection from the Works of Robert Browning*, ed. by the Author (1872: second series, 1880).
6. Ernest Dowson, *Verses* (1896).

7. Symons was attempting to persuade William Archer to include Dowson in his *Poets of the Younger Generation*, which the publisher John Lane was preparing to issue. (Symons was one of the included poets.)
8. Symons had written of Dowson (without mentioning his name) in 'A Literary Causerie: On a Book of Verses' in the *Savoy*, no. 4 (Aug. 1896) 91–3. With its description of Dowson as one who 'without a certain sordidness in his surroundings was never quite comfortable', this article was chiefly responsible for the 'Dowson Legend'. For Dowson's amused response, see *The Letters of Ernest Dowson*, ed. Desmond Flower and Henry Maas (1967) 371–2. See also Letter 72, n. 1.
9. Anna Symons (1864–1933), Arthur's sister, who, after the death of the Reverend Symons in 1898 and the break-up of the family home in Willesden, joined the Sisters of the Poor of the West London Mission. Symons told Katherine Willard (MS., 2 June 1898, Baldwin): 'She has a little money of her own, and with what my father left (for of course I would not take any of it) she will be able to live in a quiet way that will suit her quite well.'

68   To Rhoda Bowser
(MS., Columbia)

Tuesday night
[13 February 1900]   Fountain Court

Now, Rhoda, after a plunge into the ankle-deep sloppiness of the streets has made me feel that it is after all pleasant to be in my little green room by the fire, shall I confess to you my day? First I wrote six of my large MS. pages on a particular aspect of Byron[1] – "awfully good," Rhoda, as you said they were to be! – one of those bits which come out as the best things in my essays. Then I set myself to an experiment which I have been wanting to repeat. I brewed a strong dose of mescal, the drug which Ellis has been experimenting with, and which I tried a long time ago with not very much, though some, result.[2] When you were at Hastings I tried again, and it produced absolutely no effect whatever. Ellis was astonished, and thought the stuff might have got stale; so got over some more, quite fresh, which he left with me. Well, I took it at the proper intervals, eating nothing from a late breakfast until 10 tonight. This time there was some effect, but very little. I lay on the sofa by firelight, played the piano, walked about the room; and certainly I had a charming sensation, but no marvels of colour, which the stuff ought to make one see. I give it up now for good. I suppose Ellis is right when he says that my constitution is really so strong that none of these things can have their full effect on me. I ought not to be sorry that this is so – no, nor *did* I! – ought I? Well, at 10 I got so hungry that I went out in this fearful weather, had a solid meal (which ought to have nearly killed me!) then walked to Charing Cross, and have just come in dripping, but feeling singularly well. So much for artificial paradises.

Tomorrow, Valentine's Day, oddly enough, was my father's birthday. I will send you (as a valentine?) the book I told you I had got against your journey. Remember, it must not be trusted out of your own hands – you understand?

Wednesday night. [14 February 1900]

The Dolmetsches have been here, and – rejoice! – he is going to send his own man to take the great yellow handles off my desk (do you remember how you rightly hated them?) and put in their place oaken knobs, which he will have made for me, and will give me some scraps of old oak to fill up the little holes left by taking out the screws. You can imagine what a difference this will make. Then I have got some nice green velvety stuff for the piano, and am having it made. And I am even indulging in wild dreams of a series of delicious green silken cushions for the sofa. Think of that! Now advise me. How would it be to have several cushions each of a slightly different shade of green, plain green? Or would you prefer all of the same colour? For it is what *you* prefer. Please give your most careful consideration to this question.

And now to answer yours. It is so long since I read the *Master Builder* that I cannot remember all the details. I am afraid he was a little mad (he ought not to have been, but it is part of Ibsen's touch of "provinciality" to think a man of genius always a little mad) and I am sure he [Solness] never cared at all for the office-girl. But I cannot remember about the other point you refer to. Part of the skill of Ibsen lies in the ? which he leaves always in one's mind – as real life does. And now when you say that Ibsen only gives one the unhappy side of life: you are right; and there *is* another. Browning gives it, in one form; Maeterlinck, in another. Pater said to me once that Ibsen was a little bourgeois; and, for all his genius, he is. I think you have felt it, or you would never have made that last question. Ibsen is always so conscious of society. But it is possible to live one's own life, almost as if society never existed, and without too obviously "flying in the face" of society. That is what Browning sees and Ibsen does not see. – By the way, Hilda is a real woman, really called Hilda, whom Ibsen is devoted to. Brandes,[3] his great friend, told me she is only a superficial, intriguing woman, who pretends to care for Ibsen because he is Ibsen. But Brandes is a Philistine, and with a Philistine one never knows. I daresay she is better than that.

I am wondering which is "the nicest letter I ever wrote you." I remember the phrase you quote perfectly well, but I cannot at all remember into which letter I put it; and my letters to you are written so absolutely in the mood of the moment that I cannot possibly imagine which you like and which you don't like. Is not that how you wish me to write to you? I could easily make nice pieces of literature for you, and say only what I thought you would like; but I don't want to. I want, with you, to be able to say, without reflection, whatever comes into my head; and I want to feel that if I am busy you will be content with a few lines, and if I *want* to write you a long letter – like this – you will not be bored. May I?

I am hoping for a letter before I send off this; for I want to know what you think of my last poem – in fact of my two last poems, for you have not told me whether you like the one about music. Mind you always tell me what you *don't* like, for I can generally improve things once I see that they need improvement.

Thursday morning. [15 February 1900]

Your letter has come, and if I don't take care this letter of mine will never come to an end, nor you to the end of reading it! I am fully satisfied with your feeling about my poem – and, further, enchanted if it has crushed into small dust the horrible menace of the ear-rings! Quite an unintentional result, too!

Mrs. Pat has sent me tickets for the first night of her revival of *Magda*,[4] and I am asking Count Lützow, who is in town now, to go with me. I dine with Lady Charles[5] on Sunday. Such a quaint letter has just come from Laurence Tadema[6] that I enclose it for you to read. I don't keep her letters, so burn it, please, when you have read it. When I can I will get the two things of Browning I want for you, and, to please you (especially as it will only be a shilling or two!) I will get them "on commission."

Yours
Arthur

Notes

1. See Letter 67, n. 2.
2. Phyllis Grosskurth states that Ellis began experimenting with mescal in early 1897, when he was alone in Fountain Court on Good Friday, and that he introduced Yeats, Symons, and Edward Martyn to the drug: 'Ellis seems to have been the first Englishman to experiment with the drug and certainly the first European to write about it.' See Phyllis Grosskurth, *Havelock Ellis: A Biography* (1980) pp. 165–7.
3. George Brandes (1842–1927), Danish literary critic.
4. *Magda*, adapted by Louis N. Parker (1852–1944) from a play by the German dramatist Hermann Sudermann (1857–1928), opened on 19 Feb. at the Royalty Theatre. A previous production in 1896 had failed. See Mrs Patrick Cambell's *My Life and Some Letters* (1922) pp. 145–9, 189–90: Margot Peters, *Mrs. Pat: The Life of Mrs. Patrick Campbell* (New York, 1984) pp. 128–30, 184.
5. Lady Charles Beresford (d. 1922), hostess and wife of Lord Charles Beresford (1846–1919), author and naval officer, with whose career in the Navy she had little sympathy. On one occasion, Symons wrote to Rhoda (MS., postmarked 8 Aug. 1900, Columbia): 'I was at Lady Charles' on Sunday, and did not enjoy it, though Lady Eden and other pretty women were there. Somehow it all seemed empty and tedious, and I wondered

why I had come. One goes to such places, and talks generalities, and it is merely a way of filling the time, and nothing more. I wandered away by myself thinking it was a very poor way of playing at life – certainly not life at all. "To burn always with this hard gem-like flame, to maintain this ecstasy, is success in life." Do you remember Pater's "Conclusion"? Isn't that, after all, the success in life both you and I want? Shall we get it? Don't you think we might?' Symons here alludes to the famous 'Conclusion' of Pater's *Studies in the History of the Renaissance* (1873).
6. Novelist and poet (d. 1940), daughter of the painter Sir Lawrence Alma-Tadema (1836–1912) and an intimate friend of such figures as Eleonora Duse, Henry Irving, and Maeterlinck. She lived in Wittersham, Kent, where Symons later bought a cottage.

69   To Rhoda Bowser
(MS., Columbia)

Wednesday
[21 February 1900]   Fountain Court

Now let me tell you just what happened last night.[1] I took Lützow to *Magda*, and had intended to go on to sup with Lady Charles and Mrs. Craigie,[2] who had asked me to join them after some other play they were going to. It was very late when *Magda* was over, and the acting manager came up to me and asked me if I would not go on to the stage and see Mrs. Pat. I took Lützow with me and introduced him, and said to her "You were splendid: I never knew you could do anything so good!" She clutched hold of me and said: "Do you really mean that? I thought nothing ever satisfied you." Then she introduced me to her mother, a dear old Italian, 78, and still almost pretty. We had a long talk in Italian. The pretty girl who was selling programmes (you remember?) turns out to be Sylvia, Mrs. Pat's daughter.[3] Presently Mrs. Pat came up again, flung her arm round her mother's neck, and began to ask her how she had acted, etc.; then, turning to me, said, "Well, what about the play?" "The play?" I said wonderingly. "Yes, *Mariana* – the man is an idiot[4] – won't you still do it? – he insists about his name, but I'll do anything you like – have you interviewed in the papers, etc., etc." Of course there was a crowd of people, so she said, "I'll write to you in a few days and ask you to come and have a talk with me about it." I promised, and there it rests, for the moment. Of course I never got to Lady Charles's, and now I find a letter asking me to come in to tea on Sunday, and the Sunday after spend the day down at Ham, and promising to ask Mrs. Pat and Mrs. Craigie down there. Are you not pleased – and surprised – about *Mariana*? I confess it gives me a singular satisfaction, for many reasons. And particularly as I would not allow myself to make a step in her direction. Now advise me, Rhoda. My idea is – *not* to put my name *along with* Graham's but to suggest a pseudonym (what do you say to Arthur Pascoe? – my mother's name – or would you change the christian name as well, and say Mark Pascoe – i.e., my father's christian and my mother's surname? No, I don't think I'll use Mark, as my father hated the stage so much. My mother would not have minded. Do give a casting-vote). Thus it would be: "by James Graham and . . ." But if the man objects even to this, I will quietly translate the play for myself (with occasional references to his version if he has done any thing really well) and let it go under his name. As I told you I don't think it is a great work of art, though a telling play, so this is a trifling matter. The mother, who had seen Elizabeth Robins do it, thought it would exactly suit her daughter.

I wanted to write in the Browning,[5] so your sending it back pleases me very much; but hardly thought I had any right to. I will keep it by me till something occurs to me.

I can't find "Pippa Passes" in a separate form, except in an illustrated edition: which gives me a wild notion of persuading some serious publisher that there would be a great demand for a nice edition of it, simply in order that I might give you a copy![6]

Don't be surprised if some day I write to you at 147[7] from sheer force of habit. I have had to destroy a lot of envelopes because when I have written your name my hand instinctively goes on as it was accustomed.

Archer promises to read Dowson's book, which I sent him, and which he had not read. So I may have been of some use.[8]

I have written several things lately, and am reading hard at Byron's life and letters. – I want particularly to know how you like the [Pater] *Appreciations* and which best. One I think is best of all: will you choose it?

Arthur

Notes

1. That is, late Monday night (the opening night of *Magda*) and early Tuesday morning.
2. Pearl Mary Teresa Craigie (1867–1906), novelist, dramatist, and journalist, who wrote under the pseudonym of 'John Oliver Hobbes' and whose close relationship with George Moore ended after they had collaborated on two plays. Craigie wearied of Moore, who wrote disparagingly of her in his story 'Mildred Lawson' (in *Celibates*, 1895) and in *Evelyn Innes* (1898). See Margaret Maison, *John Oliver Hobbes: Her Life and Work* (1976) pp. 14–15, 36–7.
3. Symons's error: the daughter's name was Stella, who was thirteen.
4. James Graham had been chosen to translate *Mariana*, a play by the Spanish writer José Echegaray (1832–1916), a Nobel Prize winner in 1904. See Margot Peters, *Mrs. Pat: The Life of Mrs. Patrick Campbell* (New York, 1984) pp. 185–6.
5. See Letter 67 and n. 5.
6. Symons's 'wild notion' was realised some years later, when Browning's work was published by Heinemann in 1906 with Symons's introduction.
7. Rhoda had been staying at 147 Adelaide Road, Hampstead.
8. Archer decided not to include Dowson in his work, *Poets of the Younger Generation* (1902), the manuscript of which had been completed in 1899 (publication had been delayed because of the Boer War).

Arthur Symons, *c*. 1884

2 Frederick J. Furnivall, c. 1886

3 (*right*) Arthur Symons, 1891

4 (*below*) Fountain Court, the Temple

5 (*left*) Katherine Willard, 1891

6 (*right*) Frank Willard, 1908

7 (*left*) James Dykes Campbell,
14 May 1892

Some Persons of "the Nineties"
Little imagining, despite their Proper
Pride and Ornamental Aspect,
how much they will interest
Mr. Holbrook Jackson and Mr. Osbert Burdett.

8   'Some Persons of the 90s', a drawing by Max Beerbohm (1925); *front row, left to right:* Symons, Henry Harland, Charles Conder, Will Rothenstein, Max Beerbohm, Aubrey Beardsley; *back row, left to right:* Richard Le Gallienne, Walter Sickert, George Moore, John Davidson, Oscar Wilde, W. B. Yeats, and (*barely visible*) 'Enoch Soames'

9   (*left*) Lydia, *c.* 1893

10   (*below*) Empire Theatre, 1896

1 (*right*) John Lane, *c.* 1900

(*right*) Havelock Ellis and Edith Lees, 1896

13 (*left*) Rhoda Bowser, later Symons, 1897

14 (*right*) Edmund Gosse, 1896

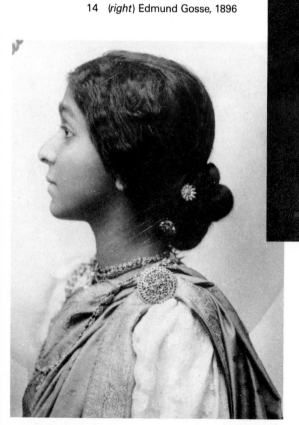

15 (*left*) Sarojini Naidu, 1906

16 (*above*) Island Cottage, Wittersham

17 (*right*) Arthur Symons and Api at Island Cottage, 1907

18 (*top left*) John Quinn (27 August
    1909), a drawing by Augustus John

19 (*top right*) Agnes Tobin (*c.* 1909), a
    drawing by Augustus John

20 (*left*) Iseult Gonne, *c.* 1914

21 Rhoda Symons in the Goetzes' garden, *c.* 1915

22 (*above*) Arthur and Rhoda Symons, *c.* 1920

23 (*below*) Arthur Symons at Island Cottage, *c.* 1920

70   To Rhoda Bowser
(MS., Columbia)

28 February 1900   Fountain Court

Rhoda! how did you know that the one thing I *nearly* asked for was a photograph?[1] This one, well, Anna says "it does not do her justice," but it brings you before me very vividly, and I have not yet accustomed my eyes to look away from it. The Henschel[2] was only 1/6, so I return the 6d. with a scrupulousness equal to your own. Always tell me when you want anything done, no matter what it is. If it is a question of buying, you shall always know exactly what everything costs, and I will take that, exactly.

Rhoda, poor Dowson is dead, and I have to-day been writing a few lines about him for the *Athenaeum*[3] – the very paper which, when he was living, cut out his name when, several times over, I brought it into my articles. It makes me rage; but pazienza! we shall not change the world. I am going to do a long article about him for the *Fortnightly*, largely personal.[4] It is so difficult to know what one may and what one may not say, isn't it? I want to be quite frank, and yet I don't want to say too much. *Isn't* it difficult? But I know one thing: I shall write something which would please him, if he could read it now. He had almost a pathetic admiration for me and for everything I did: I always looked upon it as one of the things that most really honoured me. And it happened that I was the only one among the younger men whose work he cared for.

To-day I have arranged with Pauling (Heinemann's partner)[5] for the publication of my Symbolist book. It is to be sent out on Monday. Now at last, after all this delay, I am to have my chance – so far as the war will let me. I wonder how the book will be received? I have more foes than friends, and nine-tenths of the people who write in the papers are too stupid for it to matter. And yet it is these stupid people who make what is called a reputation!

I had a chance of £800 a year dangled before my eyes to-day, and refused it, unconditionally. Tell me if I did right. Pauling told me of a literary weekly which is looking out for an editor, and said "You are the one man for it, and it means £800 a year." Of course he hasn't the power to give it to me, but he has great influence. But it would mean giving up two-thirds of my time to journalism, and having my mind occupied *all the time* with the care of the paper and the arrangments for it. The consequence would be that I should be unable to give my whole energy and the greater part of my time to writing verse and serious prose. I have been working for 12 or 13 years, often at ill-paid journalism, and it is only within the last three or four years that I have managed to get rid of most of this, and to write hardly anything but what I want to write, and slowly enough to write it really well. You would be astonished if you knew how little money I really make in the course of a year, but I have at last got to be able to make just enough to keep me going, on the proceeds of my big articles – that is, out of *my own work* and not out of pot-boilers. I shall always be a poor man, and there are many reasons why I should like *not* to be a poor man. But I think I have something to say which is worth saying, and I can only say this in my own way and at my own time. Perhaps I delude myself, and I might as well set about making money. But granting that I have that feeling, tell me, don't you think I am right in refusing even to look at a chance such as this editorship?[6] – It is curious that these problems should come up to-day of all days; in fact that so many things should occur to-day.

I will get a Daudet for you tomorrow, and send it with a volume of Ibsen, and the Spanish articles. Oh, I was forgetting about Monday. I went with Lady Charles and the French Ambassador, and we all went round to the dressing-room after;[7] but she [Mrs Campbell] had not had time to read my translation, and I had no private talk with her. The Ambassador has asked us all to lunch next week, and he is going to read out to us a play of Feuillet which he suggests my translating for her.[8]

That portrait of you varies according to the exact angle at which one looks at it. Have you noticed? By the way, would it amuse you to have the flash-light thing that Countess Lützow took of me? I put it in with the books.

And now, Rhoda, good-night. It has turned 2, and I want to do a good morning's work tomorrow.

Arthur

Notes

1. A photograph signed and dated 1897 in the Symons Papers, Princeton.
2. George Henschel (1850–1934), German-born English conductor, composer, and author of books on singing.
3. Dowson died on 23 Feb. 1900. See Symons's 'Mr. Ernest Dowson', *Athenaeum*, 3 Mar. 1900, p. 274.
4. Symons had previously written on Dowson for the *Savoy*: see Letter 67, n. 8. The article for the *Fortnightly Review* was primarily a rewriting of the *Savoy* article. See Letter 72, n. 1.
5. Sidney Pauling joined Heinemann in 1893.
6. Symons declined Pauling's suggestion, but by July, when his marriage to Rhoda was not far off, Symons sought an editorial post on a periodical without success. He wrote to Rhoda (MS., postmarked 19 July 1900, Columbia): 'Rhoda, don't be disappointed because I have failed several times already. So far from being discouraged, I am more hopeful than ever. The very fact I have come so close already to succeeding (and have got *something*, however small, each time), the respectful way in which everyone has received me, as if I am doing them a favour rather than soliciting one – no, it is far from discouraging. I am going to call on an Editor tomorrow, and failing that am going

to get Lady Charles [Beresford] to introduce me to another, whom she knows. This time I have made up my mind, and I have made up my mind to succeed *soon*. At any rate, I am putting my whole soul into the endeavour. Write and say that you don't after all quite disbelieve me.' Lady Charles provided Symons with an introduction to the publisher–editor Alfred Harmsworth: see Letter 80, n. 8.

7. Following the performance of *Magda*: see Letter 68, n. 4. 'French Ambassador': Paul Cambon (1843–1924), Ambassador to Great Britain, 1898–1920.

8. Octave Feuillet (1821–90), French author noted for his sentimental and moralistic novels and plays, an unlikely attraction for Symons, who understandably declined the ambassador's suggestion.

71   To Edmund Gosse
(MS., BL)

[4 March 1900]   Fountain Court

My dear Gosse

This hysterical, misleading, and quite untrue note on Dowson was written by Sherard,[1] in whose cottage he died, and who certainly was very kind to him at the last. Dowson was never really in want of money; he had at least a dozen attached friends (many of whose names you would know well) any one of whom was ready to do anything he could to help him. But with a thousand a year he would have lived and died exactly the same. I am bringing out all this in my *Fortnightly* article, which at the same time tells everything without disguise – if they will print it as I write it. I worked eight hours at it yesterday, and have already done most of the personal parts. I shall annoy my friends and please my enemies (always so gratifying) by pointing out that his note of delicate charm owed nothing to the disorder of his life, as, also, it was uncontaminated by it.

I had come to the conclusion that you thought my Mérimée[2] very bad; and as I had taken extreme pains to make it a close study of the man, I was disappointed.

I hope to send you my new book of essays [*The Symbolist Movement in Literature*] tomorrow. Do tell me quite frankly and quite soon what you think of it.[3] It is at all events the best I can do.

Yours ever
Arthur Symons

Notes

1. Robert Harborough Sherard (1861–1943), biographer, novelist, and journalist, the author of thirty-four books, including four books on Wilde and biographies of Zola, Maupassant, and Daudet, all of whom he knew, as well as books on social ills, such

as *The Child Slaves of Britain* (1905). Dowson died in Sherard's cottage, the final days described by Sherard in his 'Ernest Dowson', *Author*, 10 (1900) 265–8. The note alluded to has apparently been lost.

2. Symons's introduction to Mérimée's *Colomba and Carmen* (1902); rptd in *SPV*.

3. See Letter 73.

72   To Rhoda Bowser
     (MS., Columbia)

Sunday
[4 March 1900?]   Fountain Court

I worked eight hours, Rhoda, yesterday at my article on Dowson, with only an hour's interval for dinner: and I have done 20 pages of MS., which makes nearly seven pages of the *Fortnightly*. I think it is the most I ever wrote at a stretch. And *good*! It is to be in the April number. I have done most of the personal part: now I have the literary criticism to do. It is awfully outspoken, but I think it makes you like the man, and understand him. How I wish you were here that I could show you what I have written![1]

I am so glad you like that little photograph, because *I* like it; it is rather my own idea of myself. Two friends of Balfour[2] have told me I am very like him. It is unfortunate that I don't admire his photograph – but, on the other hand, he seems to me the only English politician who has intellect: so I must strike the balance! – *Dis*like yours! I like it so much that I keep it locked up in my bedroom, and look at it every night and morning. You will send me the other one, when you get it, won't you? and you won't think me too greedy for asking for it? I think the best likeness I ever had is the Comtesse de La Tour's pencil drawing which she gave Anna; and I am thinking of getting it reproduced (reduced to cabinet size) in photogravure, so as to preserve the quality of the drawing.[3]

You ask me why I make so little money, and both the reasons you suggest are true:[4] of course I am only known to a limited number, and only a limited number (though I hope a much larger one) will ever buy my books to any great extent. My books have so far brought me almost nothing. It will be better now with Heinemann, but after all it is magazine articles, translations, etc. that pay. By refusing to write at all unless I am well paid, I have finally forced a certain number of editors to pay me a higher price than they pay even to men who are much better known than I am. In this way I can concentrate myself on a few, serious things, instead of having to write hurriedly about a great many. I am getting paid better and better, and from time to time I get from America £50 for what I should get £20 for here. You know I haven't a penny except what I earn. When my father died he left me half of the little money he had put by, but there wasn't enough for two to live on, so of course I wouldn't take my share. The best of it is that when I get run down to nothing I can always put on a spurt and make whatever sum I want for the moment. I can't help thinking that this new book [*The Symbolist Movement in Literature*] will do me a lot of good in many ways. And yet, do you know, I feel absolutely indifferent: I have not the faintest curiosity to see a review, in fact I have the greatest wish not to see any.

What you ask about personal and impersonal qualities in literature is no easy question to answer, and you confuse the matter by speaking of personal *style*. Everybody who has style has a personal style. But I call Flaubert an impersonal artist because he did his utmost to keep himself out of the picture – to create beings apart from himself. Neither Pater nor Yeats nor Swinburne is impersonal in this sense. I do not quite feel that either Marius the Epicurean or the Countess Cathleen or Mary Stuart absolutely lives a vital, flesh and blood, absolutely detached life, as Madame Bovary does, as the people in Balzac, in Shakespeare do. But there are all sorts of ways of being personal. Swinburne, one must admit, is really more personal in his style than in anything: but at one time no doubt the emotions of the *Poems and Ballads* were personal to him in the sense that they completely absorbed him, even if they were only in his head. Then Yeats is personal precisely because he is a dreamer to whom realities never come quite directly, but through a kind of haze, which he puts beautifully into his work as a painter puts atmosphere into his picture. Pater was personal because the whole of his work is a perfect transcript of his way of looking at life and art, not as a dreamer nor yet with direct emotion, but as an artist, to whom everything came as a part of aesthetics.

So far from being "angry" with you for not taking my view of Pater, I should be angry with you if you did. You say "I can see what you admire in him": but that is all I want. If you liked everything, everything good even, in the same way and to the same degree, you would soon find that I should give up discussing books with you! One should *see* the merit in what is good, but then choose, choose what is one's own. And you always do that.

That you should think of me when you are by the sea, Rhoda, means to me more than you perhaps realize. Shall I tell you why? or need I?

Monday night. [5 March 1900]

I kept over this letter till to-day, and have been out all day long: in the morning I sent off my presentation copies from Heinemann's and discussed things; then caught a train down to Catford, where Dowson died, and spent the afternoon with the man [Robert Sherard] who looked after him at the last, went to the grave, etc. – a dreadful afternoon – the man just such another wreck as Dowson, half drunk and half maudlin; oh, a dreadful afternoon; then back and to a Dolmetsch concert, with a supper after, from which I have just come in at 1 in the morning; and on the door-mat I find a roll of music and a letter from (Dodo, guess!) *Adelaide Road* – 172 – Mary Carmichael's[5] setting of a silly little juvenile song of mine along with a lovely thing of Bridges which it seems to profane by its triviality. To-morrow I must return to my Dowson article again. I am scribbling these lines in my overcoat, for it is cold; and that reminds me of your "cold room." I don't like to think of your writing to me in the cold. If you haven't a fire, do as I do in the very cold weather when I want to do a little writing and don't want the bother of lighting a fire last thing: go to bed, and sit up in a dressing-gown, with a book on one's knees as a writing-desk.

So unreasonable are human beings that before there is possible time for you to reply, I shall forget that I only posted this tonight, and wonder why I don't get an answer to the letter I wrote on Sunday!

Arthur

Notes

1. When he finished his article on Dowson, Symons wrote to Rhoda (MS., n. d., Columbia): 'Will you do something for me, Rhoda? Read the Dowson very carefully and tell me how it strikes you, and if anything seems too strongly said – about drink, etc. Some of my friends want me to tone it down. It seems to me that I have not said a word too much, and think I could not tell the truth in any other way. You will see I have woven in bits of the *Savoy* article – which Dowson read and thoroughly liked.' The article, postponed until May, 'on account of so many war articles', as Symons wrote to Rhoda (MS., postmarked 20 Mar. 1900, Columbia), did not appear until June. See Symons's 'Ernest Dowson', *FR*, 67, n.s. (June 1900) 947–57; rptd in *SPV* and as the introduction to *The Poems of Ernest Dowson* (Portland, Maine, 1902), published by Thomas Mosher.
2. Arthur James Balfour (1848–1939), Chief Secretary of Ireland, 1886–92; first Lord of the Treasury, 1895–1902; Prime Minister, 1902–6. Symons wrote to Gosse on 5 Apr. 1900 (MS., Leeds): '[Balfour] is the only politician of our time, whose appreciation would be anything more to me than an agreeable and unmeaning compliment. It would be a very great pleasure indeed if you would ask me to meet him some day.' Gosse introduced Symons to Balfour in 1902.
3. The drawing of Symons remains unlocated.
4. Rhoda had written to Symons (MS., n. d., Columbia): 'Is it that such work appeals to so very limited a class – or that you are not known enough for your books to sell to any extent – if it's that – patience.'
5. Mary Carmichael (1851–1935), composer and accompanist. In a letter postmarked 20 Mar. 1900 (MS., Columbia), Symons wrote to Rhoda that he had spent a 'dreadful afternoon' at Mary Carmichael's 'and never heard my song after all! Oh, it was frightful – 30 people, all second-rate artistic people (the sort of people I loathe more than any others), affected, provincial, taking themselves and one another as if they were somebodies instead of nobodies.'

73   To Arthur Symons
   (MS., Lohf)

7 March 1900   Board of Trade

My dear Symons

The very lucky chance that I had to go to Leeds yesterday afternoon and return from it this morning has given me the rare opportunity of being able to read your *Symbolist Movement*, carefully, right through, at a single effort. Although at least half the chapters were not new to me, yet I found it a great advantage to read them in their proper order, in juxtaposition with the rest.

You must let me tell you that in my opinion you have written quite a wonderful book. It is not only certainly your best, up to now, but I do not hesitate to call it the finest product of pure criticism which has been seen in England for years. You take a wonderful position, I think, on the score of it. There is so much honesty, so much chained and balanced thought, such a distinguished and elevated, and yet graceful and supple, spirit in it all, it is so consistent, so new, so craftily moulded into one single thesis, and that thesis sustained so evenly and surely, that I do not see the other man living in England who could and would have written an analogous book so well. I ask myself – if, now, you are not the best English critic since Pater, who is? And I find no reply. As you know, I am averse to superlatives, and this means much from me.

As for myself, I am humbled by the sureness of your touch, your excellent sympathy, your firm and serious pursuit of beauty. I feel, with all my life-long passion for literature, how incapable I am of writing such a book. But I am too old, or (what is worse) too coriaceous to learn. I learn much from almost everything you write. I consider the privilege of your friendship one of the things I value highly. I have gained much, and I hope to gain much more, from having been so lucky as to know you well.

I feel that I want to speak plainly to you about this book, because, partly it comes at a time when such books must expect the maximum of negligence, and partly because the temper of our fellow-citizens grows more and more indifferent and even hostile to the pure produce of the brain. But do not be discouraged by anything. Such writing as yours, such penetration and sympathy and skill, though they may effect, or seem to effect, little at the moment, are durable.

I am, my dear Symons,

                                    Very sincerely yours
                                    Edmund Gosse[1]

Note

1. Gosse sent *The Symbolist Movement in Literature* to Henry James, who replied on 3 Apr. 1900: 'I've read it attentively. It is very intelligent & charming; & anything perceptive & liberal in this desert of Boeotian betise extremely appeals to one. I think him too solemn & Paternal [*sic*], as it were, about his people – it's Pater's manner, awfully well reproduced, without Pater's subjects. I moreover, somehow, constitutionally hate English writing on French subjects – & never so much as when it is my own. But that, I admit, we can't help, &, if we must have it, Symonds [*sic*] does it better than any one, & if you get a chance, please tell him that I've read his book with great pleasure & profit' (MS., Edmund Gosse Papers, Duke University Library).

74 To Rhoda Bowser
(MS., Columbia)

Thursday   25 Bedford Place
[15 March 1900]   Brighton

I read your letter, Rhoda, on the beach here last night about twilight, as a grey mist was coming over the sea. Can you not fancy how it completed the harmony of the time and the place? Anna was with me when your letter came, and I carried it unread in my pocket until I could send her in and read it quietly by myself. I told her afterwards about your message, and she said, "No, not even to please Rhoda!" I came down here on Monday to do my Dowson article quietly. It is done, and I return tomorrow morning. I took Anna with me, and she has been walking and sitting by the sea, and eating about three times what she eats in London, and enjoying herself considerably.

Now to answer your question. At the Ambassador's Mrs. Pat was got up in her most stylish style. But on Sunday, when I spent an hour or two at her house, she was as you say, "negligently artistic." She curled up in chairs, knelt on them, shook her head with such fury at some of the things I said that the hair on one side of her head all came down, got out books to prove to me that I was quite wrong in everything I said, talked contemptuously about "young men like you," and then asked my advice on everything she was doing! It was distinctly amusing, and we discussed various matters that *may* lead to something. But nothing with her gets settled. Now she wants *Mariana* adapted, not translated.[1] If I had had the photograph on Sunday I would have taken it, but if you send it I will seize some future opportunity: I don't know when that will be. But when you come back I shall *try* to get her to come to tea with you, so that you may really know her. She is so busy that one is never sure of her except for a matter of business; but I don't see why she shouldn't, some day, do you?

How your letter pleased me, Rhoda! I have read it over and over again. Nothing now gives me so much pleasure as your letters, and that was a specially nice one. Yes, I am always frank with you: I may often be wrong but I always say to you exactly what I feel and what I think. And I constantly find myself anticipating the mood of your letters: I did in the most precise way of this last one.

Do you remember my begging you to read Pater's *Renaissance* before his *Appreciations*? You wouldn't, but now you see why I wanted you to.

I am enclosing a very nice review of my book, by a man whom I saw once, when he came to interview me a year or two ago. I don't keep those things, so don't send it back, but send back a letter I enclose from Mme. Boissière, a delightful Provençal girl whom I met eight or nine years ago at Avignon.[2] She knew Mallarmé and she gives such a charming description of his house, and his cottage in the country, that I want to keep the letter.

I wonder how you will like my Dowson article? It ought to make twelve pages of the *Fortnightly*.

This sea-air has made me so sleepy that I must go to bed. Dodo, I kiss your hands and your lips as I say good-night. Good-night!

Arthur

Notes

1. Symons had written to Rhoda in late Feb. (MS., postmarked 22 Feb. 1900, Columbia): 'Everything is uncertain with stage arrangements until an agreement is actually signed. Graham has been revising his translation and it is always possible Mrs. Pat will end by taking that (which she can get for nothing) instead of getting what she knows will be better, but which she must pay for.' See Letter 79, n. 4.
2. Thérèse Boissière, daughter of the Provençal poet Roumanille and wife of the French poet Jules Boissière. See Letter 35, n. 3.

75 To Rhoda Bowser
(MS., Columbia)

Monday night
[26 March 1900?]   Fountain Court

"To please Dodo when she is feeling ill," I sit down at midnight, to tell her all about my visit to Swinburne, from which I have just returned. At dinner he said very little, and I was getting rather alarmed, when at last Watts-Dunton asked him if he would read me some of his prologues to Elizabethan plays. His face brightened at once, and he agreed. "You will have a worthy audience," said Watts-Dunton, pointing to me; and Swinburne gave me one of his charming little bows, smiled, and said "I am sure of it." He jumped up and as he led the way upstairs said to me: "I must say one thing, that whatever the *poetry* may be like, you will hear some good *criticism!*" Up in his study (books piled up on the floor, the sofa, the chairs, all in regular, neat rows) he lit three candles, arranged them quickly but carefully, so that the two front candlesticks, which had square stands, stood corner-ways to one another and the third, which was round, stood behind, and fitted in to the little space between them; then arranged the embroidered fire-screen so that it exactly shaded his eyes from the fire ("my eyes are so good," he said, laughing, "that they are really worth taking care of. I used to be fond of looking into the fire: I never let myself do it now") then sat down at the oak table, took out his little roll of manuscript, and opened it, his face beaming brighter and brighter. The poems were written in his shaky, clear handwriting on sheets of ordinary note paper; I could see a few, but not many, corrections. He chose first the prologue to *The Revenger's Tragedy* of Tourneur. I told him I had read the play when I was a school-boy and what an impression it had made on me; and he said "Ah, my plays at Eton were all written on the model of Tourneur and Webster. I burnt them all at the age of 16. *There* were duchesses for you and poison, and murders!" Then he began to read. His voice was much deeper than in his talk, he read in a steady sing-song, accentuating the rhymes heavily and slowly, and filling out all the emphatic words, with an evident delight in all the alliterations. Occasionally, when there was something he liked very much, he would read more slowly than ever, lift his eyes from the paper and look across at Watts-Dunton with a jubilant toss of the head, as if to say *"There's* something for you now!" You felt how intensely he felt the words, the sounds, and how he enjoyed his own poetry; but the reading was perfectly simple, sincere, absolutely genuine in its excess of emphasis. His own pleasure was almost the most striking part of it; he seemed to be actually licking his lips over sweet morsels. After the Tourneur he read a prologue to Webster's *Duchess of Malfi*, and talked a lot about the play, very interestingly, telling me how he had once read the whole play aloud to W.-D., and had only then realised how fine it was as a whole. Then I asked if he had done Ford, and he said "Yes, it comes next: *The Broken Heart*," and read that one. As he read, his little fat body swayed to and fro on the chair, bending towards the table; I watched the great shining head, the still ruddy beard, the white moustache, the red nose, the clear complexion, the eyelids (as he sat in profile) swelling out over the bright blue eye, under the great dome of forehead, the rim of long thin grey hair falling over the large ear. As the emotion of the verse excited him he clapped his hands to and fro against his legs, and clacked the heels of his boots together under his chair. He talked for a long time, gaily and delightfully, about the plays and prose writing of that period, comparing something of Dekker with Dickens. I had never seen him when he seemed so much at home, and he had never seemed so nice, so perfectly simple and childlike. Sitting there by his side I could talk to him almost easily (it is always so difficult at dinner) and he seemed still eager to talk when Watts-Dunton got up and marched me away, promising however that he would get Swinburne to read to me again another time. Downstairs he took me into a room I had never been in before, where there were a lot of Rossettis – all new to me; and I had some difficulty in getting away in time to catch the last train.

There is the night, then, that you wanted to hear about, Dodo. Has it amused you? I thought of you at the very moment when Swinburne was reading: I imagined you listening too. Now I am sure you wouldn't have thought about *me* under the circumstances: so you are pleased to take note! This is to be an entire Swinburne letter, so not another word about anything else, except to say how I hope for a letter from you tomorrow, and how I long to kiss you once, where perhaps you are still feeling pain, "between your throat and chin." Even that, you see, I say in a line out of Swinburne![1]

Arthur

Note

1. If not Swinburne, then certainly a Swinburnian phrase, suggestive of those in *Poems and Ballads* (1866).

76   To Rhoda Bowser
   (MS., Columbia)

Thursday
[29 March 1900]   Fountain Court

The crocuses are out in St. James's Park, where we walked in the rain (do you remember, Rhoda?) and it has been like Spring as I have been walking about this morning, after struggling in vain with a tedious piece of work. I will write a little to you, and then I will go back to the work again, after that change.

To-night I am to dine with Claude Monet:[1] do you know his pictures? one of the most original landscape painters of our time, who originated quite a new way of painting, almost of seeing. And on Tuesday Mrs.

Carl Meyer[2] asked me to meet Sargent,[3] and I sat by him at dinner, with Millais' daughter[4] next. Well, he is exactly what I had felt him to be: a big man, not a great man. He received me in a very hostile way (which amused me, because I knew I would melt away the ice!) and before dinner was over he was neglecting Mrs. Stuart Wortley in his eagerness to explain his ideas to me, and he has asked me to come and see his pictures on show Sunday. The man is muscular, self-assertive, sincere with just a touch of worldliness and another touch of affectation, strong, able to do everything that he conceives, but not with a subtle or beautiful mind: the incomparable craftsman.

Last night Mrs. Alfred Mond[5] took me to see *Twelfth Night,* which I had never seen, and I enjoyed it enormously. It is indeed, as Meredith says of Shakespeare, "laughter cleansing brain and heart,"[6] the divinest mingling of poetic delicacy with whole-hearted humour that I ever saw. The Bensons[7] both acted vilely, but the others were good – some excellent. Mrs. Craigie has asked me to her box on Monday for my favourite play: *Antony and Cleopatra.* I shudder to think of Mrs. Benson as Cleopatra. I once sat through a rehearsal which lasted from eleven at night till 3 in the morning merely to watch Mrs. Langtry *look* Cleopatra.[8]

Do you remember that I wanted to give you "Pippa Passes," and found there is no separate edition except an illustrated one, which would spoil it? Well, I am going to persuade a publisher into bringing out an edition – after failing once I have succeeded I think now – simply (though he little knows it, poor man!) in order that I may give you a copy!![9] And though it may be a long time before it is ready, I persist in disregarding all your warnings, and in believing that when it is ready for you, you will not be too "dead to me" to accept it! Don't grudge me at least the pleasure of believing it.

On Thursday afternoon – the 22nd. – before I had heard from you, but after I had *seen* you, I wrote some lines. Would you like me to send them?

And now let me tell you a little about my book [*The Symbolist Movement in Literature*]. They have sold about 250 copies in less than three weeks (which, all things considered, is not bad), there have been crowds of reviews, mostly stupid enough (one of them a malicious personal attack, I am told – I haven't troubled to read it), and I send you two which have come my way. I thought the *Academy* one[10] was by Mrs. Craigie: you see her reply, which is as agreeable as if she had written it. Another note may interest you. Throw away these things when you have glanced at them. Tell me frankly if it amuses you to see these things and the like. It would be undignified, childish almost, on my part, if I did not – what shall I say? – take you for granted! May I?

Oh, the *Savoys,* it is no good your sending them back out of consideration for Anna, because she deliberately gave them back to me

I don't know how long ago, not caring for them herself and guessing that I might some day like to give them away. Voilà tout!

Have you forgotten that you promised me another photograph? I want it, if you have a copy to spare, and be sure you write our names on it – on the back, mind.

Friday morning. 10 a.m.

Mariana was accepted at 2 this morning! I have a whole rigmarole to tell you about it, and all its past, present, and future transformations – but that must be for my next. Say you're pleased!

Arthur

Notes

1. French painter (1840–1926), who, in the forefront of Impressionism, advocated absolute fidelity to the visual impression.
2. Wife of Carl Meyer, Lieutenant of the City of London, a German-born businessman created a baronet in 1910.
3. John Singer Sargent (1856–1925), American painter who had settled in London, best known for his portraits of dowagers and duchesses in the Edwardian and Georgian period. Some of his paintings were on view at the New Gallery in April.
4. Alice Stuart Wortley, daughter of Sir John Everett Millais (1829–96), the Pre-Raphaelite painter.
5. In 1892, Violet Goetze (1867–1945) married Ludwig Mond's son, Alfred Moritz Mond (1868–1930), later created 1st Baron Melchett. From 1906 to 1928, he was a Member of Parliament.
6. Symons's erroneous recall of Meredith's line from 'The Spirit of Shakespeare – Continued', published in his *Poems and Lyrics of the Joy of Earth* (1883): 'Thunders of laughter, clearing air and heart.'
7. Sir Frank R. Benson (1858–1939), actor–manager and founder of a company dedicated to the presentation of Shakespeare's plays. His wife, Constance (1860–1946), appeared in many of her husband's productions. The Bensons' 'Shakespeare Season' at the Lyceum Theatre ran from February to May in 1900.
8. See Letter 30, n. 4.
9. See Letter 69, n. 6.
10. See 'A New-Old Movement', *Academy*, 58 (1900) 247.

77   To Rhoda Bowser
   (MS., Columbia)

Wednesday night
[4 April 1900]   Fountain Court

O my dear Dodo, what an extraordinary day I have had, and what a relief it is to come back at night and sit down and talk to you, as if you were really here! And yet – how I wish you really *were* here! But I mustn't think of that: let me talk a little.

First, came a letter from Mrs. Pat's business manager, suggesting fresh complications.[1] Then an amazing lunch in Pont Street with a Mrs. Duff,[2] who wanted me to write some lines out of *London Nights* in her copy of the book, and when she produced the copy it was not quite all cut! Then I decided to run through several calls I had to pay, and met the carriage of No. 1 as I came away from the door of the house where I had been lunching. After half an hour's walk I got to Hill Street, and this time met the carriage a second time, at the door of the house where I meant to call. I turned around a side street, meaning to come back and leave my card, and met it a third time! Finally I called on Gosse, about a matter of business, and something I said put him in such a towering passion that he raved at me in a way that nearly made me laugh. He said (among other amenities), "You think there's nobody in the world but you – you won't do anything for anybody – you haven't a scrap of gratitude in you. *I* have done things for you over and over again, and you don't care a jot. I never saw anybody like you." And so on and so on, to my amazement. I waited till he had calmed down, was very soothing, and before long he was apologising for what he had said. Then he told me that Balfour has become quite absorbed in my work, was going about all Sunday at his country house with my new book in his hands, has ordered all my other books, wants to know all about me, etc. etc. It would be awfully amusing to meet him and see if I can see the personal likeness which so many people see, wouldn't it?

To-night I looked in at the Empire, and suddenly realised that I was standing in exactly the place where I had stood when I came there to see you, and that it was (I believe) the first time I had been there since. I looked at the seat where you had sat, and saw you all four: I could call up quite distinctly a whole series of your looks, I can see them again now – the smile in your eyes as you turned my way, the nodding of the tassels in your hat, your fur coat open over the white blouse, the programme in your hand which you waved to and fro as a fan, something you said when Zanfretta[3] came on, your head by Nona's[4] when you were left alone. As I told you once, I don't as a rule think of you visually, but as *you*; but if I once allow myself, I can call up, I really think, exactly how you looked at almost every moment I have ever seen you. I dread my memory, for it is apt to become torturing. It is the same with words. Whenever I am "down," I begin to remember, word for word, everything you have ever said that has distressed me. And I have not Nelson's resource, with Lady Hamilton's letters. The thing that came home to me more than almost anything in his letters is one in which he says to her that he is sitting in his cabin, poring over her last letter (he was beginning to go blind) and "scratching out every unkind word." "You can't think how much prettier it looks without them!"[5] There isn't much I want to scratch out of *your* letters now, for a long long time! You don't know how much that merely negative satisfaction means to me.

Here is the poem. I have written 22 poems, every one about you or suggested by you, since December 10, and for the last month I have had to work at prose so hard that I have had no leisure to write more than a few lines.

Tell me, have you read Swinburne's *Chastelard* [1865]? If not I want you to read it. Tell me, and I will lend it to you. Also, would you not like to read a little of Verlaine's verse, in French? You ought by now to be able to make it out all right, or enough to get the real flavour. Tell me if you care to.

Have you ever read Shakespeare's sonnets?

Can you guess who this is from? "C'est très mystérieux cette chose toujours restée inexpliquée: l'ascendant d'une personne sur d'autres. Je crois que je possède cette faculté! à un très fort degré! J'ai un ascendant très marqué sur beaucoup de personnes que je connais, d'une manière différente. C'est très drôle! Il n'y a que sur vous que je n'ai aucune espèce d'influence" etc. etc. Poor dear Melodie,[6] I wish she wouldn't write to me like that. She knows so perfectly that I admire her as a musician, and as a person of quite an extraordinary number of talents, that I like her, and am pleased that she should like me; and that is all. She knows also I like her husband much more than I like her!

Thursday morning [5 April 1900]

Yours just come. Thank you so very much. You say so exactly what I feel myself that I have no longer a hesitation. You know how much I need someone clear and sure to decide for me when I begin to doubt. I write almost unconsciously, in an absorption so complete that when I come out of it I sometimes feel quite helpless, not knowing what I have done. Don't you understand? And it is then that a woman's instinct is more valuable than the judgment of no matter what man. And especially in such a case as this – because it is all a question of the right *feeling*.

I have another difficulty now, which I am afraid I must decide for myself, as it depends on a whole complication of things. Mrs. Pat decided that *no* translation of *Mariana* would do, that it must be re-written from beginning to end, all the characters made English, in fact almost a new play made on the basis of the Spanish one. Thereupon I went to Rudolf Dircks,[7] who has written plays and acted them, and asked him to help me over the "padding" – the secondary characters, etc., and some of the arrangement of the scenes. He did so,[8] and I wrote all the important part, Mariana and her lover. I sent it in. Mrs. Pat wired to me to come to supper after the theatre the very next day. She said,

"It's absolutely perfect, except –" and then she pointed out everything that I hadn't written myself! I had to tell her, and, what was worse, I had to gently insinuate it to Dircks afterwards. I promised to re-write it all, but explained that without something of the kind to work on, I couldn't have done it at all – "because it doesn't interest me." "My dear child," she said, "you'll have to find out that one has to do things that don't interest one. *I* began like that; I don't feel like it now." However, she agreed to the collaboration, as long as I rewrote everything, and I told her that I should not put my own name, but Arthur Pascoe,[9] because I could not sign with two other people, Graham and Dircks. She objected, finally consented, and told me to draw up an agreement with her manager next day: £50 to be paid down, another £50 when produced, and 1 per cent royalty when weekly gross receipts of theatre had reached £700 a week. (*Magda* must now be making half as much again.) Out of this I should have to pay Dircks. The agreement has come and the manager insists on putting "Graham and A.S.", simply. I have written back to say the names must stand as I put them. No reply. A probability of the whole thing coming to nothing over the question of signature. What am I to do? Let it drop, out of pride? Or put my name, and make such a fine play that I shan't care whose name is associated with mine? I don't see why that shouldn't be possible. It is all very bothersome.[10]

Oh, *why* didn't you jump into that train?

Here is a charming, thoughtful letter from Maeterlinck. That I want back, please.

Rhoda, my letters to you get longer and longer, and I leave out half I want to say.

Yours always
Arthur

Notes

1. Concerning Symons's adaptation of *Mariana*.
2. Possibly the wife of the artist John Robert Keitley Duff (1862–1938).
3. Francesca Zanfretta, a ballet dancer whom Shaw described as a 'gorgeous brunette' in his review of her performance in André Wormser's *L'Enfant Prodigue*. See *Music in London, 1890–1894* (1932) vol. I, p. 163.
4. One of Rhoda's two older sisters. See Letter 110, n. 10.
5. Lord Nelson to Lady Hamilton, 14 Feb. 1801. See *The Hamilton and Nelson Papers*, ed. Alfred Morrison (1894) vol. II, p. 114.
6. Elodie Dolmetsch (b. 1869), frequently called 'Melodie', was a Belgian-born musician who had married Edgard Dolmetsch in 1887. In 1895, she came to live in England with his brother, Arnold. In 1896, she and Edgard were divorced, and in 1899 she married Arnold. They were divorced in 1903. See Margaret Campbell, *Dolmetsch: The Man and His Work* (1975) p. 86.
7. Novelist, biographer, and librarian of the Royal Institute of Architects (1865–1936).
8. Symons apparently reached an agreement with Dircks with respect to payment: see Letter 80, n. 10.

9. See Letter 69.
10. See Letter 79, n. 4.

78   To Mrs Patrick Campbell
(Text: Campbell)

[mid April 1900]   Fountain Court

Dear Mrs. Campbell

I cannot help (though at the risk of seeming intrusive) writing to say how deeply sorry I am at the news I have just heard,[1] coming at the very moment when you have proved to the whole world that you are the only actress on the English stage worth listening to. It is as though you have thus to suffer to counterbalance that triumph of your art, but do remember, even while you suffer, that only suffering greatens one when one is an artist, and that you will be a greater artist in the future for every bit of suffering that you go through now. There is no other consolation for unhappiness, but may one not accept so much consolation? It is what I wish for you with all my heart.

Believe me, dear Mrs. Campbell
Always your most sincere
Arthur Symons

Note

1. Patrick Campbell (1864–1900), who had married the actress in 1884, spent several years in South Africa working for Cecil Rhodes's diamond company. He was killed in the Boer War on 5 Apr. 1900. See Margot Peters, *Mrs. Pat: The Life of Mrs. Patrick Campbell* (New York, 1984) pp. 186–9.

79   To Rhoda Bowser
(MS., Featherstone)

Tuesday
[17 April 1900]   Fountain Court

I got back last night,[1] and found your first letter; the second comes just as I was going to copy out the poem. I did about 75 miles in four days, and have come back quite red and brown. It would have been a new aspect of me, wouldn't it? (one you would have got on rather well with!) if you had seen me in a slate-grey flannel shirt and tie walking across the shingle towards Dungeness, with a wind blowing hard against me for seven miles and those frightful pebbles slipping under my feet; or in a little old inn parlour eating bread and cheese and drinking Kentish ale (one old lady of 80 gave me a little nosegay in additoin to my bread and cheese!). I finished up with Rye and Winchelsea (where I slept in a kind of immensely long loft, the roof of which I could touch with my head – all the inns were full) and then across the fields to Battle, with four or five drenching downpours, one of hail; caught the express at St. Leonards, and so home. It is odd you refer to snakes, because I saw the strangest sight on Saturday: a duck was sitting on her eggs in a little nest by the side of a dyke, far from anywhere, and as I was looking at her a little snake glided out from the grass and lay across the duck's back, as if to warm itself in the sun. The duck never moved. Presently I saw a big snake, about 3 feet long, nearby, and a little snake curled round it. The big one, the mother I suppose, moved away, and the little one came hurrying after, kissed its mother once or twice, and then slid its little body along the big snake's back, and tried to cuddle round it, pushing and pushing to try and get its body round. I never saw a more affectionate infant.

It really wasn't because I was a fiend that I didn't answer your question about Mrs. [William] Morris, but simply because other things put it, for the moment, out of my head. One can never be sure in such a matter – Mrs. Morris did not leave her husband – but as Rossetti was in love with her, and haunted by her face in his pictures, all his life, except the little while when he was *perhaps* in love with the girl he married, and that other while at the dreadful end of his life, when he was dying of insomnia and chloral, and content with an inn-keeper's fat wife, it is difficult to believe (and few people do believe) that his relations with Mrs. Morris were purely platonic.[2] Rossetti was the most passionate and the most magnetic of men; I don't know Mrs. Morris, but I know her daughter,[3] and she has a temperament like icy fire, and has always gone the way of her temperament quite frankly.

It's quite true that I delight in "mere words," but what are mere words but the expression of – something? It is only when one thinks or feels beautifully that one writes beautifully.

The reason why I wish to keep those photographs as they are, unmounted, is that I would like, one day, when the poems I write about you come to be published, to put them between the leaves of my own private copy of the book. Do you not like the idea? Yes, the one with the hand I like immensely – it's difficult to choose between that and the other. The third is not so good; why I like it is that *I* can see what the sun *meant*, as it caught you at that moment. Do you know you have given me a present which couldn't be more exquisitely to my taste, – which indeed realises a wish I thought too chimerical to mention – in giving me some likenesses of you which will be possessed by nobody but me. Thank you many times over. You always know what I like best, without my needing to tell you.

Please don't ask me to return the other. Remember it is an old friend of mine, and that it only carries *me* back to the time when I knew you first, and not to anytime before.

Mariana is, I think, really settled now. When I heard of Campbell's death I wrote off to Mrs. C. at once to say how awfully sorry I was, and told the manager that I would agree to anything she liked. So I believe the three names are to be given,[4] and I am going to make the thing really good. Almost everybody works in collaboration over plays. To go to the highest, all Shakespeare's earlier plays are merely splendid adaptations of other people's work. Now we forget that anybody but himself had a finger in them.

Yes, in June we will certainly go to the Zoo to see the serpents. I haven't been there since I was a child, and don't even know the way!

I am rather pleased that the only two books I have sent you by writers that I don't really care for much (for I admit there's a good deal in Maupassant,[5] though not a great deal) *you* don't care for – Daudet and Loti.

> Always, Rhoda, yours
> Arthur

Notes

1. Symons had spent the Easter weekend in Romney, Kent.
2. For an account of Rossetti's relationship with Jane Morris, see Oswald Doughty, *Dante Gabriel Rossetti: A Victorian Romantic* (New Haven, Conn., 1960) pp. 376–8, 396–411; *Dante Gabriel Rossetti and Jane Morris: Their Correspondence*, ed. John Bryson and Janet Camp Troxell (Oxford, 1976).
3. See Letter 66, n. 4.
4. In addition to Symons and Graham's names, the third was that of Rudolph Dircks. The difficulties over *Mariana* were settled in May, when Symons told Rhoda (MS., postmarked 14 May 1900, Columbia): 'Mrs Campbell has signed the agreement about *Mariana*, which is to be described as "translated by J. M. Graham and adapted by Arthur Symons".' However, when the play opened at the Royalty Theatre on 23 May 1901, the programme listed Graham as 'adapter' with no mention of Symons.
5. Guy de Maupassant (1850–93), French novelist and short-story writer, of whom Symons wrote: 'Everything which Maupassant wrote is interesting . . . it is too exclusively and merely interesting to be really great work' ('Guy de Maupassant' in *SPV*, p. 105).

80   To Rhoda Bowser
   (MS., Columbia)

Monday   Max Gate[1]
[6 August 1900]   Dorchester

I am so glad you are better, Rhoda. I am snatching a moment while
dressing for dinner. Just back from Weymouth, where I saw the Channel
Fleet – sea in a storm, wind terrific. Hardy is most simple and delightful,
Mrs. Hardy is nice, though homely, there is a niece staying here, Clodd,[2]
a scientific man, and A. E. Housman,[3] who wrote some verse. The
weather has been so bad we have had to stay indoors a good deal, and
Hardy has talked most interestingly. He told me a lot about George
Meredith, who read his first MS: he got only £150 a year as reader![4]
Meredith went out to the war in Italy in 1866 as "special correspondent"
for the *M. Post*, and in the intervals wrote *Emilia in England* or *Vittoria*.[5]
He was so poor he once used to read aloud to a paralytic old lady,
Dinner: I must hurry down. Wait till midnight, after we have had our
smoke in Hardy's study.

12 p.m.
   We have been for a walk in the moonlight, Hardy, Housman and I,
to an ancient British barrow. Then another talk. I am quite sleepy. Hardy
and I get on awfully well, and he wants me to come down again. He
bought my *Symbolist* book the day it came out, and showed me a marked
copy of the *Images* [*of Good and Evil*], which he seems really fond of. What
is nice about Hardy is that one can *be silent* with him so agreeably. We
sometimes walk together for ten minutes without a word, like old
friends.
   I will tell you now what I hinted at: it is the Editor of the *Saturday
Review*[6] who talks of taking me regularly on his staff. That would be
better than anything I have tried for yet. As it has existed already for 30
or 40 years there is no reason for supposing it will "go smash in a year"!
I have not seen Prothero[7] again as yet: the *S.R.* would be better I
think than anything he is likely to offer. I have just written to make an
appointment with the Editor.
   By the way, I asked Hardy just now about what Harmsworth says.[8]
He entirely disbelieves it, feels sure it is merely temporary, and that
there will soon be a great reaction, when people will be tired of wars
and the like, and quite ready to return to literature. And he points out
that some of the daily papers are giving more and more space to it, as it
is.
   You think £14 is little for the Watts.[9] Do you know that the price is a

special price paid to me, and that other people would only have been paid between £9 and £10? So I am by no means discontented with the price.

I must go to bed. I go back tomorrow. This is such a funny house – not at all like the house of a man of letters, though Mrs. Hardy reads poems to us at breakfast! Hardy isn't quite a man of genius, but he has some of the characteristics of one – especially a simple, child-like quality, united to very keen observation and a curious, interesting, rather painful quality of thought. He is a sort of cheerful pessimist. I never stayed anywhere with less constraint. I rather hate going back to the Temple.

Mrs. P[atrick] C[ampbell] wrote in a very friendly way acknowledging the receipt of *Mariana*, but hasn't had time to read it yet. Besides what I give to Dircks[10] I shall have another £30 this year. I get somewhere about £40 I believe for *La Dame aux Camélias*.[11]

Good-night, Rhoda. I hope you are sleepy as I am, or sound asleep. When will your face be quite quiet again?

Arthur

Notes

1. Symons stayed at Hardy's home from 4 Aug. to 7 Aug. 1900.
2. Edward Clodd (1840–1930), banker and author, whose books, such as *Jesus of Nazareth* (1880), brought him friendships with scientists and literary figures, such as T. H. Huxley and Herbert Spencer.
3. Poet (1859–1936), who was Professor of Latin, University College, London. Housman published his first volume of verse, *A Shropshire Lad*, at his own expense, but it did not attract wide attention until the First World War, when he was Professor of Latin at Cambridge University.
4. Meredith became a reader for Chapman & Hall in 1860.
5. It was *Vittoria* (1867); *Emilia in England* had appeared in 1864.
6. Harold Hodge: see Letter 63, n. 4.
7. George W. Prothero (1848–1922), historian and editor of the *Quarterly Review*, 1899–1922. In a letter to Rhoda (MS., n. d. Columbia), Symons quotes from a letter to Gosse from Prothero: ' "I will certainly do anything I can to get him [i.e. Symons] work. I had a notion that he was independent – he seems to have travelled a great deal, and his writing is so brilliant that one would have thought he would have got as much work as he could do – only a man who writes so well, can't write much, I fear. But I will certainly bear him in mind. If he will write again for me, I should be only too glad. – Is he too much of a swell to act as 'reader' now and then? Or has he too much taste to be a good 'taster'?" Isn't that nice, and, so far as it goes, encouraging?'
8. Alfred Harmsworth, later Viscount Northcliffe (1865–1922), editor and newspaper proprietor, founded the *Daily Mail* in 1896. In 1908, he became owner of *The Times*. Symons had seen Harmsworth on 2 Aug. when he was in quest of a post on the *Daily Mail*. After the interview, Symons wrote to Rhoda (MS., postmarked 2 Aug. 1900, Columbia): 'He laid himself out to impress me, and succeeded – by his business intelligence – which however resulted in his having nothing for me. He talked for half an hour to prove to me that no one cares any longer for literature.'
9. See Symons's 'The Art of Watts', *FR*, 74, n.s. (Aug. 1900) 188–97; rptd as 'Watts' in *SSA*.
10. Symons wrote to Rhoda (MS., postmarked 6 July 1900, Columbia): 'As for Dircks, he has a perfect right to the credit of his own share in *Mariana*. He is useful to me, and I

am quite indifferent to his claiming more or less of work of that kind. He is a very good fellow, and has often stood up for me when almost everybody was against me. Now that things have changed, and almost everybody at least pretends to be for me, I don't forget it.'

11. Symons's translation of Dumas' play was intended for inclusion in a series, 'A Century of French Romance', edited by Gosse and published by Heinemann. Symons was reluctant to sign his name to it in the 1902 edition, and later editions attribute the translation to Gosse.

81   To Rhoda Bowser
(MS., Columbia)

Saturday night
[15 September 1900]   Fountain Court

Rhoda, shall I tell you about a sad little story which has just come under my eyes? A woman knocked at my door late last night with a letter and parcel from a girl I know called Althea Gyles, an artist and poet, of uncertain but really remarkable talent (she did Yeats's bookcovers among other things). It was a landlady from a side street in the Hampstead Road, and she brought a bundle of MSS poems. The girl wrote to say she was ill in bed, had been ill for a year, thought she was going to die, and was to be moved into hospital on Monday, and before it was too late she wanted to put together a little book of her best poems. She asked me to go over them and decide; and asked if I would come and see her. I called to-day and found her lying in bed in a bare room, without a thing in the place, except five books (one a presentation-copy from Oscar Wilde) and one or two fantastic gold ornaments which she used to wear; chloral by her side, and the bed strewn with MSS. She was very white, with her red hair all over the pillow. I stayed a couple of hours, going over all her poems with her (some are full of a queer, genuine kind of poetry). As I was going to go I said, "Can I lend you any books?" She said: "I've been in bed for three weeks and I've had nothing but these old books of mine. I wish you would lend me Wm. Morris's first volume of poems."[1] Then she asked me to let her see my Dowson article (she used to know him) and said, quaintly: "When I meet him I'll tell him about it!" Then, as if she were letting out a secret she had not meant to tell, she said: "All my friends have deserted me: I've not seen a creature but the doctor ever since I've been ill. Look (she waved her hand towards the wall) I've taken down all their photographs: I've only left my own up. I don't know anybody else now." I sent her up some of the books she wanted, by special messenger, as soon as I got home, and on Monday I am going to get something else from the

London Library. I have carried off a poem (really fine) to try if I can get it into the *Saturday*. I'm awfully sorry for her, though I found her a very trying person when she was well, and she used to rather hate me, I thought. I can't imagine how she came to send for me. I'm afraid she hasn't a penny. Lady Colin Campbell[2] used to be a great friend of hers, but now she has left her, like all the rest. I can't possibly do anything for her, beyond going to see her sometimes and lending her books. Her people are rich, but she has the pride of the devil, and won't take a penny from them. I may get £2 from the *Saturday*, if they take her poem; but I doubt if it's quite to the taste of the editor.[3]

I wrote a curious thing this morning, which you may see in the *S.R.* later on.[4] Haven't any news, except an advertisement of a flat in the *Daily Telegraph*, which I mean to enquire about. If you see any London paper, keep your eye on the advts. I so rarely see one. By the way, I've just thought of *the very* hotel in Paris, close to the Avenue de l'Opera!

Did you notice the rather stupid review of my poems in the *S.R.*?[5]

I am going to try to get on with my Keats.[6] It is awfully difficult with so many things calling me in different directions. I have done 2,000 words.

I wish you were here.

Arthur

Notes

1. William Morris, *The Defence of Guenevere and Other Poems* (1858).
2. Lady Colin Campbell (1858–1911), journalist, who succeeded Shaw in 1889 as art critic of the *World*. Symons wrote to Rhoda (MS., postmarked Dec. 1900, Columbia): 'I went to see Althea yesterday. Her friends are coming back to her. She wants me to meet Lady Colin Campbell, "across her death-bed", as she says. I just chattered to her about theatres and odds and ends that are happening in the outside world, which seemed to amuse her.'
3. When Hodge accepted the poem, Symons wrote to Rhoda (MS. postmarked 19 Sep. 1900, Columbia): 'She never had a poem taken anywhere before: it will please her awfully. Yes, it wasn't without some reason that her friends deserted her. She got infatuated with a drunken brute whom no one could stand, and who of course left her as soon as he had alienated her other friends. I am only the sorrier for her because of that.' The 'drunken brute' is Symons's publisher, Leonard Smithers: see Letter 62, n. 7, and *The Letters of W. B. Yeats*, ed. Allan Wade (1954) p. 332. See, also, Gyles's poem 'For a Sepulchre', *SR*, 90 (1900) 304.
4. See Symons's 'In a Northern Bay', *SR*, 90 (22 Sept. 1900) 358; rptd in *CSI*.
5. An anonymous review of Symons's *Images of Good and Evil*: see 'Alexandrines Up-to-Date', *SR*, 90 (1900) 335–6.
6. See Symons's 'John Keats', *Monthly Review*, 5 (Oct. 1901) 139–55; rptd in *RMEP*.

82   To The Editor of the *Athenaeum*
   (21 September 1901, p. 384)

> 134, Lauderdale Mansions
> Maida Vale, W.

I wish to protest against the publication of a volume entitled 'Essays from the *Guardian*,' by Walter Pater, which has just been issued by Messrs. Macmillan and Co. This volume is uniform with the *édition de luxe* of Mr. Pater's works, and is inscribed on the back of the cover, 'The Works of Walter Pater: Essays from the *Guardian*.' On a fly-leaf we are told, "The nine papers contained in the following volume originally appeared anonymously in the *Guardian* newspaper." Now the papers in question were collected from the *Guardian* at the end of 1896 and privately printed in an edition limited to 100 copies, and offered, as the preface tells us, "to the inner circle of his (Mr. Pater's) friends." To that inner circle they had an interest of their own; it was as if a copy of a private letter had been handed about among friends, who could be relied upon to take it for what it was. But they never were a part of Mr. Pater's 'Works,' and they never should have been offered to the public under that title. They are not in the strict sense essays at all; they are merely reviews, and they were written by Mr. Pater merely as reviews. At various times Mr. Pater contributed reviews, signed and unsigned, to various papers, not only to the *Guardian*, but to the *Athenaeum*, the *Pall Mall Gazette*, the *Bookman*, the *Daily Chronicle*, the *Nineteenth Century*, and *Macmillan's Magazine*. The reviews in the *Guardian* are neither better nor worse than the reviews in the other papers. They were done to please friends (myself among others), or to express an opinion in regard to some book which had interested Mr. Pater, and they were done without the least attempt to make literature. Whole pages are taken up with quotations, and the main part of the paper on Wordsworth is taken word for word from Mr. Pater's own essay on Wordsworth contained in the volume of 'Appreciations.' No one who knew Mr. Pater will doubt for an instant that, had he been alive, he would never have consented to the publication of these reviews in a volume. So scrupulous was his rectitude towards himself and towards the public, that he was with difficulty persuaded that his most finished work was sufficiently finished for publication. To print as a part of his 'Works' a quite arbitrary selection from his literary journalism is to do a serious wrong to a writer who is no longer able to defend himself against either his enemies or his friends.[1]

> Arthur Symons

Note

1. In a letter to the *Athenaeum*, the poet Francis William Bourdillon (1852–1921) defended the publication of *Essays from 'The Guardian'*: see 'Mr. Pater's Essays from the Guardian', *Athenaeum*, 28 Sep. 1901, p. 416; Symons's response on 5 Oct. 1901, p. 453.

83   To James Gibbons Huneker[1]
(MS., Yale)

2 May 1902   134, Lauderdale Mansions

Dear Mr. Huneker

I owe many thanks for sending me the other day your article about Richard Strauss,[2] which told me much that was new to me. I should have written to you before, but I have been horribly busy, and I wanted to find time to read your *Melomaniacs* [1902], for which I also have to thank you, before writing. I have only read some of the stories yet. They are full of pungent, vivid things, nervous and subtle. You write about music as if it were alive and unhappy: strange, after the kind of musical criticism one is used to here! I try feebly now and then to say something about music, but I haven't enough knowledge to be able to do much. All the same, you might glance at a sort of imaginary portrait called "Christian Trevalga," a study of a musical temperament, which is to come out one of these days in the *Fortnightly Review*:[3] not yet, for I have something on Rodin coming out first.[4] It was written long before I saw your book, but, in a very different way, it is perhaps an attempt in the same direction.

Thank you again for the book and the article.

Yours very truly
Arthur Symons

Notes

1. American critic of the 'seven arts' (1857–1921), who, according to Arnold Schwab, 'probably quoted [Symons] more frequently than any other critic'. On a visit to London in May 1903, Huneker met Symons and Havelock Ellis, whom he also admired. For his impressions of Symons, see Huneker's 'Arthur Symons and His New Book', *Lamp*, 28 (1904) 374–8; see Schwab, *James Gibbons Huneker: Critic of the Seven Arts* (Stanford, Calif., 1963) p. 108.
2. Probably Huneker's two-part review of Hans Merians's *Nietzsche–Strauss: Also Sprach Zarathustra* in the *Musical Courier*, 44 (9 and 16 Apr. 1902) 23.
3. Symons's short story, 'Christian Trevelga', did not appear in the *Fortnightly Review* but in his *Spiritual Adventures* (1905).
4. Symons, having offered the *Fortnightly Review* an article on Rodin, wrote to Will Rothenstein (MS., 2 May 1902, Harvard): 'I have seen him, at intervals, for some ten

years, and I had an article, in French, on his drawing, in the book issued by *La Plume*; but I am only a vague sort of acquaintance. Will you, who know him so well, write and tell him that I am coming over in order to do this article as well as I can, and ask him if he will let me come to and fro to his studio, and just look and think without disturbing him?' From Paris, Symons wrote to Rothenstein, thanking him for the introduction and informing him of his meeting with Rodin (MS., 14 May [1902], Harvard). See Symons's 'Les Dessins de Rodin' (trans. Henry-D. Davray), *Auguste Rodin et son oeuvre* (Paris, 1900) pp. 47–8; and 'Rodin', *FR*, 72 (June 1902) 957–67, rptd in *SSA*.

84 To The Editor of *The Times*[1]
(20 June 1902, p. 7)

Sir: Three *matinées* of Maurice Maeterlinck's new play, *Monna Vanna*, first produced on May 17 at the Nouveau Théâtre, Paris, and since played at the Théâtre de la Monnaie, Brussels, have been announced to be given, in French, at the Great Queen-street Theatre, by the original company of the Théâtre de l'Oeuvre. The play having been submitted in the usual way to the Lord Chamberlain, the King's Reader of Plays has announced his "irrevocable" decision not to recommend it for licence. The play has been published by the Librairie Charpentier, and is now on sale in London. The name of Maurice Maeterlinck and the singular nobility of his attitude towards moral questions and questions of conduct are too well known to need more than mention. We, the undersigned, are of opinion that some protest should be made against a decision of the censorship by which the representation, in French, of a play by a distinguished French writer, of the highest moral reputation, has been forbidden in England.[2]

We are, Sir, your obedient servants,

> William Archer
> Pearl Mary Teresa Craigie
>   (John Oliver Hobbes)
> Richard Garnett
> Thomas Hardy
> Frederic Harrison[3]
> Mary St. Leger Harrison
>   (Lucas Malet)[4]
> Maurice Hewlett[5]
> Henry Arthur Jones[6]
> George Meredith
> Algernon Charles Swinburne
> Arthur Symons
> Laurence Alma-Tadema
> W. B. Yeats

Notes

1. Symons was the author of this letter of protest, the holograph of which is in the Beinecke Library, Yale. In a letter to Edward Martyn, Symons wrote on 21 June 1902 (MS., Princeton): 'Have you seen yesterday's *Times* (June 20) with the letter about Maeterlinck and the Censor? I wrote the letter and Miss Alma Tadema and I sent it round, and we got Swinburne, Meredith, Hardy, etc. to sign a protest. It is the most crazy thing the Censor has yet done.'
2. *The Times*, in a review of a private performance at the Victoria Hall on 19 June, stated that the play was neither immoral nor indecent, but noted: 'If there is such a thing as voluptuous chastity, here is its representative.' See 'The London Maeterlinck Society', *The Times*, 20 June 1902, p. 7. Symons voiced his objections to the Lord Chamberlain's decision in 'The Question of Censorship', *Academy*, 63 (28 June 1902) 21–2; rptd in *PAM*. See also Symons's '"Monna Vanna"', *Academy*, 63 (5 July 1902) 45; rptd in *PAM*.
3. Positivist philosopher, jurist, literary critic, and essayist (1831–1923), a ubiquitous publicist for social and political reform.
4. Novelist (1852–1931), the younger daughter of the novelist and clergyman Charles Kingsley (1819–75), best known for his *Westward Ho!* (1855). 'Lucas Malet' was a pseudonym derived from the surnames of two families related to the Kingsleys. She created a stir with her novel *The Wages of Sin* (1891), which was criticised as daring and unpleasant.
5. Poet, essayist, and novelist (1861–1923), whose first novel, *The Forest Lovers* (1898), a medieval romance, was an instant success.
6. Playwright and critic (1851–1929), whose provocative problem plays, such as *The Masqueraders* (1894) and *Michael and His Lost Angel* (1896), were regarded as daring at the time. He later turned to writing comedies of intrigue, producing almost 100 plays.

85   To W. B. Yeats
(MS., Yeats)

The Burtons
Fordingbridge, Hants

5 August 1902

My dear Yeats

You will have seen a review, not altogether amiable, of Lady Gregory's book in last week's *Athenaeum*:[1] I don't know who can have written it, or why I was not allowed to write something in its place.

I never thanked you for the new edition of the *Celtic Twilight* [1902], but I was glad to get it, and found many excellent new things in it. It seems to me a pity that you did not revise the old part, as I wanted you to do.

I saw Althea Gyles just before coming down here: she was irate with you, quite fat, with romantic tales of her night escape from a terrible sanatorium. Next day I met the lady *from whom* she had escaped, at Mrs. Prothero's dinner-table.[2] She fixed me with a stern eye and said "I hope you are not taken in by Miss Gyles?"

We are down here in a charming old house, near the New Forest, till the end of the month. We shall only be back in town for a few days, and then start for Constantinople. I am trying to get Heinemann to send the proofs of my new book of essays down here; he delays, and I fear the book will not be ready by the autumn.[3]

Yours ever,
Arthur Symons

Notes

1. An anonymous review of *Cuchulain of Muirthemne: The Story of the Men of the Red Branch of Ulster* (1902), translated by Lady Gregory and with a Preface by Yeats, in the *Athenaeum*, 2 Aug. 1902, pp. 146–7.
2. Mary Frances Prothero (b. 1854), wife of George W. Prothero, the editor of the *Quarterly Review* (see Letter 80, n. 7).
3. Arthur Symons, *Plays, Acting, and Music*, which appeared in 1903, published not by Heinemann but by Duckworth.

86   To Thomas B. Mosher[1]
     (MS., Princeton)

28 March [1903]   134, Lauderdale Mansions

Dear Mr. Mosher

I hope by now you have received the corrected proof.[2] I have to send you many thanks for the series of the *Bibelot*, which has already made me waste almost the whole of a day, and I fear will make me waste many more. There is hardly one of your selections which I do not applaud; a few are new to me, and these I enjoy knowing. Thanks also for the copies of my Mallarmé and for the *Guardian* essays:[3] I shall like to have the copies of my lyrics for giving away. It was I wrote that *Athenaeum* review,[4] so the list is my list, and I do not remember any more of Pater's uncollected articles, though I am sure there must be at least a few more. You may feel "absolutely certain as to the authorship" of those I named, as Pater himself told me that he had written the unsigned ones. I wish I could put you on the track of some more articles, with which you could make up an interesting little volume. I quite forget my review, and if it had any interest in itself, but perhaps you might use it as a preface if you cared to do so.[5]

The idea of Wilde's poems is a good one. I know a friend of his who has at least some of his papers (including, I *believe*, an unpublished and perhaps unpublishable autobiography, written in gaol)[6] and if you like

I could ask him if there is any unpublished verse. I doubt if there is any market here, as yet, for his work.

I wish you could bring out, in the "Pippa Passes" form, an edition of the *Cenci*.[7] It would, I am sure, be very welcome.

Do you know that there are a good many unreprinted poems by George Meredith in old numbers of *Once a Week*, etc.? Not enough, though, I think, to make even a *Bibelot*.

Yours very truly
Arthur Symons

Notes

1. Thomas Bird Mosher (1852–1923), American publisher who established a reputation by reprinting the works of British writers little known in the United States, usually reprinting without permission or payment, though Symons received eight guineas for *Lyrics* (Portland, Maine, 1903).
2. Proofs of Symons's *Lyrics*, which appeared in Oct.; 2nd edn, 1907.
3. Symons's 'Stéphane Mallarmé' (rptd from *SML*) appeared in *Bibelot*, 9 (Mar. 1903) 87–110; Mosher reprinted Pater's *Essays from 'The Guardian'* (Portland, Maine, 1897; 2nd edn, 1898).
4. See Symons's unsigned review of Pater's *Essays from 'The Guardian'* in *Athenaeum*, 12 June 1897, pp. 769–70.
5. In the following month, however, Symons wrote to Mosher (MS., 26 Apr. [1903], Princeton): 'I am afraid I cannot, for various reasons, have anything to do with the reprint of those reviews of Pater. As I said to you, I think it would be an interesting thing to do, but as I had a row with Macmillan and others when the *Guardian* reviews were wrongly and foolishly printed among Pater's *Works*, it would not be advisable for my name to be associated with this reprint, though it is done on quite different lines. I forgot about this when I suggested that my *Athenaeum* review might be used as a preface. No preface, except a few words from you, is at all needed, and my name need not be mentioned.' Mosher, in his preface to Pater's *Uncollected Essays* (Portland, Maine, 1903), kept Symons's objections in mind: 'Decidedly *not* to be ranked with Pater's published works, what we here offer should be viewed as one might view a collection of letters, if they existed, "to the inner circle of his friends".'
6. Robert Ross (1869–1918), journalist and art critic, who was Wilde's literary executor, published an expurgated version of Wilde's prison letter, *De Profundis* (1905), addressed to Lord Alfred Douglas (1870–1945), poet, journalist, and son of the Marquess of Queensberry, Wilde's antagonist. The complete letter appears in *The Letters of Oscar Wilde*, ed. Rupert Hart-Davis (1962) pp. 423–511.
7. Mosher had printed the fifth act of Shelley's *The Cenci* (1819) in the *Bibelot*, 1 (1895) 319–52, but did not issue an edition of the entire play as Symons had hoped.

87　To Gilbert Murray[1]
(MS., Bodleian)

18 July [1903]　　　　　　　　　　　　134, Lauderdale Mansions

My dear Murray

I am desperately afraid I agree with everything you say.[2] I don't quite know what we should do. Miss Craig[3] evidently will not give up: what Yeats feels now I don't know: can we, in any case, desert in a body if she insists on going on? That scarcely seems fair. I wrote to Yeats, perhaps a little more cheerfully, yesterday; I am sending your letter where I sent that one, to Coole, as the safest address, though I am not sure that he is there.[4] I shall be going abroad in a week or so, and shall probably hear nothing of what is going on. Though I shall not be able to do anything, from that distance, I won't withdraw my name *unless* both you and Yeats decide to do so. As, like you, I only joined at Yeats' request, I would retire also in that case. As Yeats never can be relied on to write a letter, I shall not be likely to hear anything from him, so may I ask you to let me know if that happens? My address, during all August, will be: au Château de Chaméane, par le Vernet-la-Varenne, Puy de Dôme.[5]

I don't feel as strongly as you do about the Committee and "running our own things." No one will complain if we give them good things: it matters so little who does them.[6]

　　　　　　　　　　　　　　　　　　Yours
　　　　　　　　　　　　　　　　　　Arthur Symons

Notes

1. Distinguished Greek scholar (1866–1957), the model for Adolphus Cusins in Shaw's *Major Barbara* (1905), translator noted for his versions of Greek tragedy, Professor of Greek at Glasgow University from 1889, and Regius Professor of Greek at Oxford, 1908–36.
2. Symons is here concerned with the functioning of the Managing Committee of the Masquers Society, which had its inaugural meeting on 28 Mar. 1903 with Walter Crane in the chair and which included Yeats, Symons, Murray, and the playwright T. Sturge Moore (1870–1944). The society intended to produce plays, masques, ballets, and other theatrical forms to create a 'Theatre of Beauty'. See Beckson, pp. 226–7.
3. Edith Craig (1869–1947), actress and director, a member of the Managing Committee of the Stage Society, 1899–1903, was the sister of the theatrical designer Gordon Craig and the daughter of Ellen Terry. As a member of the Managing Committee of the Masquers Society, she had insisted that productions be controlled by theatre people rather than by members of the Committee.
4. Yeats was indeed at Coole Park.
5. The home of the Comtesse de la Tour (see Letter 66, n. 11).
6. By late 1903, certain members of the Committee found themselves unable to devote the necessary time to planned productions. Wrote Murray to Yeats on 12 November: 'You will hear with mixed feelings that the Masquers Society is no more! As you know,

I have long been in favour of its decease'. See *Letters to W. B. Yeats*, ed. Richard J. Finneran, George Mills Harper, and William M. Murphy (New York, 1977) vol. 1, p. 131.

88 To James Joyce[1]
(MS., Cornell)

21 April 1904 134, Lauderdale Mansions

Dear Mr. Joyce

I have only just returned to England after an absence of nearly nine months in Italy, and in the midst of an immense crowd of letters I find one from you dated 14 November of last year. I am extremely sorry not to have been able to answer it sooner. What have you done with the poems?[2] If they are still unpublished, it would interest me to see them, and if I can advise you what to do with them, I will gladly.

Yours truly
Arthur Symons

Notes

1. This letter, as well as other Symons letters to Joyce in this volume, previously appeared in Karl Beckson and John M. Munro's 'Letters of Arthur Symons to James Joyce, 1902–1932', *James Joyce Quarterly*, 4 (1967) 91–101.
2. The young Joyce (1882–1941) had been taken by Yeats in early December 1902, to meet Symons at his Maida Vale residence. For an account of that meeting, see Stanslaus Joyce's *My Brother's Keeper* (New York, 1958) pp. 196–7. Symons later persuaded Elkin Mathews to publish Joyce's *Chamber Music*. See Letter 99; for Symons's friendship with and influence on Joyce, see Beckson, *passim*.

89 To Thomas B. Mosher
(MS., Princeton)

5 July 1904 134, Lauderdale Mansions

Dear Mr. Mosher \
A friend of mine, Miss Althea Gyles (whom you may know as the designer of the covers to the later editions of Yeats' *Poems* and to his *Wind Among the Reeds*)[1] has written a tiny book of verses, in which I find

great merit – a slight, fantastic, but genuine touch of lyric quality. I introduced her to a publisher here, who accepted her book, and was having it set up, when he discovered that she absolutely insisted on dedicating it "to the beautiful memory of Oscar Wilde."[2] He would have passed everything but the word "beautiful," but there he stuck, and she also, and the MS. was returned. The point is ridiculous on both sides, but she is quite unmanageable and unpractical. I told her that you had at all events no prejudices, and she begged me to write and offer to you her poems, of which of course you would have the sole copyright, on whatever terms you liked to offer. I write now to mention the matter to you. Would you care to look at the poems?[3]

I may say that she is very poor, as well as very delicate in health, and if she could make a little money it would be very welcome to her. But what she really wants is to get this little book published. She was enchanted with the form in which you had issued the *Ballad of Reading Gaol*.[4]

Yours very truly
Arthur Symons

Notes

1. See Letter 62, n. 7.
2. In a letter to Lady Gregory, postmarked 13 Dec. 1900, Yeats wrote that Althea Gyles had wept in his presence over Wilde's death: see *The Letters of W. B. Yeats*, ed. Allan Wade (1954) p. 347.
3. Mosher declined the poems, no doubt because he was primarily interested in reprinting works of established writers.
4. Oscar Wilde's *The Ballad of Reading Gaol* (Portland, Maine, 1904) in Mosher's Lyric Garland Series. In a letter to Mosher (MS., 17 May 1904, Princeton), Symons praised the edition's 'much pleasanter form than the hideous Smithers edition'.

90   To Thomas Hardy
(MS., Dorset)

Poltescoe
Ruan Minor
Cornwall

4 September 1904

My dear Hardy

I have been re-reading *Jude*[1] right through, down here, with deeper admiration than ever. It is a great book: nothing you have ever done is so fine, so solid, so complete. It seems to me as if everything else you have done is a leading up to this one book. And it seems to me that this book is one of the greatest novels in English. Only in France have they done such studies in life, and with such economy and sufficiency of art.

I wish you would clear up for me a puzzling point. On p. 97 (ed. Osgood) you quote three lines of an Oxford poet, "the last of the optimists": "How the world is made for each of us" etc. I don't recognise the lines, but they ring to me like Browning[2] – who was not an Oxford man. It is a mere curiosity, but I wish you would tell me who the poet is?

Besides reading you I have had dozens of volumes down from the London Library – 16th century poets, for an anthology I am making.[3] I have found curious traces of Wordsworth in S[amuel] Daniel,[4] of Keats in Lodge,[5] and of Shelley in Drayton – whom I have never read much, but find so attractive that I should like to re-publish his pastoral poems in some accessible form.[6] Do you know him well?

We have been here since the middle of July and are staying for nearly another month, in a thatched cottage at the very end of Cornwall, not far from the Lizard, ten miles from the railway, in a luxuriant valley close to the sea. The air is all salt and honey. I find myself writing more verse than I have written all the time I was abroad.

Yours very truly
Arthur Symons

Notes

1. Thomas Hardy, *Jude the Obscure* (1895).
2. Symons was right: the lines quoted are from Browning's 'By the Fire-Side' in *Men and Women* (1855).
3. Arthur Symons (ed.), *A Sixteenth-Century Anthology* (1905), published by Blackie & Son.
4. Poet and historian (1562–1619), best known for his sonnet sequence in *Delia* (1592). Symons may have been directed to the connection between Daniel and Wordsworth by Coleridge's discussion of Daniel, 'this wise and amiable writer', in testing Wordsworth's theory of poetic diction. See *Biographia Literaria*, ch. 18, p. 205, in the Everyman Library (1913), with an Introduction by Symons.
5. Thomas Lodge (1558?–1625), poet, playwright, and writer of romances, among them *Rosalynde* (1590).
6. Michael Drayton (1563–1631), poet, now remembered chiefly for his lengthy *Poly-Olbion* (1612–22), on English history and topography. Symons's desire to reprint Drayton's pastoral poems never materialised.

91   To Edward Hutton[1]
(MS., Harvard)

2 March [1905]   134, Lauderdale Mansions

My dear Hutton,

The Outlook has accepted my terms, and I am to do art-criticism for them regularly.[2]

I must tell you some day more in detail my own ideas about Giorgione.[3] He is the one painter I have studied minutely. D'Annunzio merely uses his name as he uses the title of the picture.[4] As for Pater, he had never made any minute study of the pictures as pictures, and accepted the received opinion at the moment when he wrote (1877) and never revised it.[5] That essay is an amazing instance of a man who gives the best interpretation of a group of pictures that has ever been given, and yet mistakes the precise authorship of almost every picture! Browning pointed out the same thing in Shelley's prose writings.[6] Tradition can mean very little when, for instance, we find Vasari in his first edition attributing the San Rocco "Christ" to Giorgione and in his second to Titian.[7] Which was the tradition? and why did Vasari change his opinion of one of the most famous pictures in Venice?

Yours sincerely
Arthur Symons

Notes

1. Historical novelist, art historian, and author of travel books (1875–1969), who became one of Symons's closest friends.
2. Symons was a contributor to the *Outlook* from 28 Jan. 1905 to 17 Feb. 1906, only occasionally failing to publish a review or article in its weekly issues. For Symons's comment on his termination as a contributor, see Letter 93.
3. Venetian painter (*c.* 1478–1510), who absorbed Symons throughout his life. See Symons's 'The Giorgiones in Italy', *LQR*, 135 (Jan. 1921) 31–9. The manuscript of an uncompleted book on Giorgione is in the Arthur Symons Papers, Princeton.
4. Gabriele d'Annunzio (1863–1938), Italian man of letters, three of whose plays Symons translated: *La Gioconda* in 1901, *Francesca da Rimini* in 1902, and *The Dead City*, performed in 1918. D'Annunzio mentions Giorgione several times in his novel *Il Fuoco* (1900), which depicts d'Annunzio's affair with Eleonora Duse. When Symons first met him at Count Primoli's, he was 'startled by his appearance: something sinister in his aspect, a certain cruelty in his perverse eyes, and then there was the intense animality of the mouth' (MS., 'Duse and D'Annunzio', Princeton).
5. Pater's essay, 'The School of Giorgione', *FR* 28 (1877) 526–38; rptd in *The Renaissance*, 3rd edn (1888). Lawrence Evans believes that the first version of 'The School of Giorgione' was written as early as 1872: see *Letters of Walter Pater*, ed. Lawrence Evans (Oxford, 1970), p. 8, n. 1.
6. See Browning's 'Introductory Essay' in *Letters of Percy Bysshe Shelley* (1852) pp. 1–44. The letters proved spurious, but Browning's essay has often been reprinted.
7. Giorgio Vasari's *The Lives of the Painters, Sculptors, and Architects* (Florence, 1550; 2nd edn, 1568; trans. 1963) vol. IV, p. 203, cites Titian as the painter of Christ bearing the

Cross (in San Rocco Church in Venice). In vol. II, p. 171, in Vasari's life of Giorgione, the unidentified translator noted: 'Modern critics accept this [i.e. Christ bearing the Cross] as a work of the master, but in the life of Titian, Vasari ascribes it to that artist.'

92   To Thomas Hardy
(MS., Dorset)

25 February 1906   134, Lauderdale Mansions

My dear Hardy

It was very good of you to remember me and to send me your second *Dynasts*.[1] I watch it as an unparalleled spectacle, which I cannot wholly accept as coming within any known limits of art, but which I wonder at, with an admiration which is forced upon me.

With my theory of poetry – on which I condemn, absolutely, the whole of Wordsworth's *Excursion* [1814], and, relatively, most narrative poems – I cannot think it is the right thing to use verse for ordinary conversation (apart from emotion) or for political speeches, or for anything relating to politics or matter removed from the elements of life. I can see that your idea is to, in a sense, transcend poetry, give a vision of life seen from a height where irony illuminates everything. Intellectually, your whole conception is a wonderful thing; artistically, I don't think it can ever be wholly achieved: the very words of the language won't allow of it, the traditions of verse won't allow of it.[2] I don't think it is the best work you can do in verse: I would give it all for "The Tramp-Woman's Tragedy",[3] but, as you have once started on it, and have shown that you can do, if not the impossible, at least something that no one would have believed possible, I am glad you are going on with it, in spite of every opinion against it: no opinion matters, only one's own feeling; and I look forward to the third part which will justify your confidence in yourself and your plan.

I believe a friend of mine and his wife, Edward Hutton, a young novelist and traveller and critic, and a very charming man, are coming to Dorchester shortly for a short visit, to get over a sort of nervous illness; and as he is a devoted admirer of you I will venture to authorise him to call on you when he is there, *unless you tell me you would rather not see anyone*, which I will quite understand and act upon.

Yours very truly
Arthur Symons

Notes

1. Thomas Hardy, *The Dynasts: A Drama of the Napoleonic Wars* (1904–8), which appeared in three separate parts, the second of which Symons alludes to.
2. For Hardy's response, see *The Collected Letters of Thomas Hardy*, ed. Richard Little Purdy and Michael Millgate, vol. III: *1902–1908* (Oxford, 1982) p. 199.
3. First appeared in *NAR*, 177 (1903) 775–8; rptd in Hardy's *Time's Laughingstocks* (1909).

93   To Edward Hutton
    (MS., Harvard)

7 May 1906   134, Lauderdale Mansions

My dear Hutton

I was very glad to hear from you, and such pleasant news. You ought to be very happy there and do good sun-warmed work. We shall soon have the terrors of moving house. The cottage also is getting on: we go down to have a look at it on the 18th.[1]

We had an amusing Easter at Bognor, in a house shadowed by a burglar. I am absurdly busy at present: have already re-written my Browning for Dent,[2] for the sake of £50 on account, and have more or less promised to do a history of English criticism for a new series of his, also for solid cash;[3] and am furthermore bringing stern accusations against him in reference to his last account with me: but, if you see the sainted villain (for he is at Florence) don't refer to this part of the matter. I am offering Constable my *Studies in Seven Arts*, and hope to get on with the Blake.[4] And all these and other undertakings won't bring in the £300 or so that I have to pay out at the present moment, much less keep me going in a flat, a house, and a cottage. But these "serious" things never worry me much.

I am glad you found anything to like in my little play.[5] Gosse was quite enthusiastic about it yesterday; and Shaw and Barker[6] both seemed really to like it. Ricketts[7] also. Barker simply *cannot* make up his mind about *Tristan* (he has just married Lillah McCarthy,[8] which may account for it). I have offered the *Harvesters* to Forbes Robertson,[9] who was very friendly about reading it. It is Gertrude Elliott[10] whom I see in it. I hear from America that Julia Marlowe[11] is to do my version of *Francesca*, and may bring it over here.[12] Heinemann has safeguarded my small royalty from the yawning gulf of d'Annunzio.

The Outlook, by the way, has chucked me for good; and I am rather glad to be out of it, though I shall probably miss my five guinea articles. I *fancy* it is money with them; but they have given me no intelligible explanation.

I thought your *Academy* review of Baudelaire surprisingly good.[13] The man, by the way, wrote to me and said *I* was responsible for his ever undertaking the work.[14] I fear I replied rather ungratefully.

Do let me hear from you sometimes. I rather envy you, being where you are.

Yours

Arthur Symons

Notes

1. In April, Symons purchased Island Cottage in Wittersham, Kent, but extensive repairs were required. At the same time, the Symonses were preparing to move from Maida Vale to a small, detached house in St John's Wood. See Beckson, pp. 240–1.
2. Dent published the revised, enlarged *An Introduction to the Study of Browning* (1906). Joseph Mallaby Dent (1849–1926) had begun as a bookbinder in 1872 before establishing his publishing house in 1888.
3. The project never materialised.
4. Constable published *Studies in Seven Arts* (1906) and *William Blake* (1907).
5. Symons's one-act play, *The Fool of the World: A Morality*, was produced on 7 Apr. 1906 at the Bijou Theatre, Bayswater, on the same programme as Villiers de l'Isle Adam's *La Révolte*.
6. Harley Granville-Barker (1877–1946), actor, producer, critic, playwright, and manager, Court Theatre, 1905–1908, where he acted in plays by Shaw and Ibsen.
7. Charles Ricketts (1866–1931), book designer and illustrator, who edited the *Dial*, 1889–97, with Charles Hazlewood Shannon (1863–1937), also a book designer. See Ricketts's *Self-Portrait: Taken from the Letters and Journals of Charles Ricketts*, comp. T. Sturge Moore and ed. Cecil Lewis (1939).
8. Actress (1875–1960) who, in addition to a career as theatre manager of The Kingsway and The Savoy, wrote her memoirs, *Myself and My Friends* (1933). She divorced Barker in 1918.
9. Johnston Forbes-Robertson (1853–1937), actor and theatre manager, did not produce Symons's play.
10. American actress (1874–1950) and wife of Forbes-Robertson, with whom she often appeared on stage.
11. English-born American actress, née Sarah Frances Frost (1865–1950), joined Edward Sothern (1859–1933) in 1904 to form a highly successful acting team noted for their Shakespearean productions. In 1911 they married and retired from the stage in 1924. See Symons's 'Great Acting in English', *PAM*, 1909 edn.
12. *Francesca da Rimini* (Symons's translation of d'Annunzio's play) was not produced.
13. See Hutton's unsigned 'Baudelaire', *Academy*, 70 (1906) 398–9, a review of Symons's *Poems in Prose from Charles Baudelaire* and *The Poems of Charles Baudelaire*, trans. F. P. Sturm (1906).
14. For a discussion of differing interpretations of Baudelaire by Symons and Sturm (1879–1942), poet, critic, and translator, see *Frank Pearce Sturm: His Life, Letters, and Collected Work*, ed. Richard Taylor (1969) pp. 16–17.

94   To Rhoda Symons
   (MS., Featherstone)

Sunday midnight
[10 June 1906]   134, Lauderdale Mansions

Dear Doë

I have just left Hardy after a very amusing evening, including *Salome*[1] –
but the dinner with Hardy was the more amusing. *Salome* was gorgeous
enough, but there was nothing new in the staging. And Hardy lays his
finger instantly on the weak point – that Herod swears his oath to
Salome *before* she has danced, and not – as in the Bible, after – that is,
under the impression of her dance. The other Wilde piece was a good
epigram in the last two lines, with mere rubbish leading up to and
delaying that epigram.

Hardy told me that in his early stories he aimed at nothing more than
pleasing the readers of the magazines for which he wrote them, and
only gradually (as I have always said) came to take himself seriously.
You will be pleased to know that he cannot read Hewlett.

I went to the Hyde Park Hotel and found no Raffalovich. Meeting
Mabel Beardsley[2] at *Salome* I found that he had changed the place to the
Hans Crescent Hotel and forgotten to let me know. I had lunch at the
Monico and tea with Anna [Symons].

I am enclosing some documents. I have asked Schiller to send us seats
for Wednesday,[3] when you will be back. Blanche expects you on
Thursday.[4] Hardy has asked me to come in tomorrow afternoon. All
the boxes are here and I have packed 4 out of 12.[5] How is Island Cottage?
Be sure you let me know which train you will come by. Anna is going
to give Sister Lily *De Flagello Myrteo* because she is so very much in
love![6]

                                                              Arthur

Notes

1. Wilde's *Salome* and *A Florentine Tragedy* were presented on the evening of 10 June 1906
   at King's Hall by the Literary Society.
2. Actress and journalist (1871–1916), Aubrey Beardsley's sister, who married George
   Bailey Wright, an actor, in 1903. While she was dying of cancer, W. B. Yeats wrote a
   series of seven poems, 'Upon a Dying Lady', which appeared in *The Wild Swans at
   Coole* (1919). Of her close relationship with her brother, alleged to have been incestuous,
   see Malcolm Easton, *Aubrey and the Dying Lady: A Beardsley Riddle* (1972).
3. Dr Max Schiller (1860–1952), Romanian-born biochemist, who married the French
   singer Yvette Guilbert (1865–1944) in 1897. Miss Guilbert was currently performing at
   the Duke of York's Theatre.
4. Jacques-Émile Blanche, the French artist, was painting Rhoda's portrait.
5. The Symonses were in the process of moving from Lauderdale Mansions: see Letter
   93, n. 1.

6. Sister Lily: probably a friend at the church mission in London where Anna worked. See Symons's unsigned review of Dr Richard Garnett's *De Flagello Myrteo* (1906) in the *Athenaeum*, 21 Apr. 1906, pp. 472–3.

95 To Edward Hutton
   (MS., Harvard)

                                                                Island Cottage
                                                                Wittersham
13 July 1906   Kent

My dear Hutton
   We have been here since Monday, and though things are not yet all in working order, we are very happy in the loveliest of all cottages. The workmen are only now going and I have done nothing yet but translate Verlaine – my old, never-failing resource: five poems in three days.
   I have written to Barnes about you, and done all I can to arrange it.[1] I hope he will agree. I have asked him to paint and paper throughout and to supply electric fittings. This is due to *us*, as tenants for $5\frac{1}{2}$ years.
   Moore's book[2] I haven't seen, but he has told me much of it. It seems to have succeeded in at least its aim at impropriety. I fear I should not wholly like it.
   My view of Ibsen will not be the usual one, and will probably meet yours nearer than you think.[3] Our marvellous grocer here has not only d'Annunzio on his shelves, but Ibsen, Hardy, Stendhal, Omar, Rossetti, Lucretius (in two translations!), Spinoza, Hume, Darwin!! And he hates education and would like to live under Marcus Aurelius! And deals in very decent groceries.
   I have just had a letter from Rostand's son, saying that "les vers des 'Twenty Songs' sont les plus émouvants qu'on ait écrits en anglais depuis Shelley" and that *Spiritual Adventures* "sont les plus belles pages, et les plus passionnés, de la littérature contemporaine," and that he and a secretary of his father want to translate both.[4] And a Japanese poet[5] writes to say, "You do not know how you are admired and loved in our younger writers of Japan," and wants my portrait for the *Iris*, a magazine of poetry: "Somehow Japan has better appreciation of poetry than other countries, I dare say." After this, I wouldn't dare say the contrary!
   I don't believe a word of what you say of *Sigismondo*.[6]
   You must both come down and see us when you are back. Who do you think *insists* on coming? MRS.[7] Watts-Dunton!
                                                                Yours ever
                                                                Arthur Symons

I have opened this to ask you to help me on two points, quite at your leisure. One is, to look at a copy of the *Smart Set* on any bookstall and tell me the London address. I want to write for a copy of my Verlaine article.[8]

The other is: can you tell me the name of a book on Balzac, in which full details are given as to the *characters*. I don't think it is by Lovenjoul.[9] I distinctly remember seeing it at the London Library, and I want to order it from them, but they are so stupid when one cannot give them precise names that I dare not write direct. I believe the man's name begins with "C." I think I told you I have bought 25 volumes for down here, and I am reading them with passion, for mere entertainment. And I begin to be curious as to who Canalis is, and if Lousteau is meant for Sainte-Beuve,[10] and if Gautier really wrote the sonnets for Lucien de Rubempré.[11]

Notes

1. Barnes was the landlord of Symons's flat in Maida Vale, which Hutton was preparing to take over.
2. George Moore, *Memoirs of My Dead Life* (1906).
3. See Symons's 'Henrik Ibsen', *QR*, 205 (Oct. 1906) 375–97; rptd in *FSC*.
4. Maurice Rostand (1891–1968), French playwright and novelist, the son of the celebrated playwright Edmond Rostand (1868–1918), best-known for *Cyrano de Bergerac* (1897). Apparently, the young Maurice did not complete his projected translation of Symons's *A Book of Twenty Songs* (1905) and *Spiritual Adventures* (1905), despite the fact that two years later he was still at work on it. In a letter to Edward Hutton on 10 Sep. 1906 (MS., Harvard) Symons wrote: 'Young Rostand has invited me to come and stay in the paternal mansion in the Basque country. He has sent me an excellent pencil sketch of himself, a beautiful poetic face, with an inscription only not too flattering to prevent me from pinning it into the cottage white-wash. He wants to translate the *Harvesters* which Olga Nethersole [the actress] read out to him, and in which finds (to his surprise, he admits) "un grand poete romantique". I wish *she* would find as much!'
5. The Japanese poet was Yone Noguchi (1875–1947), editor of *Ayamegusa – The Iris* (Tokyo, 1906), the first publication of members of the Ayame Kai – The Iris Club – which contained Japanese poems as well as English poems by Symons, Yeats, Noguchi, and others. See Shotaro Oshima, *W. B. Yeats and Japan* (Tokyo, 1965) pp. 139–40. Symons's poem 'Japan' in *Knave of Hearts* (1913) is dedicated to Noguchi.
6. Hutton's novel *Sigismondo Pandolfo Malatesta, Lord of Rimini: A Study of a XV Century Italian Despot* (1906), dedicated to Symons.
7. Symons underlined the word twice.
8. Arthur Symons, 'Aspects of Verlaine', *Smart Set*, 18 (Jan. 1906) 79–83.
9. Vicomte Charles de Spoelberch de Lovenjoul (1836–1907), French biographer and critic, author of *Histoire des oeuvres de Honoré de Balzac* (Paris, 1879).
10. Charles Augustin Sainte-Beuve (1804–69), French critic, generally regarded as a founder of modern literary criticism.
11. Like Canalis and Lousteau, a character who recurs in Balzac's series of novels, *La Comédie Humaine* (1833–50), which, in its analysis of society and its evils, as Symons states, 'proposed to do for the modern world what Dante, in his "Divine Comedy", had done for the world of the Middle Ages' (Symons's 'Balzac' in *SPV*, p. 5).

96 To George Sylvester Viereck[1]
(MS., Buffalo)

29 September 1906 Island Cottage

My dear Sir

I thank you heartily for your letter and the two books.[2] It is a great gift but a great danger to write in two languages. I don't know German well enough to venture on any criticism of your verse. I can see the influence of Swinburne, and I can see something individual. In the prose I feel Wilde, but there too is individuality. I can imagine the pleasure with which my good friend Huneker will read you. A too partial critic of mine, Mr. Lewisohn, has I see already not only read but translated you with admirable skill.[3] I am genuinely interested to hear from you and to see your aims and what you are already doing. I can't help thinking you would be wise to write only in one language. Let great journalists like George Brandes write with three pens at once: a man of letters ought to have but one pen and dip it in but one sort of ink. It is evident you could do much in either language. I am glad you knew that your work was sure to interest me, and I remain with best wishes for your success, in the true sense, very faithfully yours.

Arthur Symons

Notes

1. German–American poet, novelist, playwright (1884–1962), later apologist for Nazi Germany; father of Peter Viereck (1916–), Pulitzer Prize poet and historian.
2. Viereck's *Gedichte* (see n. 3) and *A Game at Love and Other Plays* (New York, 1906).
3. Ludwig Lewisohn (1882–1955), German-born American critic, novelist, and translator. See *Gedichte von Georg Sylvester Viereck, with an appreciation by Ludwig Lewisohn* (New York, 1904).

97 To James Joyce
(MS., Cornell)

2 October 1906 Island Cottage

Dear Mr. Joyce

I am glad to hear from you again. When I named you to Grant Richards it was before his failure: I should hardly have done it since. Still, as he has apparently begun to print your book I would be inclined to give in to him as far as you can, without vitally damaging your work.

If he signed an agreement to publish the 12 stories, why not hold him to that?[1] This I am sure you could do; and you could hold over the other two for another book later. The great thing is to get published, so that people may have a chance of reading you. I will write a line to Grant Richards advising him not to lose your book. I hope you will arrange it between you.

Now as to your poems. I feel almost sure that I could get Elkin Mathews to print them in his shilling "Garland" series. You would get little money from him, but I think it would be worth your while to take what he offered – probably a small royalty after expenses are covered. He did for me a little set of translations from Baudelaire's *Petits Poèmes en Prose* [1905]. The cost was fourteen guineas and it is now nearly covered, when my royalty will begin. Tell me if I may write and advise him to take the book. If it comes out I will give it the best review I can in the *Saturday* or *Athenaeum* and will get one or two other people to give it proper notice.[2]

I hope you are getting on well in Rome. Let me have a line promptly about the poems.

Yours very truly
Arthur Symons

Notes

1. Joyce's difficulties over the publication of *Dubliners*, which Grant Richards (1872–1948) eventually published in June 1914 (after another publisher had accepted and then rejected it), have become legendary in the history of modern publishing. See Richard Ellmann, *James Joyce* (Oxford, 1987) pp. 219–22.
2. See Symons's signed review, 'A Book of Songs', *Nation* (London), 1 (22 June 1907) 639; rptd in *James Joyce: The Critical Heritage*, ed. Robert H. Deming, vol. i (1970).

98   To Grant Richards
(MS., Gilvarry)

2 October 1906

My dear Grant Richards

I have just heard from J. A. Joyce, who seems in difficulties about his book. This one I haven't seen, but if it has anything like the talent of the verse, I do hope you will see your way to bring it out. I certainly think he ought to have a chance, though from the very little I know of him I should think he is a difficult person to deal with.

Yours sincerely
Arthur Symons

99   To Elkin Mathews
   (MS., Princeton)

9 October 1906   Island Cottage

My dear Mathews
   Would you care to have, for your Vigo Cabinet, a book of verse which
is of the most genuine lyric quality of any new work I have read for
many years? It is called "A Book of Thirty Songs for Lovers,"[1] and the
lyrics are almost Elizabethan in their freshness, but quite personal. They
are by a young Irishman called J. A. Joyce. He is *not* in the Celtic
Movement, and though Yeats admits his ability he is rather against him
because Joyce has attacked the movement. Oddly enough it is to him
that Yeats refers in the prefatory to "The Tables of the Law" in that
very series![2] He is living in Rome now, and will send you the MS. if
you would care to have it. I have only met him once, and am acting
entirely out of my admiration of his work. I consider that in offering
you this book – at my own suggestion, not his – I am offering you a
book which cannot fail to attract notice from everyone capable of
knowing poetry when he sees it. I would make a point of reviewing it
myself in the *Athenaeum* or *Saturday*,[3] and would tell others about it.

                                                    Yours sincerely
                                                    Arthur Symons

I did not after all write to Miss Neale[4] as there was nothing further to
do.

Notes

1. The title was later changed to *Chamber Music*.
2. Yeats's 'Prefatory Note' to *The Tables of the Law and the Adoration of the Magi* (1904)
   alludes to his meeting with Joyce: 'These two stories were privately printed some years
   ago. I do not think I should have reprinted them had I not met a young man in Ireland
   the other day, who liked them very much and nothing else that I have written' (p. 4).
3. See Letter 97, n. 2.
4. Violet Eveleen Neale, a friend of Dr Richard Garnett, for whose American edition of
   De Flagello Myrteo (published by Thomas B. Mosher in 1906), she contributed a Preface.

100   To Edward Hutton
     (MS., Harvard)

9 March 1907   Island Cottage

My dear Hutton
   I am distressed to hear of your infliction. Surely it is only temporary,
and not final? It is inexpressibly awful to think of. Pray tell me that your
revolver has hit a driver.[1]
   You say: scan your *Morning Post*. That is what I am thinking of doing,
in future. Would you tell me what the yearly subscription (with postage)
is, and if they send it to you when you change your address, or go
abroad? I have never subscribed to a paper of any kind in my life! One
of my reasons for wanting to see it is for *advertisements of concerts*. Do
tell me, by glancing at a number or two, if they are largely advertised
there in advance?
   I am offering my Shelley to the *Atlantic*.[2] By the way Brentano's offer
to copyright my *Cities of Italy*, and also my Spain when it comes.[3]
   Have you seen the review of my verse and prose in to-day's
Athenaeum?[4] I attribute it to [Lord Alfred] Douglas, who in the past has
gushed columnfuls of praise over my verse in particular. Why this
sudden volte-face? I don't know. When I read such things I feel inclined
to echo Shelley, when, at the end of his life, he wrote to Leigh Hunt
about a "station in modern literature, which the universal voice of my
contemporaries forbids me either to stoop or aspire to. I am, and I desire
to be, nothing."[5] It is difficult to read with patience a review in which
every criticism of technique is a confession of ignorance of that technique
which is being criticised. What my position as a poet may be is none of
my concern, but at least I know one thing, and that is my métier; and
with one possible exception, there is not a single passage quoted against
me which might not have been quoted in my favour. People are at full
liberty to complain that I do not give them the thought, or the emotion,
or whatever else they require by way of substance; but when they
complain of my technique, I feel like Whistler did when every art-critic
assured him that, whatever else he could do, he could not paint.
   I have only just read the review of *Sigismondo*, which was detained at
Clifton Hill. It is very good and just and gratifying. I am glad some
people are begining to do justice to the book.[6]
   I return Randall's amusing letter.[7]
   Do go and see *Hedda Gabler* and tell me what Mrs. Pat is like. I want
her to make a success.[8]

                                                 Yours
                                                 Arthur Symons

Notes

1. The allusion is obscure.
2. 'Shelley', *AM*, 100 (Sep. 1907) 347–56; rptd in *RMEP*.
3. E. P. Dutton published the American edition of *Cities in Italy* (1907) and Brentano's published *Cities and Sea-Coasts and Islands* (1919), which contains prose impressions of Spain.
4. 'Mr. Symons', the review states, 'is one of the most accomplished writers that we have . . . but his poetry is strown [*sic*] with discords in rhyme and infelicities of rhythm.' The reviewer alludes to Symons's prose essays as 'the diary of an attenuated taste wandering among the ghosts of beauty'. See the review of Symons's *The Fool of the World and Other Poems* (1906) and *Studies in Seven Arts* (1906) in *Athenaeum*, 9 Mar. 1907, pp. 284–5.
5. See Shelley's letter to Leigh Hunt, dated 26 Aug. 1821, in *Letters of Percy Bysshe Shelley*, ed. Frederick L. Jones (Oxford, 1964) vol. II, p. 344.
6. See review in *Athenaeum*, 26 Jan 1907, p. 97.
7. Vernon Randall (1869–1960), editor, *Athenaeum*, 1901–16.
8. Mrs Patrick Campbell opened in *Hedda Gabler*, one of her greatest successes, on 8 Mar. 1907 at the Court Theatre. See Margot Peters, *Mrs. Pat: The Life of Mrs. Patrick Campbell* (New York, 1984) pp. 266–9.

101   To Stuart Merrill[1]
(Text: Guiette)

26 April 1907   10, Clifton Hill

My dear Merrill
    It is like good old times to hear from you – times that I have recalled in dedicating my translated poems to Verhaeren. Do you never come to London now? I have not gone abroad lately, partly because I do not make much money and partly because we have an adorable little late 16th century cottage (all old oak beams and white wash) in Kent. I will put in a postcard of it. The old man who stands outside cannot read or write, and has the most exquisite manners – besides being a man-of-all work.
    Now what can I tell you that would be of use? I am Cornish on both sides, and was born in Wales, Feb. 28, 1865. I was married in 1901. I went to Paris first in 1889, when I only knew Remy de Gourmont. I met Verlaine in 1890, and from that time saw him frequently. In November 1893 he stayed with me in the Temple, when he was giving his lecture.
    I travelled a good deal for some years: in 1894 I was out of England, in France and Italy, for nine months; in 1898, I spent six months in Spain; 1897 I went to Russia. After my marriage, in 1902 I went with my wife to Constantinople, visiting Germany, Austria, Hungary, Serbia, and Bulgaria on the way. In 1903 we spent the summer in Auvergne and the autumn and winter in Italy.

The Savoy ran for a year: Jan. to Dec. 1896. Crackanthorpe,[2] Dowson, and Lionel Johnson are dead, and of course Beardsley; none of the others, I think. Among these were Verlaine, George Moore, Yeats, Shaw, Gosse, Selwyn Image, Havelock Ellis.

The people who went to the "Crown" were very casual: Dowson and Johnson were generally there.

You ask about my critical work. The best of it is in *The Symbolist Movement in Literature* (1899). *Studies in Prose and Verse* (1904 – the *Portraits Anglais* are chiefly out of this) and *Studies in Seven Arts* (1906) which is about all the arts *except* literature (essays on Rodin, Whistler, Wagner, Duse, the Ballet, etc.). I have just finished a big book on William Blake.

Besides my published verse I have written (in verse) a four act play on Tristan and Iseult, a three act modern play *The Harvesters*, and two one act plays, of which *Cleopatra in Judaea* is to be performed on May 6.[3] The others I have not yet succeeded in getting acted, and I don't want to publish them till they have been acted.

In my youth I cared most for Browning and Rossetti, then for Baudelaire, and then, most of all, for Verlaine, who taught me more than any other. Verlaine learnt from English poetry secrets which he has taught to English poets.

I take it as [a] great favour, that you are doing this article about me. There is no other man in France who *could* judge my verse as you can.

When are you going to publish a book? I have seen nothing since *Les quatres* [sic] *Saisons*.[4]

> Yours ever
> Arthur Symons

Notes

1. At this time, Merrill (see Letter 58, n. 7), who was writing an article on Symons, had asked him for biographical information.
2. Hubert Crackanthorpe (1870–96), short-story writer and editor of the *Albemarle*, 1892–3. In despair over the break-up of his marriage, he committed suicide by drowning in the Seine. See David Crackanthorpe, *Hubert Crackanthorpe and English Realism in the 1890s* (1977) 139–43; Symons, 'Hubert Crackanthorpe' in *SPV*.
3. Symons's *Cleopatra in Judaea* was performed at the Bijou Theatre, Bayswater: see the review, 'English Drama Society', *The Times*, 9 May 1907, p. 3.
4. Merrill's *Les Quatre Saisons* (Paris, 1900) is in the tradition of confessional literature.

102 To George Sylvester Viereck
(MS., Iowa)

28 May 1907 Island Cottage

Dear Mr. Viereck

Your book[1] has reached me and I have been greatly interested in reading it. It is astonishingly clever, and is sure to have success. For my personal pleasure I find it much too emphatic and I feel the influence of Swinburne much too strongly. As a model he is fatal. But I am sure you will soon shake off his influence. I can't help hoping you will also shake off what seems an influence from modern German art. It leads you to prefer sounding rhetoric, as in pieces that have been most praised, like "Aiogyne",[2] to the subtler qualities of poetry. Your considerable faculty for rhythm has not yet become individual. You say you are aiming at a new form. That is essential, but I do not think you have yet got it. But all such experimenting is useful, for some day you may suddenly discover that you have done a new thing without knowing it. I don't at all know from this book what you are going to do. You are at present much too conscious. Is there anything here that would come under the best definition ever made of poetry: that it should be "overheard"?[3] I find in it any amount of substance, and a certain kind of form mastered, but I do not find the really instinctive expression of an individuality. You will probably go through a kind of technical period before you get to this: all depends on whether you get through this period and come out on the other side. You have force and exuberance, and Blake said "Exuberance is beauty."[4] It isn't, of course; but he meant that we can't get the richest beauty without it.

Believe me, with all best wishes, yours very truly

Arthur Symons

Notes

1. George Sylvester Viereck, *Nineveh and Other Poems* (1907).
2. 'Aiogyne: a Vision of Woman', which contains the lines:

> The sinuous glory of your hair,
> The chiselled marble of your breast, . . .
> Your body is with wonders filled,
> And you creation's masterpiece.

3. An allusion to John Stuart Mill's essay, 'What is Poetry?' (1833), which states that 'eloquence is *heard*; poetry is *over*heard'.
4. From William Blake's *The Marriage of Heaven and Hell* (1793), Pl. 10.

103 To Edward Sothern[1]
(MS., Museum, NY)

22 July 1907   Island Cottage

Dear Mr Sothern

I am sending you by book post, at Miss Marlowe's request, a copy of my article as it is to appear in the new edition of a book of mine called *Plays, Acting, and Music*. It is enlarged from the paper as published in the *Monthly Review*,[2] so please do not let any of the unpublished part be quoted in print. It is just for you to see, for your own pleasure (if it can give you any) a little of the admiration I had for you both.

We have had Miss Marlowe and Miss McCracken[3] with us, in this little cottage, for nearly a week, and I only wish I could think we had made them as happy as they made us. Your name was continually among us, and I feel as if I know you better than when you were in London. I gather from what was said that it is not *certain* that you, as well as Miss Marlowe, will return to London for next season. I wish I could feel assured of it. You will realise that I have a close personal interest in the matter (for I could never see with pleasure anyone but you in my old man in *The Harvesters*)[4] but it is not *only* because I want to see you in my play. I do honestly think that you and Miss Marlowe ought to come back together, not separately, and to repeat the attack upon London with all the culminating effect of two blows struck twice in the same place. No first attempt here is ever quite a success. But if you abandon the ground you have so far occupied, it will be an experiment left unfinished, and, I am sure, a rare pity. I believe the actors here are positively afraid of you both: what you do is like an awful exposure of them, and they more or less feel it. On the other hand, many people regret that they have not seen you, or only at the end. Henry James, for instance, whom we lunched with at Rye yesterday, was saying how much he regretted his absence, and hoped to be in London when you came again. I should be astonished if a second season did not establish you firmly here. You have an even harder game to play than Miss Marlowe, for a Hamlet, a Malvolio, is not readily accepted where less thoughtful and original representations are familiar and admired. If you persist, you *must* have your own way, for it is impossible that such things can be denied or disproved.

Well, so I hope you will both come back and really conquer. I don't pretend that the eager desire of such a delight as seeing my play acted as you would act it does not add some heat to that hope; but it was alight before any thoughts of myself came into it. Whatever I can do to help I will – though I fear my power in the matter is small. I think the *Figlia di Iorio* would attract, and if arrangements can be made I shall be glad to do what I can to make it playable in English.[5] I am sure the rhythmless metre in which the English version now exists could never be spoken on the stage. My idea is a mingling of prose and verse, but I must get the book and look at it again.

Miss Marlowe read out my play one evening. I had no idea till then that what I had written was so good! It seemed to come to life as I had dreamed it before I began to write it. There was not a cadence I had meant which she did not catch and render, nor a word into which she did not put warmth.

You will certainly never get to the end of this letter; but read bits of it here and there. I am quite sure I was not to tell you how your rhymed chronicle of London was read out to us over the supper table, and how we laughed and delighted in it.

Very sincerely yours
Arthur Symons

Notes

1. See Letter 93, n. 11. Sothern had returned to America, having completed with Miss Marlowe a six-week season of Shakespearean plays at the Waldorf Theatre, London, which began on 22 Apr. 1907.
2. Symons's 'Great Acting in English' – principally concerned with Sothern and Marlowe – appeared in the *Monthly Review*, 27 (June 1907) 12–17; incorporated in his privately printed pamphlet with the same title and included in *PAM* (enlarged, rev. edn, 1909).
3. Elizabeth McCracken (b. 1876), author and companion of Miss Marlowe.
4. Completed in 1905, *The Harvesters*, which Symons thought his best play, was never performed.
5. Symons did not undertake a translation of d'Annunzio's *La Figlia di Iorio: Tragedia Pastorale* (Milan, 1904).

104   To Edward Garnett[1]
(MS., Texas)

11 October 1907   Island Cottage

My dear Garnett

I thank you for sending me your play with its brave preface and telling attack.[2] The play is not only a good piece of work, simple and human, but there is nothing in it that one would have dreamed of a Censor nosing. I hope some of the dramatic critics will take it up. The Censor is bound to collapse at last: but when? Yours will not be the final blow, but it is a good hard one. Are you within the law in printing his letter?

By some accident probably two copies reached me. Tell me if I shall send on the second elsewhere.

I am getting very much absorbed in Conrad, and offered to write on him for the *Century*. The refusal seemed to say that to write about "a contemporary novelist" was not to offer a worthy subject to a magazine which itself published fiction.[3]

Thank you again for the play.

Very truly yours
Arthur Symons

Notes

1. Dramatist, essayist, and biographer (1868–1937), the son of Dr Richard Garnett.
2. Garnett's *The Breaking Point* (1907) had been suppressed by the Lord Chamberlain's office on grounds of indecency – the plot concerns a girl who believes she has been made pregnant by her lover. The play was given a private performance by the Theatre Stage Society on 6 Apr. 1908 at the Haymarket Theatre. See George Jefferson, *Edward Garnett: A Life in Literature* (1982) pp. 118–21.
3. Symons had written to Richard Watson Gilder (1844–1909), poet, biographer, and editor of the *Century Illustrated Monthly Magazine* (New York): 'I want to write a study of Joseph Conrad, whom I am more and more coming to think unique among novelists who write in English, for qualities which are lacking in all our native novelists. I do not think he is yet placed in his due position, either here or in America' (MS., 18 September 1907, NYPL). Symons offered the essay to *Scribner's Magazine* and to the *Quarterly Review*, both of which also refused it. It finally appeared in the *Forum*, 53 (May 1915) 579–92; rptd in *DP*. See Beckson, pp. 252–3.

105 To George Sylvester Viereck
(MS., Iowa)

13 October 1907   Island Cottage

Dear Sir

I have read your novel[1] with more satisfaction, I think, than any of your other work. The idea is original and the form is well wrought, brought to an end which justifies and explains the whole course of action. The idea is one I quite believe in, in the metaphorical sense, and more: I have often said that the general intelligence of England has suffered that we may have one Shakespeare and one Coleridge. But you have made a really impressive story out of a symbol. It rather suggests Wilde, but Wilde would have spoilt it by decoration and left it vague in the end. There is certainly force in it, and it insists on being read straight through.

Yours very truly
Arthur Symons

Note

1. George Sylvester Viereck, *The House of the Vampire* (New York, 1907).

106   To Edmund Gosse
     (MS., Leeds)

9 January 1908   10, Clifton Hill

My dear Gosse
   I have read your Ibsen [1907] straight through, and find it quite the best thing I have seen on the subject. We differ on one or two fundamental points – *Brand* and *Ghosts* especially. It seems to me almost a blasphemy to call that tract "one of the great poems of the world," and I am sure you are wrong about *Ghosts*.[1] But for the main part I find you wholly just and instructive – absolutely broad criticism, showing us Ibsen the Norwegian. You are very generous to Archer, who is of course not a critic at all, though a good stout beast of burden.[2] The book is delightful to read – only not a *Father and Son*.[3] I shall never be able to tell you quite how much I like, and, I think, understand that book.[4] I wish I had had it to write about, but as I told you, I never heard of its appearance till long afterwards.
   One can never talk at a party, however pleasant; but I certainly hope to meet you more by yourself before long.

                                         Yours ever
                                         Arthur Symons

Notes

1. Gosse comments on *Ghosts*: 'I confess, for my part, that it seems to me deprived of "poetic treatment", that is to say, of grace, charm, and suppleness, to an almost fatal extent . . . the dialogue seems stilted and uniform, the characters, with certain obvious exceptions, rather types than persons' (p. 164).
2. Gosse states that thirty-six years ago he had discovered Ibsen's early metrical writings, that he had 'the privilege of being the first person to introduce Ibsen's name to the British public' (p. vii). But, he adds, it was Archer (with whom Gosse had translated such plays as *Hedda Gabler* and *The Master Builder* in the early 1890s) who was 'the introducer of Ibsen to English readers'. For a quarter of a century, Archer was the 'protagonist in the fight' to secure for Ibsen 'the recognition due to his genius' (p. viii).
3. Edmund Gosse's *Father and Son: A Study of Two Temperaments* (1907), an autobiography published anonymously.
4. No doubt, Symons is alluding to Gosse's Nonconformist religious upbringing, similar to his own.

107   To Thomas Hardy
     (MS., Dorset)

4 March 1908   Island Cottage

My dear Hardy
  When I had finished, tonight, the reading from beginning to end of
your *Dynasts*,[1] I wrote on the flyleaf a line of your own:

Unprecedented and magnificent.

There is nothing else to say. The whole effect of it is so great, so epical,
that all petty criticism becomes useless, I see now all that I did not see
at the beginning. Most of what here and there seemed, in passing,
faults – *literary* faults – seem, at the end, to be but so much rough,
needful mortar, building the vast structure. It is impossible for me to
say in detail what has thrilled me from end to end; how deeply
imaginative I have found what first seemed to me trivialities; how you
have made poetry of a unique kind; how the whole effect would have
been lost if you had written it all on any higher a level of speech – I
mean in the more deliberately prosaic parts, for there is the finest poetry
you have ever written in some of the songs, and rhymed lyrics of the
Pities (such as the magnificent one on p. 281 of the last volume "The
eyelids of eve" and that in vol. 2, p. 267 "They come beset by riddling
hail"). The grand choral ending is indeed an ending of all things. But I
can't tell you with what joy I assured myself, after some doubting by
the way, that you have done the immense thing you set out to do; not
that *you* can have any doubt of it, but I had to come to my own
conclusion for myself. Now I see that you have "crowned the edifice"
of the whole work of your lifetime. Everyone will see it, if not now, in
time.[2]

Yours always
Arthur Symons

Notes

1. See Letter 92, n. 1.
2. For Hardy's response, see *The Collected Letters of Thomas Hardy*, ed. Richard Little Purdy
   and Michael Millgate, vol. III: *1902–1908* (Oxford, 1982) p. 305.

108   To Julia Marlowe
     (MS., Museum, NY)

Sunday
29 March 1908   Island Cottage

Dear and kind friend, will you be angry and not understand, or may I tell you and be understood, and so forgiven? It is impossible for us to have another dog (we have already refused one from a friend). We were both too fond of ours to ever try to replace him.[1] It may all be very foolish, but there it is. Rhoda has not yet got over the shock, which made her seriously ill. I never spent so terrible a time as after that Christmas. I have bought her a pony, as she is fond of driving, not as any sort of substitute but as a distraction. She feels that to have another dog would be unbearable. So we are condemned to refuse your kind and loving gift, with infinite thanks and regrets. I enclose Mr. Sothern's letter. He has been most kind, and, as you see, will find "King Solomon" a good home. I must tell you a story which has some analogy with ours. A beautiful young girl, one of our friends, had a tiny child which died of a horrible accident. It was kicked to death in its perambulator by a runaway horse. The mother held the broken body in her arms for eight hours until it died, without a word or tear. The people about her thought she was heartless, and her husband insisted that she should have another child. The other child has come, and she is unable to care for him or take the slightest interest. It is that same feeling which will not allow us to run such a risk. Things go, one can never replace them. We must turn to other things.

Please don't be cross with us, or say anything more about the matter. Your letter caused "real tears."

Which leads me to your address on the art of the theatre.[2] Every word in it rings true, and one hears the voice. There are subtleties that no one but you could discover or half-reveal. I say half because they are deeper than words. You have written a beautiful defence and definition of the art of the theatre, and it will remain – shall I say as a document? It is more than that, but it is that also.

And now good-bye, and all our thanks and good wishes and hopes, and all our love to you.

                                                    Yours
                                                    Arthur Symons

Notes

1. On Christmas Day, 1907, their dog, Api, which they had acquired in February when it was two months old, suddenly died. Symons, who was much attached to him, wrote

Songs for Api and fifteen prose poems entitled *For Api*, which were privately printed in two pamphlets in 1913 and reprinted in vol. III of Symons's *Collected Works* (1924).
2. An address entitled 'The Art of Play-Acting', delivered on 21 Feb. 1908, before the Idler Club of Radcliffe College.

109   To Edmund Gosse
(MS., Leeds)

28 April 1908   Island Cottage

In the first place, my dear Gosse, let me assure you that you are entirely wrong in what you say about yourself. Your last book[1] has been universally recognised for what it is, the best you have ever written. In France, which we both care for so much, you are more and more known and admired. The attention of critics is of course no sign of anything but their lack of judgment. The popular people you name (even Shaw) will be forgotten much sooner than they or anyone thinks. None of them have the one essential thing – the sense of beauty. That is what condemns Shaw forever. Alfred Nutt[2] wrote to me only the other day, begging me to write against the Chesterton & Belloc Co. Ltd.,[3] from just your point of view. I replied that I neither would nor could – in the first place because I had not read a single book of any one of them. It is very wrong and idle to speculate about the consequences of one's death, but one thing *you* are sure of: to live as one who had many friends, which is better than having the voices of an increasing crowd.

The Romantic Movement is the same book which I told you of before. I am still at it, finding gaps and filling them up. Such a book is never really finished.[4]

"The Splendid Shilling"[5] is on my list, and Dobson told me of a "Crooked Sixpence," which parodies it.

What weather! scarcely a good day since we came here. But we have both been unusually well in spite of it. We come to London for a short time on Thursday. I hope very much to see you there.

Yours ever
Arthur Symons

Notes

1. See Letter 106.
2. Publisher and folklorist (1856–1910), a founder of the Irish Texts on Society in 1898.
3. Hilaire Belloc (1870–1953), French-born English essayist, historian, biographer, poet, and novelist, who, from 1906 to 1910, was a Member of Parliament. In 1911, he and his friend and collaborator, G. K. Chesterton (1874–1936), author of over 100 books in

literary biography, criticism, verse, drama, and fiction, founded the weekly political newspaper, *Eye Witness*, which Belloc edited. Because of Chesterton and Belloc's Roman Catholic viewpoint and anti-Fabian socialism, Shaw called their enterprise 'The Chesterbelloc' (in *Pen Portraits and Reviews* [1932]).

4. On 5 Apr. 1908, Symons told Gosse (MS., Leeds) that he hoped that *The Romantic Movement in English Poetry* (1909) would be 'the best prose book that I have done (I have been working at it for 10 or 12 years)'.

5. By John Phillips (1676–1709). Symons was preparing an anthology, *A Book of Parodies* (1908), in which Phillips's 'The Splendid Shilling' appears (pp. 47–54).

110 To Rhoda Symons
(MS., Columbia)

Garlant's Hotel
Suffolk Street
[postmarked: 26 June 1908]   Pall Mall

Dear Rhoda

I shall be very glad to get back. I have done nothing but go to and fro and see people. But I was right to come up. I have had a long talk with Mrs. Conder,[1] and two lovely fans are reposing in my chest of drawers, on their way to be photographed. But – the Spanish cloak! You never saw anything so wonderful – a real white silk shawl, painted in scores of little panels around the border. It is Mrs. Conder's, done for her, and few people have ever seen it. I carried it to Mansell's[2] wrapped up in [a] silk handkerchief, which looked like a workman's dinner, and I take it back to her on Saturday morning.

Nothing can be done for Conder in Germany, and she is bringing him back, to a sanatorium at Virginia Water.[3] She is very anxious for me to come down and see him.

Hutton and I went tonight to see Maud Allan[4] and Yvette [Guilbert] (standing at the back of the stalls). Yvette simply wipes Maud out like a sponge.

I take the Botticelli to the Monds tomorrow.[5] Salting[6] came in to have another look at it while I was at the Carfax [Gallery]. Davies[7] went and professed to see nothing in it. Mrs. Conder told me he had given £200 to Huth![8] She said he was sickening beyond words.

I have had an extraordinary letter from John[9] – really a fine piece of writing – but of a frankness!

I went up last night to thank the Watkins – only Charlie and Faith were there.[10] Nona's absence was taken for granted.

I am writing this at 12 o'clock on the bed with an impossible pen.

A

Notes

1. Stella Maris Conder (d. 1912), wife of the artist Charles Conder, who married her in 1900.
2. Pioneers in the manufacture of photographic art reproductions.
3. See John Rothenstein, *The Life and Death of Conder* (1938) p. 238. Of Conder, who died in 1909, Symons later wrote in *Confessions: A Study in Pathology* (1930): 'on one of my nights of insomnia, I wept all night – so excited were my emotions by so tragic a death of one of my most intimate friends, himself a painter of an exquisite and perverse genius' (p. 64).
4. Dancer, actress, and costume designer (1879–1956), currently appearing at the Palace Theatre. Though she never appeared in a production of Wilde's *Salome*, her dance called 'The Vision of Salome' created a sensation in 1918, as described in Michael Kettle's *Salome's Last Veil: The Libel Case of the Century* (1977).
5. Which Botticelli painting Symons took to show Ludwig Mond is unknown. In Mond's library at The Poplars, there were two Botticellis among a number of well-known masterpieces. See Jean Goodman, *The Mond Legacy* (1982) p. 70.
6. George Salting (1836–1909), Australian-born collector of art, who gave the bulk of his collection to the Victoria and Albert Museum in London.
7. Randall Davies (1866–1946), author and art critic.
8. Louis Huth, art collector and friend of George Salting.
9. Augustus Edwin John (1878–1961), Welsh-born portrait painter, etcher, and author. For John's account of their friendship, see his *Chiaroscuro: Fragments of Autobiography* (1952) p. 233, which is less sympathetic than his earlier 'Fragment of an Autobiography – X', *Horizon*, 8 (1943) 140; see also Michael Holroyd's *Augustus John: A Biography* (1975) *passim*.
10. Charles Watkins, a solicitor who died of cancer in 1925, was the husband of Rhoda's sister, Nona, who committed suicide shortly after his death. Faith was another of the Bowser sisters.

111 To Edward Hutton
(MS., Featherstone)

[postmarked: 28 September 1908]

Grand Hotel Brun
Bologna

Dear Huton: in entire confidence let me tell you that Rhoda and I have [been] quarelling[sic] about the most about small things[sic] all through the journey. To my relief she insists on going straight back to London via Milan and Paris. I shall feel very lonely. I hate being alone in a foreign country. Is there any chance of your being able to come to me? You would make money[?] in the journey and wherever we went and[?] in France on the back[?]. Think of it over [and] tell me directly. I would be graful[sic] if you could.[1]

Yours ever
AS

Note

1. Evidence of Symons's mental breakdown is obvious in the strangely contorted handwriting with numerous letters and words omitted and sentences oddly constructed.

112   To Rhoda Symons
(MS., Columbia)

[postmarked: 1 October 1908]   Ferrara

Dear beloved Dodo

[D]umpling's delicious dar[l]ing dollie. I am in Ferrara and awake all night with stif[f] fingers and face. I am copying and writing poems to distract myself. I had [a] nasty journey. Train always stopping. Men trying to take my ticket to pay them twice over. Odiously altogether.

The place is lovely with [a] fine church and a huge palace with a moat, but[t]ressed arch over the moat. There are gardens and narrow streets and squares. I got a carriage and saw all Ferrara.

I hope to get away from this unholy place: and to find better air and dr[e]am of sleep on the Perugian heights.

Your devoted
AS[1]

Note

1. Roger Lhombreaud's *Arthur Symons: A Critical Biography* (1963) in giving a transcription of this letter, has many errors (see p. 240).

113   To William Butler Yeats
(MS., Berg)

[early October 1908]   10, Clifton Hill

Dear Mr. Yeats

Though of late years Arthur greatly regretted not seeing you more often, you were the man nearest to him, and the one he honoured and admired most. His mind has given way. It happened in Italy. I sent two male nurses to bring him home. Risien Russell,[1] the best man in London, saw him yesterday, he says it is general paralysis. There is no hope – he will not let me keep him at home, and indeed it is impossible, he wants to lock me into a room with him. So today we take him to a private doctor's home,[2] where he will be extremely well looked after. I feel stunned and quite incapable of doing anything – he has devoured your collected edition[3] which he found on his return – murmuring 'beautiful – beautiful' – it is terrible – perhaps sometime you will go and see him at Crowborough – it would be more than a kindness on your part.[4]

> Yours gratefully for all
> you have been to him –
> Rhoda Symons

Notes

1. Dr J. S. Risien Russell (1864–1939), who examined Symons upon his return from Italy and recommended immediate hospitalisation. Erroneously, Rhoda wrote 'Rizien'.
2. See Letter 115.
3. Yeats's *The Collected Works in Prose and Verse*, 8 vols (Stratford-on-Avon, 1908).
4. Yeats, responding to Rhoda's letter, called Symons 'the best critic of his generation', adding: 'He has been always the most sympathetic, and understanding of friends, a man of true wisdom' (MS., postmarked 13 Oct. 1908, Lohf). Yeats visited Symons in 1909 two or three times after his transfer to Brooke House and rarely thereafter, perhaps the result of his distress over his friend's transformation, for which he held Rhoda principally responsible (see Beckson, pp. 263–4). On 29 Oct. 1917, Rhoda wrote to John Quinn (MS., Quinn): 'Yeats, who was A.'s closest friend in old days, who begged for a winter's home with him in the Temple (and – need I say – got it!) when he was homeless – and who often enough came, in the early days of our marriage, to ask A. (for W.B.Y.'s ear was never a perfect one) if a certain line scanned . . . now studiously avoids meeting him.'

114   To Rhoda Symons
(MS., Columbia)

17, Hanover Terrace
Regent's Park
N.W.

21 October 1908

My dear Mrs. Symons

I hope I do not need to tell you how deeply I sympathise with you. The terrible event has scarcely been out of my mind since I heard of it.

Perhaps it is best that I should tell you clearly what I have done: –

1. I have made application for a grant for your husband from the Royal Literary Fund, of the council of which I am a member. This application will be read at the next meeting of the Council, which meets about the middle of November. I have already privately laid the matter before many of the members, and have in every case met with sympathy.

2. I have presented the matter fully to the Prime Minister, who is giving his attention to it.

You will understand that I cannot tell, and ought not to guess, what will be done.[1] But I am extremely sanguine that efficient help will be given. This, however, is the only answer I can give to your questions at present.

For the moment, you must look to your friends to tide you over the immediate need. You are perfectly at liberty, indeed I should wish you, to tell anyone who inquires, what it is that I am endeavouring to do.

I can assure you that I should not allow the matter to be removed from my mind for a single day, and that I shall work for poor Arthur as keenly as I should for my own son.

Do keep up your spirits as well as you can under this appalling affliction, and believe in the zeal of your friends. I am, with deepest sympathy, most sincerely yours,

Edmund Gosse

Note

1. Gosse was indeed successful in securing a lifelong grant from the Royal Literary Fund in 1909 and a Civil List pension in 1913, but Symons was resentful towards Gosse for the amount of the pension: see Beckson, pp. 273, 280–1.

115 To Edward Hutton
(MS., Harvard)

[early November 1908]   [Brooke House]

Dear Hutton

I must tell you of my awful adventure in Italy. I will never go there again. I was imprison[ed] in a deep dungeon with manacles on hands and feet and no food and a wooden bed. They got me out and took me to a stable[?] next to an asylum[?] where I was clean out of all recognition. They called it the House of Repose and Song. Then one after another down to Dr. Griffin[1] of Crowborough – weird name – healed my hands with great skill and sent me away to London a cleansed leper.

I hope to see you soon working[?] in your usual way, and your wife, and I will climb[?] the multitude of stairs and open the door of your little flat and take dinner with[?] you.

Always yours, caro amico mio
A.S.[2]

Notes

1. Dr A. Watson Griffin, at whose institution at Beacon Court, Crowborough, Sussex, Symons remained for several weeks in October. Of Symons's condition, Dr Griffin wrote to Rhoda (MS., 18 Oct. 1908, Columbia): 'You may rest contented that Mr. Symons is happy and occupies himself in constant scribbling and reading various poems of Byron, Burns, etc. and they are all beautiful – much too beautiful – in his mind.' On 2 Nov. Symons was certified as insane upon his transfer to Brooke House.
2. Compare our transcription with Roger Lhombreaud's in his *Arthur Symons: A Critical Biography* (1963) p. 245.

4
Years of Decline: 1909–35

When Symons entered the mental home at Crowborough, Rhoda was worried about their financial situation. The late Mrs Lucy Featherstone, Symons's sister-in-law, declared that the Symonses' financial problems were more imaginary than real,[1] but Rhoda appears to have thought them sufficiently serious to make an effort to secure extra income. Almost immediately, she wrote to Prime Minister Balfour, whom she knew personally, requesting a Civil List pension. He replied that 'it was an unbroken rule that an ex-First Lord of the Treasury makes no requests in such matters to his successor', suggesting that Rhoda write to Gosse, who, he said, was in a better position to plead on Symons's behalf (MS., Columbia). Thanks chiefly to a recommendation from Gosse, Symons was awarded a grant from the Royal Literary Fund for the remainder of his life and in 1913 a Civil List pension (see Letter 114, n. 1).

Meanwhile, despite the doctors' gloomy prognosis, Symons was slowly improving. By the spring of 1909, he had recovered sufficiently to permit outings in the company of an attendant and usually the poet and translator Agnes Tobin, who had left her home in San Francisco for England soon after she had heard of Symons's illness. With such people as John Quinn, Ezra Pound, or Augustus John, they dined at the Café Royal, Claridge's, Trevoglio's or the Carlton, and visited theatres and art galleries.

In February, 1910 Symons was permitted to stay in rooms at 74 Fitzjohn's Avenue, Hampstead, and in April he returned to his cottage in Wittersham. Although from this time he became something of a recluse, many of his old friends came to visit him. Yvette Guilbert, Ellen Terry, Mrs Patrick Campbell, Vladimir de Pachmann, Julia Marlowe, Edward Sothern, Havelock Ellis, and Edward Hutton all came for brief visits, and one day Agnes Tobin brought André Gide to see him. Symons was also fortunate in having Laurence Alma-Tadema as a neighbour, and Henry James and Joseph Conrad lived not far away. At this time, Symons's friendship with Conrad was a crucial source of comfort.

Despite such frequent visitors, Rhoda found Symons's instability difficult to cope with and, with the oncoming winter of 1910–11, she found life at Island Cottage increasingly bleak. In a letter to Huneker on Christmas Eve (MS., 24 Dec. 1910, Dartmouth), she wrote:

[Arthur] keeps wonderfully well, tho' there is no reasoning power, and he is apt to fly into ungovernable rages a propos of nothing – of course Mr. Huneker, as you can well guess, it is *terrible* for me – I am with him all day and every day – and here, in a tiny country village, at this time of year you can imagine *how* deadly it is – I read enormously – and I try to shut my brain to everything connected with this horror which has fallen on us – the man-nurse I have here says there is no doubt about the diagnosis – that it's simply a matter of time – Arthur reads and translates all day long – his work, with the exception of an occasional quite perfect lyric, is worthless – but what a blessing that he is unconscious of that and that he can occupy himself – we go over and see Joseph Conrad occasionally – Arthur has a passionate admiration for him –

Gradually Symons began to regain some of his working rhythm, but though his literary output was not as prolific as it had been before 1908, the amount which he did produce after this date is nevertheless considerable. Some of it, such as *The Romantic Movement in English Poetry* (1909), however, had been written before his breakdown. *Knave of Hearts* (1913), a volume of poems, had also been written before 1908. The post-breakdown work is often rambling and undistinguished, though on occasion Symons's former brilliance is apparent.

Though the grant from the Royal Literary Fund was helpful, it could provide only a modest living. For a time, Rhoda contemplated journalism as a means of supplementing their income, but, deciding that she was more likely to make her way as an actress, she made her debut in April 1912, at the Liverpool Repertory Theatre in Alfred Sutro's *The Perplexed Husband*. Her success in the theatre was modest, at best, though she did appear in about a dozen plays in the West End. Despite the small financial rewards, her career provided her with a legitimate escape from a domestic situation that at times was unbearable.[2]

Symons's activity in the ensuing post-breakdown years was extraordinary: among his critical studies, *Figures of Several Centuries* (1918), *Colour Studies in Paris* (1918), *Cities and Sea-Coasts and Islands* (1919), *Studies in the Elizabethan Drama* (1920), and *From Toulouse-Lautrec to Rodin* (1929) are the best, all of them containing essays which Symons had published in various journals before his breakdown. His work on Baudelaire, however, most of which was undertaken after his illness, is very poor indeed. His *Baudelaire: Prose and Poetry* (1925), a collection of translations into English, compares most unfavourably with his earlier translations of Verlaine, those, for example, included in *Knave of Hearts*,[3] while his *Charles Baudelaire: A Study* (1920) reflects Symons's own fascination with the bizarre and his own preoccupation with sin and damnation.[4] *Studies in Strange Souls* (1929), an account of Rossetti and Swinburne, and his poetry, *Lesbia and Other Poems* (1920), *From Catullus, Chiefly Concerning Lesbia* (1924), and *Jezebel Mort and Other Poems* (1931), are not especially noteworthy from the literary point of view, but they do have some interest for the psychologist, for they reveal Symons's reversion to the pietistic faith of his Wesleyan parents.

That he was obsessed by a consciousness of his sinfulness and imperfection is apparent from a letter written by Rhoda to her husband upbraiding him for his feeling of moral and spiritual inadequacy:

> If you realise *acutely** that you are an *eternal, perfect** expression of God – that realisation – if it is complete enough – is bound to cure you – keep constantly in your consciousness that you are now – always were – and always will be a son of God, therefore – *necessarily* perfect. That's what the Greeks meant when they wrote 'Know thyself'. The constant realisation that *Now* are we the Sons of God brings healing. 'Where the Spirit of the Lord is there is liberty' – (Liberty from disease and unhappiness).[5]

Though Symons became increasingly religious and withdrawn during his later years, he did not spend all of his time at Wittersham. There were the periodic trips to London to visit art galleries and attend the theatre, and on several occasions he spent time with Havelock Ellis in Cornwall. In addition, in the 1920s he went to France several times, in 1921 with Rhoda, in 1924 with Ellis, when they saw Gide, Joyce, and Vincent O'Sullivan, the American novelist who had moved in Symons's circle in the 1890s. O'Sullivan wrote to Rhys recalling his meeting with Symons: 'He did not seem to have changed much from the days in Fountain Court, either physically or mentally. He seemed in fact to have remained in Fountain Court.'[6]

During these years, an important friendship was that with the American art patron, John Quinn, who, according to his biographer, B. L. Reid, described Symons to Huneker as 'the best critic in England since the death of Pater' and who bought Symons's manuscripts in order to assist him financially regardless of their intrinsic value.[7] Deeply appreciative, Symons wrote to Quinn (MS., 17 May 1920, Quinn): 'You know you are the most generous man I have ever met.' When writing his *Confessions* in the 1920s, Symons praised Quinn as one who 'stood by me as no other man would have stood by me; he almost literally kept me alive by the cheques and the cables he sent me'.[8] But Symons's expectations that Quinn would buy an endless number of his manuscripts and his almost continual stream of requests for favours of various kinds began to weary and exasperate Quinn by the early 1920s.[9]

After 1925, Symons became increasingly isolated as his old friends died one by one, and although he still went up to London occasionally, visiting his old haunts, he was very much a part of a nearly forgotten past. John Betjeman once saw him in the Café Royal, looking 'very old and very grand',[10] but Symons knew no one, and no one spoke to him. Still, he was not forgotten by Joyce, to whom Symons was still his arbiter in poetry: in a letter from Paris, Rhoda wrote of her meeting with Joyce: '– he wants me to bring back his verse, written recently – for you to read and advise upon – said he hadn't the courage to show it to you –.'[11]

In the 1920s, Rhoda became increasingly unstable, constantly changing apartments in London in order to escape from noise. She remained on the stage until 1925 (her final appearance was in a minor role in William Congreve's *The Mourning Bride*, which was given a single performance at the New Scala Theatre on 22 November). Unable any longer to obtain theatrical employment, she told Symons in 1928: 'Fate has been against us, my dear – and there is little left for either now – *you've* done something anyway, I've failed utterly' (MS., postmarked 12 Apr. 1928, Columbia). After many years of illness, she died of leukemia on 3 November 1936.

The relationship between Arthur and Rhoda, though never placid, was none the less based on mutual affection and respect. She once wrote to him (MS., postmarked 9 May 1931, Columbia):

> It's a curious thing that when I'm with you I get exasperated. When I'm away from you I realise that you are the only person in the world I love – and you understand me – tho' you are so extraordinarily inexpressive as a being – I feel so often that I'm dashing my mind and soul against – a stone wall – it is, I believe, that you *cannot* let what you think and feel emerge except on paper.

And Symons replied (MS., Featherstone):

> I have always been restless and nervous, and have had relatively little peace in my life. . . . I have every desire to comfort you and I have always comforted you as much as I possibly could. My mother certainly did that for me, and I often wonder how much I myself gave her comfort. And I have been fated to live almost always alone, even when I am with others. I have often wished I could have been different from myself; which most artists do when they get into despair.

Notes

1. Interview with the late Mrs Lucy Featherstone by John M. Munro. Symons was expected to provide a living, despite Rhoda's private wealth (inherited from her

father, a Newcastle shipbuilder). At her death in 1936, she left an estate of over £43,000.
2. The isolation of Wittersham and the difficulty in getting roles in plays made Rhoda turn to various people with appeals for help. In response to her letter, Henry James offered to introduce her to the actor–manager Gerald du Maurier, adding:

> I can well imagine your desire to provide for yourself in London rather than face those conditions at Wittersham. . . . But I rather feel that managers are just like editors, publishers and such like, whom, after long years of the occasional effort to approach on behalf of friends with articles and books to bring to light, I have always observed to do purely and simply what suited themselves only, and what they have thought would pay, without a grain of real difference to my appeal or recommendation. . . . Your trade and his [du Maurier's], like that of all those of us who practice the arts of the recreational sort, has fallen on bad days – and I hear that this awful Lusitania for instance has emptied the theatres. (MS., 15 May 1915, Lohf)

3. For a discussion of Symons as a translator, see Ruth Z. Temple, *The Critic's Alchemy: A Study of the Introduction of French Symbolism into England* (New Haven, Conn., 1953) pp. 135–52.
4. See T. S. Eliot's evaluation of Symons's study in 'Baudelaire in Our Time', *For Lancelot Andrewes: Essays on Style and Order* (1928).
5. MS., *c.* 1933, Columbia. The words marked with an asterisk are underlined twice by Rhoda. Her quotation ('Where the spirit of the Lord is . . .') is from II Corinthians 3:17.
6. Ernest Rhys, *Letters from Limbo* (1936) pp. 284–5.
7. B. L. Reid, *The Man from New York: John Quinn and His Friends* (New York, 1968) pp. 31, 462.
8. Arthur Symons, *Confessions*, p. 72. Symons also wrote that Quinn struck him by 'something sinister, strange, not quite normal, in his aspect; by something morbid, very peculiar and very original' (p. 70).
9. See Letter 147, n. 6.
10. See Betjeman's 'On Seeing an Old Poet in the Café Royal', *Collected Poems*, enlarged edn (1970) p. 61.
11. MS., 19 Mar. 1926, Columbia. Joyce's poems were undoubtedly those published in *Poems Penyeach* (Paris, 1927). Whether Joyce actually sent them to Symons is unknown.

116   To Thomas B. Mosher
    (MS., Princeton)

17 March 1909   Stoke Newington

Dear Mr. Mosher

I thank you deeply for your kind letter – alas, there is no possible hope of recovery for my husband. I am in rooms here, to be near the private asylum where he is. It is General Paralysis of the Insane. The specialist says he will only live a few months longer.[1] He insists that it is due solely to hereditary taint (there was insanity in Arthur's mother's family) and that it has taken this particular form owing to his peculiarly over-sensitive nervous organization. Arthur had never had the disease which usually accounts for General Paralysis[2] – he is perfectly quiet and clings to me like a little child – he is just gradually fading away. I shall be very glad to receive the five guineas of which you speak. The government has made a grant for his maintenance during the rest of his life.

There is one thing quite clear, Mr. Mosher – my husband was the *most sincere* artist that ever lived – he sought after one thing and one thing only – perfection – I think he found it.

Yours very sincerely
Rhoda Symons

Notes

1. Agnes Tobin (1864–1939), American poet and translator of Petrarch, a close friend of Symons and Conrad, who dedicated *Under Western Eyes* (1911) to her, had informed Shaw of Symons's illness and the doctor's diagnosis; he wrote to her on 16 June 1909 that doctors were generally wrong in their judgements concerning 'General Paralysis of the Insane': 'There is not the slightest sign of lunacy about A.S.' See Shaw's letter in *Agnes Tobin: Letters – Translations – Poems, With Some Account of Her Life* (San Francisco, 1958) p. 78.
2. That is, syphilis.

117   To Rhoda Symons
    (MS., Columbia)

                                                                 [Brooke House]
[postmarked: 20 April 1909]   [Clapton]

I have written 1,500 words on Swinburne. Here is the sentence:
Swiftness, a bird's wing; loftiness a mighty oak; anger, the soul and

body of hell resurrected by the vitality of a passionate rage; beauty, the sea, the land, the skies – beauty is the wind; an elegant, exquisite, delicious – what word can express? – powerful, imaginative, a beautiful, radiant style – words, cadences, new rhymes, new metres; a new world exhibited in all its splendour, lust, passion, love, tragedy, humour, with the sky; he mirrors[?] and shadowed with white clouds, set as a secret veil between heaven and earth; hell being under the volcanoes, the fires that are sent up by the messengers of Satan. All this is a spectacle for God and man to wonder at. Life, consecrated by a love of all lovely things, children (whom he loved, adored, and worshipped) the whole covering of the earth with manifold beauty, wonderful as is the created world: all things, fair and foul, God and Satan, wrath and passion, love of nature, love of all things that are pure, beautiful, swift and powerful; an atmosphere that is balanced over the enormous gulf where tragic games are enacted, revealed by words of fire; a vitality, stupendous in the reverence of heroes; description of children, of all their sweetnesses, their little heroisms, their feet, their names, rhymes of a clear wit, as of a mystical, enchanted child; dramas that are too magnificent for any stage since Greece, excepting, he said, the Globe.
Of *Poems & Ballads* (age 29)

His sensuality was like a mighty current of diabolism, devouring with its teeth the lust and perversity which had never before been described with so serene and so beautiful a style.
The *Duce* [?] – fierce attack on *Napoleon the Third*.
Sir Olive [?] in anger, vituperatious, deserved, words so passionately angry, that one's intimate vitals are thrilled through with it.

> (You will find that accidentally the words make blank verse!!)

118 To André Raffalovich[1]
(MS., Northwestern)

[May 1909]   [Brooke House]

Dear André

I have only now found your address. Very many thanks for the new flowers: no one seems to know the name of those wonderful blue flowers.

As I have not his address will you thank Father Gray for those splendid Dürers and for the Pater book [which] has your name and my name in it. I remember meeting Pater at your house. He who was then John Gray repeated one of his poems. A certain expression passed over

Pater's face and he asked Gray to say it over again. "The rest was silence."[2]

Just the same when Rhoda and I met Whistler peering at the Chigi Botticelli at Colnaghi's.[3] He came back and sat beside us, and said nothing.

I was delighted to see Mabel [Beardsley] again. She shook my hand three times as she was going away!

Very sincerely yours
Arthur Symons

Notes

1. Raffalovich had visited Symons at Brooke House in May.
2. The famous last line – slightly altered by Symons's change from present to past tense – spoken by Hamlet when he dies (v.ii.358).
3. The 'Chigi Botticelli' was a reference to Botticelli's painting *Madonna and Child of the Eucharist*, once owned by Prince Chigi of Rome and sold to Mrs Isabella Gardner for a reported £12,000. It was on show for two weeks in November 1901 at Colnaghi & Co., the London art dealers who had acted as Mrs Gardner's agents. The painting is now in the Gardner Museum, Boston. For the controversy surrounding the sale, see Louise Hall Tharp, *Mrs. Jack: A Biography of Mrs. Isabella Stewart Gardner* (New York, 1965) pp. 221–3.

119 To Marie Allgood[1]
(MS., Texas)

Brooke House
Upper Clapton, N.E.

12 June 1909

Dear Miss Allgood

I cannot refrain from writing to you and of repeating how splendid was your acting of Pegeen.

I have always realised that Synge was a man of genius: mysterious, "shadowy" indeed, the man and his work. What originality of invention, what perfection of pure Irish style, what strange and wonderful characters, which, for the first time I saw living on a stage. Every play of his that I have read is the product of so strange and so various an imagination. Yeats read me, a week or two ago, some extremely fine poems and prose translations. His death, sad and terrible as it was, may, as I think, be the seal, inscribed *Finis*, set on his last manuscripts. You who mourn him must realise that his name will remain among those writers whose names survive death, and remain: Triumph.

Yours, with sincere admiration,

Arthur Symons

Note

1. Irish actress (1887–1952), who used the stage name of 'Maire O'Neill', created the role of Pegeen in *The Playboy of the Western World* by the Irish playwright John Millington Synge (1871–1909) at the Abbey Theatre in 1907, at which time she was engaged to Synge. On 7 June 1909, she appeared in a revival of the play at the Court Theatre, presented by the Irish National Theatre Society.

120   To Rhoda Symons
(MS., Featherstone)

25 August 1909   Clapton

My dear one

Alas and alas that you went away so soon! So I must tell you what happened.

We went to John's studio at 3. The Quinn was finished: a very fine living portrait: 5 days![1]

Then I turned over heaps and heaps of designs, and he gave me a delightfully sensual nude, with the sketch of a head on the back.

Then – in half an hour (I sitting as still as a statue) he did a magnificent drawing of me – almost more living than myself – the eyes marvellous! – and what fat cheeks! – mouth! etc. It is full face. I crossed my knees and put my left hand around my chin. His eyes went up and down every minute – his hand went and went with a strength and precision that I never believed any human being could do. He sat on a stool in shirt and trousers, the sleeves turned up, holding the block between his knees with his left hand. I sat on the edge of the platform.

Then, a few minutes after, I sat on the chair, upon it half-sideways with my eyes turned to his. He sat on a high stool. Another half hour – another totally different – but both magnificent – the latter gave, in a few strokes, my left hand with the rings on it.

Then John said: "I am going away for three weeks or so, and when I come back I will do a portrait of you."[2] Now what do you think of that? Then Hugh Lane's,[3] then Carlton for dinner, then the Empire where Lydia Lopokova,[4] a Polish dancer – was, as I said to John, the perfection of Beauty: and he said: divine!

Then we went back to the Carlton and had a few drinks (I mean the three of us.) Then I put on the red silk tie and John said: "I must do another drawing." He seized Quinn's bill and dashed off a diabolical half-face of me!!!

Then he said: "I must do some more drawings." So Agnes Tobin, and John Quinn, Arthur Symons and Augustus John are going on

Friday to the White City[5] – where he will see a collection of chef d'oeuvres.

> All quite sober!
> What my booful love puts into 2 sides of a card
> makes her love *gloat* over it!

Now please ask Mrs. Mond[6] again:

> Maint page epris du hasard,
> Maint seigneur et maint Ronsard
> Epieraient pour le deduit
> Ton frais reduit!

what these last two lines are?

Well, I am doing all I can to give pleasure to John.[7] I sent him a copy of the London[8] to A.J. with all the gratitude that is within me: from A.S. (I put the names, of course). And I enclosed a letter in French calling him "le seul Rabelais qui existe, l'abstraction de quintessence." And suddenly this morning out came a *magnificent* poem of 12 lines which I shall write on the [Yeats?] Coll[ected] Ed[ition].

Sometime I want to have these drawings framed: he said at the Chenil Gallery they should be done. Do you think Mrs. Mond would feel at all inclined to pay for them later on for the frame of the portrait?

I wrote to Aggie for some MS. paper, note-paper, envelopes – all gone but a few. None so far. I do not like these envelopes.

Marlowe's *Hero and Leander*:

> But as her naked feet were slipping out
> The half appeared, the other half was hid.

After that, Doë will have to read the whole poem.

This shall go tonight with no more than the deepest love of

Mimos

Notes

1. Quinn had commissioned John to paint his portrait, which now hangs in the Edna Barnes Salomon Room of the New York Public Library. See B. L. Reid, *The Man from New York: John Quinn and His Friends* (New York, 1968) p. 73.
2. John's portrait of Symons (now owned by Mr Peter Salm of New York) was reproduced as the frontispiece to *Poems*, vol. I, of the *Collected Works of Arthur Symons* (1924). For John's memories of Symons as a sitter, see 'Fragment of an Autobiography – X', *Horizon*, 8 (1943) 139–40.
3. Hugh Lane (1875–1915), Irish art dealer and collector, the nephew of Lady Gregory.
4. Ballerina (1892–1981), later a dancer in Diaghilev's company, who married the economist

John Maynard Keynes in 1925. In an unpublished memoir, Symons describes what
was apparently his first meeting with her at the Savoy Hotel on 9 Oct. 1918: 'Tiny,
perfectly beautiful, delicious beyond all conception, imaginative. . . . Nor have I ever
seen anyone of her kind who took to me so instantly – more and more – as the hour
and a half went on – with that Russian sensitive sense that we have qualities alike.
She shares so many of my tastes and loves. And during all that time we were utterly
unconscious of anything but ourselves' (MS., 'Lydia Lopokova', Princeton).
5. A large open-air arena in Hammersmith, built in 1908 for exhibitions and sports events.
6. Mrs Ludwig Mond, née Frida Lowenthal (1847–1923), who married the industrialist
Ludwig Mond in 1866. Symons dedicated *Studies in Prose and Verse* (1904) to her.
7. John, however, wrote to Quinn on 18 Dec. 1909 (MS., Quinn): '[Symons] has developed
a tremendous affection for me, which I find as embarrassing as it is undeserved. He
never suspects that there can be no complete understanding between us, and one can't
be frank with an invalid.'
8. Probably *London: A Book of Aspects* (1909); rptd in *CSI*.

121   To Rhoda Symons
(MS., Featherstone)

[late September 1909]

[Brooke House]
[Clapton]

My most beloved one

I had a dream last night. A number of prisoners were walking along
a road, roped together. I was in the first row. The gaolers were throwing
heavy sticks at us. One just missed me. Then we all stopped. Another
[*sic*] one of them said: Have you ever translated a poem? I said: Yes.
He said: Have you got it on you? I said: Yes. So he said: Will you read
it? So I replied: If you will take this rope off me and let me sit down in
the dust and go on without me, I will read it. So he said: Yes. So all
said: Yes. So off went the rope, down I sat in the dust, and read – no
doubt – a translation of Villon.

So there the dream left me – of course they went on and left me there
free to go wherever I wanted to go. So is not that dream a symbol?
October 1![1]

So to continue: my planets – Scorpio, Herschel, Venus and the Moon.
Herschel and Venus reigned over Bianca – perversity and passion.[2]
Venus and the Moon reigned over you – love and passion. Scorpio
caught me in Italy. Now Venus and the Moon came to me (the Moon to
you) and these are the powers of the sky and the Dream is the power
of the earth.

So that is for you and for you alone.

Now also remember that Scorpio came to me in a dream as a beautiful
serpent, and that Herschel has set me on the passionate and perverse

poems of the East. So Symbol after Symbol. All that means an immediate
and eternal freedom.

All my love and passion to Doë's love and passion.

From her own
Mimos

Notes

1. It was on this day in 1908 that Symons had been in Ferrara, Italy, where he was imprisoned in the Castello Vecchio.
2. Symons uses the name 'Herschel' to refer to the planet Uranus after its discoverer Sir William Herschel (1738–1822). Lydia (or 'Bianca', as Symons sometimes refers to her in various poems in *London Nights*) was, according to Symons, the illegitimate offspring of a Spanish gypsy and was, at nineteen, a dancer at the Empire Theatre, where Symons first saw her. She was his mistress from late 1893 to 1896, when she married a man of wealth. Distraught, Symons wrote a series of poems suggested by Yeats, *Amoris Victima* (1897), and later privately printed a prose account of his affair in the similarly titled (but misprinted) *Amoris Victimia* (1940), which he had written at the time of the affair (a portion of the holograph is in the Lohf Collection; another holograph, obviously a copy in Symons's post-breakdown handwriting, is in the Symons Papers, Princeton). For another version of his affair, see 'Lydia' in *Memoirs*; see, also, Yeats's *Memoirs*, ed. Denis Donoghue (1972) p. 98.

122   To Augustus John
(MS., John)

[Brooke House]
[Clapton]

[late 1909]

Dear Augustus John

after a beastly night – what a tremendous present from you awaited
me!

Tremendous thanks to Augustus John

For the wonderful gifts he has heaped upon
(Each worth more than a million)
Arthur Symons: for we both are Don
Quixote! And the same Sun hath shone
on Arthur Symons and Augustus John!

This is a morning prelude: I wait until night comes on to continue
this letter. Only I must say that the C.B. translations, having arrived at
the number of 80, stopt. So I am writing notes for an essay on C.B.[2]

Frequently had he frequented Hell, whose abominations he had observed, with eyes as piercing as an eagle's. And in his eyes there is also an hallucination, a deadly fixity, in which depths of thought, sensation, despair, passion, seem to commit adultery with those she-Devils whose eyes had fastened upon his eyes, with an equal fascination. On the sardonic smile of his tight-closed lips there is Satan's scorn of the world, and his own laughter. Wrinkles curl downwards from the distended nostrils that seem to breathe scents, perfumes, and the bestial subtlety that exhales from a woman's flesh.

I hear that our [?] Agnes is taking me for some jaunt this evening. I am more than anxious to meet you again and soon. I have written "The World's Dance," "Lais to Aphrodite," "The Spanish Monk" – and – a sonnet – "Hell and the Serpent."[3]

"The Idolatrous Madonna" has arrived at the height of 33. The 31st will become the end of what may be a long series: it ends:

> That but the candles witness, as their lights
> Illuminate our abominable frights.

Le meilleur[?]:

> Her serpent's mouth, her mad breasts, and her reins.

You can imagine how often I shall take out these photogravures and gloat over each and return and gloat again and again.

Everlasting thanks for these gifts that your genius created!

Always yours
Arthur Symons

Notes

1. Perhaps a sketch of Symons by John: see Letter 120.
2. Possibly Symons's 'Charles Baudelaire: Poet, Critic and Man of Letters', *VF*, 5 (Sep. 1915) 43. Symons's translations of Baudelaire and his full-length study appeared much later: *Charles Baudelaire: A Study* (1920) and *Baudelaire: Prose and Poetry* (1925).
3. None of the poems alluded to in this letter was published.

123   To Augustus John
     (MS., John)

[mid-April 1910]   Island Cottage

Dear John

You wrote me a letter of immortal beauty – so imaginative and one tremendous sentence. I got here on the 7th (lucky day!).[1] Only now occurs to me to write to you after a wretched night and *such* a poem on Lucifer!

> Great Satan, help me, Lucifer of Men!

Your letter I shall never forget: it is by me now.[2]

I was astonished on returning here at last to find so lovely a transformation of this study where I write, and the other room: Blake, Rodin, John; crucifixes, mirror, brass plates; treasures brought from many countries – and the most splendid of all cottages – *here*! Certain is it that sometime you must come to stay here. Here there is perfect peace, wind from the sea, lawn, orchard, and a place to refresh one and to stir one's imagination into freer flights-winged. This in the next letter.

We saw a lovely golden-haired Welsh Gypsy – 20 or so – as we drove past. She smiled and I lifted my hand in a gesture that she understood. We are sure to meet her again. A poem written in the form of Spanish-Gypsy tales.

Here, a Gypsy proverb that I translated:

> We are not used to live as a Christian log:
> We are used to live as a savage dog.

Splendid!

I shall enclose a few things I wrote before I came here. Here an attempt in one of my *Cantares a la Española*:

> Yo quiero, estrella de mar,
> Juanita, mia cariña,
> Por mi corazon y alma,
> Mia hermosa niña.

---

27 Gypsy books have I here.

Open hearth and wood-fire – the sap exuding and that scent and sound of its crackling – its superb colour.

Won't *your* work be superb!
Don't forget some time or other a drawing on *Lesbia in Old Age*.[3]
The only prose I have written here is on *Modern Love*.[4]
How I remember Marseilles – La Cannebière – the forest – and the ill-famed houses and the inveterate whores.

At last I have attained leisure, the wood and air and space and solitude, the world vanished, one's own world here: a world – some new invented world – to create. Why not, August John?

But, what is *my* world in the love and passion of two beings united again and forever after all the abominations of the ghastly past. One becomes also natural and primitive: God unbeaten and hearts in God.

Only one woman exists for me, who is here. Only two men exist for me: Rodin and you.

So let there be eternal luck for these famous four!

Always yours
Arthur Symons

Notes

1. On 7 Apr. Symons returned to Island Cottage, which he had not seen for eighteen months.
2. John had written to Symons (MS., Mar. 1910, Lohf): 'You have triumphed over the Devil and all his imps and confounded the grey-bearded and hydrocephalous doctors.'
3. A poem that appeared in *Knave of Hearts* (1913). Apparently John did not do the drawing.
4. Possibly included in his 'George Meredith: With Some Unpublished Letters', *Forum*, 68 (Oct. 1922) 817–34; rptd in *FR*, 93, n.s. (Jan. 1923) 50–63.

124 To Augustus John
(MS., John)

[late April 1910]   Island Cottage

[first page missing]

You will know, after that scorpion of mine bit me in Italy, and, worse than he, a man-scorpion laid hands on me in London, still less and less clutching me, that all the freedom, wildness, possession of nakedness, seduction, sin, perversity, all these years that one remembers fatally and superbly, has wrenched me from the sight of naked beauty, the actual possession, and that thus, my mental faculties turned inwards and my brain also, only abstract, lustful, unnatural and illusive and visionary, ghastly also, things can find their way out of my imagination into forms of verse. It is the unnaturalness of things which obsessed me, and stirs up all the devil in me intö flaming wrath [?].

And so, my aversion to London being definite, my only desire of a favourable future, which certainly beams before me, even on such a day of snow as this is: to go abroad (with her, of course) and, of all places in the world, to Spain. So (private to you, John) if any possibility of the return of the money, or some of it, that we first and for so many years possessed, should return, and the way be at last clear before us as it was before, there – devils or no devils – do we and shall we go.

I have written "The Gypsies' Song",[1] in triple rhymes, with the refrain:

> (The serpent's tail).
> (We follow the trail).

It is a vision and an imagination.

Then "The Lesbians", with double rhymes in each stanza repeated as: tresses, caresses, wine-presses, guesses. *Salome* (ages and ages passed through me while I was writing it):

> I am the virgin of all virgins, I,
> Salome, daughter of Herodias,
> The slyest snake that ever curled in grass,
> Coloured and painted as the images
> Of idols, wife of Herod, and his sly
> Harlot, painted as woven tapestries
> Of curious and abominable dyes,
> That gaze upon as she gazes on
> The wrinkled ruinous ruin of the worm
> Of worms incarnate, Herod, the infirm
> King of the Kingdom of the ruinous sun.

And the end!

> Past virginal delights, till all is flame
> Before me and around me, and within
> This body of mine, a sin desiring sin.

Now, my fancy is for the last thing I have written: natural? So here I copy it for you. Now, this was a vision from a marvellous drawing of an aged snake in Blakes's *Vala*.[2] So, in this case, why not imagine, that, in the future, this one thing, if it appeals to you as it seems to me, should have your name on it, in this real, vague, imaginary new book of verses of mine? It would be a passionate pleasure to me.

Yours always
Arthur Symons

Notes

1. This poem and 'The Lesbians', mentioned later in this letter, are probably among those poems written and destroyed by Symons after his release from Brooke House.
2. Symons had probably seen Blake's drawing in *The Works of William Blake: Poetic, Symbolic, and Critical*, ed. Edwin John Ellis and William Butler Yeats (1893) vol. III, p. 11 of the *Vala* facsimile.

125   To Rhoda Symons
(MS., Columbia)

6 February 1911   Island Cottage

Dearest Rhoda

Yesterday was splendid. A[gnes Tobin] hired a car from Rye and we went to the Conrads.[1] A. and C. talked at such a rate that I imagined how on earth I was to edge in words between them: about Poland, Polish, California, etc. Finally my triumph came. Exit all but C. and I. He said to A.: I must talk with *A*.! And such a talk we had. He said: How living you look. Your beard gives you un air distingué, a poetical distinction. Then I read him "Crimen Amoris."[2] He sat close beside me on the sofa, and listened, breathing hard. One or two interruptions came: up went C., door shut: back: then: magnificent! what a magnificent translation. So I read over in a sonorous voice the 1st stanza and then the last in its lovely nuances (adores; implores). Then C.: I am transported.

Then money. He said: I have had £300 for the serial rights of my novel:[3] think of those awful creatures who get thousands. I may get altogether £1,000 out of it. Mais, I am always under the water. (He was walking to and fro, smoking.) I am not content with my novel. It has no end. It sickens me when I have to sit down to my desk and write so many thousand words for a short story – for money. (He put his hand over his forehead: All is here!) But how can I go on?

I reminded him of my thing on him[4] and he said, with such curious emotion: When you publish another book, you won't forget me? Certainly not, said I.[5]

Then, as we left, to return to Laurence's,[6] said C.: Au revoir, cher! and I answering him. Wasn't it lovely?

I saw A. off to London at 5:30. Isn't it awful that Sir H.[7] cometh here from Friday to Monday? Be sure that our lunch on Sunday will be the 3, not the 4!

Arthur

Notes

1. In 1910, Symons first met the Conrads, who had recently bought a farmhouse near Ashford, Kent. In his *Notes on Joseph Conrad* (1925) p. 13, Symons errs in dating their first meeting as 1911. Jessie Conrad (1874–1936) was the author of two memoirs of her husband: *Joseph Conrad as I Knew Him* (1926) and *Joseph Conrad and His Circle* (1935).
2. From Verlaine's *Jadis et Naguère* (Paris, 1884).
3. Joseph Conrad, *Under Western Eyes* (1911), dedicated to Agnes Tobin, was serialised simultaneously between Dec. 1910 and Oct. 1911, in *NAR*, vols 192–4, and *ER*, vols 7–9.
4. Symons's article on Conrad, rejected by two periodicals. See Letter 104, n. 3.
5. In Apr. 1911, Symons wrote to Gordon Craig about Conrad: 'how astonishing a creature is he – a Hamlet, if you like – with all his wisdom and nerves, and vision also. As the man (whom I have met continually) so are his works. I am Cornish, he is Polish: the two races' (MS., n. d., Bibliothèque Nationale, Paris).
6. Laurence Alma-Tadema's house in Wittersham.
7. Sir Herbert Thompson (1859–1944), Egyptologist and author, who later encouraged Rhoda to go on the stage.

126   To Rhoda Symons
   (MS., Columbia)

[postmarked: 23 May 1911]   Island Cottage

Dearest Rhoda

How splendid to hear Kreisler:[1] so I wait till tomorrow. What can I do but wait? Rien que ça.

I too have had a splendid time with Bullen.[2] He was his old self, the same charm, walking, drinking, smoking, talking, and reciting verses of immense length from Lucretius in Latin, Milton, Arnold, Swinburne, and how many others. We talked incessantly – on every sort of thing. One book that he read through in the study and in the orchard was my 1629 Sanchez de Matrimonio,[3] of which he explained, in bursts of laughter, all the hidden mysteries contained in that book. I read him my verses on *Don Juan*, which he compared with Blake's *Prophetical Books*. And a few translations also.

We had midnights: and how Bullen and I drank that brandy as he became more and more excited. We quarrelled like two fiends about Milton and M. Arnold. Nothing mattered: mood and mood, opinion and opinion. Yesterday a jaunt to Rye, lunch at the Mermaid (young Paine[4] took us in his wagonette). And we strolled in the streets and sat in the garden at the back, talking of Marlowe, Rowley,[5] and who knows how many other men and books. I lunch with him today, he leaves afterwards. Our food and our wine were better than what we had at Rye.

So I have written but a few verses and translations. The days fled. But how I waited for your letters!

A lovely one from Stella [Conder].

The day when he came was so cold that a fire had to be lighted, for the whole day.

Alors, je suis toujours votre aimant.

Arthur

Notes

1. Fritz Kreisler (1875–1962), Austrian violinist and composer, who became an American citizen in 1943, was currently giving recitals at Queen's Hall. See Symons's 'Kreisler: A Summing Up', *SR*, 104 (2 Nov. 1907) 539–40.
2. Arthur Henry Bullen (1857–1920), founder of the Shakespeare Head Press of Stratford-upon-Avon in 1904 and editor of Shakespeare's works in 1910, had – Symons writes – 'an imagination of a curious kind – one that came and went, as when the winds toss winter leaves. . . . His whole nature was in certain senses almost Elizabethan, so deeply it seemed to me rooted in that rich and abundant soil' (*Memoirs*, p. 122).
3. *Aphorismi Matrimonio* (Madrid, 1629) by Tomás Sánchez (1550–1610), Spanish Jesuit and author.
4. A neighbour of the Symonses.
5. William Rowley (1585?–1626), actor and dramatist, who collaborated with Thomas Middleton (1580–1627) on their best-known play, *The Changeling* (1621). See Symons's 'Middleton and Rowley' in *SED*.

127   To John Quinn
   (MS., Quinn)

c/o Miss Agnes Tobin
1 December 1911   Curzon Hotel

Dear Quinn

In September I was in Kent. At the end of October in Wales with John Sampson,[1] where I had a splendid holiday, seeing Mat the Gypsy, talking in Romani and learning more. In London now, but the address above is safer.

Thanks for Hearn's book.[2] It has brilliant things in it, touches of colour (why do the Americans spell such a word as this wrong?) and charm and something exotic, derived, I think, from Gautier and others. I don't deny him originality.

I am glad you bought that magnificent Puvis:[3] a treasure for you.

You write of John: he has vanished.

Max has written an amusing sort of novel,[4] but I find tragedy and comedy too mixed, sometimes absurdly.

I have by me a fragment of a letter of yours to Agnes Tobin; asking her to ask me if I had a manuscript, which I should be willing to sell to you. I have here the MSS. of my essay on Conrad (which extends to 80 pages, excessively revised and rewritten) which has a history. The typewritten copy was sent to the *Quarterly*, and returned by Prothero, with an insolent letter, also pencil marks on the pages. (I may add that Henry James was the one who coincided with Prothero.) I rubbed out the pencil marks, sent the thing to Conrad, who wrote me an enormous letter, entirely approving (with all his foreign grace and using such words as gratitude) what I had written, advising me to omit two references to two American novelists (one Mark Twain). This I did. Since then, nothing has happened to the essay. But, for the last year and more Conrad has been the one friend whom I wanted, whom I saw continually. He, of course, is anxious for the publishing of the thing (which I have since revised) in some American magazine.[5] This I am uncertain enough about.

As for the manuscript, it, if bought, would be in your hands, which would not prevent the printing of what is now finally revised.[6] This you must keep as a secret, as Conrad himself does not know how I have brought back the thing to what it should have been in the end of 1908.

The reason why I want you to send an answer c/o A.T. is that she and I could talk over the affair together (in case you have the least inclination in buying it) before I submit the question to my wife, who must decide in all such affairs as these. Myself, I do not think she would be averse to it, as, naturally, she is always in want of money: a delightful extravagance in one who (and I formerly!) has always been extravagant.

If necessary I could have Conrad's opinion about it: which I imagine would be unnecessary. For I know his pleasure in selling some of his MSS. to you.

As for my publishing a new book, there is one, begun in 1900, and now finished at last, which I certainly intend to see the light of day (or of the world, if you like) as soon as it becomes possible.[7]

Yours

Arthur Symons

Notes

1. Romany scholar and author (1862–1931), who, from 1892 to 1928, was Librarian of the University of Liverpool. In 1905, he edited Blake's works and in 1926 published *The Dialect of the Gypsies of Wales*.
2. Lafcadio Hearn (1850–1904), American writer, settled in Japan in 1890, taking citizenship in 1895 and establishing himself as a major Western interpreter in *Japan: An Attempt at Interpretation* (1904). Quinn had sent Symons a copy of *Leaves from the Diary of an Impressionist: Early Writings of Lafcadio Hearn* (New York, 1911).
3. Pierre Puvis de Chavannes (1824–98), French mural painter associated with the Symbolists. Quinn had just purchased his painting *The Beheading of John the Baptist* (1869), now in the Barber Institute of Fine Arts, Birmingham, England.
4. Max Beerbohm's *Zuleika Dobson; or an Oxford Love Story* (1911).
5. See Letter 104, n. 3.
6. On 9 Mar. 1912 Quinn responded favourably to Symons's offer and subsequently purchased the essay on Conrad for £35. The manuscript is now in the Rosenbach Museum and Library, Philadelphia.
7. The new book is probably *Knave of Hearts* (1913).

128 To Julia Marlowe
(MS., Museum, NY)

17 February 1912
(my month on the 28th)[1]   [Island Cottage]

Dear Julia

You wrote a lovely letter to Rhoda, which *I* am going to answer. And how we admire the two images of you: the actress for me, the woman for her. Splendid you must be as that cruel creature[2] (I first saw Irving, and met him only then after the performance, in *Macbeth*, with Ellen Terry). As I, he was Cornish, and he had that imagination which made him the greatest actor of his time. Ah! how far off is America, so no chance of seeing both of you in that magnificent drama. But surely when you come to England we *must* somehow meet – meet and talk! I am overflowing with ideas and how few can understand them. Certainly there is Conrad, the greatest novelist living, Polish, whom we have seen at intervals for two years or so; and he has been a great friend and even admirer of me and my work. I cannot tell you how much he is to me.

Julia Marlowe, forget not that Marlowe was born at Canterbury Feb. 26: 1564, two days (so long ago!) before me! And the best thing I have written lately is a long essay on him.[3]

I had a splendid holiday in North Wales with John Sampson and the Gypsies at the end of September. From youth I have had a passion for them. And twice have I seen *Carmen* a ballet with Bizet's music, and at the first rehearsal talked as well as I could in Spanish with several of the Spanish dancers. Maria la Bella is lovely and tragic.

How amused were we about Georgette![4] I fear also that Maeterlinck has failed since many years: even from the time when he read me some of *Monna Vanna*, and I said to myself: rhetoric!

As for a dog, no. The one we had was too wild to live longer than he did, and his death was one of our tragedies.[5]

But to end, in no such sad a strain, here are words from Conrad, which every artist, such as you, must feel, if one despairs at times: "Courage – courage – quand même!"[6]

And I am yours always

Arthur Symons

Notes

1. Symons's birthday.
2. Julia Marlowe and Edward Sothern opened a season of six Shakespearean plays (*Macbeth* was their greatest triumph) at the Broadway Theatre in New York on 3 July 1911.
3. See 'A Note on the Genius of Marlowe', *ER*, 36 (Apr. 1923) 306–16; rptd as 'The Genius of Marlowe' in *CR*.
4. Georgette Leblanc (1876–1941), French actress, singer, and author; the wife of Maurice Maeterlinck. In connection with her debut in Debussy's opera, *Pelléas and Mélisande*, based on her husband's play (Boston Opera House on 10 Jan. 1912), she gave several amusing interviews to the press. See Mary Carolyn Crawford, 'The Wife of Maeterlinck', *Theatre Magazine* (New York) 15 (1912) 86–7.
5. See Letter 108.
6. See Conrad's letter to Symons, dated 11 Dec. 1911, in G. Jean-Aubry, *Joseph Conrad: Life and Letters* (1927) vol. II, p. 137.

129 To Joseph Conrad
(MS., Yale)

13 May 1912   Island Cottage

Dear Conrad

I am enchanted to know that you are coming before long. Let the weather be as glorious as this. Don't any of you be surprised if my wife is not here on the day you fix. Just now she is in town. But be certain of my hospitality to welcome so long expected a friend. Do let me have a word or a wire – soon!

I have a reason for wanting to have a conversation with you about an important affair of mine:[1] in which you come in, and your advice also. If such a thing as I imagine shall come to pass, it will give me a most lucky chance of showing myself and my work to the world: to speak figuratively. And this is one reason why I am so anxious for your apparition here; not aureoled as St. Joseph.

One thing will please you – that I have been writing an essay on Flaubert, at intervals, since my return; and that it is intensely concentrated.[2] Scarce a note have I made, a few translations, as the superb dance of Salome;[3] and some of the wonderful aspects, passions, agonies and ecstasies in *Salammbô*:[4] that intoxicated vision of the mysterious East. Imagine, mon cher, that I have compressed [Flaubert's] *Bouvard et Pécuchet* into five or six pages, without a quotation.

I dined with [Augustus] John just before I left London: at midnight, *Carmen*, Café Royal, and (what I hope is a promise) that the August will venture his way down here chez moi, seul!

Yours always
Arthur Symons

Notes

1. A projected collected edition of Symons's works to be published by Constable but later abandoned because of copyright difficulties. See Beckson, pp. 276–7.
2. This was apparently never completed.
3. Symons wrote several poems on Salome after his breakdown. See 'Salome' in *Lesbia and Other Poems* (1920) and 'Studies in Strange Sins (After Beardsley's Designs)' in *Love's Cruelty* (1923). See, also, Letter 124.
4. Symons wrote the introduction to Flaubert's *Salammbô* in an edition published by Grant Richards in 1901; rptd in *SML*, 1919 edn, and in *FSC*.

130 To Rhoda Symons
(MS., Columbia)

1 June [1912]   Island Cottage

Ghost of Shakespeare still singing
Dearest Bird of the green Eyes

Conrad was caressingly kind. Voux avez l'air très bien, plus raffiné, plus jeune: et tout le reste. He was intensely absorbed in my *Collected Edition*:[1] listened to every detail; gave me some wise hints; and never have we had such a conversation, so natural, so simple, and for several hours. He was just the same, somewhat less nervous, but with all his vitality. He said a splendid thing: We overleap two centuries.

We had an Italian lunch and [Vin des] Grave[s] and several cups of coffee and cigarettes, and then tea. And then – imagine! – that long before then Peter was sent back with Weaver[2] and Conrad drove me back in the funniest little car I ever saw. He bought it or hired it for a year – awfully cheap. And his childish enjoyment at this new adventure was amusing. I am so prudent! Triomphe, Conrad? He stayed here for about a quarter of an hour and I showed him various things in the way of the books. He thought the idea wonderful.

When he comes over next with Jessie [Mrs Conrad] he will bring back my essay on him and give me his opinion.

And he told me two strange affairs of his. He got £40 for the Titanic, which he wrote in 48 hours.[3] Before then he had sold the MS of *The Outcast of the Islands* (of immense length, 800 pages or more) and for only £40.[4] I said: Well, the world is odd and fantastic enough.

A propos of the ring the stupid Emily[5] evidently opened the case, dropped the ring under the bed, and there left [it] in her idiocy.

Conrad is most curious to see [Augustus] John when he comes here.

Yes, an immense joy in getting away from the Gu-ts.[6]

So, all the news, all good news, certainly.

And your Arthur sends you his

Love

Notes

1. See Letter 129, n. 1.
2. Peter was a horse, and Weaver was the Symonses' servant.
3. Joseph Conrad, 'Some Reflections, Seamanlike and Otherwise, on the Loss of the *Titanic*', *ER*, 11 (1912) 304–15; rptd as 'Some Reflections on the Loss of the *Titanic*' in his *Notes on Life and Letters* (1921); and 'Some Aspects of the Admirable Inquiry', *ER*, 11 (1912) 581–95; rptd as 'Certain Aspects of the Admirable Inquiry into the Loss of the *Titanic*' in *Notes*.
4. Conrad's *An Outcast of the Islands* had been published in 1896.
5. The Symonses' maid.
6. Symons's jesting reference to Sigismund Goetze (1866–1939), a painter, and his wife, Constance, at whose home near Regent's Park Rhoda had been staying. His sister Violet had married Alfred Mond: see Letter 76, n. 5.

131 To Mabel Beardsley Wright
(MS., Princeton)

21 July 1912   Island Cottage

Dear Mabel

I hear that you are resting somewhere, so I send on this letter c/o Mr. E. Mond. And I hear that you are as exquisite as ever.

Don't forget the days of the *Savoy*! Nor do I forget when I first met you and Aubrey: July 30th 1895, at 7.30.[1] His letter is before me. What ages ago! And yet, one doesn't forget. Nor I, that I have been fond of you, as I never was of Aubrey: *à cause, à cause d'une femme*! But I want you to be rejoiced by hearing that next year an edition of my works will be printed by Constable, and that in one volume (*Figures of Several Centuries*) amidst Casanova, St. Augustine, Baudelaire, Rossetti, Emily Bronte, Pater, Villon, Meredith, Swinburne, etc., etc. will be the exact Beardsley book, taken from the treacherous hands of Dent, and so find its place at last. And that is one of many books (not yet to be known except to few) containing my four tragedies and enough MSS. and printed and unprinted material to make most of it copyrighted. Augustus John and Conrad have been told of it – both enchanted.

The last time I dined with John was when he came up from his manor especially to see me. Then *Carmen* (my 8th time, usually alone) then Café Royal, drinks, cigarettes, conversation until midnight turned us out. That was splendid.

I can't imagine why I never saw you when I was in London. I was most anxious, and got no chance.

I wonder if you saw Maria la Bella in *Carmen*? Simply lovely, and dramatic: was eight times enough for me? *Nunca! Jamais!*

I have just sent some verses of mine to Yvette [Guilbert] on Toulouse-Lautrec: a man of bizarre genius. She must have known him. I failed somehow. And, so like me, fou de la musique, I have sent for *la Valse des Roses* of Olivier Metra,[2] simply because I wrote in Paris in my 1892 verses you know

Olivier Metra's Waltz of Roses

for my enchantress, La Mélinite.[3] I can't get back the rhythm of that strange girl's dancing, but the swing of the music – and a night.

I send you my Casanova.[4] Keep it.

Croyez-mois chère et belle amie,

toujours votre
Arthur Symons

Notes

1. Symons had evidently forgotten that he had first met Beardsley in 1893, as revealed in a letter to Horne, postmarked 24 Aug. 1893: 'I saw Lane tonight, who brought Beardsley to the Crown [a public house]: the thinnest young man I ever saw, rather unpleasant and affected' (Ian Fletcher, 'Symons and Beardsley', *Times Literary Supplement*, 18 Aug. 1966, p. 743). In his *Aubrey Beardsley* (1898), Symons also errs in dating his first meeting with Beardsley – citing the year 1895.
2. Jules Louis Olivier Metra (1830–89), French composer of popular dance music, operettas, and ballet scores.
3. Symons first saw the dancer La Mélinite (the subject of his poem, 'La Mélinite: Moulin

Rouge', in *London Nights*) in May 1892, at Le Jardin de Paris: see 'Lautrec and the Moulin Rouge', *PN*, p. 4. She was born Jeanne Richepin (1868–1943) but took the name 'Jane Avril' when she began to dance at Le Jardin de Paris and the Moulin Rouge.
4. Probably his article 'Casanova at Dux', *NAR*, 175 (Sept. 1902) 329–46, in which Symons revealed his discovery of two missing chapters in Casanova's *Mémoires*.

132   To Rhoda Symons
(MS., Columbia)

[postmarked: 10 December 1912]

[Island Cottage]
[Wittersham]

Dearest: I am enchanted that you *will* come here on the 15th. You *do* need change, and here you will get rest. Why wait for the Florentines?[1] They may be here any time.

Conrad this morning came in looking splendid (as he said of me) – for more than an hour. He said that between the 15th and the end he would come here or take us back. Both were in joyous mood – so I played him twice over [one] of our favourite dances of Vezeli. He told me that he was alone in London for two years; and for that reason he went every night to the Empire or Alhambra, and that when any horrid thing came on, he went to [the] promenade and talked with the cocottes and gave them drink. Much like me!![2]

He read my War:[3] très bien, my cher.

Then I showed him a letter I had written in French for sending to Duse. He read it twice over, corrected only a few words, and said to me: It is an adorable letter. Now can you find her address in Florence? Might not Ellen Terry know it?

Now, I imagine how you behaved (jumped or not?) when the *Box*[4] came?

Last night was curious. I had a strange dream about Whitman – what he had done and written. I felt very miserable until I saw that Peter's head eagerly [?] against the window!

A book of verse of Yone Noguchi[5] from Japan, sending love to you.

Arthur

Notes

1. Presumably an allusion to an appointment between Rhoda and Lady Florence Alexander, wife of Sir George Alexander (1858–1918), actor and theatre manager; and Florence Beerbohm (1876–1951), actress and wife of Max Beerbohm. Earlier, Rhoda had written to Symons (MS., postmarked 4 Dec. 1912, Columbia): 'Tomorrow I lunch with Essie and Alfred Sutro at Garrick Club to meet *Max*, his wife – and the Alexanders!!!!'

Esther Sutro (d. 1934), artist and author, was the wife of Alfred Sutro (1863–1933), popular playwright and translator of Maeterlinck.
2. See Letter 53.
3. Possibly 'On War', later published in the *Nation* (New York), 106 (15 June 1918) 702, or the manuscript of 'A Proposal for the Utilisation of War', printed by Roger Lhombreaud in 'Documents and Detection', *News Letter of the British Council*, no. 6 (1953) 59–60.
4. Tickets for a performance of *Art and Opportunity* by Harold Chapin (1886–1915) at the Prince of Wales's Theatre (the play had opened on 5 Sep. and closed on 14 Dec.). Rhoda wished to see the actress Marie Tempest (1864–1942) in this production.
5. See Letter 95, n. 5.

133   To John Quinn
(MS., Quinn)

28 September 1913   Island Cottage

Dear Quinn

I got your cheque for £1 and cashed it in London. I was there for a week; saw my wife acting dramatically in *Joseph and his Brethren* at His Majesty's Theatre: the one real actress on the stage.[1] I took with me a Spanish woman Señora Mercedes, and talked some Spanish. Went one night to the Empire, found myself by the side of 3 Maoris from the Tahiti Islands, whom I knew by the paintings of Gauguin. Three girls, and the strangest animals I ever saw, talking in a melodious language. I kept my midnight (like Falstaff), dined someone at Kettner's; had many adventures; spent an awful lot of money. It was exactly the change I wanted, just as you your month in the woods. How glad I was to hear of that. To be on the sea or in the woods gives one more liberty than anything else.

My *Knave of Hearts* will soon be printed by Heinemann. Before sending you a copy, I send the rough proofs; for which I think you might give a fair price, considering the fact that you will see not only my corrections but many scribblings of Yeats, all utterly wrong. I was unaware that he had seen them, which made [me] rather angry. The thing ought to amuse you: a sort of revenge, on my part, against Yeats![2]

I received the MS. of the Pétrus Borel.[3] I have not yet had it typewritten. The woman who had done some for me doesn't understand French. I found one in the Strand where I intend to send the MS. But, as a matter of fact, money spent does not return. So perhaps, as I imagine that you intend to buy the MS., you might send me a cheque in advance of a few pounds. If so, I should like to be certain, if, in that case, whether I could send on the cheque to the bank in Lombard St.

and if they would send me the amount here. I have no bank and shall not be in London for quite a long time.

I had a letter from John, but he did not come up to see me when I was in town.

I spent most of yesterday at Conrad's. He was in splendid form, and found me the same. I don't think that either he nor I were ever so much our own selves. And I think both enjoyed it immensely.

Yours

Arthur Symons

Don't forget the Verlaine *Sagesse* in facsimile.[4]

Notes

1. *Joseph and His Brethren*, by Louis Parker, opened on 2 Sep. with Rhoda in the role of Serah. Huneker wrote to Quinn on 8 Dec. 1913: 'Rhoda Symons is in "Joseph and his Brethren" with Tree and Maxine Elliott (i.e. she is in the mob. Poor Arthur!)' (*Letters of James Gibbons Huneker*, ed. Josephine Huneker [New York, 1922] p. 164).
2. Invited, presumably, by the publisher to read proofs, Yeats made some obvious corrections in punctuation, which Symons accepted, but Symons rejected most of Yeats's suggested revisions of the verse. See Bruce Morris, 'Symons, Yeats, and the *Knave of Hearts*', *Notes and Queries*, 31, n.s., (Dec. 1984) 509–11. The corrected proof sheets with Symons's scratching out of Yeats's suggestions are in the Symons Papers, Princeton.
3. French poet, novelist, and short-story writer (1809–59), whose stories in *Champavert: Contes immoraux* (1833), Symons remarked, anticipated Huysmans's *A Rebours* (1884) in their depiction of Decadence. See Symons's 'Petrus Borel', *Forum*, 53 (June 1915) 763–75; rptd in *CSP*.
4. Symons had asked Quinn to reproduce *Sagesse* from the manuscript, writing on 10 Aug. 1913 (MS., Quinn): 'When Verlaine was with me in Fountain Court [1893] I lent him my own copy of that book for his conference.'

134   To Rhoda Symons
        (MS., Columbia)

[postmarked: 29 September 1913]   [Island Cottage]

Carissima mia

Si, son motto buono. Diceva Conrad: Voi siete perfettamente buono. Ho parlato a voi con molto laudato.[1] Thought as an actress you would go far. – I got there at 12.30. We sat under a shed. I showed him the proof:[2] immensely delighted by it. But perfectly furious against H[einemann] whom he imagined (as I) had not reserved the copyright in America. He said I can't live without my American sales. Mention this to H. and see which is right.

Conrad was more himself than ever: proud of his work, praising my art as aesthetic, exactly like the prose of Flaubert: What a compliment! He got excited over *The Secret Agent* [1907]; told me lots about it. As I said entirely ironical. He: I showed an utter contempt for those Nihilists. The murder and the rest made it. My quality, as a foreigner, is that of the art of narration, which distinguishes me from any other novelist. (Think of *Lord Jim*!) I write laboriously, go over my work. I write by images, which I have some trouble in putting into words. (Every poet also! but more by instinct.) Nor can I write without adventures.

And we were less nervous, on the whole, than usual. The lunch was spaghetti, venison with vegs. and a sweet. I had half a tumbler of Graves and of soda-water.

[Augustus] John said: *I* want to go and see the play! (Yours.)[3] John is just a little afraid of Conrad, but entirely devoted to him. At tea C. got depressed (nervous) wouldn't eat or drink. John with a subtle smile got off his stool, put the plate and the tea cup before him, then returned. No use. C. was all right when he saw me off. Au revoir et bon voyage!

He showed then his hatred against women in general. He said: I don't want praise from my wife nor any woman; with a great scowl. There, I can't just fathom him.

Certainly from 12.30 to 5.15 both equally enjoyed the visit. He showed me, naturally, many of his moods and sensations.

Methuen has printed and bound 15000 copies of his novel *Chance*, but it will appear in the spring.[4] I wonder how many copies of *my* verses H. will print![5]

Your p.c. gladdened me when I got back at 7 – especially about your throat. Quite wise in buying those books.

Here's a bizarre card! Perhaps you and Essie [Sutro] might venture there as an adventure.

Sarojini: "I am sorry to say that I am feeling very ill and stupid and I am just going off to the doctor – worse luck!"[6]

Conrad's nicknames for the 2 servants here: The Hag and the Nymph! As imaginative as true!

> Buono notte!
> Suo Arthur

Notes

1. Yes, I am very good. Conrad said: You were perfectly good. I spoke of you with high praise.
2. Symons's *Knave of Hearts* (1913).
3. See Letter 133, n. 1.
4. Actually, Conrad's *Chance* appeared later in 1913.

5. Heinemann printed 1250 copies of *Knave of Hearts*.
6. Sarojini Chattopâdhyây Naidu (1879–1949), Indian poet and later political leader, whose poem 'Eastern Dancers' Symons published in the *Savoy* (Sep. 1896) and to whose volume of verse, *The Golden Threshold* (1905) he had written the introduction. Mrs Naidu had arrived from India in June for an extended stay to undergo medical treatment, apparently on the Continent. See John M. Munro's 'The Poet and the Nightingale: Some Unpublished Letters from Sarojini Naidi to Arthur Symons', *Calcutta Review*, 1, n.s. (1970) 136–46.

135   To John Quinn
(MS., Quinn)

30 January 1914   Island Cottage

Dear Quinn

I was really glad to have your opinion on my *Knave*; best praise after Conrad's – whose *Chance* is his finest after *Lord Jim* – as I wrote to him. I got that wonderful *Sagesse*, which I prize greatly. Lady Gregory's book amused me – I liked her praise of you;[1] for the rest, what unabashed self-conceit on her part, and how shameless her showing up of Yeats!

Many thanks for the £20.[2] Quite [a] fair price, it seems to me. I shall cash it at the bank the last week in February. It will interest you to know that on February 28 I shall be 49. My father and mother (Mark Symons and Lydia Pascoe) both belonged to old Cornish families (with a strain of French blood also), and I was born at Milford Haven in Wales – oddly, nine miles along the coast from where Augustus John was born!

I saw Huneker for a few minutes when I was in London some months ago.

I have been in town for a holiday of a week – came back on the 19th. Dinner at Pinero's,[3] plays, Empire, etc. At Sarojini's I met Yone Noguchi who gave me a Japanese translation of my *Symbolist Movement* – jolly enough to be in Jap language!

But I found good luck in calling by chance on Dr. Hyslop,[4] the best doctor living, who had done something for me before – lately [?]. In a few minutes I told him exactly where my nerves were – on the right. He took (for the first time) my blood-pressure; found it abnormally high; reduced it some days after to more or less normal: then said to me: "I will cure you entirely! that is, gradually." I certainly believe in him. Question of time. Also he has given me some nerve-stuff to take 3 times a day. So I begin to feel just very slightly [?] relieved. He found me, of course, enormously well in regard to general health: just remains the damnable *question des nerfs*. And, as both my wife and Sarojini believe in this – perhaps final – cure, so do I.

I shall write to you again, early in March, after my return from London.

Yours

Arthur Symons

Notes

1. Writing in *Our Irish Theatre* (1913) of the arrest of the Irish Players in Philadelphia in 1911, when they presented Synge's *The Playboy of the Western World*, Lady Gregory says of Quinn, who gave legal assistance: 'The Company are in a state of fury, but they adore John Quinn and his name will pass into folk-lore' (p. 231).
2. Quinn had purchased the manuscript of Symons's essay 'Middleton and Rowley', which had appeared in *The Cambridge History of English Literature*, ed. A. W. Ward and A. R. Walter (Cambridge, 1910) vol. VI, 58–80; rptd in *SED*.
3. Arthur Wing Pinero (1855–1934), actor and playwright, noted for his well-made 'problem plays', such as *The Second Mrs Tanqueray* (1893). His popularity, however, declined with the emergence of the 'New Drama' of Ibsen and Shaw. He was knighted in 1909.
4. Theophilus B. Hyslop, M:D. (1864–1933), a specialist in psychiatry, was a teacher and author of books on art, genius, and insanity.

136 To Julia Marlowe

(MS., Museum, NY)

2 April 1914   Island Cottage

Dear Julia

Here I am in the study. Window open on this day when all the birds are singing in rapture: and why not I? One feels the spring in one's veins. Conrad was here yesterday – both complained of the dreary March. I have just come in from a walk, after playing Wagner on the piano: glorious his pieces!

Every month I go up to London: how many adventures I have had there, here and in Wales! I wander about the streets, the Strand, the Embankment, with the same old pleasure as before – as Lamb before me (who was born in the Temple, where I lived for ten years).

Whenever I shall have the extreme delight in seeing you again, dear Julia! You will find me absolutely different from what I was during that horrid – I won't say what! I have, of course, in every real sense recovered absolutely. It amazes me how that Risien Russell admitted to Sarojini [Naidu] – a little Indian Princess, an old flame of mine, who is now in London, whom I see here and there, that he had entirely misunderstood my case. So quite a change for me – against me whom my friends the gypsies call *drabingo* (prisoner!).

Rhoda and I long for you seeing both of you. But have you seen my *Knave of Hearts*, Heinemann published last November? I had so few copies to send, dear! It was dedicated to Rhoda – unprinted poems from 1891–1908, with translations from Verlaine, and from the Latin of Catullus. 163 pages, and copyrighted in America! So if not, do buy it on some bookstall – read it on the sea!

Till next we meet I am your fervent friend

Arthur Symons

137   To John Quinn
(MS., Quinn)

3 May 1914   Island Cottage

Dear Quinn

I have not [had] one single hour till now for answering your splendid letter and thanking you for the cheque which I cashed at your bank. But in my whole week in town I lived chiefly on what I call "Cassy's money."[1] But my one unspiritual adventure was on the 30th at the Café Royal at midnight when I saw perhaps the most extraordinary girl of her kind whom I had seen. I was drinking and smoking; she also. As she came past me I caught hold on her; down she sat beside me: Helen her name, a model for one thing, a gadfly for another. She was dressed in a barbaric fashion: small, nervous, black eyes and hair: and somehow knew my name. Later when she passed me again, I got up and said: "Helen of Troy, will you do me a favour? That is dine with me to-morrow night at the Cavour?" "Absolute!" said she. And the next night was more than absolute!

I am tremendously glad that you accepted my proposition in regard to a book on Conder.[2] It will take me a long time in doing it: it shall be done finally. For one thing I rather wonder if I shall have any chance in seeing the Baroness de Meyer[3] in London. Nor am I certain whether or not I should write to her.

As for the *Jargon*[4] there are only 12 ballads which I have translated, and I am not yet satisfied by them. They need much revision and thinking over before any question of typewriting. (The 500 pages were the *Jargon Dictionary*.) If I write an introduction it will be quite a small one.

The letter I had in Paris about Conder was from Augustus.

You will be glad to hear that my wife will be in Paris for a good long holiday, which she certainly needed. She will be seeing Rodin, Yvette and others – and finding again that fascination which one always has when one returns to Paris.

It will indeed be splendid if you can get me £20 from either American magazine.

I return to the Conder. One of his letters was written in 1905 after his return from Spain – it covers 2 pages. The 2nd – a quite long one – is dated 2 December 1905 – very original and full of his unique charm. Is it worth while having these 2 letters photographed or not? There is a man here who could do that job if need were. Give me your opinion.

One of Stella's (Ap. 29. 1907) I will copy for printing – on Conder's malady. From 2 others I shall quote a few lines – of much less importance, yet of some interest. – Also I shall quote several lines of Mabel Beardsley's "A New Watteau," in *The Rambler* of 1901, which have her peculiar fantastic quality.[5] Just possible I may be able to see her when next in London: she has been dying for years, yet still alive. In that case she will surely tell me a few anecdotes on Conder. I don't yet know if this will be feasible.

I find I have pencil notes on what Stella told me in 1907. I may also quote a few lines from [Jacques] Blanche's "Beardsley" in *Antée* of that year.[6]

Sarojini is that lady of eminent Indian birth whom I met as a girl 16 years ago.[7] ("Strange to think by the way," she was one of a few girls whom I made love to in different years who would have married me. But I was dead against those affairs.) She is adorable; we, so foreign, vagabond about, heedless of the observance of strangers. I saw her nearly every day in town. No question yet of the adventure in Cornwall. I hope to be again in town on May 30, that is if [Sir Herbert] Thompson has bought the tickets for *Boris Godonov* at the Royal Opera. He told me last Monday that we was almost certain of getting them.

So full is my life now, as it was many years ago, that I shall be in London June 13 for Pachmann's concert and to meet him comme d'autrefois.[8] Mais, hélas, as Verlaine wrote in his poem on me:

> . . . Ils ont raison, et nous aussi,
> Symons, d'aimer les vers et la musique
> Et tout l'art, et l'argent mélancolique
> D'être si vite envolé, vil souci![9]

You will be glad to hear that Heinemann entertains the idea of printing my *Tragedies* (not one word ever printed) I think in the autumn.[10] He will of course get dramatic rights and print the whole book in America. For years I have set my heart on having them acted. Now certainly there is a chance of it.[11] And, whenever this book is printed, you (who of course will have a copy) perhaps might aid me in relation to American actors or possibly – as you seem to know everyone – catch hold of that invaluable, perhaps uncaptuable, Frohman.[12] – I intend to send the typewritten plays to Heinemann, for him to read them at his leisure, soon after his return from Leipzig; then, when next in town, to discuss the affair with him – quite an old friend of mine. And I shall try to get an advance – something reasonable on the royalties. I have had nothing from *Knave of Hearts* (too early) but I imagine that he will be as decent as ever he was.

Just come on a small life of Roubiliac (from whom Conder was descended) – a French sculptor (born 1702)[13] in an old book *Nilvickers*[?], 1828. A few facts will come in well, as no one knows them.

As you sent me *The Independent* I shall send them in a few days a little essay on John Synge which I wrote lately.[14] I think they might print it. It is concentrated.

Ave atque Vale!

Yours
Arthur Symons

Notes

1. Payment for his article on a dancer at the Alhambra Theatre: see Letter 49, n. 1.
2. Symons wrote to Quinn on 7 Mar. 1914 (MS., Quinn) that he was thinking of writing a 'small book' to be entitled *Charles Conder: Notes and Impressions*. Of Conder, Symons wrote: 'I knew him from about 1893 till 1907. We spent 2 months together in Dieppe (in the same lodging-house) in 1895. We were almost inseparable; never a day went by but we were in the Casino, dining, bathing, gambling, (I admit to two women only!) – he painting, I writing, in his room and on the sand.' Symons never completed the book; possibly his memoir, 'Charles Conder' (in *Memoirs*), was a beginning.
3. Baroness Olga Alberta de Meyer (d. 1931), the wife of the Baron Adolf Edward de Meyer of Saxony (d. 1977), later a professional photographer, was a prominent figure in Edwardian society, to whose home in Cadogan Gardens came such figures as Somerset Maugham, Arthur Wing Pinero, and Charles Conder. See Robert Brandan (ed.), *De Meyer* (1977).
4. *Le Jargon et jobelin de François Villon*, ed. Lucien Schone (Paris, 1888).
5. The Conder article appeared on 24 Aug. 1901, pp. 1311–14.
6. Jacques Blanche, 'Aubrey Beardsley', *Antée*, 2 (1907) 1103–22.
7. Symons met her eighteen years before in 1896.
8. Vladimir de Pachmann (1848–1933), Russian pianist, was the inspiration for Symons's story 'Christian Trevalga' in *Spiritual Adventures*. Symons also wrote several articles on him, among which are 'Pachmann and Paderewski', *SR*, 106 (11 July 1908) 44–5; and 'Pachmann: Pianist', *VF*, 5 (Dec. 1915) 55. In an unpublished memoir, dated 29 September 1918, Symons described him 'as wonderful as ever. I never saw him so mad as he is now after a year's seclusion. He began in a most uneasy manner – then

seemed to say: "I won't play the piano": put his hands in his pockets and goes back into the artists' room. He returns – plays Mozart divinely – Chopin as he always did. In one word: absolute perfection of this man of an abnormal and inhuman genius' (MS., 'Vladimir de Pachmann', Princeton).

9. From 'Fountain Court', dedicated to Symons, in Paul Verlaine's *Dedicaces* (Paris, 1894).
10. Symons's *Tragedies* (containing *The Harvesters*, *The Death of Agrippina*, and *Cleopatra in Judaea*) appeared in 1916.
11. Of the plays in *Tragedies*, only *Cleopatra in Judaea* was produced. See Letter 101, n. 2.
12. Charles Frohman (1860–1915), American theatre manager and producer.
13. Louis François Roubillac (1702–62), French sculptor, who migrated to England around 1720, where he achieved fame. His busts of Hogarth, Colley Cibber, and Handel are in the National Portrait Gallery.
14. The essay on Synge did not appear in Symons's lifetime. See Karl Beckson, 'Arthur Symons on John Millington Synge: A Previously Unpublished Memoir', *Eire-Ireland*, 21 (Winter 1986) 77–80.

138   To James Joyce
      (MS., Cornell)

29 June 1914   Island Cottage

Dear Mr. Joyce

No, I have not forgotten you. I still have your verses here. I find a great deal to like in *Dubliners* – unequal as the short stories are – but original, Irish, a kind of French realism, of minute detail, sordid; single sentences tell: I like the kind of abrupt style in the book. "Counterparts" is quite fine – grim humour – a sense of Dublin as I saw it – a lurid glare over it. It gave me a sensation of Fountain Court and the pubs. But the best is the last:[1] the end imaginative.

I have been wandering for the last 3 years as usual. Last November Heinemann printed my *Knave of Hearts* – verse and translations.

By the way, not long ago an American magazine printed a MS. of mine called "Notes on the Sensations of a Lady of the Ballet"[2] – which I wrote in Fountain Court. So in return I send you a copy.

                                        Yours sincerely
                                        Arthur Symons

Notes

1. 'The Dead', which concludes James Joyce's *Dubliners* (1914).
2. See Letter 49, n. 1.

139   To John Quinn
     (MS., Quinn)

10 August 1915   Island Cottage

Dear Quinn

I had fairly forgotten your aspect – when suddenly sprang before me your very image – John's splendid drawing. I see as ever I did the penetrating eyes, firm mouth, and strong chin. And – as I write – you stare at me in the old fashion. So that I keep.

The *North American* prints my final Verlaine this September.[1] And they ask me to send them some more of my MSS. "We beg you to remember that we shall always be happy to have the privilege of considering whatever article you may produce." That word – production – this aiming [?] to make new experiments in prose: to make a study of one's sensations (after – dare one say? – Lamb!). But I shall probably send them first an essay (made out of my notes) "The Giorgiones in Italy"; which, as Italy is fighting gloriously in the war, they are likely to accept.[2]

I imagine you will see in the September *Vanity Fair* my perverse prose on Yvette Guilbert.[3]

A woman – one of "my women" (as John says) has given me the 1st edition of Pater's *Studies in the History of the Renaissance* – with its wonderful ribbed pages – so unusual to one's touch: to me perhaps the rarest book of prose ever written.

I have an etching of Félicien Rops that he gave me in Brussels in 1896 – I was with Dowson. Huysmans praises it in his *Certains* [1904]. It is eight and a half inches broad – ten and a half high. It is quite indecent. A prostitute of the Parisian kind stands half-naked – with the usual black stockings gartered at the knees – showing her sex; in an amazing attitude of self-admiration before her mirror. Behind the glass is an infamous monkey holding in its hands its Priapus. The whole thing is prodigiously fine.

August 24

Dear friend, yours is a wonderful letter and the £35 quite a windfall for me. It is more than "fair!"

I shall answer all your questions later – in detail. I have to think over these affairs carefully. One thing: my wife has just said to me: "You have improved enormously during this year!" That is quite certain.

                                                 Yours
                                                 Arthur Symons

I have written a story – tragic, passionate, sensational – one whole midnight in Paris – "The Sinister Guest" – 25 pages. The characters – in the Opera and the Café Anglais – are myself, Toulouse-Lautrec, Cléo de Merode, Lola de Valanée, Faavelte Pranzol (one of my actual mistresses in Paris!) and Fortunio-type of abnormal depravity.[4] That I shall fire off across the Atlantic perhaps to *Lippincott's*.[5]

Notes

1. Arthur Symons, 'Some Unpublished Letters of Verlaine', *NAR*, 202 (Nov. 1915) 748–56.
2. Published in *LQR*, 135 (Jan. 1921) 31–9.
3. Symons, 'Yvette Guilbert', *VF*, 5 (Dec. 1915) 55.
4. Fortunio, the eponymous hero of Gautier's novel, first serialised as *L'Eldorado* (1837); in book form: *Fortunio* (1838).
5. Symons's 'The Sinister Guest' appeared in *ER*, 29 (Aug. 1919) 105–19.

140   To John Quinn
       (MS., Quinn)

2 December 1915   Island Cottage

Dear Quinn

Here is the man's letter. I can't for a moment imagine that even you would care to give such a price for the invaluable MS. of Baudelaire as 7.000 francs. If by any chance you do so – let me have it sent to me here for me to examine before I send it to you in America from London.

So – as my friends give me certain gifts for the New Year (yours will be my *Figures*[1] – as soon as they are out) you might do me the immense favour in buying from the man in Paris some Balzacs, and Stendhal etc. I give a list of a few that I most desire to possess.

The Boston *Transcript* has printed some of my Fountain Court prose – Nov. 13.[2] I suppose they pay for such MS. No cheque yet but the paper. The Balzacs I bought from Jaske[?] varied from 10/- to 5/-.

Dec. 9

I have just returned from the Savoy – after one week. I wrote to ask John to dine with me – not a word! I wrote to a certain woman I had not seen for years – not a word! I had two amazing adventures. 1. Pachmann who (for an hour in his room) uttered Rabelaisian words – of an unspeakable nature. 2. I made love to a young Spanish dancing-girl – *una bailarina española de Sevilla* – as lovely as sin and with the whitest flesh I have ever seen in any girl.

I won't let you know what the *Gitana* said to me and I to her – as we spoke in Spanish and French. Now for Vladimir. We sat in a corner alone. He: *I love Fucking!* with an immense chuckle. I: Yes, I also. *Mais fornication simple et extraordinaire!* Whereupon he actually hugged [me] in his arms, rubbed his cheek on mine – with bursts of Rabelaisian laughter. I veritably imagine his desire was – for *me* – to sleep with him that night! (I might – I might not, as John might have said on such an occasion!)

Before then he said I was mad – he was mad – assez – pas beaucoup – as he wrote down some notes of music. And this man of genius said: You are a great poet – after Dante! (I might have blushed at such a compliment.)

To jump from this Rhoda said to me at the Savoy that she had taken the flat she wanted so much and for a fairly long lease. Good for her nerves to have a home in London: with this and that for change.

Dec. 14

For several days I have been laid up with an atrocious cold – caught in London. The weather is awful! Impossible to amuse oneself anywhere. Still I have bought an original letter of Villiers – a beauty – and a jolly one of Jenny Colon – the actress that Nerval was in love with.[3] It begins: Mon Dieu, Monsieur!

Thanks for the *Atlantics*!

As I have had no word from Paris in regard to Descaves'[4] collection I send you this list of a few *rare* books that I am sure it would "amuse you" to buy for me. As of course you will write to Descaves – that makes the books cheaper – *francs* = shillings; that is, for him to send them to me here. – That will be one of your real acts of friendship to me.

Have you done anything more in regard to my *Cities*?[5] the new one?

As this letter is probably the last I shall write you this year I wish you every possible kind of Good Luck! So wish the same to your friend

Arthur Symons

I want to get rid of a certain nightmare. That is *Superwomen: A Farce*. So I send you the whole MS. and the typed copy. It is – of course – a thing never to be printed – never to be acted. Yet it has a value of its own: a satirical quality – paradoxes – a farcical action – amusing dialogues – hits at various living people.[6]

So it is for you to assign to it whatever price you think to be fair. The question is for you to read it – then make up your mind as to its pecuniary value.

Notes

1. Arthur Symons, *Figures of Several Centuries* (1916).
2. 'Arthur Symons' Juvenile Verses', *Boston Evening Transcript*, 13 Nov. 1915, Pt 3, p. 9; rptd as 'Notes on My Poems', *Athenaeum*, Mar. 1916, pp. 111–12.
3. Gerard de Nerval (1808–55), French writer, about whom Symons had written in *The Symbolist Movement in Literature*, and whose mental breakdown he compared to his own (see *Confessions: A Study in Pathology*, pp. 2–3). The letter by Jenny Colon to which Symons refers, is addressed to a theatrical impresario, and is presently in the Lohf Collection.
4. Lucien Descaves (1861–1949), French playwright.
5. Symons had apparently asked Quinn to help him find an American publisher for his manuscript of *Cities and Sea-Coasts and Islands*. Brentano's published it in 1919.
6. The unpublished manuscript, dated 25 Mar. 1908, is now in the Humanities Research Center, University of Texas, Austin. Two of the 'various living people' that the play 'hits at' are Yeats and Augustus John. For a discussion of the play and its background, see Beckson, pp. 250–1 and 370, n. 4.

141 To John Quinn
(MS., Quinn)

29 December 1915   Island Cottage

Dear Quinn

With this book I send you the enclosed note that Rhoda wrote at my request.[1] It gives her definite idea of my case: which we both think was more or less misunderstood by these doctors.

Our idea is this: that you, my dear friend, are certain to know if there are any great specialists in regard to the nerves – to this particular case of mine – in America – that ever come – for some important reason – to England. If so – there is one rich woman in London[2] who would probably pay some – or most – of the "Fee" that is usually fabulous. My wife would also pay a reasonable amount of money: that is, if such a man as you know will ever cross the Atlantic so as to give me – at least – one more chance of being – in a sense "cured".

As my last chance does depend simply on this – I leave this entirely in your own hands to do whatever you can for me: that is to say, in recovering over again *just*[3] what does not remain to me of my old self.

Yours ever
Arthur Symons

Notes

1. Rhoda's note is as follows: 'Seven years and 3 months ago Mr. Arthur Symons had a mental breakdown – the best specialists in London – Drs. Risien Russell – Savage –

Hyslop etc – diagnosed it as a case of galloping "general paralysis" – for one year he was completely out of his mind – since that time he has recovered to a very great extent – though not altogether – still childish – without any reasoning power – and complains of nervous twitchings in various parts of the body – A certain wastage is to be noticed – there is slight paralysis of the speech, and the handwriting is noticeably affected – but he walks well –'. George Henry Savage, M.D. (1842–1921), prolific author and editor of *Journal of Mental Science.*

2. Probably Mrs Ludwig Mond: see Letter 120, n. 6.

3. Symons underlined this word twice.

142   To John Quinn
   (MS., Quinn)

4 August 1916   Island Cottage

Dear Quinn

Arthur Brentano sent me the two new agreements on the 2nd from Paris. A friend motored me to Conrad's on the 3rd. I spent most of the day with him; he signed the Agreement next to my name; this I sent yesterday with a letter of mine to Brentano in Paris. He thinks *Tristan* will have a success. He also means to dispose of an edition in sheets in London.[1]

Conrad was enchanted with the *Toy Cart*: he thought it might be turned into a libretto for music. I fear there is now no musician anywhere who would attempt this.

His adventure in Poland took him more than an hour to relate; incredible – amazing – terrible.[2] One: "There were 25,000 stinking Jews on the stairs up which I went to have my passport vised. I had to wait 5 hours in the corridor – thought I would never get in nor out. Finally I enter. The man flings up his hands and says: 'I can't! I can't!' " In Vienna he just escaped being arrested; "had I been (said he) I shouldn't have been here." Back at home he's ill for 3 months – [phrase illegible]. I never saw him in better spirits than on that afternoon.

So he found me: his friend and yours.

Arthur Symons

Notes

1. Arthur Brentano (1858–1944), American publisher and bookseller, issued Symons's *Tristan and Iseult* (New York, 1917); Heinemann issued it in England in the same year.
2. Conrad had gone to Poland in July 1914, after an absence of nearly twenty years. Shortly thereafter, the First World War broke out. While Polish friends were attempting to exert influence with Austrian authorities on his behalf (war between Austria and England not yet having been declared), Conrad and his family went to Zakopane,

Austria, a four-hour journey from Cracow. The American Ambassador in Vienna, Frederick C. Penfield, secured exit visas, and Conrad left Austria for Milan. See Frederick R. Karl, *Joseph Conrad: The Three Lives* (New York, 1979), pp. 761–2.

143 To John Quinn
   (MS., Quinn)

                                                              Ritz Hotel
21 June 1918   Piccadilly

Dear Quinn

I write to you after a gorgeous dinner here. Just seen John – who dines with me on Tuesday night. I had an hour's conversation with him in his house in Chelsea – a fine little Dutch house he designed. I saw on one wall an oil painting of his – and said to him – the ripest [?] and deepest in colour of any of his paintings with a kind of richness [?] and archaism [?]. The moment he saw me [he] said: "You look fine!" So did he. I look forward enormously for [*sic*] our dinner.

Yesterday I went to Pachmann's concert – the whole house packed full. He was more wonderful than ever. I went round – he embraced me on the throat! Said, "Kiss me!" I didn't! He was certainly possessed with the sense of his own genius. Then I went for the first time [with] Ysaÿe[1] – who said to me he had never heard Pachmann play before. "He is a Poet – an Interpreter – he is unique!" cried he. So he certainly is.

I lunched with Bullen on Wednesday – quite amusing as an adventure.

I shall send to [you] insured by sea my translations.

I have had a nice letter from the Editor of *Vanity Fair*[2] – I used you before in sending him some prose I wrote in Venice in 1894. He prints it[3] and will send me eight guineas and wants me to send him a list of "a dozen possible articles – in that way we can manage always to have something by Arthur Symons in our magazine." The words delighted me. Do you know him? I sent him two I had done – with hints for more – such as "Night in the Savoy," "Notes on Music Halls," etc.

Curiously quiet here – so few people.

My wife sent you my D'Annunzio article.[4] I send the scrawled MS. with this – as my first journalism for years.

John and I talked of the Romani *Lubait* harlots – he gave me an amusing story of his adventure with one at Marseilles. She was too corrupt even for him!

John never turned up – the only time he has ever failed in an assignation with me.

I return to the cottage tomorrow the 22nd.

I have had many adventures – certainly. I must surely send off those translations. It is midnight!

Bien à vous
Arthur Symons

Notes

1. Eugène Ysaÿe (1858–1931), Belgian violinist and composer whom Symons first heard in 1899, when he wrote to Rhoda: 'He played a Bach and a Mozart concerto. He was simply marvellous – different from anyone I had ever heard, with a tone like gold and like steel at once. He stood there, calmly possessed by the devil, looking about him with a vague and wondering glance which saw nothing, a grotesque, impossible figure [he was over six foot four], with his vast white face and one long lock of black hair dangling into one eye, really as if he was not even conscious that he was playing – and what playing it was!' (MS., postmarked 30 May 1899, Columbia). See Symons's 'Ysaÿe' in *PAM* (1928 edn).
2. Frank Crowninshield (1872–1947), editor, *Vanity Fair*, 1914–36.
3. Arthur Symons, 'On the Genius of Degas', *VF*, 10 (May 1918) 60, 90–4; rptd in *FTTR*.
4. Arthur Symons, 'Gabriele d'Annunzio', *Land and Water*, 70 (30 Aug. 1917) 14–17.

144   To John Quinn
(MS., Quinn)

10 December 1918   13, Queen's Gardens, W.

Dear Quinn

Many thanks for your voluminous letter and the clear memorandum of your account with me.

As for my wife the operation was a most complicated one;[1] for three days they thought she would never survive; thanks to her wonderful constitution and the great care they had of her in the hospital she is very slowly but certainly recovering: that is, from the date of the operation, October 24th, till now – more than seven weeks. How she endures this interminable length of time she knows no more than I do. It is a question of patience – and she was ever restless and nervously active – as I always have been – I of course much more so. There is no chance of her leaving before the end of January – if even then. On account of the pain in one of her legs – the result of the operation – she can only just move a little in her bed. In regard to food she has been kept alive by the wonderful attention of her older sister. In regard to nursing she has been kept alive by Nurse Brennen – Irish – a Godsend to her – who feeds her at intervals every night. As I have promised to pay for whatever she has to be paid – that is as long as Rhoda is in hospital – I fear the amount will be immense; yet nothing in the world gives me – as it gives her – more satisfaction than the fact that I shall certainly be able to pay whatever I have to pay to Brennen.

As for me, as the result of a bad cold, I began spitting up blood the week before last; so my famous doctor[2] examined me thoroughly: declared me "Clear as a bell; perfectly all right, except that by coughing I had made my throat raw." So he gave me a mixture which has stopped the blood-spitting and almost the remains of my cold. You can imagine my intense relief – after such nervous terrors as have always beset me. In fact he said I was living the life I ought to lead now – going out and seeing people and ballets and dining out and getting as much amusement as I can under these conditions.

You do amuse me about Lydia [Lopokova]: quite true as I have lately found out myself that "baby stare" is – far from being innocent! She is no more wicked than the generality of Russian women. (She calls her canary "The Pimp!") I taxi both of them to the hospital this Thursday.

If you – that is I – mention Baudelaire to Diaghileff,[3] he always answers: "C'est un Monsieur!" "Qu'elles crèvent!" I have heard him say of these Russian dancers. So you see I'm learning a lot about Life.

I want to ask you one thing. As Rhoda will still be in hospital on *January the 19th* which is her birthday and our marriage-day that you would cable her some comforting message: coming from you it will give her a thrill of pleasure.

I shall finish this letter to-morrow – as I shall write later as to the MSS. I still have here. Your prices are *certainly*[4] most reasonable; so send them as you intend to. With Rhoda's advice I sent a cable to Belasco[5] last Friday in regard to *The Toy Cart* – which he is certain to answer.

I never see John at all – I don't know for what reasons. In any case I have all but finished my one act tragedy: *Cesare Borgia*.[6] It is tremendously alive and essentially dramatic.

Yours always
Arthur Symons

P.S. I enclose these to show how vilely and stupidly I and my book have been attacked – more spite.[7]

I shall write to Maunsel and ask if he has found a publisher in America;[8] if not perhaps you might easily find one for me; of course neither Brentano nor Dutton. I find in his letter 22 August he says he intends to "submit *The Toy Cart* to a publisher who issued Synge by arrangement with us." You ought to know who he is.[9] I have written him a note in regard to these questions.

Conrad writes: "I saw that nasty and stupid article which a man like you may disregard. That vol. is full of charm and contains many pages of rare distinction and luminous like pearls, which – as we know on high authority – are not appreciated by swine. Let them grunt!'' That's the great man who writes to me from his heart.

Vera Donnet,[10] who has taken the Haymarket Theatre for two years says she will produce my *Cleopatra* on my next birthday: February 28th.[11]

Notes

1. Rhoda Symons, who had been operated on for an unspecified growth, was hospitalised until 4 Mar. 1919.
2. Dr Theophilus Hyslop: see Letter 135, n. 4.
3. Sergei Pavlovich Diaghilev (1872–1929), Russian ballet impresario, who, in 1909, founded the Diaghilev Ballet Russe in Paris.
4. Symons underlined this word twice.
5. David Belasco (1859–1931), American playwright and theatre manager, who declined Symons's offer of *The Toy Cart*.
6. Later published with Symons's other plays, *Iseult of Brittany* and *The Toy Cart*, in 1920 by Brentano.
7. Possibly including the review of *Colour Studies in Paris* in *SR*, 126 (1918) 1110–11, which begins: 'This is a collection of essays dating in some cases from the last century, and all obviously anterior to the cataclysm which for a time has rendered impossible the attitude of artistic – and slightly inhuman – detachment by which they are characterized.'
8. Maunsel published *The Toy Cart* simultaneously in Dublin and London in 1919; it was not published in the United States.
9. John W. Luce & Co., Boston.
10. Russian-born director and theatre manager.
11. There is no record of a production of *Cleopatra in Judaea* in 1919.

145   To John Quinn
(MS., Quinn)

[late September 1919]   Oxford

Dear Quinn

I have spent a week here – an absolute enchantment – these marvellous gardens, the ancient colleges: I saw Brasenose where Pater lived, right on the Bodleian. I spent yesterday with Robin de la Condamine;[1] spent several hours with Robert Bridges in his house and on a bench under the sun – where I write now – Worcester Gardens. A wild Arab boy has taken me over Oxford – we boated down the river.

Rhoda triumphed as the villainous Eliska in the Drury Lane melodrama – she acted in a perversely imaginative way and looked as lovely as wicked.[2] She is in every act, so she has hired a car to take her there and back – simply invaluable as the part is a heavy one. I often go in with her and back at nights.

Ask Dutton in my name to send you *Studies in the Elizabethan Drama,* as it is not yet published here: a book I have always wanted to see in print.

Chaundry & Son, 104 High Street, Oxford, showed me all Wilde's first editions, with signed old letters of his to Smithers and some dedicated to Mrs. Brown-Potter.[3] To me these [have] no value.

Yours

Arthur Symons

Hydera [?][4] tells me buggery is notorious in Keble College and that there used to be Dons with painted faces that had midnight abominations in dimly lit rooms draped in black. I have come on several bawdy-houses on nights when I wander in the streets. It is in the air.

Notes

1. Spanish actor (1878–1966) who used the name 'Robert Farquharson' on the English stage. In an unpublished essay entitled 'The Question of *The Dead City'*, an account of a production of d'Annunzio's play in Symons's translation presented by the Stage Society at the Court Theatre on 24 and 25 Feb. 1918, Symons writes that Farquharson's performance showed 'a kind of rare and wandering genius, sinister, sombre, perverse and passionate' (MS., Princeton).
2. Rhoda appeared in *The Great Day,* by Louis Parker and George R. Sims, which opened on 12 Sep. 1919 and ran for ninety-eight performances. (The heroine was played by Sybil Thordike.) On 13 Sep. the *Daily Sketch* reported: 'Miss Rhoda Symons is very much to be complimented on her humorous, as well as intense, adventuress'.
3. Mrs Cora Brown-Potter (1859–1936), American actress, later theatre manager, took an option on Wilde's scenario for a play (which he had planned to write with Frank Harris, who later used the scenario to write *Mr. and Mrs. Daventry*). See *The Letters of Oscar Wilde*, ed. Rupert Hart-Davis (1962) p. 830.
4. Unidentified.

146   To Arthur Symons
    (MS., Reading)

9 April 1920   121, Ebury Street

My dear Symons

I have just read the letter you wrote to Mr. Werner Laurie,[1] saying that you could not write a book about me for him. Of course, if a book were written about me, I would prefer that you were the writer rather than anybody else, but my present concern is not with the book, but our personal relations. I have often wished to ask you to come here to dinner and spend an evening with me talking over old times, but have not done so for one reason or another; and I have often felt angry with myself for my negligence and seeming heartlessness to an old friend. And once more I buried myself in my writings and forgot everything else, sometimes for weeks, sometimes for months. I neglect everything for these writings, all my friends; I have only got to live a little longer not to have one left in the world. I hope that when you return to town you will come to see me. You will find me just as glad to see you as I used to be when we both lived in the Temple.[2]

Sincerely yours,
George Moore

Notes

1. Thomas Werner Laurie (1866–1944), the publisher, who, having been the manager of the T. Fisher Unwin publishing company, established his own publishing firm in 1904, when he became a principal publisher of George Moore's works.
2. On 4 July 1920, Moore, responding to a letter sent by Symons, said that he could not invite him to dinner because of difficulties with his domestic help and recalled his past clashes with Symons over literary matters: 'I hope that when we do meet our literary opinions will not conflict too violently. I remember your saying to me – You dislike Hardy for certain things and I like him in spite of those things. I have been looking into his writings lately and his stories seem to me to be the squalid imaginings of a village schoolmaster who has seen a few melodramas at Drury Lane' (MS., State University of New York, Buffalo).

147   To John Quinn
    (MS., Quinn)

13 January 1921   13(3), Queen's Gardens

Dear Quinn

I can imagine your relief after that chimera disappeared.[1] This I heard last night at the Café Royal where I sat in the midst of 12 people – Anita for one.[2] To-day there is chance for Rhoda to act in some plays in the Garrick Theatre.[3] Lizzie had told me my fortune in which I get mixed with a dark man: *question d'argent*. This manager thinks of producing *The Toy-Cart* with Rhoda as Vasantasene. I hear from Gwen and imagine she will send you some of her paintings.[4] I hope our *Baudelaire* may have a big sale.[5] You will be as delighted as we are with the hand-made copies. Only – as I confess to you most things – I start this year with only £219.19.0 in my bank.[6] One of the reasons is the huge amount of money I spent in Paris.[7] That was well spent – as I never enjoyed such a holiday as we had. The next visit depends on how much money I can go on making. It is exasperating to have one's MS. returned from many magazines. Still, as I believe as I always did in my own work, better times and better chances may come.

Don't be alarmed with my passing attack of sciatica. I am as always a vigorous walker; am on the whole not in the least troubled with indigestion; I am moderate in regard to food and wine; and am either wandering, or having siestas, or meeting exotic people, or writing or translating. Also, I generally have good nights. Yet, as I don't write (as Conrad for one has to) pot-boilers, and am even now not anything like as popular as I ought to be, – having been always, I am aware, difficult to deal with – the question as to how to earn my living grows more and more ominous. I am neither lamenting nor complaining – though I have too many reasons for having to do so – often enough – but am stating simple facts. Ezra Pound – who was here – told me *The Dial* can print nothing of mine for half of this year.[8] I send MS. to various papers here – all sent back; and the stuff they print is to me unreadable: verse that is no more verse than the line I am writing.

Mathews has sent you some more of my MS. Later I want to send you – besides the seven MS. I sent – as many original MS. as I have of the *Lesbia*.

I have been invited to dine next week with the manager of *Scribner's*. Perhaps he may consider the question of using some of my prose in his magazine or some new book of mine.

L'Intersigne I translated from Villiers de l'Isle-Adam.[9]

As I wished you a very satisfactory New Year which you also wish me – why should not this year prove satisfactory?

Very sincerely yours
Arthur Symons

After going to Paris again, this spring, I may be able to finish my book on Toulouse-Lautrec.[10]

Notes

1. Who or what the 'chimera' was remains unknown.
2. A casual acquaintance at the Café Royal.
3. Nothing came of this.
4. Gwen John (1876–1939), painter, who, like her brother Augustus, studied at the Slade School of Fine Art, London, 1895–8. In 1903, she went to France, where, during her residence of more than thirty years, she became one of Rodin's models and lovers. On 27 Dec. 1919 (carbon copy of typewritten letter, Quinn), Quinn wrote to Symons: 'I am a great admirer of her work and I agree with you that she has genius. In fact I think she is a greater artist than John. John is entirely too facile.' For Gwen John's

relationship with the Symonses, see Susan Chitty, *Gwen John: 1875–1939* (1981) *passim*.
5. Symons's *Charles Baudelaire: A Study* (1920).
6. Symons's financial difficulties were beginning to have an effect on Quinn, who wrote to Ezra Pound in late January 1921: 'I have Symons on my back with his recklessly extravagant wife. . . . His wife must have an apartment in London. She must have a motor car. She must go to Paris with him. And I am supposed to pay the bills. Well, I won't' (quoted in B. L. Reid, *The Man from New York: John Quinn and His Friends* (New York, 1968) p. 480).
7. Symons had spent May and June of 1920 in Paris.
8. Pound was an 'agent' and correspondent for the *Dial* (Chicago) between 1920 and 1923. See Nicholas Joost, *Scofield Thayer and The Dial: An Illustrated History* (Carbondale, Ill., 1964) pp. 166–70.
9. First published in *La Revue des lettres et des arts* (Paris) Dec. 1867; rptd in *Contes cruels* (Paris, 1883).
10. The book was never completed.

148   To John Quinn
(MS., Quinn)

7 September 1921   Island Cottage

Dear Quinn

I was almost annihilated by the refusal of Doubleday to publish my *Notes and Impressions*;[1] worse, yesterday, when Brentano returned to me the whole MS. of my *Wanderings* he had kept for two years;[2] and that, after cabling one year ago: "Publishing *Cesare Borgia*[3] now *Wanderings* later. Brentano's." Besides this, in their letter of August 28, they practically stated their intention of never publishing any more of my books. This seems to me infamous: considering the fact – not only of my name – but that I find it more and more impossible to earn enough money to keep me alive. What with no more royalties, and few chances of printing my prose in English magazines, with certainly much more chances[4] in American magazines such as *Vanity Fair*, the expenses we have to incur terrify me as they did Baudelaire. In fact, it seems to me most uncertain if any American publisher will print *Notes and Impressions*. I have heard nothing so far in regard to that book. I wrote Conrad yesterday in regard to these questions. He, who has made a colossal fortune: I, who never had any private income, who never made any kind of fortune! You wrote: "You ought to protect yourself." I only wish I could. How can I with so many enemies at my gates? Everything exasperates me. I have had bad luck ever since I returned from Paris. In spite of letter after letter I cannot induce Dutton to send me £40 for *Baudelaire* and £50 for my Villiers versions – in spite of his written statements to this effect. Rhoda has seen a nerve specialist in London who warns her to avoid all worry – so difficult for her to avoid and to avoid any nervous crisis. I hate the thought of returning to London and the winter that ensues.

To add to these tragedies, Iseult,[5] that beautiful girl, tells me to-day that her daughter Dolores (who was my godchild) died in June in the excessive heat. She is heart-broken.

Yours ever
Arthur Symons

Notes

1. This consisted of previously published essays, 'a big book that begins with Swinburne and da Vinci and ends with Paul Verlaine' (Symons to Quinn, 14 Apr. 1921, MS., Quinn). Conrad had suggested that it be sent to Doubleday.
2. Symons's *Wanderings* (1931) was never published in the United States.
3. See Letter 144 and n. 6.
4. Apparently, Symons meant to write 'not many more chances'.
5. Iseult Gonne (1894–1953), the illegitimate daughter of Maud Gonne (1864–1953), Irish actress, journalist, and ardent supporter of revolutionary causes in Ireland, whom Yeats loved and made the subject of many poems. In 1920, Iseult, whom Symons described to Quinn as 'strangely exotic' (MS., 13 Oct. 1918, Quinn), married the Irish novelist Francis Stuart, after refusing an earlier proposal from Yeats.

149   To John Quinn
   (MS., Quinn)

13 October 1921   13(3) Queen's Gardens

Dear Quinn

I am delighted to hear about your adventures in Paris. As for me, for the first time in my life, poverty stares me in the face. This is partly the result of the £80.0.0 I spent in Paris and other expenses. My bank account is reduced to almost zero. There are other tragedies in store for me. I cannot live without distraction: what distractions can I look forward to now? Indeed how can I pay for a dinner in the Café Royal? What with my intolerable vitality which gives me little in the way of rest, and the impossibility of staying indoors for one whole day, I dread this winter more than ever. I am over 56. I am aware that I am incurable. I am rarely invited out; in fact I have only three or four *real* friends in London. These – such as John – I rarely meet. I have always to endure a throbbing in the right foot and a tingling as if pricked by needle-points. I am tolerated because I have a name. Rhoda who cannot exist without acting has had no engagement this year. I wrote to Barrie – this is his mean answer.[1] He has a *platonic* passion for young girls:[2] he won't even lift a finger to help either of us in our precarious position. To have to endure such humiliations, to have to endure poverty and the results of poverty – as for no fault of mine I have to do – is almost enough to drive one mad: not that I imagine this for a moment.

Instead of taking taxis as I used to, I shall have to go by train into town, which always exhausts me: there's no question of buying any more books. The whole summer – tropical in regard to heat – has caused us nothing but disturbances. The street-noises are worse than ever.[3] In any case, in this Hell of a city one must go on existing. I never felt so lonely as I do now; always some nervous pain – that varies. The chief question to us now is: is it possible for us to get through this winter without some kind of ruination? Up to now I have been only too glad to use as much money as I could in household expenses; the question is, again: in what manner can I contrive to make money – enough, that is, to keep myself going. This is worse than an Incubus. I have sent many MS. to American magazines, several of which have been accepted. I want you to see mine on "Dancing" in *The Forum*.[4] For that I shall get £20. I send you separately something you will like.

Believe me, dear Quinn, yours always

Arthur Symons

Notes

1. A typescript of Barrie's 'mean answer' is in the John Quinn Collection, The New York Public Library:

| | Adelphi Terrace House |
| 22 September 1921 | Strand |

My dear Symons

  Yes, of course, if there was anything I could do to help your wife on the stage, I should be very glad. I don't know of anything tho [sic] at present, I have nothing coming myself that would have a suitable part – indeed I am not writing plays at all, and I live too out of the world of the stage to know much of what is going on there. But should I hear of anything I would do my best. I was very sorry you are not well yourself.

Yours sincerely
J. M. Barrie

2. His 'platonic passion' was particularly for young actresses. See Andrew Birkin, *J. M. Barrie and the Lost Boys* (1979) p. 44.
3. Symons's increasing obsession with motor traffic resulted in a letter to the Editor of *The Times*, part of which states: 'Surely the noise of motor traffic, and above all, of motor horns, is not only offensive to many, but is a grave danger to one portion of the community, who are assuredly deserving of some consideration' (27 Aug. 1928, p. 13).
4. Arthur Symons, 'Dancing as Soul Expression', *Forum*, 66 (Oct. 1921) 308–17.

150   To Iseult Gonne
(MS., Northwestern)

22 May [1922]   13(3) Queen's Gardens

Dear Iseult
    Your prose is lovely – so is the sonnet in a different way. I hope to go
to Paris early in June:[1] one stifles here for lack of air. I suppose there is
no chance of your being there – to wander on wonderful nights in
adorable Paris? If so do let me know for certain. I may be staying where
the Sotherns the actors are in Paris – near where Rodin had his atelier.[2]
John has been in Spain for more than a month – he will have a wonderful
time there. I have met the Welsh tramp poet Davies,[3] who is an amazing
animal and very Celtic. He hopes to be also in Paris – for the first time
and he not knowing one word of French! Exotic Iris[4] is to be found
night after night in a Café [in] boulevard Montparnasse. I am anxious
to meet her again – most of all in Paris. An American magazine sent
back an essay of mine on Rodin as being "too erotic for their readers"!
He was apart from his immense genius erotic.[5] So one has to swear:
Damnation! Do send me more of your prose and of your verse and
believe me

                                                Yours ever
                                                Arthur

Notes

1. Symons was apparently not in Paris during June.
2. Rodin had more than one studio in Paris, but he generally entertained visitors at 182
   rue de l'Université, near the Quai d'Orsay.
3. W. H. Davies (1871–1940), Welsh poet, whose *Autobiography of a Super-Tramp* (1908)
   appeared with a preface by Shaw. Symons had reviewed Davies's first volume of verse,
   The Soul's Destroyer and Other Poems (1905), in 'A Poet of the Lodging-House', *Outlook*,
   16 (19 July 1905) 129 – a review for which Davies was grateful (see Beckson, p. 302).
4. Iris Tree (1897–1968), a poet, the daughter of the actor–manager Herbert Beerbohm
   Tree. Her biographer describes her as 'the most truly Bohemian person I have ever
   known: totally unconcerned about public opinion, material matters and conventional
   society' (Daphne Fielding, *The Rainbow Picnic: A Portrait of Iris Tree* [1974] p. 13).
   Augustus John, in a letter to John Quinn (MS., 3 Apr. 1915, Quinn), referred to her as
   'a fine wench, with pink hair'.
5. In a letter to Herbert Horne, Symons wrote of Rodin: 'It appears that having used up
   the resources of one organ in his devotion to women, he has had recourse to another
   organ; and that in that respect he is insatiable, his preference being for extreme youth'
   (MS [May 1892] Dugdale).

151   To John Quinn
   (MS., Quinn)

15 September 1922   Island Cottage

Dear Quinn

   I was delighted and depressed when I read your letter. I have felt for
so many years almost the same symptoms you describe – awful pains,
exasperations: and, as for me, these exasperations make me more
restless than I ever was. The sudden death of Sir Charles Ryall[1] was an
immense loss to us and to I know not how many hundreds whom he
cured by his flawless operations. He was Irish by origin, he had genius;
he was the kindest man in the world; it is incredible that we shall never
see him again.
   I am making hardly any money – no sales from my books either here
or in America: I get a few essays printed now and again. On account of
the long delay of *The Forum* in sending me cheques to the value of
perhaps £60, I have put this affair in the hands of Pinker.[2] No dealer
will buy any of my MSS. I am trying to sell the entire MS. of *The Toy-
Cart* (1908) of about 160 pages, which I value at £50.
   It is a damned thing to be condemned by one's nerves and one's
imagination to go on writing – without the least chance of making my
living; while all I want is to go abroad and escape this horrible and vile
London, in which I have lost almost all interest. My only chance of
enduring this winter is – if I can by some means contrive to make
enough money – to spend part of it in Biarritz, which is less expensive
in the winter; the climate is glorious; it is near the Pyrenees; it is on the
border of Spain; and if I contrive to get there I may perhaps stay with
some of my Spanish friends and have another chance of wandering
with them over Spain.
   It will be most kind of you to have sent to my London address (3
Queen's Gardens) the entire MS. of *Notes and Impressions* you have so
carefully kept for me. Then I can discuss with Joseph Anthony[3] the
question of The Century Publishers issuing this book. Also please try
and sell Barrie's letter[4] and the MS. of my *Charles Baudelaire*.
   We spent a day with Joseph Conrad. He was sinister, one mass of
writhing nerves; irritable and impatient – yet always the man of genius.
   Have you read Yeats' wonderful pages in the September *Dial* of his
and my adventures – which are authentic, which surge before me? I am
of course the Rhymer he refers to.[5] It is nearly a year since I saw
Augustus John. Very many thanks for your cheque of £20. Just had
cheque for £1.7.0 from Brentano. Disgraceful!

                                    Always yours sincerely
                                    Arthur Symons[6]

Notes

1. The distinguished surgeon (d. 1922) who had operated on Rhoda in 1918.
2. James B. Pinker (1863–1922), literary agent, who had been handling Symons's business affairs since 1907.
3. The London manager of the Century Co.
4. See Letter 149, n. 1.
5. See Yeats's 'More Memories [xxxiii–xliii]', *Dial*, 73 (1922) 284–302; rptd in his *The Trembling of the Veil* (1922), dedicated to Quinn, 'My friend and helper and friend and helper of certain people mentioned in this book'. When Symons wrote to Quinn that he was planning to write his own confessions, the latter replied on 21 July 1923: 'I think it will make a fascinating book, worthy to stand with Yeats's *Trembling of the Veil*, which, as you say, is a real masterpiece. I knew that you were the rhymer [*sic*] that Yeats referred to' (carbon copy of typewritten letter, Quinn).
6. This typewritten letter with Symons's autograph signature contains a statement written in his hand at the bottom of the last page, referring, apparently, to the typewriting service that he used: 'They omitted some of my best sentences.'

152   To Rhoda Symons
(MS., Munro)

Sunday
31 May [1925]   [Paris]

Dear Rhoda

You said you were glad as I always am to be at the Cottage. In your letter you speak of wanting to sell it. I tell you one thing: you promised me there was no question of it this year, as you know I have an enormous mass of work to do when I return there which I could do nowhere else. Were you to do what I refer to I know to a certainty that all our luck would leave us – with at least almost to a certainty. I have several reasons for saying what I am bound to say: certain ominous things have happened to me here, which have given me fear. I have never been more serious than I am now. Yesterday I met at Natalie's[1] (besides Rachilde[?],[2] Ch. Dachet[?],[3] and Vincent O'Sullivan[4]) a Vampire, and a kind of Monstre[?], the Baroness Deslandes[5] – [with] a childlike grace – with the most evil eyes I have ever seen; she spoke French and English with perfection, but always in a state of nervous agitation. She took me home with her to 16 Villa Central, 83 rue d'Arthur, where she kept me to dinner. She is abnormal, has travelled immensely, has known almost everyone, such as D'Annunzio and any numbers[?] of others. She is as monstrous as Messalina.[6] And *she has double sight.* She has also *double vision.* She told me things about myself, about my future, at least for this year, which I dare not at the present tell you – for these things must never be written down. You and I cannot help believing in these signs and omens. You also know the state of nerves I am always in, and that I don't want to be upset, most of all in Paris and in Brittany. So don't send me any more disturbing letters as the one you sent me. – Your news in regard to Caliban[7] certainly distressed and disturbed me. *Send me better news of him*! All this did not keep me awake. Besides this, apart from the fascination of Paris, life here is very trying – an incessant noise – and yet I must be in the open air. For heaven's sake do relieve my mind, my nerves, and my imagination, by saying that the Cottage will remain in our possession at least this year if not longer. I don't want to be kept awake by these apprehensions – which I prefer not to have.

Yesterday I spent two hours alone with Ida Rubenstein[8] in her lovely house. She was reclining on a couch, as she could not go out of doors then. She has a unique fascination, a magical charm, an adorable voice. She spoke in French and English. I showed her Gabriele's letter – we talked about the man and his work. She still adores him as she adored Duse who had – as I also said to her – a purity of genius and of imagination which was unique. She wants me to send her *Knave of Hearts* with the Verlaine versions, and *Sea-Coasts and Cities and Islands*[9] – so as to compare her travels with mine. You can imagine how sweet and simple[?] she was with me: the radiant smile, the sudden gestures, her instinct, animation, her glorious hair, her absolute grace. I may see her again; for she said, "I hope this is not the last time I shall see you when you are in Paris."

I went last night to the Moulin Rouge, where there was a magnificent spectacle. I lunch today at Voltaire with O'Sullivan, who wants to give me more information in regard to Brittany. I lunched Joyce yesterday at La Pérouse – he can talk as he did then, wonderful. He also has a fascination of his own – we got on splendidly – the same race for one thing.

There came to me a chance of their giving *Francesca* in London. Ida R. said to me she meant to produce the play here almost at once.[10] She will stay [with] Gabriele in Italy and tell him about me – so she promised and so she will. She is evidently a woman of genius.

Do answer this letter as soon as you have got it and send me better news and no more of those disturbances I hate to have to deal with. In any case if by chance I were to go on to Saint Malo they will forward on your letter.

Joyce thought the image of you I showed him during our lunch was wonderful and absolutely foreign – which it is. Like me in a different sense!

I am ever
Arthur

Notes

1. Natalie Barney (1876–1972), American-born writer and expatriate who lived most of her life in Paris, where, on the Left Bank at 20 rue Jacob, she established a salon which, for sixty years attracted noted French, American, and English writers. She was, moreover, 'unquestionably the leading lesbian of her time' (George Wickes, *The Amazon of Letters: The Life and Loves of Natalie Barney* [New York, 1976] p. 7).
2. The pseudonym of Marguérite Vallette (1860–1953), French novelist and biographer.
3. Unidentified.
4. American poet, novelist, and biographer (1868–1940), who lived in France for most of his life.
5. Baroness Ilse Deslandes, one of Natalie Barney's lovers, a hostess to artists and writers, painted by Burne-Jones, whose biographer, Penelope Fitzgerald, describes her as 'a tiny, formidable blonde Jewish *lionne*, mysterious as to age and provenance, given to strange gestures and long, swimming, short-sighted glances' (*Edward Burne-Jones: A Biography* [1975] p. 221).
6. Valeria Messalina (d. AD 48), wife of the Roman Emperor Claudius, who executed her because of her greed and lust.
7. One of Symons's cats.
8. Russian-born French actress, dancer, and theatrical manager (1885–1960), once hailed as 'Queen of the Stage' in Europe.
9. Symons inadvertently errs in his own title: it should be *Cities and Sea-Coasts and Islands*.
10. We are unable to find a record of a production at that time of d'Annunzio's play, *Francesca da Rimini*, translated by Symons.

153   To Warner Taylor[1]
(Text: Taylor)

[late 1931?]

Dear Mr. Taylor

Has any imaginative critic ever absolutely fathomed what is most essential in that particular form we call Style? The problem has always been one of a kind of spiritual or unspiritual vexation to all those who had endeavoured to define it. There have been infinite attempts, and not one has been flawless. One thing is certain: that the style or the rhythm of verse, that rhythm which distinguishes it from prose, has never been traced with any certainty to its origin. Compare, for instance, Fitzgerald's translation of *Omar Khayyám* with Rossetti's translation of the early Italian Poets.[2] Rossetti was a poet of creative genius, and in these translations we see him forming his own style in his reproduction of these medieval poets of his own country. Again, the style of Rabelais is primitive and elemental, and almost unsurpassable.

As for me, I had never written any prose that satisfied me, nor had I achieved a style that seemed to me original, until, when I was seventeen, I read Pater's *Studies in the History of the Renaissance*, which opened a new world to me, or, rather, gave me the key or the secret of the world in which I was living. It taught me that life (which had seemed to me then of so little moment) could be made a work of art, and I caught from it an unlimited curiosity. From that moment the question of style resolved itself into a certainty that mine, on the whole, would never vary. It has always been subtle and complex, and I have always had the gift of excitement, both in verse and prose, and I can express that excitement with a terrible justice. And, apart from this, one of my most poignant excitements came over me when in Paris I heard Yvette Guilbert sing *La Soulerde*. I felt a cold shiver run down my back, and I could hardly endure the pity of it. And it was I who persuaded the manager of the Empire to bring her over to London. I have been a rebel and a wanderer, to whom the visible world existed, very actively; and there was the vision rising in one's eyes and the passion rising in one's heart.

Without technique, perfect of its kind, no one is worth considering in any art. The rope-dancer or the acrobat must be perfect in technique before they appear on the stage at all. We have come to value technique for the violence (as, for instance, in Kreisler) which it gives into the hands of those who possess it, in their assault upon the nerves. We have come to look upon technique as an end in itself, rather than as a means to an end. One should begin to create one's art at that point where faultless technique leaves off.

I have never admired rhetoric, and yet certain great writers have taken advantage of it, such as Sir Thomas Browne and De Quincey, whose style becomes that of Ruskin, and is what is frankly called prose poetry, a lucky bastard, glorying in the illegitimacy of its origin. Browne, famed for his *Hydriotaphia*,[3] in which there are touches of the "divine spark," could not get away from an atmosphere of all-pervading oddity and quaintness. His work, one night, draws to a natural close. "To keep our eyes open longer were but to act our Antipodes. The huntsmen are up in America!"

You wrote: "words that laugh and cry." I turn at once to Meredith's masterpiece, *Modern Love*, which is packed with imagination of so nakedly human a kind that every word burns into one like the touch of a corrosive acid. The poem laughs and cries, with, at times, an acuteness of sensation carried to the point of agony at which Othello sweats words like these:

> O thou weed,
> Who art so lovely, fair, and smell'st so sweet,
> That the sense aches at thee, would thou hadst ne'er been born!
> [IV.ii.67–9]

Baudelaire observed profoundly that "in one word, every character in Balzac, down to the very scullions, has genius.'"[4] It is actually Balzac himself. His style is passionate and visionary, magnetic and magnificent, and, when his words become flesh and blood, he is the lyric poet. I have often considered whether, in the novel, perfect form is a good or even a possible thing, if the novel is to be what Balzac made it: he, who can only be compared with Shakespeare, because his mind is nearer to what is creative in the poet's mind than that of any other novelist, has created in Père Goriot the equivalent of King Lear: for Goriot is a Lear at heart, and he suffers the same tortures and humiliations. When I read Shakespeare, I never think of his incomparable style, but of his immortal Genius. The rhythm of one of his plays speaks to the blood like wine or music: it is with exultation, with intoxication, that I see or read *Antony and Cleopatra*; it gives me exactly the same intoxication as when I heard Vladimir de Pachmann play the piano, as when I heard Wagner's *Tristan*.

I have an extraordinary memory, which can be as vivid as visions: so had Verlaine and Swinburne, but we all used it for different purposes. Vidocq remembered almost every face he had seen.[5] To Rossetti memory was a curse. He wrote:

> Is memory most of miseries miserable,
> Or the one flower of ease in bitterest hell?[6]

Dante makes Francesca da Rimini say in Hell:

> There is no greater woe
> Than to remember how our gladness fled
> Into our misery; this your guide doth know.
> If you are fain to know of the roots outspread
> Of our first love that led to endless night,
> I will do as one that weeps for the words she said.
> We read one day for our supreme delight
> Of Launcelot, how Love seized him, furious:
> We were alone and knew not of Cain's spite.[7]

And it is I who wrote these lines:

> This (need one dread? nay, dare one hope?)
> Will rise, a ghost of memory if
> Ever again my handkerchief
> Is scented with White Heliotrope.[8]

I must mention Borrow, who had a peculiar kind of genius, at once creative and inventive, normal and abnormal, and a most original style, who, in *Lavengro*,[9] referring to his complication of *The Newgate Trials*, quotes this sentence, which was written by Henry Simms, who had been executed at Tyburn, "So I went with them to a music booth, where they made me almost drunk with gin, and began to talk their flash language, which I did not understand." Borrow adds: "I have always looked upon this sentence as a masterpiece of the narrative style."

You refer to the barrier between the trained mind and the sheet of blank paper one stares at. Stendhal knew what that meant, he who confessed that to him style was a kind of purgatory. For he said: "Often have I reflected for a whole half-hour in order to place an adjective before or after a substantive."[10] Flaubert, possessed of an absolute belief that there exists but one way of expressing one thing, one word to call it by, one adjective to qualify, one verb to animate it, gave himself superhuman labours for the discovery, in every phrase, of that word, that verb, that adjective. Compare his style, in each of his books, and you will find that each book has its own style; that style, which had every merit, becomes what it was by a process very different from that of most writers careful of form. He is so difficult to translate because he has no fixed rhythm. And yet he invents the rhythm of every sentence. One day Conrad (a man of genius, whose fascination was unique, and whose own style was inimitable and often exasperating) standing in my study many years ago, having read these sentences, in an article of mine on *Salammbô*, looked up at me with surprise and expressed his delight in finding that I was the first to discover, what he had wondered at, the secret of Flaubert's rhythm.[11]

"On thinking a subject through before beginning to write." What else can one do? No subject is ever "made to one's hand." It is Poe who has said all that is essential in regard to this question. "A skilful literary artist has constructed a tale. If wise, he has not fashioned his thoughts to accommodate his incidents; but having conceived, with deliberate care, a certain unique or single *effect* to be wrought out, he then invents such incidents – he then combines such events as may best suit him in establishing this preconceived event. If his very initial sentence tends not to the outbringing of this effect, then he has failed in his first step. In the whole composition there should be no word written of which the tendency direct or indirect is not the one pre-established design."[12] Here is the test: "The Cask of Amontillado." "The thousand injuries of Fortunato I had borne as I best could; but when he ventured upon insult, I vowed revenge."

I have never had any barrier before [me] when I began to write. D'Annunzio often had. He told me when I was with him in Rome in 1898 that he usually worked for twelve hours every day, but that, when his inspiration failed him, he would stare at the blank page on his desk, until in despair he would go out and wander along the Corso. And he would speak of his life in Pescara. "I used to return to my silent and deserted house at ten, and sit there, devouring my utter despondency. I hid my real life, and I hid my real art. Never was a creature more mutable than I; never creature more restless, more at peace with itself." He still desires beauty with the rage of a lover; and, to him, sex is the supreme beauty and passion a supreme art. A man of creative genius, his style, partly founded on Aretino,[13] is intensely original, and much more lyrical than that of his verse, and I can see the tenacity of his will in the perfection of his rhythms: and in the style, as in the man, the exclusive predominance over him of beautiful physical things, gestures, perfumes, and a kind of tyranny of the senses. Art begins when a man wishes to immortalize the most vivid moment he has ever lived.[14]

Yours truly

Arthur Symons

Notes

1. American Professor of English and author (1880–1958), who taught at the University of Wisconsin. For one of the sections in his anthology of essays, Taylor invited such authors as Lord Dunsany, Frank Swinnerton, Sinclair Lewis, Ludwig Lewisohn, Llewelyn Powys, and Symons to respond by letter to various queries regarding style.
2. *Rubaiyat of Omar Khayyám, the Astronomer-Poet of Persia* (1859), trans. Edward FitzGerald (1809–83); *The Early Italian Poets from Ciullo d'Alcamo to Dante Alighieri* (1861), trans. Dante Gabriel Rossetti.
3. Better known by its subtitle, *Urn Burial* (1658), by Sir Thomas Browne (1605–82), physician and author.
4. See Charles Baudelaire, 'Exposition Universelle, 1855', *Oeuvres Complètes*, ed. Yves-Gerard Le Dantec (Paris, 1954) p. 692.
5. Eugène François Vidocq (1755–1857), French detective who joined the Paris Sûreté in 1809 after a life of crime. Symons's incomplete translation of Vidocq's *Memoires d'un Forcat*, 4 vols (Paris, 1828–9) and a typescript, 'Eugène François Vidocq: A Study in Criminology' are in the Symons Papers, Princeton.
6. 'Memory', *Collected Works of Dante G. Rossetti*, ed. W. M. Rossetti (1886) vol. ii, p. 371.
7. From the 'Inferno' of *The Divine Comedy*, 5.121–9.
8. From 'White Heliotrope' in *LN*.
9. See Letter 13, n. 7.
10. From *Correspondance de Stendhal, 1800–1842*, Preface by M. Barres (Paris, 1908) vol. iii, p. 57.
11. Symons's 'Gustave Flaubert', an introduction to *Salammbô* (1901); rptd in *FSC* and *SML*, 1919 edn.
12. Symons was apparently quoting from memory. See 'Tale Writing – Nathaniel Hawthorne', *The Complete Works of Edgar Allan Poe*, ed. James Harrison (New York, 1902) vol. xiii, p. 141.
13. Pietro Aretino (1492–1556), Italian playwright, whose plays and letters are known for their coarse, satiric wit.
14. Symons quoting himself: see *SPV*, p. 290.

154 To Augustus John[1]
(MS., John)

[mid July 1935]   Island Cottage

Dear John

I have been waiting for the last news of your son before writing to you.[2] It must have been a terrible shock: no one knows what an infinity of bodies the Sea has seized on. Bessie, our Dorset maid, said to me that as a rule a body was washed up at the end of nine days. There must have been some consolation for you to know what you have just known. You once said to me: Those who create must always believe in Immortality.

Yours ever
Arthur Symons

Notes

1. A typed letter (signed by Symons), apparently typed by Symons himself, for errors abound. These have been corrected here.
2. Henry John, Augustus John's son by his first wife, Ida, who had died after giving birth to him in Paris in 1907, went swimming off Newquay in Cornwall on 24 June and never returned. His body was found on 5 July; an inquest returned a verdict of accidental death. See Michael Holroyd, *Augustus John: A Biography* (1975) pp. 555–6.

5

Epilogue

After Rhoda's death in 1936, Symons was cared for by Mrs Bessie Seymour, their housekeeper since 1921, to whom Symons wrote a note dated 10 February 1940: "I have always had a profound admiration for you going back to a certain year in which Mrs Symons was not well and she often said to me that your devotion to her was almost divine and that without you she would not have lived as long as she did. And for your devotion to me and I know that without you I should never have lived as long as I have."[1]

During the Second World War, Symons moved into her home in St John's Wood, London, but in 1944 returned to his beloved Island Cottage, where he caught a chill, which developed into pneumonia. On 22 January 1945, he died, and was buried in a small, isolated cemetery some 500 yards from the Wittersham churchyard.[2]

His funeral was sparsely attended, and obituary notices generally adopted the faintly patronising tone appropriate to literary failures.[3] Aestheticism was out of fashion, and Symons's achievement seemed to belong to a distant age whose concerns were trivial compared to those of the generation just emerging from a world war. But the *Times Literary Supplement* editorialised at length on the passing of 'the last of the eminent aesthetic writers', whose 'special contribution' was his revelation of the significance of French Symbolist writing, and aptly summarised his contribution to English literature. 'The seclusion of beauty', the *Times Literary Supplement* noted, manifested itself in its purest state in 'the critical writings of that subtle and responsive spirit, Arthur Symons'.[4]

Notes

1. The signed note, typewritten and corrected in ink, is now in the possession of Mrs Diana P. Read, Bridport, Dorset. On p. 306 of his *Arthur Symons: A Critical Biography* (1963), Roger Lhombreaud rewrites the final sentence of Symons's note.
2. Lhombreaud erroneously locates the gravesite in the Wittersham churchyard (p. 307).
3. See Richard Jennings, 'Arthur Symons', *New Statesman*, 17 Feb. 1945, p. 15.
4. 'Arthur Symons', *Times Literary Supplement*, 3 Feb. 1945, p. 57.

Appendix A

INDEX OF WRITERS OF LETTERS (OTHER THAN SYMONS)

Appendix B

* Letters once in these collections are now untraceable.

Northwestern	Northwestern University
Pennsylvania	University of Pennsylvania
Princeton	Princeton University
Quinn	John Quinn Memorial Collection, Rare Book and Manuscript Division, New York Public Library
Rhys	Ernest Rhys, *Letters from Limbo* (1936) pp. 200–3
Taylor	Warner Taylor, ed., *Types and Times in the Essay* (New York, 1932) pp. 360–4
Texas	Humanities Research Center, University of Texas (Austin)
Yale	Beinecke Library, Yale University
Yeats	Michael Yeats

Appendix C

In 1932, the *British Journal of Medical Psychology* published a psychological study of Symons by a Louis Bragman,[1] which greatly distressed Havelock Ellis. In a letter to the assistant editor, Dr John Rickman, Ellis wrote of Bragman:

> I do not know who he is, American? I do not find his name in the Medical Register, or in the American Who's Who. His essay shows a wide knowledge of the *literary* sources, and is quite a reasonable deduction from those sources. *At the same time it is completely misleading*. He evidently has no personal knowledge of the case, which (though A.S. has no knowledge of ever having had syphilis) was accepted generally by the specialists as G.P. and they anticipated his death in a few months. He is alive still, more than 20 years later, and living at home in freedom though (contrary to what Mr. Bragman believes) his mental health has never been completely restored; he has never been in any respect his old self, whence a source of error for Mr. Bragman who has taken too literally what A.S. has written about himself in the years since his breakdown.
>
> I have known A.S. intimately for over 40 years, though I do not now see him much, and also have been able to view him with a psychological eye. I shared chambers in the Temple with him for 10 years, and travelled with him all over Europe. I am therefore rather shocked at the impossible person he is represented by Mr. B. to be, certainly a person with whom I, with my quiet and respectable ways of living, could not have associated, or found so entirely delightful a companion as in old days I always found A.S. to be.
>
> I am also rather shocked at finding a study of this kind – even if it were more reliable than it is – written about a man who is still living and moving in good society. I have not ventured to tell him about it.[2]

Included with this letter to Dr Rickman was a lengthy one to Louis Bragman:[3]

24, Holmdene Avenue
Herne Hill
August 13th 1933   London, S.E. 24.

Dear Sir,

As I have been a near friend of Arthur Symons for some forty-five years (his wife would probably say, for most of the time his nearest friend) I have been much interested in your "Case of A.S.", all the more so since I am myself something of a psychologist and so have been able to observe A.S. in a double capacity. I knew him before he left his early home; when he came to London we shared the same chambers when I was myself in London and I travelled with him in half a dozen countries.

I admire the way in which you have equipped yourself for the task with literary material. It is, however, most unfortunate that you write without personal knowledge (and none of the writers you quote were more than very slightly acquainted with A.S.)[4] and without clinical knowledge of the case, for you leave out of account the essential question of its specific nature.

Should you think of reprinting your study it may be as well if I comment on a few of the points where you have been led astray. I do not wish to imply that the number of such points involves any discredit. I think that you have been as careful as possible, and that they were inevitable. You were not able to correct the two main sources of error: (1) that in A.S. to an unusual extent the man and the artist are distinct, though the artist in him is completely genuine and not a pose; and (2) you have not been able to allow for the fact that a man whose brain has been so shaken as was A.S.'s cannot afterwards be accepted as completely reliable in his statements regarding his early life or indeed at any point. Up to his breakdown in 1908, he seemed to everyone entirely sane and normal and balanced, although, as was natural, he possessed the Celtic[5] temperament of eager vivacity; his mind was singularly precise, sensitive, and accurate. He has never been the same since. This is obvious in his writings, they never reach the same level as his earlier work, even though he fortifies them by embodying earlier work, and they are full of careless errors; he cannot even quote a French sentence correctly now, or scarcely even translate it without gross mistakes. This accounts for many points where you have been led astray.

In the second sentence of your second paragraph, the statement about the psychosis at 41 is correct;[6] all the other statements need qualification. I do not know what are the "glaring factors" for ill-adjustment in his child-hood which you have in mind; and I think his sister would be equally at a loss to enumerate them; it was the normal home of a Wesleyan Minister, and he never made any serious complaint of it except that he was not in sympathetic touch with his father, but his mother was of congenial temperament and he got on well with his sister, though they had few tastes in common.

While it is quite true that A.S. frequently noted (as in writing of J. A. Symonds, a man of completely different temperament) and quite correctly, how often writers find in their work an "escape" from themselves, Gribble (speaking with little or no personal knowledge) was wrong in supposing that that was the case with A.S.[7] As also he was wrong in supposing A.S. moulded by Methodism, which made no impression on him at all. He *reacted* to it but was from the first quite impervious. A.S., like so many young people in a rather uncongenial home, was pleased to "escape" from it. But he did so quite easily, and, before his breakdown, thoroughly enjoyed himself and his life; it was an entirely happy life in all respects, from which he had not the faintest wish to "escape". So far from being an "escape" from himself, his work was an immensely enjoyed part of himself, and of the nature of a natural interest, and it also came easily to him. No one could enjoy life more than A.S. with his vivacious Celtic temperament; he was very sociable, had crowds of friends in the best social circles; in spite of an occasional adventure, he had no temptation to debauchery or to excess of any kind, and after marriage in 1900[8] to a wife to whom he has always been completely devoted, his life has been in every respect extremely regular.

It is incorrect to speak of his "madness" as congenital. There was slight nervous trouble in child-hood which passed off completely before puberty, and he was altogether sane in every respect until the attack of 1908 from which he has never *completely* recovered. So that everything he has said of himself since that date must be taken *cum grano*, though he was quite reliable before then.

It is a mistake also to regard A.S. as a "symbolist"; a mistake probably due to the fact that he was always much interested in the French "symbolists", and inclined to extend that term widely. A very slight examination of his poems will show that they are not of "symbolist" kind, but might much better be termed "realist".

That A.S. was "always in frail health" is completely wrong. He was not grossly robust, but always impressed me by what I called his delicate strength; like delicately wrought iron, I used to think of his personality and his work; he had no serious illness and seemed never to know fatigue. I was myself fairly healthy, but on our long continental tours together I was occasionally rather upset by a night journey; he never was; and only once (in Moscow) did I ever know him to suffer even from indigestion.

When he left home for good in his early twenties to live in London it was not for "five years" but for good. Until a year ago he has had a fixed home there and a cottage in the country and divided his time between them. For the first ten years I rented two rooms in his chambers in the Temple to occupy whenever I came to London. There was no "search without an aim" and certainly no "torture". He was equally at home in London and Paris and Rome; it was a great joy to him to have so large a field for art and study open to him; he had endless schemes of work; he wrote so well that it was easy for him to make money; he did regular and much appreciated journalistic work from the first; and even before he came to London he was making many excellent friends. It is wrong to suppose that "his world and his companions were exotic", even though he was always pleased to meet "exotic" people. Most of his friends were not "exotic". His wife is very English, so am I; so was "Bianca". All his nearest friends have been British. Welby who never knew A.S. before his breakdown is completely mistaken if he asserts (I do not recall the passage), that A.S. "lived in the most wicked and wanton quarters of cities with their depraved and perverted inhabitants".[9] His tastes have always been refined and aesthetic; he has always stayed at comfortable (even luxurious) hotels in the best quarter of a city and has never lived with "depraved and perverted" people, however much interest he may have felt in them from outside.

p. 352 "I inherited madness"[10] is not strictly correct. An uncle, or some other collateral relative, is said to have been insane. The "recurrent spell of amnesia" seems imaginary. "Music in Venice" *is* definitely pathologic; it reveals excessive hyperaesthesia and is quite unlike Symons' normal personal and restrained style of writing. "The woman he was with" in Italy at this crisis was his wife; I cannot imagine how this mistake occurred; for he never at any time travelled with any other woman.

A.S.'s resentment of the "tyrants" of the asylum you correctly represent as without foundation. He was at Brook[e] House (where I visited him), treated with all consideration, and with constant attention from his wife and loving friends. It may be called a "temporary psychosis" for it became possible to give him freedom, but he has never been the same A.S. of old. All the finest reactions of his delicate intelligence were permanently impaired, and his intellect crippled, while he has ever since been liable to suffer from various nervous symptoms.

p. 358. Symons was never a drug addict, and there is some mistake about his trying haschish with J. A. Symonds, though he once or twice did with another author.[11] The sonnet "The Absinth[e] Drinker"[12] was written after he and I had tried an absinth outside a Parisian cafe, and I doubt if either of us ever tried it again.

The concluding paragraph is misleading.[13] The visible world has always been a keen and delightful reality for Symons, and until his breakdown few people had experienced less of the "harshness of life".

With best regards,
Very truly yours,
(Signed) Havelock Ellis.

Notes

1. Louis J. Bragman, 'The Case of Arthur Symons: The Psychopathology of a Man of Letters', *British Journal of Medical Psychology*, 12 (1932) 346–62.
2. Typescript copy dated 13 August 1933, University of Reading Library.
3. Typescript copy containing corrections and additions in ink, University of Reading Library.
4. Among the authors quoted are James Gibbons Huneker, Padraic Colum, and Paul Elmer More.
5. Ellis, in ink, added in the margin: 'Cornish which is different from either Irish or Gaelic.'
6. Symons was forty-three at the time of his breakdown.
7. See Francis Gribble's 'The Pose of Mr. Arthur Symons', *FR*, 90 (1908))pp. 127–36.
8. Symons married Rhoda in 1901.
9. The passage is by Bragman; it is not a quotation from T. Earle Welby's *Arthur Symons: A Critical Study* (1925), though Bragman attributes the idea to Welby.
10. From Symons' *Confessions* (1930) p. 1.
11. For Symons's description of his taking haschish with Symonds, see *Memoirs*, p. 117. Symons also took the drug with Yeats, according to a postcard postmarked 17 December 1896, sent from Paris, to Henry-D. Davray (Queen's).
12. From Symons's *Silhouettes* (1892).
13. Bragman had written: 'The so-called schizoid individual, with his restricted fields of interest, requires satisfaction from highly coloured contrasts. This is based chiefly on a poor hold on reality and a need for morbid stimulation, almost, in order to retain his interest. It is through this morbid stimulation that Arthur Symons obtained his satisfactions as an antidote for the harshness of life' (p. 362).

Select Bibliography of Symons's Works

Because *The Collected Works of Arthur Symons*, 9 vols (London: Martin Secker, 1924; rptd New York: AMS Press, 1973) is incomplete and revised or cut, the reader should also consult original editions. *The Collected Works* contain the following:

I	*Poems: Days and Nights, Silhouettes, London Nights, Amoris Victima*
II	*Poems: Images of Good and Evil, The Loom of Dreams, The Fool of the World and Other Poems, Love's Cruelty*
III	*Poems: Knave of Hearts, Lesbia and Other Poems*
IV	*William Blake*
V	*Spiritual Adventures*
VI	*Tragedies: Tristan and Iseult, The Harvesters*
VII	*Tragedies: The Death of Agrippina, Cleopatra in Judaea, The Toy Cart*
VIII	*Studies in Two Literatures* (incorporating *The Symbolist Movement in Literature*)
IX	*Studies in Seven Arts* (incorporating 'Aubrey Beardsley').

The original editions of Symons's major works are here listed in chronological order:

1886   *An Introduction to the Study of Browning* (London and New York: Cassell; rev., enlarged, 1887).

1889   *Days and Nights* (London and New York: Macmillan).

1892   *Silhouettes* (London: Elkin Mathews and John Lane; rev., enlarged, London: Smithers, 1896).

1895   *London Nights* (London: Smithers; rev., 1897).

1897   *Amoris Victima* (London: Smithers; New York: Richmond).

1897   *Studies in Two Literatures* (London: Smithers).

1898   *Aubrey Beardsley* (London: Unicorn Press; rev., enlarged, London: Dent, 1905).

1899   *The Symbolist Movement in Literature* ([delayed publication: 5 March 1900] London: Heinemann; rev., London: Constable, 1908; rev., enlarged, New York: Dutton, 1919).

1899   *Images of Good and Evil* ([delayed publication: May 1900] London: Heinemann).

1902   *Poems*, 2 vols ([published: December 1901] London: Heinemann; New York: John Lane).

1903   *Plays, Acting, and Music* (London: Duckworth; rev., enlarged, London: Constable, 1909; New York: Dutton, 1909).

1903   *Cities* (London: Dent; New York: Pott).

1904   *Studies in Prose and Verse* (London: Dent; New York: Dutton).

1905   *Spiritual Adventures* (London: Constable; New York: Dutton).

1905   *A Book of Twenty Songs* (London: Dent).

1906   *The Fool of the World and Other Poems* (London: Heinemann; New York: John Lane, 1907).

1906   *Studies in Seven Arts* (London: Constable; New York: Dutton).

1907   *William Blake* (London: Constable; New York: Dutton).

1907   *Cities of Italy* (London: Dent; New York: Dutton).

1908   *London: A Book of Aspects* (privately printed by Edmund Brooks [less than twelve copies for copyright in the USA]; 2nd printing, 1909).

1909   *The Romantic Movement in English Poetry* (London: Constable; New York: Dutton).

1913   *Knave of Hearts, 1894–1908* (London: Heinemann; New York: John Lane).

1916   *Figures of Several Centuries* (London: Constable; New York: Dutton).

1916   *Tragedies* (London: Heinemann; New York: John Lane).

1917   *Tristan and Iseult: A Play in Four Acts* (London: Heinemann; New York: Brentano's).

1918   *Cities and Sea-Coasts and Islands* (London: Collins; New York, Brentano's 1919).

1918   *Colour Studies in Paris* (London: Chapman & Hall; New York: Dutton).

1919   *Studies in the Elizabethan Drama* (New York: Dutton; London: Heinemann, 1920).

1919   *The Toy Cart: A Play in Five Acts* (Dublin and London: Maunsel).

1920   *Lesbia and Other Poems* (New York: Dutton).

1920   *Cesare Borgia, Iseult of Brittany, The Toy Cart* (New York: Brentano's).

1920   *Charles Baudelaire: A Study* (London: Elkin Mathews; New York: Dutton).

1923   *Love's Cruelty* (London: Secker; New York: Boni, 1924).

1923   *Dramatis Personae* (Indianapolis: Bobbs-Merrill; London: Faber & Gwyer, 1925).

1923   *The Café Royal and Other Essays* ([delayed publication: January 1924] London: Beaumont Press).

1924   *The Collected Works of Arthur Symons*, 9 vols (London: Secker).

1925   *Studies on Modern Painters* (New York: Rudge).

1925   *Notes on Joseph Conrad, with Some Unpublished Letters* ([delayed publication: February 1926] London: Meyers).

1926   *Parisian Nights: A Book of Essays* (London: Beaumont Press).

1926   *Eleonora Duse* (London: Elkin Mathews; New York: Duffield/London: Elkin Mathews and Marrot, 1927).

1927   *A Study of Thomas Hardy* ([delayed publication: February 1928] London: Sawyer).

1929   *Studies in Strange Souls* (London: Sawyer).

1929   *Mes Souvenirs* (Chappelle-Réanville, Eure, France: Hours Press).

1929   *From Toulouse-Lautrec to Rodin, with Some Personal Recollections* (London: John Lane; New York: King, 1930).

1930   *Confessions: A Study in Pathology* (New York: Fountain Press/Cape & Smith).

1930   *A Study of Oscar Wilde* (London: Sawyer).

1931   *Wanderings* (London and Toronto: Dent).

1931   *Jezebel Mort and Other Poems* (London: Heinemann).

1932   *A Study of Walter Pater* (London: Sawyer).

1977   *The Memoirs of Arthur Symons: Life and Art in the 1890s*, ed. Karl Beckson (University Park, Pennsylvania and London: Pennsylvania State University Press).

Index

The abbreviation AS refers to Arthur Symons. Boldface entries indicate biographical information.

275